AN EXEGETICAL SUMMARY OF
MATTHEW 17–28

AN EXEGETICAL SUMMARY OF
MATTHEW 17–28

David Abernathy

SIL International®
Dallas, Texas

©2015 by SIL International®

ISBN: 978-1-55671-390-3

Library of Congress Control Number: 2015936949
Printed in the United States of America

Copies of this and other publications of SIL International®
may be obtained through distributors such as Amazon,
Barnes & Noble, other worldwide distributors and, for
select volumes, www.sil.org/resources/publications:

SIL International Publications
7500 West Camp Wisdom Road
Dallas, TX 75236-5629, USA

General inquiry: publications_intl@sil.org
Pending order inquiry: sales_intl@sil.org
www.sil.org/resources/publications

PREFACE

Exegesis is concerned with the interpretation of a text. Thus, exegesis of the New Testament involves determining the meaning of the Greek text. Translators must be especially careful and thorough in their exegesis of the New Testament in order to accurately communicate its message in the vocabulary, grammar, and literary restraints of another language. Questions occurring to translators as they study the Greek text are answered by summarizing how scholars have interpreted the text. This is information that should be considered by translators as they make their own exegetical decisions regarding the message they will communicate in their translations.

The Semi-Literal Translation

As a basis for discussion, a semi-literal translation of the Greek text is given so that the reasons for different interpretations can best be seen. When one Greek word is translated into English by several words, these words are joined by hyphens. There are a few times when clarity requires that a string of words joined by hyphens have a separate word, such as "not" (μή), inserted in their midst. In this case, the separate word is surrounded by spaces between the hyphens. When alternate translations of a Greek word are given, these are separated by slashes.

The Text

Variations in the Greek text are noted under the heading TEXT. The base text for the summary is the text of the fourth revised edition of *The Greek New Testament,* published by the United Bible Societies, which has the same text as the twenty-sixth edition of the *Novum Testamentum Graece* (Nestle-Aland). Dr. J. Harold Greenlee researched the variants and has written the notes for this part of the summary. The versions that follow different variations are listed without evaluating their choices.

The Lexicon

The meaning of a key word in context is the first question to be answered. Words marked with a raised letter in the semi-literal translation are treated separately under the heading LEXICON. First, the lexicon form of the Greek word is given. Within the parentheses following the Greek word is the location number where, in the author's judgment, this word is defined in the *Greek-English Lexicon of the New Testament Based on Semantic Domains* (Louw and Nida 1988). When a semantic domain includes a translation of the particular verse being treated, **LN** in bold type indicates that specific translation. If the specific reference for the verse is listed in *A Greek-English Lexicon of the New Testament and Other Early Christian Literature* (Bauer, Arndt, Gingrich, and Danker 1979), the outline location and page number is given. Then English equivalents of the Greek word are given to show how it is translated by those commentaries which have translations of the whole Greek text and, after a semicolon, by twelve major versions. "All versions" refers only to those versions used in the lexicon. "All translations" refers to both the versions and the commentaries used in the lexicon. Sometimes further comments are made about the meaning of the word or the significance of a verb's tense, voice, or mood.

The Questions

Under the heading QUESTION, a question is asked that comes from examining the Greek text under consideration. Typical questions concern the identity of an implied actor or object of an event word, the antecedent of a pronominal reference, the connection indicated by a relational word, the meaning of a genitive construction, the meaning of figurative language, the function of a rhetorical question, the identification of an ambiguity, and the presence of implied information that is needed to understand the passage correctly. Background information is also considered for a proper understanding of a passage. Although not all implied information and background information is made explicit in a translation, it is important to consider it so that the translation will not be stated in such a way that prevents a reader from arriving at the proper interpretation. The question is answered with a summary of what commentators have said. If there are contrasting differences of opinion, the different interpretations are numbered and the commentaries that support each are listed. Differences that are not treated by many of the commentaries often are not numbered, but are introduced with a contrastive 'Or' at the beginning of the sentence. No attempt has been made to select which interpretation is best.

The Use of this Book

This book does not replace the commentaries that it summarizes. Commentaries contain much more information about the meaning of words and passages. They often contain arguments for the interpretations that are taken and they may have important discussions about the discourse features of the text. In addition, they often have information about the historical, geographical, and cultural setting. Translators will want to refer to at least four commentaries as they exegete a passage. However, since no one commentary contains all the answers translators need, this book will be a valuable supplement. It makes more sources of exegetical help available than those to which most translators have access. Even if they had all the books available, few would have the time to search through all of them for the answers.

When many commentaries are studied, it soon becomes apparent that they frequently disagree in their interpretations. That is the reason why so many answers in this book are divided into two or more interpretations. The reader's initial reaction may be that all of these different interpretations complicate exegesis rather than help it. However, before translating a passage, a translator needs to know exactly where there is a problem of interpretation and what the exegetical options are.

ABBREVIATIONS

COMMENTARIES AND REFERENCE BOOKS

BAGD   Bauer, Walter. A Greek-English Lexicon of the New Testament and Other Early Christian Literature. Translated and adapted from the fifth edition, 1958 by William F. Arndt and F. Wilbur Gingrich. Second English ed. revised and augmented by F. Wilbur Gingrich and Frederick W. Danker. Chicago: University of Chicago Press, 1979.

BECNT   Turner, David L. Matthew. Baker Exegetical Commentary on the New Testament Grand Rapids: Baker Books, 2008.

BNTC   Filson, Floyd V. The Gospel According to St. Matthew. 2d ed. Black's New Testament Commentary. London: Adam and Charles Black, 1971.

CC   Gibbs, Jeffrey A. Matthew 1:1–11:1. Concordia Commentary. Saint Louis: Concordia Publishing House, 2008.

Gibbs, Jeffrey A. Matthew 11:2–20:34. Concordia Commentary. Saint Louis: Concordia Publishing House, 2010.

EBC   Carson, D. A. Matthew. The Expositor's Bible Commentary. 2 vols. Grand Rapids: Zondervan. 1995.

ESVSB   English Standard Version Study Bible. Wheaton: Crossway Bibles Div, Good News Publishers, 2008.

ICC   Davies, W. D. and Dale C. Allison, Jr. The Gospel According to Saint Matthew. The International Critical Commentary. 3 vols. Edinburgh: T. & T. Clark, 1988, 1997, 2004.

LN   Louw, Johannes P., and Eugene A. Nida. Greek-English Lexicon of the New Testament Based on Semantic Domains. New York: United Bible Societies, 1988.

Lns   Lenski, R. C. H. The Interpretation of St. Matthew's Gospel. Minneapolis: Augsburg, 1943.

My   Meyer, Heinrich August Wilhelm. Critical and Exegetical Handbook to the Gospel of Matthew. New York: Funk and Wagnalls, 1884.

NAC   Blomberg, Craig L. Matthew. New American Commentary. Nashville, TN: Broadman, 1992.

NIBC   Mounce, Robert H. Matthew. New International Biblical Commentary. Peabody, MA: Hendrickson, 1991.

NICNT   France, R. T. The Gospel of Matthew. New International Commentary on the New Testament. Grand Rapids: Eerdmans, 2007.

NIGTC   Nolland, John. The Gospel of Luke. The New International Greek Testament Commentary. Grand Rapids: Eerdmans, 2005.

NTC   Hendriksen, William. Exposition of the Gospel According to Matthew. New Testament Commentary. Grand Rapids: Baker, 1973.

PNTC   Morris, Leon. The Gospel according to Matthew. Pillar New Testament
       Commentary. Grand Rapids: Eerdmans, 1992.
TH   Newman, Barclay, and Philip C. Stine. A Handbook on The Gospel of
       Matthew. New York: United Bible Societies, 1988.
TRT   Carlton, Mathew E. The Gospel of Matthew. Translator's Reference
       Translation. Dallas, TX: SIL International, 2001.
WBC   Hagner, Donald A. Matthew, 2 vols. Word Biblical Commentary.
       Dallas: Word Books, 1993, 1995.

GREEK TEXT AND TRANSLATIONS

GNT   The Greek New Testament. Edited by B. Aland, K. Aland, J.
       Karavidopoulos, C. Martini, and B. Metzger. Fourth ed. London,
       New York: United Bible Societies, 1993.
LXX   The Septuagint. The Greek translation of the Jewish Scriptures,
       translated between 300–200 BC in Alexandria, Egypt.
CEV   The Holy Bible, Contemporary English Version. New York: American
       Bible Society, 1995.
ESV   The Holy Bible, English Standard Version. Wheaton: Crossway Bibles
       Div, Good News Publishers, 2001.
GW   God's Word. Grand Rapids: World Publishing, 1995.
KJV   The Holy Bible. Authorized (or King James) Version. 1611.
NASB   New American Standard Bible. La Habra, CA: Lockman Foundation,
       1995.
NCV   New Century Version. Dallas: Word Publishing, 1991.
NET   The NET Bible. New English Translation, New Testament. Version
       9.206. www.bible.com: Biblical Studies Press, 1999.
NIV   The Holy Bible, New International Version. Grand Rapids: Zondervan,
       1984.
NLT   The Holy Bible, New Living Translation. Wheaton, IL: Tyndale House,
       1996.
NRSV   The Holy Bible: New Revised Standard Version. New York: Oxford
       University Press, 1989.
REB   The Revised English Bible. Oxford: Oxford University Press and
       Cambridge University Press, 1989.
TEV   Good News Bible, Today's English Version. Second ed. New York:
       American Bible Society, 1992.

GRAMMATICAL TERMS

act.	active	mid.	middle
fut.	future	opt.	optative
impera.	imperative	pass.	passive
imperf.	imperfect	perf.	perfect
indic.	indicative	pres.	present
infin.	infinitive	subj.	subjunctive

EXEGETICAL SUMMARY OF MATTHEW 17–28

DISCOURSE UNIT—17:1–13 [CEV, ESV, GW, NASB, NCV, NET, NIV, NLT, NRSV, TEV]. The topic is the transfiguration [ESV, NASB, NET, NIV, NLT, NRSV, TEV], Moses and Elijah appear with Jesus [GW], Jesus talks with Moses and Elijah [NCV], the true glory of Jesus [CEV].

DISCOURSE UNIT—17:1–8 [ICC]. The topic is the Son of God transfigured: a greater than Moses.

17:1 **And after six days Jesus takes Peter and James and John his brother and leads**[a] **them up to a high mountain alone.**[b]

LEXICON—a. pres. act. indic. of ἀναφέρω (LN **15.176**) (BAGD 1. p. 63): 'to lead up' [BAGD, BECNT, BNTC, LN, NICNT, NIGTC, NTC; ESV, GW, NASB, NET, NIV, NLT, NRSV, REB, TEV], 'to bring up' [BAGD, CC, LN, PNTC, WBC; KJV], 'to take up' [BAGD; NCV]. The verb phrase 'leads them up' is translated 'they went up' [CEV]. This verb means to bring or lead up [LN].

  b. κατ' ἰδίαν (LN 28.67) (BAGD 4. p. 370): 'alone' [NIGTC, WBC], 'privately' [BAGD, CC, LN; NET], 'apart' [BNTC; KJV], 'by themselves' [BECNT, NICNT, PNTC; ESV, NASB, NCV, NIV, NRSV, REB], 'to be alone' [NLT], 'to be alone with them' [NTC], 'where they could be alone' [CEV, GW], 'where they were alone' [TEV]. The phrase κατ' ἰδίαν 'according to that which is private' is an idiom pertaining to what occurs in a private context or setting in order to keep it from being made known publicly [LN].

QUESTION—Why does the account in Luke 9:28 say 'about eight days later' instead of 'after six days'?

  Both Matthew and Mark apparently are using an exclusive reckoning that counts only the intervening days, whereas Luke may be using an inclusive reckoning [My, NTC]. Luke's description is a Greek way of expressing that it was about a week later [EBC]. Luke's report is not necessarily precise, as he says 'about eight days later' [My, NTC]. Both expressions mean 'about a week later' [NAC].

QUESTION—Why does Matthew mention that this happened just six days later?

  He is connecting this event with what Jesus had said a week earlier about the Son of Man coming in his kingdom [EBC, NICNT], and both passages must be read together [EBC]. This event and Jesus' statement at the end of chapter 16 should be linked together [Lns, NICNT, NIGTC, PNTC].

QUESTION—What is the function of the historical present tense 'leads'?

  It helps to engage the reader's imagination in a dramatic new development [CC, NICNT]. It gives emphasis to the correlation between 16:28 and this event [NIGTC]. It makes the account more vivid [PNTC, TH].

QUESTION—What mountain might this have been?

It could have been Mt. Meron [EBC, NAC, NICNT, NTC, WBC], which is the highest mountain in Galilee, having an altitude of over 3,900 feet [NAC, NICNT], or perhaps Mt. Hermon [BNTC, NIBC]. It is unlikely to have been Mt. Tabor, which was occupied at the summit [EBC, Lns, NAC, NIBC, NICNT, NTC, PNTC, WBC], or Mt. Hermon, which is too high and cold [EBC], and too far away [EBC, Lns, NAC].

17:2 And he-was-transfigured[a] before[b] them, and his face shone[c] like the sun, and his clothing became white[d] as the light.

LEXICON—a. aorist pass. indic. of μεταμορφόομαι (LN 58.16) (BAGD 1. p. 511): 'to be transfigured' [BAGD, BECNT, BNTC, NTC, PNTC, WBC; ESV, KJV, NASB, NET, NIV, NRSV, REB], 'to be transformed' [CC, NICNT, NIGTC], 'to be completely changed' [CEV], 'to be changed in appearance' [LN]. The passive verb phrase 'he was transfigured' is translated, 'Jesus' appearance was changed' [NCV]. It is also translated as an active verb phrase: 'a change came over Jesus' [TEV], 'Jesus' appearance changed' [GW]. This verb means to take on a different physical form or appearance [LN].

b. ἔμπροσθεν (LN 83.33) (BAGD 2.c. p. 257): 'before' [BAGD, BECNT, BNTC, CC, LN, NICNT, NTC, PNTC, WBC; ESV, KJV, NASB, NET, NIV, NRSV], 'in front of' [LN, NIGTC; CEV, GW], 'in their presence' [REB], 'in the sight of' [BAGD]. The phrase 'before them' is translated 'while they watched' [NCV], 'as the men watched' [NLT], 'as they looked on' [TEV]. This preposition describes a position in front of an object, whether animate or inanimate, which is regarded as having a spatial orientation of front and back [LN].

c. aorist act. indic. of λάμπω (LN 14.37) (BAGD 1.b. p. 466): 'to shine' [LN; all translations except GW, NCV], 'to become bright' [GW, NCV], 'to shine out, to shine forth, to gleam' [BAGD], 'to give light, to bring light' [LN]. This verb means to shine or to produce light, as in the case of heavenly bodies, lightning, candles, torches, etc. [LN].

d. λευκός (LN **14.50**) (BAGD 1. p. 472): 'white' [LN (79.27); all translations except NRSV, REB, TEV], 'bright' [BAGD, **LN** (14.50)], 'shining' [BAGD, LN], 'brilliant, gleaming' [BAGD], 'radiant' [LN (14.50)], 'light color' [LN (79.27)]. The phrase 'white as the light' is translated 'dazzling white' [NRSV, TEV], 'brilliant white' [REB]. This adjective describes being bright or shining, either of a source or of an object which is illuminated by a source [LN (14.50)].

QUESTION—What does it mean that he was 'transfigured'?

The verb itself does not communicate the nature of the event [NICNT, PNTC]. It was not a matter of changing form, but of having an added dimension of glory [NICNT]. His physical appearance was significantly altered [WBC]. He appeared in heavenly glory [PNTC]. Light emanated from within him [ICC]. His own divine glory shone out from within so that he was luminous and radiant [Lns, My].

QUESTION—What is the significance of this event?

The change of his appearance shows that Jesus is more than just a human teacher, and his association with Moses and Elijah shows that he is the Messiah, and again identifies as God's Son [NICNT]. This event was primarily for the benefit of Jesus' disciples, who were able to glimpse his pre-incarnate glory [EBC]. The disciples came into direct contact with the glory of God's immediate presence [WBC]. It is intended to be a foretaste of the transformation that the bodies of believers will experience at the end [ICC].

17:3 **And behold[a] Moses and Elijah appeared[b] to them talking-together[c] with him. 17:4 And answering Peter said to-Jesus, "Lord, it-is good for-us to-be here; if you-wish[d] I-will-make here three shelters,[e] one for-you and one for-Moses and one for-Elijah."**

TEXT—Manuscripts reading ποιήσω ὧδε 'I will make here' are given a B rating by GNT to indicate it was regarded to be almost certain. Some manuscripts omit ὧδε 'here' as do NTC; NET, NIV, NLT. Some manuscripts read ποιήσωμεν ὧδε 'let us make here' and this reading is followed by KJV. Some manuscripts read ποιήσωμεν 'let us make' which is followed by CEV.

LEXICON—a. ἰδού (LN 91.13) (BAGD p. 370): 'behold' [BAGD, BECNT, BNTC, CC, WBC; ESV, KJV, NASB], 'look' [BAGD, LN, PNTC], 'see' [BAGD], 'listen, pay attention' [LN], 'suddenly' [NICNT; GW, NLT, NRSV], 'all at once' [CEV], 'just then' [NIV], 'then' [NIGTC, NTC; NCV, NET, TEV], not explicit [REB]. This particle is a prompter of attention and it serves to emphasize the following statement [LN].

   b. aorist pass. indic. of ὁράω (LN 24.1) (BAGD 1.a.δ. p. 578): 'to appear' [BAGD, BECNT, BNTC, CC, NIGTC, NTC, PNTC, WBC; all versions except CEV, REB, TEV], 'to become visible' [BAGD], 'to be seen' [LN]. The phrase 'Moses and Elijah appeared to them' is translated 'they had a vision of Moses and Elijah' [NICNT], 'they saw Moses and Elijah appear' [REB], 'the three disciples saw Moses and Elijah' [TEV], 'Moses and Elijah were there' [CEV].

   c. pres. act. participle of συλλαλέω (LN 33.157) (BAGD p. 776): 'to talk with' [BAGD, BECNT, LN, NICNT, PNTC, WBC; all versions], 'to converse with' [BAGD, BNTC], '(to be) in conversation with' [NIGTC], 'to be engaged in conversation with' [NTC], 'to converse, to speak with" [LN], 'to speak together' [CC], 'to discuss with' [BAGD]. This verb means to converse with someone [LN].

   d. pres. act. indic. of θέλω (LN 25.1): 'to wish' [BECNT, BNTC, LN, NICNT, NIGTC, NTC, PNTC; ESV, NASB, NIV, NRSV, TEV], 'to desire' [LN], 'to want' [CC, LN; GW, NCV, NET, NLT], 'to like' WBC,

REB], 'to will' [KJV], not explicit [CEV]. This verb means to desire to
have or experience something [LN].

e. σκηνή (LN 7.9) (BAGD p. 754): 'shelter' [BECNT, CC, NICNT, NIGTC,
NTC, PNTC; CEV, NET, NIV, NLT, REB], 'tent' [BAGD, LN; ESV,
GW, NCV, TEV], 'dwelling' [NRSV], 'booth' [BAGD, BNTC], 'shrine'
[WBC], 'tabernacle' [KJV, NASB], 'lodging' [BAGD]. This noun
denotes a portable dwelling of cloth and/or skins that is held up by poles
and fastened by cords to stakes [LN].

QUESTION—What is the function of the exclamation ἰδού 'behold'?

It indicated emphasis [EBC, NICNT, NIGTC, PNTC, WBC]. It marks a new
development [CC]. It indicates that something remarkable is about to be
described [WBC]. It draws attention to the unexpected appearance of Moses
and Elijah [PNTC]. It emphasizes the marvel of what the disciples
experienced in this event [EBC]. It conveys dramatic effect [NICNT].

QUESTION—What is it that Peter is answering?

It only means that Peter spoke [BECNT, EBC, NICNT, NTC; CEV, ESV,
GW, NASB, NCV, NET, NIV, NLT, NRSV, REB, TEV]. Peter was
responding to the situation [Lns, My, NIBC, PNTC, WBC], not to something
that anyone has said [Lns]. This verb is used in a very general sense here
[Lns].

QUESTION—What is the significance of the presence of Moses and Elijah?

They represent the law and the prophets [BNTC, EBC, Lns, My, NAC,
NIBC, NTC, PNTC, TRT, TH, WBC], Moses being the great lawgiver and
Elijah being one of the greatest prophets [NIBC, PNTC]. It is as though the
law and the prophets are bearing witness to Jesus [TH]. Both men
represented prophecy as well as law [Lns]. They lived at the two greatest
periods of OT miracles [NAC]. Their presence together signifies that Jesus'
ministry is in harmony with the OT [WBC], or that OT revelation is fulfilled
in Jesus [PNTC]. Both are key prophetic figures [BECNT]. Both men had
experienced the glory of God on Mt. Sinai [ICC, NICNT, WBC], both ended
their earthly life in the context of a supernatural event, both suffered
rejection from their own people, and now because of Jewish expectations
that they would both return in the last days, their presence symbolizes the
coming of the messianic age [NICNT]. They were both expected to appear
as forerunners of the Messiah [BECNT, NAC]. Jesus, Moses, and Elijah are
in partnership in the grand sweep of God's purposes in that Moses is Jesus'
predecessor, bringing the law that Jesus fulfils, and Elijah is Jesus' precursor
through John the Baptist [NIGTC]. Moses does represent the OT law, but
Elijah's presence indicates that the end-time reign of God has begun to break
through [CC].

QUESTION—Why would Peter think that it was good for them to be there?

He sensed that they were experiencing something wonderful [EBC, Lns,
NIGTC]. He probably felt that it was good for them to be there so that they
could do whatever needed to be done, such as prepare shelters [NICNT].

QUESTION—Why did Peter propose to build shelters?

He may have felt that they should provide accommodation for such important visitors [BNTC, NICNT, NIGTC]. He may simply have wanted to be hospitable [BECNT]. He may have intended that as an honorary gesture, or felt compelled to commemorate this event [WBC], or simply had a concern to protect them from the cold [NTC] or from the heat of the sun [NICNT]. Since the Feast of Tabernacles, in which Jews lived in such shelters, had eschatological associations, Peter may have become convinced that the messianic age was about to dawn and he wanted to express gratitude for that [EBC]. He wanted Moses and Elijah to be able to stay longer so as to extend the experience as much as possible [Lns, NAC]. He does not want the brilliant vision to fade [BNTC].

QUESTION—What would a σκηνή 'shelter' consist of?

It would be some kind of hut made of branches and leaves [My, NICNT, NTC, PNTC, TRT, WBC].

17:5 While he-was- still -speaking behold a- bright[a] -cloud overshadowed[b] them, and behold a-voice from the cloud speaking, "This is my son, the beloved,[c] in whom I-am-well-pleased.[d] Listen[e] to-him."

LEXICON—a. φωτεινός (LN **14.50**) (BAGD p. 872): 'bright' [BAGD, BECNT, BNTC, LN, NIGTC, NTC, PNTC, WBC; all versions except TEV], 'shining' [BAGD, CC, **LN**; TEV], 'radiant' [BAGD, LN, NICNT]. This adjective describes that which is bright or shining, either of a source or of an object which is illuminated by a source [LN].

b. aorist act. indic. of ἐπισκιάζω (LN **14.62**) (BAGD 2. p. 298): 'to overshadow' [CC, **LN**, NICNT; ESV, GW, KJV, NASB, NET, NLT, NRSV], 'to cast a shadow over' [REB], 'to come over' [TEV], 'to come down over' [WBC], 'to cast a shadow upon' [LN], 'to cover' [BAGD, BECNT, BNTC, NTC, PNTC; NCV], 'to envelope' [NIGTC; NIV]. The phrase νεφέλη φωτεινὴ ἐπεσκίασεν αὐτούς 'a bright cloud over-shadowed them' is translated 'the shadow of a bright cloud passed over them' [CEV]. This verb means to cause a shadow by interposing something between an object and a source of light. In this verse the bright cloud was interposed between the sun and Jesus (and his disciples). The shining cloud may be more like a covering than a shadow [LN (14.62)]. The reference to this shining cloud is also discussed in LN 14.50 and 14.49. It could refer to the cloud as being bright or shining, either as the source of the shining or as the object which is illuminated by a source: 'while he was talking, a shining cloud came over them' [LN (14.50)]. Another possibility is that it was similar to what happened in 1 Kings 8:11 when the ark had been set up in the Most Holy Place of the Temple. A cloud had filled the house of the Lord so that 'the priests could not stand to minister because of the cloud, for the glory of the Lord had filled the house of the Lord' (1 Kings 8:11). The cloud was a bright, cloud-like object which represented the personal presence of God. In the case of

Matthew 17:5, which is generally regarded as a reference to the Shekinah presence of God, the cloud would not be merely reflecting light but would be the source of light [LN (14.49)].

c. ἀγαπητός (LN 58.53) (BAGD 1. p. 6): 'beloved' [BAGD, BECNT, BNTC, CC, NICNT, NIGTC, NTC, PNTC, WBC; ESV, KJV, NASB, NRSV, REB], 'only beloved' [BAGD], 'dearly loved' [NLT], '(my) own dear' [CEV, TEV], 'one dear' [NET], 'only, only dear' [LN]. This adjective is translated as a verb phrase: 'whom I love' [GW, NCV, NIV]. This adjective describes one who is the only one of his or her class, but at the same time is particularly loved and cherished [LN]. This first sentence of the quotation is exactly the same as God's words to Jesus in 3:17.

d. aorist act. indic. of εὐδοκέω (LN 25.87) (BAGD 2.a. p. 319): 'to be well pleased with/in' [BAGD, BECNT, BNTC, CC, NTC, PNTC, WBC; ESV, GW, KJV, NASB, NIV, NRSV], 'to be very pleased with' [NCV], 'to be pleased with' [LN; CEV, TEV], 'to take delight in' [BAGD; REB], 'to take great delight in' [NET], 'to come to delight in' [NIGTC], 'to take pleasure in' [LN]. The phrase ἐν ᾧ εὐδόκησα 'in whom I am well pleased' is translated 'who brings me great joy' [NLT]. This verb means to be pleased with something or someone [LN].

e. pres. act. impera. of ἀκούω (LN 31.56) (BAGD 4. p. 32): 'to listen to' [BAGD, BECNT, CC, LN, NICNT, NIGTC, NTC, PNTC; all versions except KJV], 'to hear' [BNTC, WBC; KJV], 'to accept, to listen and respond, to pay attention and respond, to heed' [LN], 'to follow' [BAGD]. This verb means to believe something and respond to it on the basis of having heard [LN].

QUESTION—In what way did the cloud overshadow them?

The luminous cloud was still capable of casting a faint shadow [EGT]. The cloud symbolized the Shekinah glory, the very presence of God [BECNT, EBC, ICC, PNTC, WBC]. Since the cloud itself was full of light, the word 'overshadowed' probably means the cloud 'covered them with its brightness' rather than 'covered them with its shadow' [PNTC, TH]. Luke 9:34 says that a cloud came and overshadowed them and adds that as 'the cloud 'was overshadowing them' the disciples were afraid 'as 'they' (either Jesus, Moses, and Elijah, or everyone present) entered into the cloud'. Then the disciples heard the voice from the cloud speak to them. Here in Matthew, almost all of the translations seem to imply that the bright cloud remained above all of them, but some translations and commentaries seem to say that probably Jesus, Moses, and Elijah were enveloped by that cloud [ICC, My, NIGTC, NTC, PNTC], or all of them were [Lns, TH, WBC; NIV].

QUESTION—What does ὁ ἀγαπητός 'the beloved' mean?

It means that Jesus is the only beloved, or uniquely beloved, Son of God [NICNT, WBC]. It expresses the Father's great love for the Son [NTC]. God's favor rests on him [NIBC]. It is a messianic title [PNTC]. It means that he is *chosen* [Lns]. This term reflects the wording of the Septuagint

Greek translation of Gen 22:2 which describes Isaac as Abraham's *only son, whom he loves* [WBC].

17:6 **And having-heard (this) the disciples fell on their faces[a] and were-greatly[b] -afraid.[c] 17:7 But Jesus approached and having-touched them said, "Rise and do- not -be-afraid." 17:8 And having-lifted-up[d] their eyes they-saw no-one except Jesus himself alone.[e]**

LEXICON—a. The idiom ἔπεσαν ἐπὶ πρόσωπον αὐτῶν 'fell on their faces' [BNTC, CC, NICNT, NIGTC, NTC, PNTC, WBC; ESV, REB, similarly KJV] is also translated 'they fell face down' [BECNT], 'they fell face down on/to the ground' [GW, NASB, NIV, NLT], 'they fell flat on the ground' [CEV], 'they fell to the ground' [NCV, NRSV], 'they threw themselves down with their faces to the ground' [NET], 'they threw themselves face downward on the ground' [TEV].

    b. σφόδρα (LN 78.19) (BAGD p. 796): 'greatly' [BAGD, LN], 'extremely' [BAGD], 'exceedingly, violently, terrible' [LN]. This adjective describes a very high point on a scale of extent, and in many contexts it implies vehemence or violence [LN]. See next entry for translations.

    c. aorist pass. indic. of φοβέομαι (LN **25.252**) (BAGD 1.a. p. 862): 'to be afraid' [BAGD, **LN**], 'to fear' [LN], 'to become frightened' [BAGD]. The phrase ἐφοβήθησαν σφόδρα 'were greatly afraid' [PNTC] is also translated 'were extremely afraid' [CC, **LN**], 'were much afraid' [BNTC], 'were sore afraid' [KJV], 'were so afraid that' [CEV], 'were so frightened that' [NCV], 'were exceedingly frightened' [NIGTC], 'were terribly frightened' [NTC], 'were overcome with fear' [NRSV], 'were overwhelmed with fear' [NET], '(they fell) terrified' [NIV], '(fell) in terror' [REB], 'were terrified' [BECNT, NICNT, WBC; ESV, GW, NASB, NLT], 'were so terrified that' [TEV]. This verb means to be in a state of fear [LN].

    d. aorist act. participle of ἐπαίρω (LN **24.34**) (BAGD 1. p. 281): 'to lift up' [BAGD, BNTC, CC, NIGTC; ESV, KJV, NASB], 'to lift' [WBC], 'to raise' [NTC, PNTC; REB]. The phrase ἐπάραντες...τοὺς ὀφθαλμοὺς 'having lifted up their eyes' is translated 'when they looked up' [BECNT, **LN**, NICNT; NCV, NET, NIV, NLT, NRSV], 'they looked up' [TEV], 'they raised their heads' [GW], 'when they opened their eyes' [CEV]. This idiom means to direct one's attention to something by looking closely at it, to notice, to look [LN].

    e. μόνος (LN 58.51) (BAGD 1.a.γ. p. 527): 'alone' [BAGD, BECNT, BNTC, CC, LN, NICNT, NIGTC, PNTC, WBC; NASB, NCV, NET, NRSV], 'only' [BAGD, NTC; CEV, ESV, KJV, NLT], 'all by oneself' [LN], not explicit [GW, NIV, REB, TEV]. This adjective describes the only item of a class in a place [LN].

QUESTION—What is the nature of their fear?

It was terror [BECNT, BNTC, CC, NAC, NICNT, NTC, TH, WBC; ESV, GW, NASB, NLT, REB, TEV], but there may have been an element of worship mixed with the fear [NAC, WBC].

QUESTION—What is communicated by the phrase αὐτὸν Ἰησοῦν μόνον 'Jesus himself alone'?

Jesus is of central importance [BECNT, EBC, NICNT], all the emphasis is on him [PNTC], and they must focus on him alone [NAC]. Jesus alone now occupies center stage, and he is the only one who can complete and fulfill salvation history [WBC]. All other revelation pales in comparison with him, and has only a supporting role [EBC]. Jesus alone is the revealer, and he alone is to be obeyed [BECNT]. After the dazzling and frightening vision it signals a return to the normal state of affairs [NICNT].

DISCOURSE UNIT—17:9–13 [ICC]. The topic is Elijah and John.

17:9 And (as) they were-going-down from the mountain Jesus commanded them saying, "Tell the vision[a] to-no-one until the Son of Man is-raised[b] from (the)-dead." **17:10** And the disciples asked him saying, "Then why do- the scribes -say that Elijah must[c] come first?"

LEXICON—a. ὅραμα (LN 33.488) (BAGD 1. p. 577): 'vision' [BECNT, BNTC, LN, NICNT, NIGTC, PNTC, WBC; ESV, KJV, NASB, NET, NRSV, REB, TEV], 'the sight' [CC], 'what you have seen' [NTC; GW, NIV, NLT], 'what they had seen' [CEV, NCV]. This noun denotes an event in which something appears vividly and credibly to the mind. Although it is not actually present, it implies the influence of some divine or supernatural power or agency [LN].

b. aorist pass. subj. of ἐγείρω (LN 23.94): 'to be raised' [BECNT, CC, NICNT, NIGTC, NTC, PNTC; CEV, ESV, NET, NIV, NLT, NRSV, REB, TEV], 'to be brought back to life' [GW], 'to be raised to life, to be made to live again' [LN]. This aorist passive is translated 'has risen' [BNTC; NASB, NCV], 'is risen' [WBC], 'is risen again' [KJV]. This verb means to cause someone to live again after having once died [LN].

c. pres. act. indic. of δεῖ (LN 71.34) (BAGD 1. p. 712): 'must' [BAGD, BECNT, BNTC, LN, NICNT, NIGTC, PNTC, WBC; all versions except TEV], 'to be necessary' [BAGD, CC, LN], 'to have to' [NTC; TEV]. This verb describes that which must necessarily take place [LN].

QUESTION—Why was it necessary that they not tell anyone about the vision?

Jesus did not want a shallow messianic zeal that was primarily political to grow [BECNT, EBC, Lns, My] and develop into a messianic uprising [NIBC]. The transfiguration could be understood in proper perspective only in light of the resurrection [NAC, NTC]. The strongest evidence for Jesus being the Messiah will be the resurrection, so if this vision is reported at this time it would stir up a misguided messianic zeal that might bring about a serious disillusionment when Jesus is crucified [EBC]. Enthusiasm about

Jesus' glory should not be allowed to divert him from the path of suffering [NAC].

QUESTION—Why did the disciples ask this question?

In their thinking Elijah should have already come if Jesus truly is the Messiah [BNTC, EBC, NTC, PNTC]. They wanted to know if the teaching of the scribes about Elijah was true, since it did not seem that Elijah had actually come before Jesus, the Messiah, had appeared [My]. They already expected that Elijah was supposed to come and restore all things, but they could not fit the possibility of Jesus' suffering and death into any framework that included such restoration [EBC]. Since Elijah had appeared in the transfiguration vision, they did not understand why the restoration Elijah was supposed to bring would be delayed, and why Jesus would have to suffer [BECNT]. They were concerned that the scribes could reject Jesus as the Messiah by saying Elijah had not yet come [NIBC, NTC]. They were wondering if the coming of Elijah was limited to his brief appearance at the transfiguration, which did not seem sufficient to fulfill what the scribes were saying would occur [Lns].

QUESTION—What does 'first' refer to?

Elijah was expected to appear before the coming of the Messiah [Lns, My, NAC, NIBC, NTC, PNTC, TH, TRT], who would then establish his kingdom [My]. Elijah was to come before the Day of the Lord [BECNT, BNTC, CC, NICNT, WBC]. The coming of the Messiah is the same as the coming of the Day of the Lord [PNTC].

17:11 And answering he-said, "Elijah does-come and will-restore[a] all (things);[b] **17:12** but I-say to-you that Elijah already came, and they-did-not -recognize[c] him but did to him whatever they-wanted; so also the Son of Man is-about-to suffer by[d] them." **17:13** Then the disciples understood[e] that he-spoke to-them about John the Baptist.

LEXICON—a. fut. act. indic. of ἀποκαθίστημι (LN 13.65) (BAGD 1. p. 91): 'to restore' [BAGD, BECNT, BNTC, CC, LN, NIGTC, NTC, PNTC, WBC; ESV, KJV, NASB, NET, NIV, NRSV], 'to reestablish' [BAGD], 'to set right' [REB], 'to set to rights' [NICNT], 'to get ready' [CEV, NLT, TEV], 'to put in order' [GW], 'to make something the way it should be' [NCV], 'to cause again to be' [LN]. This verb means to change to a previous good state [LN].

b. πᾶς (LN 59.23): 'all things' [BECNT, BNTC, CC, NIGTC, PNTC; ESV, KJV, NASB, NET, NIV, NRSV], 'everything' [NICNT, NTC, WBC; CEV, GW, NCV, NLT, REB, TEV], 'all, every, each' [LN]. This pronominal adjective describes the totality of any object, mass, collective, or extension [LN].

c. aorist act. indic. of ἐπιγινώσκω (LN 27.61) (BAGD 1.c. p. 291): 'to recognize' [BNTC, LN, NICNT, NTC, PNTC, WBC; all versions except KJV], 'to acknowledge' [BAGD, BECNT], 'to know' [CC, NIGTC; KJV], 'to give recognition to' [BAGD]. This verb means to identify newly acquired information with what had been previously learned or known [LN].

d. ὑπό with the genitive (LN 90.1) (BAGD 1.b. p. 843): 'by' [BAGD, LN], 'by means of' [NIGTC], 'of' [KJV]. The phrase ὑπ' αὐτῶν 'by them' is translated 'at their hands' [BECNT, BNTC, NICNT, NTC, PNTC, WBC; ESV, NASB, NET, NIV, NRSV, REB]. The phrase πάσχειν ὑπ' αὐτῶν 'to suffer by them' is translated 'to be treated badly by them' [CC], 'they will/are going to make...suffer' [CEV, GW, NCV, NLT], 'they will also mistreat' [TEV]. This preposition indicates the agent or force, whether person or event [LN].

e. aorist act. indic. of συνίημι (LN 32.5) (BAGD p. 790): 'to understand' [BAGD, LN; all translations except NLT], 'to realize' [NLT], 'to comprehend' [BAGD, LN], 'to have insight into, to perceive' [LN], 'to gain insight into' [BAGD]. This verb means to employ one's capacity for understanding and thus to arrive at insight [LN].

QUESTION—What is meant by the statement 'Elijah does come'?

1. He is affirming the scribes' expectation about the coming of Elijah, but informs them that it has already happened [EBC, BNTC, CC, Lns, My, NIBC, NICNT, NTC, PNTC, WBC]. The future tense verb 'will restore' refers to the continuation of a work that John began during his ministry [PNTC].

2. It appears that he is saying that Elijah will come again in the future [BECNT, NIGTC]. It is possible, though not completely clear, that the description of two witnesses in Revelation 11:3–6 anticipates that one of those witnesses will be Elijah himself [BECNT, NAC].

QUESTION—In what sense did John the Baptist restore anything, much less all things?

The ministry of John the Baptist brought about a deep change for a large number of people [Lns, My, NAC, NTC]. The future hope of restoration has already begun with the ministry of John [CC]. He did fulfill all of his mission of bringing about justice and true worship, but since he was a true prophet like those of the OT, he was persecuted and killed [EBC].

QUESTION—Who is included in the 'they' who did not recognize John, and who persecuted him?

'They' refers to the Jewish people generally and the leaders in particular who did not recognize him [EBC, Lns, NTC, PNTC], and it was the leaders who rejected him [EBC, NAC, NTC]. It is indefinite [NIGTC].

DISCOURSE UNIT—17:14–18:35 [PNTC]. The topic is Christ at work.

DISCOURSE UNIT—17:14–27 [NICNT]. The topic is back to the present: frustration and accommodation.

DISCOURSE UNIT—17:14–23 [NASB, NIV]. The topic is the healing of a boy with a demon [NIV], the demoniac [NASB].

DISCOURSE UNIT—17:14–20 [ICC; CEV, ESV, GW, NCV, NET, NLT, NRSV, TEV]. The topic is Jesus cures a demon-possessed boy [GW], Jesus heals a demon-possessed boy [NLT], Jesus heals a sick boy [NCV], Jesus heals a boy with a demon [ESV, TEV], Jesus heals a boy [CEV], Jesus cures a boy with a demon [NRSV], the disciples' failure to heal [NET], Jesus heals an epileptic [ICC].

17:14 **And (when they) had-approached the crowd, a-man came to-him kneeling-down (before) him** **17:15** **and saying, "Lord, have-mercy-on[a] my son, because he-is-epileptic[b] and suffers[c] terribly;[d] for often he-falls into the fire and often into the water.** **17:16** **And I-brought him to-your disciples, but they-were- not -able to-heal[e] him."**

LEXICON—a. aorist act. impera. of ἐλεέω (LN 88.76) (BAGD p. 249): 'to have mercy on' [BAGD, BECNT, BNTC, CC, LN, NIGTC, WBC; all versions except CEV, REB], 'to show mercy on' [LN, NICNT], 'to have pity on' [REB], 'to take pity on' [NTC, PNTC; CEV], 'to be merciful toward' [LN]. This verb means to show kindness or concern for someone in serious need [LN].

b. pres. mid. or pass. (deponent = act.) indic. of σεληνιάζομαι (LN **23.169**) (BAGD p. 746): 'to be an epileptic' [BNTC, **LN**, NIGTC, NTC, WBC; ESV, NRSV, REB, TEV], 'to have seizures' [BECNT; NET, NIV, NLT], 'to suffer epileptic seizures' [LN], 'to have epilepsy' [CEV, NCV], 'to be subject to fits' [NICNT], 'to be moon struck' [BAGD, CC], 'to be a lunatic' [PNTC; KJV, NASB]. The phrase σεληνιάζεται καὶ κακῶς πάσχει 'he is epileptic and suffers terribly' is translated 'he suffers from seizures' [GW]. This verb means to suffer epileptic seizures, and in ancient times this was associated with the supernatural power of the moon [LN].

c. pres. act. indic. of πάσχω (LN 90.66) (BAGD 2. p. 634): 'to suffer' [BECNT, CC, LN, NICNT, NIGTC, NTC, PNTC, WBC; ESV, GW, NCV, NET, NIV, NLT, NRSV], 'to be sick' [BNTC], 'to be ill' [NASB], 'to be vexed' [KJV], 'to experience' [LN], 'to be in an evil plight, to be badly off' [BAGD]. The phrase καὶ κακῶς πάσχει 'and he suffers terribly' is translated 'and he suffers harm' Matthew 17:15 [**LN**], 'he has a bad case' [CEV], 'he has bad fits' [REB], 'he has terrible attacks' [TEV]. This verb means to undergo an experience, usually difficult, and normally with the implication of physical or psychological suffering [LN].

d. κακῶς (LN **20.18**) (BAGD 1. p. 398): 'terribly' [CC, NICNT, WBC; ESV, NET, NLT, NRSV], 'greatly' [NIV], 'severely' [BAGD, NTC], 'badly' [BAGD, NIGTC], 'horribly' [BECNT], 'grievously' [PNTC], 'very much' [NCV], 'very (sick/ill)' [BNTC; NASB], 'sore (vexed)' [KJV], not explicit [CEV, GW, REB, TEV]. This adverb describes having experienced harm [LN]. This may be a reference to a type of epileptic seizure [LN].

e. aorist act. infin. of θεραπεύω (LN 23.139): 'to heal' [BNTC, CC, LN, NIGTC, WBC; CEV, ESV, NET, NIV, NLT, TEV], 'to cure' [BECNT, LN, NICNT, NTC, PNTC; GW, KJV, NASB, NCV, NRSV, REB]. This verb means to cause someone to recover health, often with the implication of having taken care of such a person [LN].

QUESTION—Who were the people who approached the crowd?

Since a new section begins here, it may be necessary to identify by name the persons involved: 'When Jesus and his disciples came back down the mountain to where the crowd was' [TH]. Two translations explicitly state that the people who came to the crowd were 'Jesus and his disciples' [CEV], 'Jesus and his followers' [NCV].

QUESTION—Does the man worship Jesus when he kneels and calls him 'Lord'?

Kneeling shows humility [EBC, NTC], reverence [NTC], respect [PNTC], entreaty [CC, EBC, NICNT, PNTC], even worship [CC]. When the man calls him 'Lord' he is making a Christological confession [NIBC]. Calling him 'Lord' expresses reverence, but it is not an acknowledgment of his deity or divine sonship [Lns]. The man may not have fully recognized all that Matthew's readers would have understood by the title 'Lord' [EBC].

17:17 And having-answered Jesus said, "O unbelieving[a] and perverse[b] generation, until[c] when will-I-be with you? Until when will-I-endure[d] you? Bring him here to-me." **17:18** And Jesus rebuked[e] it/him and the demon went-out from him and the boy was-healed from that hour.[f]

LEXICON—a. ἄπιστος (LN 31.98) (BAGD 2. p. 85): 'unbelieving' [BAGD, BECNT, BNTC, NIGTC; GW, NET, NASB, NIV, REB, TEV], 'faithless' [BAGD, CC, NICNT, NTC, PNTC; ESV, KJV, NLT, NRSV], 'unfaithful' [WBC], 'to be unbelieving, to be lacking in trust' [LN], not explicit [CEV]. This adjective is translated as a statement: 'you people have no faith' [NCV]. This adjective describes someone as not believing and it implies that he refuses to believe [LN].

   b. perf. pass. participle of διαστρέφω (LN 88.264) (BAGD 1.b. p. 189): 'to be perverted, to be led astray, to be misled' [LN]. This passive participle is translated as an adjective: 'perverse' [BECNT, BNTC, NIGTC, NTC, PNTC; KJV, NET, NIV, NRSV, REB], 'perverted' [**LN**, NICNT; NASB], 'depraved' [BAGD, WBC], 'crooked' [CC], 'twisted' [ESV], 'corrupt' [GW, NLT], 'wrong' [TEV]. This is translated as a statement: 'your lives are all wrong' [NCV]. The phrase 'unbelieving and perverted generation' is translated 'you people are too stubborn to have any faith' [CEV]. This verb means to cause someone to depart from correct behavior and thus engage in serious wrongdoing [LN].

   c. ἕως (LN 67.119) (BAGD II.1.c. p. 335): 'until, to' [LN]. The phrase ἕως πότε 'until when' [CC, NIGTC] is also translated 'how long' [BAGD, BECNT, BNTC, NICNT, NTC, PNTC, WBC; all versions except CEV,

NET, NRSV], 'how much longer' [CEV, NET, NRSV]. This adverb refers to the continuous extent of time up to a point [LN].

d. fut. mid. indic. of ἀνέχομαι (LN 25.171) (BAGD 1.a. p. 65): 'to endure' [BAGD; NET, REB], 'to bear with' [BAGD, CC; ESV], 'to put up with' [BAGD, BECNT, BNTC, NIGTC, NTC, PNTC, WBC; CEV, GW, NASB, NIV, NLT, NRSV, TEV], 'to be patient with' [LN; NCV], 'to have patience' [LN], 'to suffer (someone)' [KJV]. This verb means to be patient with someone in the sense of enduring possible difficulty [LN].

e. aorist act. indic. of ἐπιτιμάω (LN 33.419) (BAGD 1. p. 303): 'to rebuke' [BAGD, BECNT, BNTC, CC, LN, NICNT, NTC, PNTC, WBC; ESV, KJV, NET, NASB, NIV, NLT, NRSV], 'to speak sternly to' [NIGTC; CEV, REB], 'to order' [GW], 'to command' [NCV], 'to give a command to' [TEV], 'to reprove, to censure' [BAGD], 'to denounce' [LN]. This verb means to express strong disapproval of someone [LN].

f. ὥρα (LN 67.199) (BAGD 3. p. 896): 'hour' [LN], 'time' [BAGD]. The phrase ἀπὸ τῆς ὥρας ἐκείνης 'from that hour' [BNTC, CC, PNTC, WBC] is also translated 'from that very hour' [NIGTC; KJV], 'from that moment' [BECNT, NICNT; NET, NIV, NLT, REB], 'from that very moment' [NTC], 'at that very moment' [TEV], 'at that moment' [GW], 'right then' [CEV], 'from that time on' [NCV], 'instantly' [ESV, NRSV], 'at once' [BAGD; NASB]. This noun denotes the twelfth part of a day, measured from sunrise to sunset (in any one day the hours would be of equal length, but would vary somewhat depending on the time of the year) [LN].

QUESTION—What is the rhetorical effect of ᵊΩ 'O' with the vocative?

It expresses solemnity [Lns] and deep emotion [EBC, Lns]. Here it expresses frustration and disappointment [TRT].

QUESTION—To whom is Jesus' lament about unbelief and perversity primarily addressed?

1. Jesus addressed his disciples [BNTC, CC, Lns, My, NIGTC], but he also sees the same problem that the disciples have to be characteristic of the entire generation of people then living [BNTC, Lns, My, NIGTC, NICNT].

2. He addressed the whole crowd, including the disciples [EBC, ICC, NAC, NIBC, NTC, PNTC, TH]. He was making a general statement about the people of that day [EBC, PNTC, TH].

3. He addressed the crowd, but not his disciples [BECNT].

QUESTION—What was the nature of their problem?

Their minds were turned away from resolute faith in God [NTC]. They were spiritual dwarfs, lacking an attitude of trust in God and twisted in their thinking [PNTC]. Their lack of trust in God make the faith that they had weak and ineffective [ICC]. They needed to focus on who Jesus is and what he says, and ask him for his help and saving power, and relying fully on him [CC]. Their unbelief resulted from the moral failure of neglecting and distorting the evident truth available to them [EBC]. They had no faith and were confused about what is right and what is wrong [TH].

QUESTION—To whom is the plural imperative 'bring him here to me' addressed?

It is addressed to the nine disciples who had not been with Jesus on the mountain [CC, My, NICNT]. It is addressed to the boy's father and to the nine disciples [Lns, PNTC].

QUESTION—To whom or what did Jesus address his rebuke?

He rebuked the demon [BECNT, BNTC, My, NTC, PNTC, WBC; CEV, ESV, GW, KJV, NCV, NET, NIV, NLT, NRSV, TEV]. He spoke to the boy himself [NICNT, NIGTC, TH], but was addressing the demon that was in the boy [NICNT]. His rebuke of the boy reveals the presence of the demon [NIGTC].

17:19 Then the disciples having-approached Jesus privately said, "Why (were) we not -able to-cast- it -out?" **17:20** And he-said to-them, "Because of your little-faith.[a] Truly I-say to-you if you-have faith like[b] a-seed[c] of-mustard,[d] you-will-say to this mountain, 'Move[e] from-here to-there.' and it-will-move; and nothing will-be-impossible[f] for-you."

TEXT—Manuscripts reading ὀλιγοπιστίαν 'small faith' are given an A rating by GNT to indicate it was regarded to be certain. Manuscripts reading ἀπιστίαν 'unbelief' are followed by KJV.

LEXICON—a. ὀλιγοπιστία (LN **31.95**) (BAGD p. 563): 'little faith' [BECNT, CC, NTC, WBC; ESV, NET, NRSV], 'small faith' [PNTC], 'limitedness of faith' [BAGD], 'littleness of (your) faith' [NASB], 'poverty of faith' [BAGD], 'lack of faith' [NICNT], 'to not have enough faith, to have limited faith' [LN]. The phrase τὴν ὀλιγοπιστίαν ὑμῶν 'your little faith' is translated 'you had/have so little faith' [BNTC; GW, NIV], 'you do not have enough faith' [**LN**; CEV, NLT, TEV], 'your faith is too small' [NCV, REB]. This noun denotes the state of having little or inadequate faith [LN].

b. ὡς (LN 64.12) (BAGD II.3.b. p. 897): 'like' [BAGD, BNTC, CC, LN, PNTC; ESV], 'as' [LN, NTC; KJV], 'as small as' [WBC; NIV], 'even as small as' [NLT], 'no larger than' [CEV], 'no bigger than' [REB], 'the size of' [BECNT; GW, NASB, NET, NRSV], 'only the same size as' [NIGTC], 'as much as' [NICNT], 'as big as' [NCV, TEV]. This adverb indicates a relatively weak relationship between events or states [LN].

c. κόκκος (LN 3.35) (BAGD 1. p. 440): 'seed' [BAGD, LN; all translations], 'grain' [BAGD]. This noun denotes the kernel part of fruit [LN].

d. σίναπι (LN 3.20) (BAGD p. 751): 'mustard' [BAGD; all translations], 'mustard plant' [LN]. This noun denotes a large herb noted for its very small seeds and in some instances growing to a height of three meters (about ten feet).

e. aorist act. impera. of μεταβαίνω (LN 15.2) (BAGD 1.a.β. p. 510): 'to move' [BECNT, BNTC, NICNT, NIGTC, NTC, PNTC, WBC; all versions except KJV, TEV], 'to go' [TEV], 'to go across' [CC], 'to remove' [KJV], 'to move from one place to another, to change one's location, to depart' [LN], 'to go over, to pass over' [BAGD]. This verb means to effect a change of location in space, with the implication that the two locations are significantly different [LN].

f. fut. act. indic. of ἀδύνατος (LN 71.3) (BAGD p. 19): '(to be) impossible' [BAGD, LN; all translations except CEV, NCV, TEV], 'to be powerless, to be disabled' [BAGD]. The phrase 'nothing will be impossible for you' is translated 'everything would be possible for you' [CEV], 'all things will be possible for you' [NCV], 'you could do anything' [TEV]. This verb describes something as being impossible, presumably because of a lack of power to alter or control circumstances [LN].

QUESTION—To what mountain does the demonstrative adjective 'this' refer?

It refers to the mountain on which Jesus had been transfigured, and which they had just descended [BNTC, NAC, NIGTC, TH].

QUESTION—In his statement about the sufficiency of even a small amount of faith was Jesus implying that the disciples had no faith at all?

Their problem was not so much that they had a small amount of faith, but that the faith they had was so impoverished [EBC, PNTC]. Their faith was not persistent [NTC]. The main point about the mustard seed is its growth potential, and like the mustard seed, even if their faith was very small, it could grow tremendously [CC]. Though they had too little faith, at least they had some faith [NIGTC]. In this situation the disciples had failed to apply any faith at all [NICNT].

QUESTION—How literally did Jesus intend them to take his statement about moving mountains?

Jesus was using a proverbial expression about accomplishing what appears to be impossible [CC, EBC, ICC, My, NAC, NIBC, NIGTC, PNTC]. This promise is to be taken figuratively, not literally [BECNT, CC, My, Lns, NAC, NTC]. The statement is limited by the context, which refers to accomplishing kingdom work for which they had been granted authority [BECNT, CC, EBC, NAC, NTC]. He is saying that there are unlimited resources available to the believer for carrying out the will of God [PNTC, TRT], but not for things that are not the will of God [TRT].

17:21 [**But this kind will not go out except through prayer and fasting.**]

TEXT—Many ancient manuscripts omit verse 21. GNT omits it with an A rating, indicating that the text is certain. Only KJV includes it as part of the text. It is included in brackets by NAB.

DISCOURSE UNIT—17:22–18:35 [NIGTC]. The topic is status and behavior in the 'royal family'.

DISCOURSE UNIT—17:22–23 [ICC; CEV, ESV, GW, NCV, NET, NLT, NRSV, TEV]. The topic is Jesus again foretells that he will die and come back to life [GW], Jesus talks about his death [NCV], Jesus again predicts his death

[NLT], Jesus speaks again about his death [CEV, TEV], Jesus again foretells his death and resurrection [ICC; NRSV], Jesus again foretells death, resurrection [ESV], second prediction of Jesus' death and resurrection [NET].

17:22 (While they were) gathering[a] in Galilee Jesus said to them, "The Son of Man is-about to-be-handed-over[b] into (the) hands of men, **17:23** and they-will-kill him, and the third day he-will-be-raised.[c]" And they were-greatly[d] -distressed.[e]

TEXT—Manuscripts reading συστρεφομένων 'gathering' are given a B rating by GNT to indicate it was regarded to be almost certain. Manuscripts reading ἀνατρεφομένων 'abiding' are followed by KJV.

LEXICON—a. pres. pass. participle of συστρέφω (LN 15.125) (BAGD 2. p. 795): 'to gather' [BAGD, BECNT, BNTC, NICNT, NIGTC, PNTC; ESV, NCV, NLT, NRSV], 'to gather together' [CC, LN; NASB, NET], 'to gather around (him)' [WBC], 'to be gathered' [BAGD], 'to go about together' [REB], 'to move about together' [NTC], 'to travel together' [GW], 'to go from place to place' [CEV], 'to come together' [BAGD; NIV, TEV]. This verb means to cause to come together, whether of animate or inanimate objects [LN].

    b. pres. pass. infin. of παραδίδωμι (LN 37.12) (BAGD 1.b. p. 614): 'to be handed over' [BAGD, BECNT, CC, LN, NIGTC; CEV, GW, NCV, REB, TEV], 'to be delivered' [BAGD, BNTC, NTC, PNTC; ESV, NASB], 'to be betrayed' [NICNT, WBC; KJV, NET, NIV, NLT, NRSV], 'to be given over' [BAGD], 'to be delivered to the control of' [LN]. This verb means to hand someone over into the control of others [LN].

    c. fut. pass. indic. of ἐγείρω (LN 23.94) (BAGD 2.c. p. 215): 'to be raised' [BAGD, BECNT, CC, NICNT, NIGTC, PNTC, WBC; ESV, NASB, NET, NRSV], 'to be raised again' [KJV, REB], 'to be raised from the dead' [NCV, NLT], 'to be raised up' [NTC], 'to be raised to life,' [LN; NIV, TEV], 'to rise' [BAGD, BNTC], 'to rise to life' [CEV], 'to be brought back to life' [GW], 'to be made to live again' [LN]. This passive verb means to be caused to live again after having once died [LN].

    d. σφόδρα (LN 78.19) (BAGD p. 796): 'greatly' [BAGD, BNTC, LN; ESV, NET, NRSV], 'extremely' [BAGD, CC], 'exceedingly' [LN, NIGTC; KJV], 'deeply' [BECNT, NTC; NASB], 'very' [BAGD, PNTC, WBC; CEV, GW, TEV], 'utterly' [NICNT], not explicit [NCV, NIV, NLT, REB]. This adjective describes a very high point on a scale of extent and in many contexts implying vehemence or violence [LN].

    e. aorist pass. indic. of λυπέομαι (LN 25.274) (BAGD 2.a. p. 481): 'to be distressed' [BAGD, LN, NIGTC, NTC; ESV, NET, NRSV], 'to be grieved' [BECNT, BNTC, CC; NASB], 'to be dismayed' [NICNT], 'to be sad' [BAGD, LN, PNTC; CEV, GW, TEV], 'to be sorry' [KJV], 'to be sorrowful' [BAGD, WBC], 'to be filled with sadness' [NCV], 'to be filled with grief' [NIV, NLT, REB]. This verb means to be sad as the result of what has happened or what one has done [LN].

QUESTION—Does the passive participle συστρεφομένων 'gathering' have the active voice meaning of 'moving about' or the middle voice meaning of 'gathering'?

1. It has the middle voice meaning of 'gathering' [EBC, BECNT, BNTC, CC, NIBC, NICNT, NIGTC, PNTC, TH, WBC; ESV, NASB, NCV, NET, NIV, NLT, NRSV, TEV].
2. It has the active voice meaning of 'moving about' [Lns, NTC; CEV, GW, REB].

QUESTION—Who is the agent of the passive infinitive παραδίδοσθα 'to be handed over'?

It is ambiguous [BECNT, EBC, TRT], and probably intentionally so [EBC]. The passive voice suggests that God is the agent [BECNT]. He was handed over by divine providence [NIGTC]. It refers primarily to God, though in a secondary sense it also refers to men, including Judas [ICC]. It also hints at Judas' role in the betrayal [BECNT, Lns]. It can mean no more than to be handed over [NIBC], but can also refer to Judas' betrayal of Jesus [NIBC]. This refers to Judas' role in Jesus' arrest [NICNT].

DISCOURSE UNIT—17:24–27 [ICC; CEV, ESV, GW, NASB, NCV, NET, NIV, NLT, NRSV, TEV]. The topic is the temple tax [ICC], paying the temple tax [CEV, GW], Jesus talks about paying taxes [NCV], payment of the temple tax [NLT, TEV], the temple tax [ESV, NET, NIV], the tribute money [NASB].

17:24 And (when) they had-come into Capernaum, the (ones) collecting[a] the two-drachma[b] (tax) approached Peter and said, "Does- not your teacher -pay the two-drachma (tax)?"

LEXICON—a. pres. act. participle of λαμβάνω (LN **57.65**) (BAGD 1.d. p. 464): 'to collect (taxes)' [BAGD, LN], 'to receive taxes' [BAGD]. This participle is translated 'those who collected' [BECNT, BNTC, WBC; NASB], 'the men who collect/ed' [CC; NCV], 'the collectors' [NICNT, NIGTC, NTC, PNTC; all versions except KJV, NASB, NCV], 'they that received' [KJV]. This verb means to collect what is due, normally in terms of taxes and interest, with the possible implication of extortion [LN].

b. δίδραχμον (LN **57.181**) (BAGD p. 912): 'two-drachma tax' [BECNT, CC, LN; ESV, NASB, NIV], 'temple tax' [**LN**, NICNT, WBC; CEV, GW, NCV, NET, NLT, NRSV, REB, TEV], 'tribute money' [KJV], 'double drachma' [BNTC, NIGTC], 'double drachma tax' [NTC], 'didrachma' [PNTC], 'two drachma piece' [BAGD]. This noun denotes a tax of two drachmas that was required of every male Jew each year as a kind of Temple tax. The two-drachma coin referred to in this verse was approximately equivalent to two denari [LN].

QUESTION—What is the expected answer to the question "Does not your teacher pay the two-drachma tax?"

The form of the question shows that the answer anticipated would be 'yes, he does' [BECNT, ICC, NAC, NIBC, NICNT, NIGTC, PNTC, TH, TRT], but the tone of their question appears to express doubt that Jesus actually pays the tax [My]. They are inquiring about this because they think that Jesus might consider himself exempt from the tax [Lns, NICNT, NTC].

QUESTION—What was the purpose of the two-drachma tax?

It was paid by Jewish adult males for the upkeep of the temple [BECNT, BNTC, EBC, ICC, LN, Lns, My, NAC, NIBC, NICNT, NIGTC, NTC, PNTC, TH].

17:25 **He-says, "Yes." And having-come into the house Jesus anticipated[a] him saying, "What do-you-think[b] Simon? From whom do the kings of the earth receive taxes[c] or (the) poll-tax[d]? From their (own) sons[e] or from strangers[f]?"**

LEXICON—a. aorist act. indic. of προφθάνω (LN 67.29) (BAGD 1. p. 724): 'to anticipate' [BAGD, BNTC, LN, NIGTC], 'to speak first' [BAGD, BECNT, LN, NICNT, NTC, PNTC; ESV, NASB, NET, NRSV, TEV], 'to intercept' [CC], 'to forestall' [REB], 'to come to (him)' [WBC], 'to go up to (Peter)' [CEV], 'to be ahead of, to be in advance' [LN], 'to prevent' [KJV ('prevent' meant 'to precede' when the KJV was published)]. The phrase προέφθασεν αὐτὸν ὁ Ἰησοῦς λέγων 'Jesus anticipated him, saying' is translated 'before he could speak Jesus asked him' [GW, similarly NCV, NLT], 'Jesus was the first to speak' [NIV], 'Jesus spoke to him first' [**LN**]. This verb means to do something at a point of time which immediately precedes another point of time [LN].

   b. pres. act. indic. of δοκεῖ (impersonal form): (LN **31.30**) (BAGD 3.a. p. 202): 'to think' [BAGD, BECNT, BNTC, CC, LN, NICNT, NIGTC, NTC, PNTC; all versions except REB, TEV], 'to believe' [BAGD], not explicit [REB]. The question Τί σοι δοκεῖ; 'What do you think?' [**LN**] is also translated 'What is your opinion?' [TEV], 'How does it seem to you? [WBC]. This verb means to hold an opinion based upon appearances which may be significantly different from reality [LN].

   c. τέλος (LN **57.179**) (BAGD 3. p. 812): 'tax' [BAGD, LN; CEV], 'duty' [BAGD, **LN**, NICNT; NIV], 'customs' [BAGD, BECNT; KJV, NASB], 'custom duties' [CC, PNTC], 'duties' [TEV], 'revenue' [BNTC, LN, WBC], 'dues' [NIGTC], 'toll' [NTC; ESV, NET, NRSV], 'fee' [GW]. The phrase τέλη ἢ κῆνσον 'taxes or the poll tax' is translated 'different kinds of taxes' [NCV], 'tribute money' [REB]. The phrase ἀπὸ τίνων λαμβάνουσιν τέλη ἢ κῆνσον 'from whom do (the kings) receive taxes or the poll tax?' is translated 'do (kings) tax (their own people, etc.)' [NLT]. This noun denotes payments customarily due a governmental authority [LN]. The term τέλος differs from κῆνσος (57.180) in being somewhat more generic in meaning. In certain contexts τέλος may refer to various kinds of direct taxes, customs duties, and tribute money, but in contexts such as this verse in which κῆνσος also occurs, τέλος probably refers primarily to customs duties, while κῆνσος refers to a direct poll tax upon all adult males [LN].

d. κῆνσος (LN 57.180) (BAGD p. 430): 'poll tax' [BAGD, BNTC, CC, LN; NASB], 'tax' [BAGD, BECNT, LN, NICNT, NIGTC, NTC, WBC; ESV, GW, NET, NIV, TEV], 'tribute' [PNTC; KJV, NRSV], 'fee' [CEV], not explicit [NCV, NLT, REB]. This noun denotes a tax paid by each adult male to the government [LN].

e. υἱός (LN **11.69**, 10.42): 'son' [BNTC, CC, LN (10.42), NICNT, NIGTC, NTC, PNTC; ESV, NASB, NET, NIV], 'citizen' [**LN** (11.69)]. This plural noun is translated 'children' [BECNT, WBC; KJV, NCV, NRSV], 'family members' [GW], 'people' [CEV, REB], 'their own people' [NLT], 'citizen of the country' [TEV]. This noun denotes an immediate male offspring [LN (10.42)], or it may denote a member of a sociopolitical group with some presumed ethnic relationship [LN (11.69)].

f. ἀλλότριος (LN 11.74) (BAGD 1.b.β. p. 40): 'stranger' [BAGD, BECNT, CC, LN, NICNT; KJV, NASB], 'foreigner' [LN, NTC; CEV, NET, TEV], 'alien' [BNTC; REB], 'outsider' [PNTC], 'others' [NIGTC, WBC; ESV, NCV, NIV, NRSV], 'other people' [GW], 'people they have conquered' [NLT]. This noun denotes a person from another geographical or cultural region and/or one not known to members of the socio-political group in question [LN].

QUESTION—What is the difference between τέλος 'tax' and κῆνσος 'poll tax'?

Τέλος 'tax' probably refers to customs on the movement of goods [BNTC, ICC, Lns, My, NIGTC, NICNT, NTC PNTC, TRT], and was indirect and local [NIBC]. The κῆνσος 'poll tax' was a 'head' tax imposed on individuals [BNTC, ICC, My, Lns, NIGTC, NICNT, NTC, PNTC, TRT], and was normally paid to the imperial treasury [NIBC]. The two terms used together refer to the whole range of taxation [BECNT, NIGTC].

QUESTION—What is the intended contrast in 'from their own sons or from strangers'?

1. It is between the children of the king and others in his kingdom [BECNT, CC, EBC, ICC, Lns, My, NIBC, NICNT, NIGTC, NTC, PNTC, WBC; GW, KJV, NASB, NCV, NIV, NRSV].
2. It is between the citizens of the king's country and foreign subjects [TH, TRT; CEV, NLT, REB, TEV].
3. It is between the children of the king and foreign subjects [BNTC].

17:26 (He) having-said, "From foreigners," Jesus said to-him, "Then the sons are exempt.[a] **17:27** But so-that we- not -offend[b] them, having-gone to (the) lake cast a-fishhook and take the first fish coming-up, and having-opened its mouth you-will-find a-stater;[c] having-taken that give to-them for[d] me and you."

LEXICON—a. ἐλεύθερος (LN 37.134) (BAGD 2. p. 250): 'exempt' [BECNT, BNTC, NTC; GW, NASB, NIV, REB], 'free' [BAGD, CC, LN, NICNT, NIGTC, PNTC, WBC; ESV, KJV, NET, NLT, NRSV], 'independent, not bound' [BAGD]. The phrase ἐλεύθεροί εἰσιν 'are free' is translated 'don't have to pay' [CEV, NCV, TEV]. This adjective pertains to being free [LN].

b. aorist act. subj. of σκανδαλίζω (LN **25.179**) (BAGD 2. p. 753): 'to offend' [BECNT, BNTC, CC, LN, WBC; KJV, NASB, NASB, NIV, NLT, TEV], 'to cause offence to' [NIGTC; REB], 'to give offense to' [BAGD; ESV, NRSV], 'to ensnare' [NTC], 'to be a snare to' [PNTC], 'to cause to stumble' [NICNT], 'to cause to be offended' [**LN**], 'to create a scandal' [GW], 'to upset' [NIV], 'to cause trouble' [NCV], 'to anger, to shock' [BAGD]. This verb means to cause someone to experience anger and/or shock because of what has been said or done [LN].

c. στατήρ (LN **6.80**) (BAGD p. 764): 'stater' [BAGD, BNTC, CC, LN, NIGTC, NTC, PNTC], 'coin' [**LN**, WBC; CEV, GW, NCV, NRSV, TEV], 'stater coin' [BECNT], 'silver coin' [NICNT; REB], 'large silver coin' [NLT], 'four drachma coin' [NET, NIV], 'shekel' [ESV, NASB], 'piece of money' [KJV]. This noun denotes a silver coin worth two didrachma or approximately four denarii [LN].

d. ἀντί with the genitive (LN **90.37**) (BAGD 3. p. 73): 'for' [BAGD, BECNT, BNTC, **LN**, NICNT, NIGTC, NTC, PNTC, WBC; all translations except CEV, TEV], 'worth enough for' [TEV], 'in exchange for' [CC], 'on behalf of' [BAGD, LN], 'in place of' [BAGD], not explicit [CEV]. This preposition indicates a participant who is benefited by an event, usually with the implication of some type of exchange or substitution involved [LN].

QUESTION—What did Jesus mean when he said, 'Then the sons are free'?

Jesus acknowledged that the temple tax was an obligation to God, but since he is the unique Son of God, he is exempt. Yet even though he is exempt, he will pay the tax so as not to offend the collectors [EBC, NTC, PNTC]. The sons are also the Christians, the children of God by adoption [WBC]. If Jesus refused to pay the tax, people would conclude that he rejected all that the temple stood for and would then turn away from him and his message of salvation [PNTC].

DISCOURSE UNIT—18:1–19:2 [BECNT, EBC, NICNT]. The topic is discourse 4: values and relationships in the kingdom community [BECNT], living together as disciples: the discourse on relationships [NICNT], fourth discourse: life under kingdom authority [EBC].

DISCOURSE UNIT—18:1–35 [NAC, WBC; REB]. The topic is implications for the Church: humility and forgiveness [NAC], the fourth discourse: life in the community [WBC], teaching about the kingdom [REB].

DISCOURSE UNIT—18:1–14 [ICC]. The topic is on children and little ones.

DISCOURSE UNIT—18:1–10 [NLT]. The topic is the greatest in the kingdom.

DISCOURSE UNIT—18:1–9 [NCV, NET, NIV]. The topic is who is the greatest? [NCV], questions about the greatest [NET], the greatest in the kingdom of heaven [NIV].

DISCOURSE UNIT—18:1–6 [ESV, NASB]. The topic is who is the greatest? [ESV], rank in the kingdom [NASB].

DISCOURSE UNIT—18:1–5 [CEV, GW, NRSV, TEV]. The topic is greatness in the kingdom [GW], who is the greatest? [CEV, TEV], true greatness [NRSV].

18:1 **At that time the disciples came to Jesus saying, "Who then[a] is greatest[b] in the kingdom of the heavens?" 18:2 And having-called a-child he-stood him in (the) midst of-them 18:3 and said, "Truly I-say to-you, unless you-are-changed[c] and become like children you will- certainly not - enter the kingdom of the heavens.**

LEXICON—a. ἄρα (LN **89.46**) (BAGD 2. p. 103): 'then' [BAGD, BECNT, BNTC, LN, NTC, PNTC; NASB], 'therefore' [CC], 'so' [LN, NICNT], 'indeed' [WBC], not explicit [NIGTC; CEV, ESV, GW, KJV, NCV, NET, NIV, NLT, NRSV, REB, TEV]. This conjunction indicates the result to be inferred from what has preceded it [LN].

    b. μέγας (LN 87.22) (BAGD 2.b.α. p. 498): 'great' [BAGD, LN], 'important' [LN]. This comparative form is translated as a superlative: 'greatest' [all translations]. This adjective describes being great in terms of status [LN].

    c. aorist pass. subj. of στρέφω (LN 13.63) (BAGD 2.b. p. 771): 'to be changed' [BAGD, LN], 'to change' [BAGD, BECNT; CEV, GW, NIV, NRSV, TEV], 'to revise one's ways' [WBC], 'to turn' [BNTC, CC, NIGTC, NTC; ESV], 'to turn around' [NICNT; NET, REB], 'to turn from your sins' [NLT], 'to be turned' [PNTC], 'to be converted' [BAGD; KJV, NASB], 'to be turned into' [LN]. The phrase ἐὰν μὴ στραφῆτε 'unless you are changed' is translated 'you must change' [NCV]. This verb means to cause something to turn into or to become something else [LN].

QUESTION—When does this take place?

'That time' links this with the preceding account [CC, EBC, Lns, NAC, NIBC, NICNT, NTC, PNTC, TH]. It happened immediately after it and continues a similar line of thought [NTC]. All that is related in 17:24–18:35 occurred on the same day [Lns]. It refers specifically to the time when Jesus was having the conversation with Peter narrated in the preceding context [My].

QUESTION—What relationship is indicated by the conjunction ἄρα 'then'?

There is a close connection with what had been said in the immediately preceding passage. Since they have the significant status as sons of God (17:26), then who would be the greatest of them? [CC, PNTC]. If the sons of the kingdom are free and the kingdom itself will be a great privilege, then the next question is 'Who will be greatest?' [BNTC]. However, others think the word 'then' has no significant function other than to perhaps enliven the language [NIGTC] and this conjunction is not even translated by CEV, ESV, GW, KJV, NCV, NET, NIV, NLT, NRSV, REB, TEV.

QUESTION—When did they think this kingdom would be established?

They thought his kingdom would soon be established [CC, Lns, My, NAC, NICNT, PNTC, WBC]. The issue about being greatest 'in the kingdom of heaven' concerns the people of the kingdom, that is, those who make up the church. So it is unlikely that the eschatological kingdom is meant here [WBC]. They had become increasingly aware that Jesus was the Messiah, and they thought that the messianic kingdom was just around the corner [PNTC]. They probably thought, 'Why is Peter regarded as chief among us? Who is going to be chief in the coming kingdom?' [ICC].

QUESTION—Who was the child Jesus called to stand before the disciples?

Some modify the noun παιδίον 'child' with the adjective 'little' [BNTC, NTC, PNTC, WBC; GW, KJV, NCV, NIV, NLT]. The child was probably a small child [PNTC], yet old enough to come when Jesus called [BECNT]. This child was probably no more than ten years old [TRT]. The noun παιδίον 'child' is neuter, so it is not known whether the child was male or female. [CC, NICNT, NIGTC].

QUESTION—What is the function of Jesus' opening words, 'Truly I say to you'?

It is a solemn introduction [BECNT, CC, EBC, Lns, My, NICNT, NTC, PNTC] that stresses the importance of what is being said [CC, NIGTC, TH, WBC].

QUESTION—In what way must the disciples be changed?

They must change from their present conduct [EBC, NIBC] and become like little children [WBC]. They must become indifferent to status or greatness [NAC, TH], and have a radical change of attitude, turning from sin, especially pride about prestige, and adopting an attitude of humility [BECNT]. It is a radical change of orientation such that one will no longer be concerned about personal status, but will start over on a completely new footing [NICNT]. They had to turn from worldly ambition [NTC]. It meant seeing themselves to be in need of a fresh new start, and with courageous humility begin their religious lives all over again [ICC]. This expresses the concept of repentance, of changing one's ways [CC, My, PNTC, WBC].

QUESTION—Was Jesus expressing doubt about whether they might enter the kingdom of heaven?

He is telling them that if they seek greatness according to the world's values, they will *not* enter the future heavenly kingdom [BECNT, BNTC, EBC, My, NIBC, NTC, PNTC, WBC]. The double negative here is emphatic [BECNT, My, NTC, WBC]. He is restating what he has taught them before about entering the kingdom and being saved [CC]. He is not expressing doubt about whether or not they were citizens of God's kingdom [NICNT, NIGTC], but he is warning them not to become complacent and that their concern for status and importance is incompatible with the values of that kingdom [NICNT]. They must sustain that new orientation and recognize the challenge it presents in its implications for life [NIGTC].

QUESTION—What trait or quality of children was Jesus primarily focusing on in this statement?

A child is held up as an ideal of humility [BNTC, EBC, Lns, NIGTC]. He is referring to a child's lack of concern for social importance [BECNT, EBC, ICC, My, NIBC, PNTC, TRT, WBC]. This does not refer to a return to the state of childhood. The pretentious attitude of the disciples, who are each hoping for the highest position within the kingdom, is being contrasted with the lack of pretension of children, who are humble and unconcerned about status [TH].

18:4 So whoever humbles[a] himself like this child, this-one is the greatest in the kingdom of the heavens. **18:5** And whoever welcomes[b] one such little-child in my name welcomes me.

LEXICON—a. fut. act. indic. of ταπεινόω (LN **88.56**) (BAGD 2.b. p. 804): 'to humble oneself' [BAGD, BECNT, BNTC, CC, NIGTC, PNTC, WBC; ESV, KJV, NASB, NET, NIV, REB, TEV], 'to humble' [BAGD, **LN**], 'to become humble' [BAGD, NTC; NLT, NRSV], 'to be humble' [CEV], 'to make oneself humble' [NCV], 'to take the lowly position (of this child)' [NICNT]. The phrase ὅστις ταπεινώσει ἑαυτὸν ὡς τὸ παιδίον τοῦτο 'whoever humbles himself as this child' is translated 'whoever becomes like this little child' [GW]. This verb means to cause someone to be or to become humble [LN].

b. aorist mid. (deponent = act.) subj. of δέχομαι (LN 34.53) (BAGD 1. p. 177): 'to welcome' [BAGD, BECNT, LN, NICNT, NTC; CEV, GW, NET, NIV, NLT, NRSV, TEV], 'to receive' [BAGD, BNTC, CC, LN, NIGTC, PNTC, WBC; ESV, KJV, NASB, REB], 'to accept' [LN; NCV]. This verb means to accept the presence of a person with friendliness [LN].

QUESTION—What does it mean 'to humble' oneself?

It is to humble oneself to the point of having no more social status than a child [BECNT, EBC, NICNT, TH], who is dependent on and subject to others [NICNT]. It is to have no concern or pretensions about one's status [NIBC], to be humble and unassuming [My], to turn from worldly ambition [NTC], to consider oneself insignificant [TH]. Humility is to be content with a low status, and it is the opposite of seeking position and power [WBC]. It is to acknowledge one's own dependence and powerlessness [CC, NAC, PNTC], yielding to God's will [Lns].

QUESTION—What does it mean to receive or accept such a child in Jesus' name?

It means to accept someone, whether child or adult, because he or she is Jesus' disciple [BECNT, CC, EBC, NAC, NTC, TH, TRT, WBC], and 'Jesus' name' expresses the sum of that person's belief and confession [My]. It is to receive someone as though he or she were Jesus himself [NIGTC]. To receive anyone to whom Jesus has united himself is like receiving Jesus at the same time [ICC]. It is to accept someone because that is what Jesus would do [PNTC]. In so doing they accept Jesus' message and become disciples themselves [NAC]. Welcoming anyone who belongs to Jesus is to welcome Jesus himself [BNTC, NTC]. It means to treat one of his disciples hospitably because that disciple is ministering in Jesus' name [WBC]. To receive a humble, lowly, weak disciple because of what Jesus has taught is to receive that disciple in Jesus' name [CC, Lns]. In this context, it is about accepting literal children [ICC, Lns, NIBC, PNTC], although this could be extended to include adults who have humbled themselves as such a child [Lns].

DISCOURSE UNIT—18:6–10 [GW]. The topic is causing others to lose faith.

DISCOURSE UNIT—18:6–9 [CEV, NRSV, TEV]. The topic is temptations to sin.

18:6 But whoever causes- one of these little-ones who-believe in me -to-sin,[a] it-would-be-better for-him that a-donkey[b] millstone be-hung-from around his neck and he-be-caused-to-drown[c] in the depths of-the sea.

   LEXICON—a. aorist act. subj. of σκανδαλίζω (LN 88.304) (BAGD 1.a. p. 752): 'to cause to sin' [BAGD, BECNT, BNTC, LN, NTC, PNTC; ESV, NCV, NET, NIV], 'to cause to fall into sin' [NLT], 'to cause to stumble' [CC, NICNT, NIGTC, WBC; CEV, NASB], 'to put a stumbling block before' [NRSV], 'to cause to lose faith' [GW, TEV], 'to cause the downfall' [REB], 'to offend' [KJV]. This verb is a figurative extension of meaning of the verb that means 'to cause to stumble' and means to cause to sin, with the probable implication of providing some special circumstances which contribute to such behavior [LN].

   b. ὀνικός (LN **4.32**) (BAGD p. 570): 'of a donkey' [LN]. The phrase μύλος ὀνικός 'a donkey millstone' [CC, NIGTC] is also translated 'an ass's millstone' [ICC], 'a millstone turned by a donkey' [LN], 'a millstone worked by donkey power [BAGD], 'a millstone that a donkey causes to go round (rotate) by pulling on a shaft' [LN], 'a millstone' [KJV, REB]. Most translations indicate the significance of it being 'a *donkey* millstone': 'a heavy millstone' [BECNT, NICNT, NTC; NASB], 'a large millstone' [BNTC, WBC; NCV, NLT, TEV], 'a huge millstone' [NET], 'a great millstone' [ESV, NRSV], 'a heavy stone' [CEV], 'a large stone' [GW, NCV]. This adjective is derived from the noun ὄνος 'donkey' and means 'pertaining to a donkey' [BAGD, LN].

   c. aorist pass. subj. of καταποντίζω (LN **15.117**) (BAGD p. 417): 'to be drowned' [BAGD, **LN**; all translations except CEV], 'to be thrown (into the ocean)' [CEV], 'to be made to sink' [BAGD, LN]. This verb means to cause something or someone to sink into deep water [LN].

   QUESTION—Who are these 'little ones'?

   1. Jesus is still referring to the little ones like the child who was discussed in verse 2, whether children or humble disciples who believe in him [PNTC].

They are actual young children who believe in him [BNTC; GW]. Some make a discourse break after this verse [ESV, NASB].

2. Now the focus is on Jesus' disciples, who are still described as 'little ones' [BECNT, CC, EBC, ICC, My, NAC, NICNT, NIGTC, NTC, PNTC, TH, WBC], a title that speaks of their lowly status [NICNT, PNTC, WBC], or their vulnerability to stumbling into ruin with regard to their faith [CC], or their childlikeness [Lns]. 'Little ones' describes his disciples, though here he is probably referring to those who were most vulnerable [NAC]. It is the average church member, who could be led into error by false teaching [NIBC]. Some make a discourse break before this verse [NIGTC, TH; CEV, GW, NRSV, TEV].

QUESTION—How does he cause the little ones to sin?

He seriously damages or destroys their faith [CC, ICC, My, NAC, NIBC, NICNT, TH, TRT, WBC]. He destroys them spiritually [Lns]. He entices them into moral corruption that brings eternal judgment [BECNT], or into any sin that would bring judgment [NTC, PNTC]. He rejects or ignores Jesus' followers in such a way that they are impeded in their discipleship [EBC].

DISCOURSE UNIT—18:7–11 [NASB]. The topic is stumbling blocks.

DISCOURSE UNIT—18:7–9 [ESV]. The topic is temptations to sin.

18:7 Woe[a] to-the world because-of the things-that-cause them-to-sin.[b] For (it-is) inevitable[c] (that) the-causes-for-sin come, but woe to-the man through whom the cause-for-sin comes.

LEXICON—a. οὐαί (LN 22.9) (BAGD 1.b p. 591): 'woe, alas!' [BAGD], 'disaster, horror' [LN]. The clause οὐαὶ τῷ κόσμῳ 'woe to/unto the world' [BECNT, BNTC, CC, NICNT, NIGTC, NTC, PNTC, WBC; ESV, KJV, NASB, NET, NIV, NRSV] is also translated 'alas for the world' [REB], 'the world is in for trouble' [CEV], 'how horrible it will be for the world' [GW], 'how terrible for the world] [TEV], 'how terrible for the people of the world' [NCV], 'what sorrow awaits the world' [NLT], This particle refers to a state of intense hardship or distress [LN].

b. σκάνδαλον (LN 88.306) (BAGD 2. p. 753): 'that which causes someone to sin' [LN], 'temptation to sin, enticement to apostasy' [BAGD]. The clause ἀπὸ τῶν σκανδάλων 'because of the things that cause them to sin' is translated 'because of the things that lead people to sin' [PNTC], 'because of (its) stumbling blocks' [NICNT; NASB. NET, NRSV], 'for the stumbling blocks it brings' [WBC], 'from the causes of stumbling' [CC, NIGTC], 'because of the things that cause them/people to sin' [NCV, NIV], 'because of things that cause sin'[BECNT], 'because of the way it causes people to sin' [CEV], 'because of temptations to sin' [BNTC], 'because of its temptations' [NTC], 'because it causes people to lose their faith' [GW], 'because it tempts people to sin' [NLT], 'that there are things that make people lose their faith' [TEV], 'for temptations to sin' [ESV], 'because of offences' [KJV], 'that any of them should be made to fall' [REB]. This noun is a figurative extension of meaning of 'trap' and denotes that which, or the one who, causes someone to sin [LN].

c. ἀνάγκη (LN **71.38**) (BAGD 1. p. 52): 'inevitable, necessary, must' [BAGD], 'bound to happen' [**LN**], 'inevitability, what is bound to be, to have to be' [LN]. The clause ἀνάγκη ἐλθεῖν τὰ σκάνδαλα 'it is inevitable that the causes for sin come' is translated 'it is inevitable that stumbling blocks come' [NASB], 'it is necessary that stumbling blocks come' [NET], 'there is a necessity that causes of stumbling come' [NIGTC], 'the causes of stumbling come as an inevitability' [CC], 'stumbling blocks are bound to occur, [NICNT], 'things that cause sin must come' [BECNT], 'things that lead to sin must come' [PNTC], 'temptations are inevitable' [NLT], 'temptations must come' [NTC], 'temptations are bound to come' [NRSV], 'it is necessary that temptations come' [BNTC; ESV], 'it must needs be that offences come' [KJV], 'such things must come' [NIV], 'such things will/must happen' [NCV, REB], 'such things will always happen' [TEV], 'situations that cause people to lose their faith will arise' [GW], 'there will always be something to cause people to sin' [CEV]. This noun denotes necessity as a law of human experience [LN].

QUESTION—Is the word 'woe' used as a lament or as a warning?

1. In both places in this verse this word is used to express warning [BECNT, CC, EBC, NTC, TH, WBC]. It is a proclamation of coming judgment [EBC, Lns]. In both places 'woe' expresses the fact that misery will come on individuals as well as the world for the causes of stumbling they present [WBC].

2. The first 'woe' in this verse expresses lament or regret that the world is beset by so many things that cause people to sin, but the second 'woe' expresses blame and condemnation for those who cause others to sin [My, NICNT, TRT].

QUESTION—What is meant by ἀνάγκη 'inevitable'?

It means that such things are inevitable in a fallen world [BECNT, EBC, Lns, My, NAC, NICNT, NIGTC, NTC, PNTC, TH, WBC]. However, the fact of inevitability does not reduce the guilt of someone who causes others to fall into sin [BECNT, EBC, ICC, My, Lns, NAC, NIGTC, NTC, PNTC, WBC].

18:8 And if your(sg) hand or your foot causes- you -to-sin, cut- it -off and cast (it) from you; it-is better for-you to-go-into life crippled or lame than having two hands or two feet to-be-cast into the eternal fire. **18:9** And if your eye causes you to sin, pluck- it -out[a] and cast (it) from you; it-is better for-you to-enter into life having-one-eye than having two eyes to-be-cast into the Gehenna of-fire.[b]

LEXICON—a. aorist act. impera. of ἐξαιρέω (LN 85.43) (BAGD 1. p. 272): 'to pluck out' [NTC, PNTC, WBC; KJV, NASB], 'to gouge out' [BECNT; NIV, NLT], 'to tear out' [BAGD, BNTC, CC, NICNT; ESV, GW, NET, NRSV, REB], 'to take out' [BAGD, LN, NIGTC; NCV, TEV], 'to poke out' [CEV], 'to remove' [LN]. This verb means to take something out of its place [LN].

    b. γέεννα (LN 1.21) (BAGD p. 153): 'Gehenna, hell' [BAGD, LN]. The phrase τὴν γέενναν τοῦ πυρός 'the Gehenna of fire' [NIGTC, WBC] is also translated 'fiery Gehenna' [BNTC, CC], 'the fires/fire of hell' [CEV, NCV, NIV, NLT, REB, TEV], 'hellfire' [NICNT; GW, KJV], 'the fiery hell' [NASB, NET], 'the hell of fire' [BECNT, NTC, PNTC; ESV, NRSV]. This noun denotes a place of punishment for the dead. The Greek term γέεννα is derived from a Hebrew phrase meaning 'Valley of Hinnom,' a ravine running along the south side of Jerusalem and a place where the rubbish from the city was constantly being burned. According to late Jewish popular belief, the last judgment was to take place in this valley, and hence the figurative extension of meaning from 'Valley of Hinnom' to 'hell.' In most languages γέεννα is rendered as 'place of punishment' or 'place where the dead suffer' or 'place where the dead suffer because of their sins' [WBC].

QUESTION—How do verses 8–9 differ from Matthew 5:29–30?

    In chapter 5, practically the same warning is given, but there the offending members of the human body are the right eye and the right hand, and it was given in the context of the enticement of sexual lust. Here the contrast is broader [NICNT, NIGTC, WBC]. In both occurrences the point is the desirability of drastic action to overcome the instrument of sinning [BECNT, NAC, PNTC, WBC]. In 5:29–30 Jesus challenges them to deal radically with lust, and here he challenges them to deal just as radically with pride [EBC].

QUESTION—Is there a difference between being cast into τὸ πῦρ τὸ αἰώνιον 'the eternal fire' and being cast into τὴν γέενναν τοῦ πυρό 'the Gehenna of fire'?

    Both expressions refer to the same place of final destruction. In verse 8 they will be sent to hell 'where the fire doesn't go out', and in verse 9 they will be sent to that same hell, 'where the fire is' [TH].

DISCOURSE UNIT—18:10–14 [CEV, ESV, NCV, NET, NIV, NRSV, TEV]. The topic is a lost sheep [NCV], the lost sheep [CEV], the parable of the lost sheep [ESV, NET, NIV, NRSV, TEV].

18:10 See (to it that) you(pl)-do- not -despise[a] one of-these little-ones; for I-say to-you that their angels in heaven always[b] see[c] the face of my Father in the heavens.

LEXICON—a. καταφρονέω (LN **88.192**) (BAGD 1. p. 420): 'to despise' [BAGD, BECNT, BNTC, CC, **LN**, NICNT, NIGTC, PNTC; ESV, GW, KJV, NASB, NRSV, REB, TEV], 'to look down on' [BAGD, LN, NTC; NIV, NLT], 'to treat with contempt' [BAGD, WBC], 'to disdain' [NET], 'to think of as worth nothing' [NCV], 'to be cruel to' [CEV], 'to scorn' [BAGD, LN]. This verb means to feel contempt for someone or something because it is thought to be bad or without value [LN].

   b. διὰ παντός (LN **67.86**) (BAGD A.II.1.a. p. 179): This phrase is translated 'always' [BAGD, BNTC, **LN**, NICNT, NTC, WBC; all versions except NASB, NRSV, REB], 'continually' [BAGD, BECNT, LN, NIGTC, PNTC; NASB, NRSV, REB], 'constantly' [BAGD, CC, LN]. The idiom διὰ παντός 'through all' refers to duration of time, either continuous or episodic, but without limits [LN].

   c. pres. act. indic. of βλέπω (LN 24.7) (BAGD 1.a. p. 143): 'to see' [BAGD, BECNT, BNTC, CC, LN, NIGTC, NTC, PNTC; ESV, GW, NASB, NET, NIV, NRSV], 'to behold' [WBC; KJV], 'to look at/on' [BAGD, NICNT; REB], 'to be with' [CEV, NCV], 'to be in the presence of' [NLT, TEV]. This verb means to see, and frequently in the sense of becoming aware of or taking notice of something [LN].

QUESTION—What is meant by 'despising' one of them?

   It means to consider such a person to be unimportant [Lns, TH, TRT], and of little worth [WBC]. It means to treat them with disrespect [EBC], disdain [BECNT, ICC, NIBC, NTC; NET], or contempt [BECNT, NTC, WBC]. It means to fail to take them seriously or to consider their needs as being important [Lns, NIBC, NICNT]. It is to see the potential loss of one of them who might be led astray as being a matter of little concern [NIGTC].

QUESTION—Who were 'these little ones'?

   This refers to any disciple of Jesus [EBC, EGT, NIGTC], Such disciples were members of the Christian community WBC]. This takes up the mention of little ones in verse 6 where Jesus' disciples are described as 'little ones' [NIGTC]. Another thinks this still refers to children [ICC].

QUESTION—Who were 'their angels' who always see the face of Jesus' Father in heaven?

   1. This passage does not provide sufficient information for us to conclude that each child or believer has one or more guardian angels [CC, Lns, NAC, NICNT, NTC, PNTC, WBC].The angels mentioned here are in the presence of God representing the interests of believers [BECNT, NIBC, NIGTC, PNTC]. If even the very angels in God's presence are concerned with the 'little ones', how much more should fellow Christians be concerned for one another [WBC].

   2. These are guardian angels [ICC, My, TRT]. This refers to the guardian angels of children, and it gives proof that he still has literal children in

mind. It gives an additional reason for reverencing the Christ-like qualities of children [ICC]. Another thinks that both children and adults have angels God has assigned to help them [TRT].

3. 'Angels' refers to the spirits of believers who have died and are now in the presence of God. The little ones on earth must not be despised since their destiny is the unshielded glory of the Father's presence. The present tense, 'they always see' shows that Jesus is dealing with a class of such people, not individuals [EBC].

18:11 [[For the Son of Man has come to save what was lost.]]

TEXT—GNT omits verse 11 with a B rating, indicating that the omission of the text is almost certain. Only KJV translates it as part of the text. NASB includes it in brackets, and BECNT translates it, but comments that it is probably not original.

DISCOURSE UNIT—18:12–14 [GW, NASB, NLT]. The topic is the lost sheep [GW], the parable of the lost sheep [NLT], ninety-nine plus one [NASB].

18:12 **What do you(pl) think? If a certain man owns a hundred sheep and one of them goes-astray,[a] will-he- not -leave the ninety nine on the mountain[b] and having-gone he-will-seek the one-going-astray?** **18:13** **And if he-happens to-find it, truly I-say to-you that he-rejoices over it more than over the ninety nine not having-wandered.** **18:14** **Likewise it-is not (the) will before your Father in (the) heavens that one of these little-ones perish.[c]**

LEXICON—a. aorist pass. subj. of πλανάομαι (LN 15.24) (BAGD 2.a. p. 665): 'to go astray' [BAGD, BECNT, CC, NTC, PNTC, WBC; ESV, NASB, NET, NRSV], 'to be gone astray' [KJV], 'to stray away' [BNTC], 'to stray' [GW, REB], 'to be led astray' [NIGTC], 'to get lost' [NCV, TEV], 'to wander away' [NICNT; NIV, NLT], 'to wander off' [CEV], 'to wander about' [BAGD, LN]. This verb means to move about, without definite destination or a particular purpose [LN].

b. ὄρος (LN 1.46) (BAGD p. 582): 'mountain' [BAGD, BECNT, BNTC, LN, NIGTC, NTC; ESV, KJV, NASB, NET, NRSV], 'hill' [BAGD, CC, NICNT, PNTC, WBC; GW, NCV, NIV, NLT], 'hillside' [CEV, REB, TEV]. This noun denotes a relatively high elevation of land, in contrast with βουνός 'hill' (1.48), which is by comparison somewhat lower [LN].

c. aorist mid. subj. of ἀπόλλυμαι (LN 21.32): 'to perish' [BECNT, BNTC, CC, LN, NIGTC, NTC, PNTC, WBC; ESV, KJV, NASB, NLT], 'to be lost' [LN, NICNT; CEV, GW, NCV, NET, NIV, NRSV, REB, TEV]. This verb means to be lost, in the religious or spiritual sense [LN].

QUESTION—What is the function of Jesus' question 'What do you think?'

It is an invitation to reflect seriously about what he is about to discuss [NIGTC, PNTC, WBC]. It is used to arouse interest and focus attention [ICC, NTC], and elicit their agreement with the point he will make [NTC]. It gives rhetorical emphasis, but also reminds the reader that it was in fact the disciples' wrong understanding of things that even made the discussion

necessary. It can also remind the reader that in the bigger picture of
Matthew's gospel the Father sent his Son as a shepherd to seek the lost sheep
of Israel as well as to save others [CC].

QUESTION—Does the illustration of the lost sheep refer to believers who have
fallen into error, or to people who have never been believers?

This is about believers [BECNT, BNTC, CC, EBC, ICC, Lns, My, NAC,
NIBC, NICNT]. The 'wandering' consists of having left close fellowship
with other believers and not living in consistent obedience [NAC]. It refers
to people who have belonged to the community of believers, though they
may or may not have really been true believers [NTC]. The wandering one
has not fallen into apostasy, but into sin more generally [EBC].

QUESTION—What is the 'perishing' that he does not want?

This refers to ultimate or eternal ruin [BNTC, My, NIBC, WBC], being lost
eternally [TH], to spiritual disaster of lasting consequence [NICNT], to
eternal loss [PNTC], to being condemned by God [NAC]. It is the opposite
of salvation [Lns, NTC].

DISCOURSE UNIT—18:15–35 [ICC]. The topic is reconciliation and
forgiveness.

DISCOURSE UNIT—18:15–22 [NET]. The topic is restoring Christian
relationships.

DISCOURSE UNIT—18:15–20 [ESV, GW, NASB, NCV, NIV, NLT, NRSV].
The topic is dealing with believers when they do wrong [GW], when a person
sins against you [NCV], if your brother sins against you [ESV], the brother who
sins against you [NIV], reproving another who sins [NRSV], discipline and
prayer [NASB], correcting another believer [NLT].

DISCOURSE UNIT—18:15–17 [CEV, TEV]. The topic is a brother who sins
[TEV], when someone sins [CEV].

18:15 "If your(sg) brother sins against you(sg), go reprove[a] him between
you and him alone. If he-listens-to you, you-have-gained[b] your brother.

TEXT—Manuscripts reading εἰς σέ 'against you' are included in brackets by
GNT and given a C rating to indicate that choosing it over manuscripts that
omit those words was difficult. It is included by CC, NTC, PNTC; CEV,
ESV, KJV, NCV, NIV, NLT, NRSV, TEV, and is also accepted as original
by ICC, Lns, My, and NAC. It is included in brackets by BECNT and WBC,
both of which view it as probably original. It is omitted by BNTC, NICNT,
NIGTC; GW, NASB, NET, REB, though BNTC views it as expressing the
implied meaning, regardless of whether or not it was in the original text.

LEXICON—a. aorist act. impera. of ἐλέγχω (LN 33.417) (BAGD 3. p. 249): 'to
reprove' [BAGD, BNTC, CC, NIGTC, PNTC], 'to correct' [BAGD], 'to
rebuke' [LN, WBC], 'to show someone his fault' [BAGD, NTC; NASB,
NET, NIV, TEV], 'to tell someone his fault' [ESV, KJV], 'to point it out'
[BECNT], 'to point out what was wrong' [CEV], 'to point out the

offense/fault' [NLT, NRSV], 'to tell someone what he did wrong' [NCV], 'to confront' [NICNT; GW], 'to take the matter up with someone' [REB]. This verb means to state that someone has done wrong, with the implication that there is adequate proof of such wrongdoing [LN].

b. aorist act. indic. of κερδαίνω (LN 57.189) (BAGD 1.b. p. 429): 'to gain' [BAGD, BNTC, CC, LN, NIGTC, WBC; KJV], 'to regain' [BECNT; NET, NRSV], 'to win' [NICNT, NTC, PNTC; NASB], 'to win back' [CEV, GW, NLT, TEV], 'to win over' [NIV, REB]. The phrase ἐκέρδησας τὸν ἀδελφόν σου 'you have gained your brother' is translated 'you have helped that person to be your brother or sister again' [NCV].

QUESTION—Does the word 'brother' mean that the other person is part of the community of believers?

Jesus is dealing with problems within the community of believers [BECNT, BNTC, CC, EBC, ICC, Lns, My, NAC, NICNT, NIGTC, NTC, PNTC, TH, WBC].

QUESTION—What does the verb 'gain' mean here?

The person is restored to God's kingdom [My, NTC]. It is to free him from his sins, and thereby save him [Lns]. It indicates that the offending brother was in danger of falling away from faith altogether, which the confrontation and restoration is intended to prevent [CC]. It is to restore him or her to fellowship as one's brother or sister [PNTC, TH; NCV], or to fellowship with the community of believers [NIGTC].

18:16 But if he-does- not -listen, take with you one or two (others) in-addition,[a] so-that by (the) mouth of two or three witnesses every matter[b] may-be-established.[c] **18:17** If he refuses-to-listen[d] to-them, tell the church; and if he also refuses-to-listen to-the-church, let-him-be to-you(sg) as the Gentile[e] and the tax-collector.

LEXICON—a. ἔτι (LN 59.75) (BAGD 2.b. p. 316): 'in addition' [BAGD, LN], 'others' [BECNT, BNTC, NIGTC, WBC; all versions except KJV, NASB], 'others as well' [NICNT], 'still' [CC], 'more' [BAGD, PNTC; KJV, NASB], 'also' [BAGD], 'besides' [LN], not explicit [NTC]. This adverb indicates the state of something being in addition to what already exists [LN].

b. ῥῆμα (LN **13.115**) (BAGD 2. p. 735): 'matter' [BAGD, BECNT, CC, **LN**, NTC, PNTC, WBC; NET, NIV], 'charge' [NICNT; ESV], 'accusation' [GW, TEV], 'case' [NCV, REB], 'fact' [NASB], 'complaint' [CEV], 'thing, event' [BAGD, LN], 'word' [NIGTC; KJV, NRSV]. The phrase πᾶν ῥῆμα 'every matter' is translated 'everything' [BNTC], 'everything you say' [NLT]. This noun denotes a happening to which one may refer [LN].

c. aorist pass. subj. of ἵστημι (LN 76.21) (BAGD II.1.d. p. 382): 'to be established' [BNTC, CC, LN, NIGTC, NTC, PNTC, WBC; ESV, KJV, NET, NIV], 'to be confirmed' [BECNT; NASB, NLT, NRSV], 'to be verified' [GW], 'to be sustained' [NICNT], 'to be proved' [NCV], 'to be proven true' [CEV], 'to be settled' [REB], 'to be upheld' [TEV], 'to put into force' [LN]. This verb means to establish as validated and in force [LN].

    d. aorist act. subj. of παρακούω (LN **36.27**) (BAGD 3. p. 619): 'to refuse to listen' [BECNT, BNTC, **LN**, NICNT, NIGTC, NTC; all versions except GW, KJV, TEV], 'to refuse (someone)' [PNTC], 'to ignore' [CC; GW], 'to not listen' [WBC; TEV], 'to neglect to hear' [KJV], 'to refuse to obey' [LN]. This verb means to refuse to listen to and hence to disobey [LN].

    e. ἐθνικός (LN 11.38) (BAGD p. 218): 'Gentile' [BAGD, BECNT, BNTC, CC, LN, NICNT, NIGTC, WBC; ESV, NASB, NET, NRSV], 'pagan' [LN, PNTC; NIV, NLT, REB, TEV], 'unbeliever' [CEV], 'heathen' [BAGD, LN; GW], 'heathen man' [KJV], 'a person who does not believe in God' [NCV], 'foreigner' [NTC].

QUESTION—What was the function of the two or three witnesses?

    1. They were to be witnesses of the confrontation [EBC, My, NAC, NICNT, PNTC, TH, WBC], to assist the process of reconciliation [NIBC], to emphasize the seriousness of what was happening and add their wisdom to help solve the problem [BECNT], to protect the person being reproved from being mistreated by the process [TH]. Additional people with integrity can insure that the views of each of the parties are represented fairly if the matter has to come before the church [NAC]. They were to be witnesses of what the offending brother actually said so that he would not be able to evade it later [My].

    2. They were to be witnesses who knew that the behavior in question really happened and was wrong [CC, NIGTC, NTC], but they are also to be eyewitnesses that the confrontation was done properly [NTC], or to emphasize to the offending party that the matter is serious [NIGTC].

QUESTION—Are the witnesses needed to begin the process of excommunication?

This is the second step in winning back the brother who has sinned based on Deuteronomy 19:15, "Every accusation may be upheld by the testimony of two or more witnesses" [TH]. This is about excommunication [EBC, CC, Lns, My, NAC, NIBC, NICNT, WBC], but with reconciliation still being a possibility [BECNT, CC, ICC, Lns, NAC, NICNT, NIGTC, NTC]. Restoration is still the primary goal [NAC, NTC]. They were not there to convince the man of his fault, rather they would be witnesses to the confrontation if the case must go before the whole church [EBC]. Such an individual should be considered as having expelled himself, and the church simply acknowledges his choice [Lns]. The offending brother has chosen to be estranged from the group and from the one whom he offended, so his choice is to be acknowledged for what it is [PNTC].

DISCOURSE UNIT—18:18–20 [CEV, TEV]. The topic is prohibiting and permitting [TEV], allowing and not allowing [CEV].

18:18 Truly I-say to-you(pl), whatever you bind on the earth will-be bound[a] in heaven, and whatever you loose[b] on the earth will-be loosed in heaven.

TEXT—Manuscripts reading Ἀμὴν λέγω ὑμῖν 'Truly I say to you' are given a C rating by GNT to indicate that choosing it over a variant text that omits ἀμὴν 'truly' was difficult. It is omitted by CC, NICNT, NTC; ESV, KJV, NASB, NCV, NIV, NLT, REB. It is included by BNTC, NIGTC, PNTC, WBC; NET, NRSV, and is included in brackets by BECNT, GNT. It is unclear whether CEV, GW, TEV accept this variant or not.

LEXICON—a. perf. pass. participle of δέω (LN 37.46) (BAGD 4. p. 178): 'to bind' [BAGD], 'to prohibit, to not allow, to not permit' [LN]. The phrase ἔσται δεδεμένα ἐν οὐρανῷ 'will/shall be bound in heaven' [BECNT, BNTC, NIGTC, NTC, PNTC; ESV, KJV, NIV, NRSV] is also translated 'will/shall be forbidden in heaven' [NLT, REB], 'will be prohibited in heaven' [TEV], 'God will imprison' [GW], 'God in heaven…will not allow anything you don't allow' [CEV]. Some translations keep the perfect passive attributes prominent: 'shall/will have been bound in heaven' [CC, WBC; NASB, NET], 'will have been tied up in heaven' [NICNT], 'will be the things God does not allow' [NCV]. The verb 'to bind' has the extended meaning of to exercise authority over something on the basis that it is not legitimate. There are a number of different interpretations of the implication of the nearly verbatim statement 16:19, so translators should carefully review this passage in various commentaries [LN].

b. aorist act. subj. of λύω (LN 37.47) (BAGD 5. p.484): 'to loose' [BAGD, BECNT, BNTC, CC, NIGTC, NTC, PNTC; ESV, KJV, NASB, NIV, NRSV], 'to untie' [NICNT], 'to allow' [LN; CEV, NCV, REB], 'to set free' [GW], 'to release' [NET], 'to permit' [LN; NLT, TEV]. This verb means to exercise authority over something on the basis of its being legitimate [LN].

QUESTION—What is the significance of the change from second-person singular address in vv.15–17 to plural address in 18–19?

It indicates a broadening of the scope of what Jesus is talking about, as here it involves the whole believing community [CC, Lns, NICNT]. The plurals are addressed to the apostles, but where the grammar is in the singular it is addressed to individual believers [My].

QUESTION—What are the differences and similarities between this statement and the similar one in 16:19?

They are very similar, though this one is addressed to the group of disciples whereas in 16:19 it was addressed only to Peter [BECNT, BNTC, CC, ICC, Lns, My, NAC, NIBC, NIGTC, NTC, PNTC, TH, WBC]. This passage specifically addresses church discipline, whereas in chapter 16 he was dealing more generally with questions of conduct [WBC]. Here he is describing retaining apostles to teach and preach Christ in such a way as to

open or shut access to God's kingdom [CC]. Note: For questions about
binding and loosing in this passage, see comments on 16:19.

QUESTION—What do 'binding' and 'loosing' describe?

Loosing is forgiving sins, and binding is retaining them in the case of
unrepentant sinners [BECNT, BNTC, Lns, NAC, TRT, WBC]. Binding
would be ruling against the brother accused of wrongdoing, and loosing
would be ruling in his favor, absolving him of any wrongdoing [NIBC,
probably ICC]. The consequence of binding is that an unrepentant sinner is
excluded from the community, and the consequence of loosing is that the
person may continue in fellowship in the community [BECNT]. It has to do
with decisions made corporately by the believing community about right and
wrong behavior [My, NICNT, NIGTC, PNTC], and how that applies
practically in specific incidents [NICNT, NIGTC, PNTC]. Binding is
forbidding believers to violate principles of good conduct, and loosing
involves permitting what is in keeping with such principles of behavior
[NTC].

18:19 **Again, truly I-say to-you that if two of you agree[a] on the earth
concerning every matter that they-shall-ask, it-will-be-done for-them by my
Father in the heavens. 18:20 For where two or three having-been-
gathered[b] in my name, I-am there in their midst.**

LEXICON—a. aorist act. subj. of συμφωνέω (LN 31.15) (BAGD 2.a. p. 781):
   'to agree' [BAGD, BECNT, BNTC, NICNT, NTC, PNTC; all versions],
   'to agree together' [CC, NIGTC], 'to agree with' [LN], 'to be of one
   mind, to be in agreement' [BAGD]. This verb means to come to an
   agreement with someone, often implying a type of joint decision [LN].

   b. perf. pass. participle συνάγω (LN 15.125) (BAGD 2. p. 782): 'to be
   gathered together' [BAGD, BECNT, BNTC, CC, LN, WBC; KJV,
   NRSV], 'to be gathered' [NIGTC, NTC, PNTC; ESV], 'to gather
   together' [NASB, NLT], 'to come together' [NICNT; CEV, GW, NCV,
   NIV, TEV], 'to meet together' [REB], 'to be assembled' [NET], 'to be
   brought together' [BAGD], 'to be called together' [BAGD, LN]. This
   verb means to cause to come together, whether of animate or inanimate
   objects [LN].

QUESTION—What is the function of πάλιν 'again' in this passage?

It indicates that he is continuing to discuss church discipline [NIBC, TH,
WBC]. It indicates another significant comment is being added to what was
just said [Lns, NICNT]. It indicates a shift in topic [PNTC].

QUESTION—What specifically is being promised regarding answered prayer?

In this setting it is not a promise regarding any prayer on which two or three
believers agree. Jesus is referring to any judicial matter [EBC, NAC]. This
concerns prayers for guidance in matters of church discipline [CC, BECNT,
EBC, Lns, NAC, NIBC, NIGTC, NTC, TH, TRT, WBC]. Others take this to
be a broad promise concerning a variety of things, though we must recognize

that it is qualified by other conditions elsewhere such as praying in faith, in Jesus' name, and in accordance with God's will, etc. [NTC, PNTC].

QUESTION—What relationship is indicated by γάρ 'for' in verse 20?

It indicates an explanation and support for what is said in verse 19 [NIGTC], or a reason for what was what was just said [Lns, PNTC].

QUESTION—What is meant by 'gathering in Jesus' name'?

It means to come together under his rule [WBC]. It means to gather together as Jesus' followers [TH, TRT], as his disciples representing him [NICNT], in keeping with his revelation [Lns]. It means to come together to earnestly discover and do his will [BNTC]. It is their coming together on the basis of who he is and what he has done, as those who are baptized in the triune name, and who teach and learn all Jesus taught [CC]. It indicates a commitment to him and all he has done and stands for [NIGTC]. It means gathering to call on his name or with him as their reason for coming together; 'name' stands for the person [PNTC]. It means to come together in close fellowship with him at his direction and in keeping with what he has revealed about himself [NTC]. When praying in his name, the prayer of the community, however small, becomes as though it were the prayer of Jesus himself [ICC]. It is to confess and honor Jesus himself [My].

QUESTION—What is the point of Jesus' promise about his presence with two or three believers?

He is present with them as they carry out their business, especially that of church discipline [BECNT, BNTC, EBC, WBC]. His presence is the basis for their authority to declare what God's will is or to have their prayers heard [NICNT]. It relates to the Immanuel, 'God with us' promise in 1:23 [BECNT, CC, EBC, NAC, NICNT, NIGTC, WBC], and also to the promise of Christ's continued presence that will be given later in 28:20 [BECNT, CC, EBC, NICNT, WBC]. This is not about the minimum number required in order for Jesus to be present, rather he makes this promise to assure them that he will be present with them even when as few as two or three are gathered in his name. It is particularly relevant for when they meet to exercise shepherding care and concern for wayward members [CC].

DISCOURSE UNIT—18:21–35 [CEV, ESV, GW, NASB, NCV, NIV, NLT, TEV]. The topic is personally forgiving others [GW], an unforgiving servant [NCV], the parable of the unforgiving servant [ESV, TEV], the parable of the unforgiving debtor [NLT], the parable of the unmerciful servant [NIV], the official who refused to forgive [CEV], forgiveness [NASB].

DISCOURSE UNIT—18:21–22 [NRSV]. The topic is forgiveness.

18:21 Then having-approached Peter said to-him, "Lord, how-often will-my brother sin against me and I-forgive him? As-many-as[a] seven-times?"
18:22 Jesus says to him, "I-say to-you not up to seven-times but up to seventy times seven.[b]

LEXICON—a. ἕως (LN 59.21) (BAGD II.4. p. 335): 'as many as' [BAGD, BNTC, NICNT, NIGTC, WBC; ESV, NCV, NET, NRSV, REB], 'up to' [BECNT, LN, NTC, PNTC; NASB, NIV], 'until' [CC], 'till' [KJV], 'as much as' [LN], not explicit [GW, NLT, TEV]. The phrase ἕως ἑπτάκις 'Up to seven times?' is translated 'Is seven times enough?' [CEV]. This preposition indicates the extent of a quantity [LN].

b. ἑβδομηκοντάκις (LN **60.74, 60.77**) (BAGD p. 213): 'seventy times' [BAGD, **LN** (60.74, 60.77)]. The phrase ἕως ἑβδομηκοντάκις ἑπτά 'up to seventy times seven' [**LN** (60.77), NIGTC, NTC, WBC; ESV, GW, KJV, NASB, NLT, REB, TEV] is also translated 'up to seventy-seven times' [BECNT, BNTC, CC, **LN** (60.74), NICNT, PNTC; CEV, NCV, NET, NIV, NRSV]. This adjective describes seventy occurrences [LN (60.74)], or to seventy multiples of a quantity, and in this verse 'seventy times seven'. One should not, however, interpret this to be referring to a specific number, such as 490, but simply an unusually large number with symbolic significance of being totally adequate or complete. [LN (60.77)].

QUESTION—Does this question, and Jesus' answer to it, assume repentance on the part of the offender?

Jesus' answer assumes that the person needing forgiveness is repentant [BNTC, NAC, WBC]. If there is no real repentance, the principles of discipline in verses 15–18 must be followed [NAC]. No apology is stated here [ICC, NICNT, NIGTC]. The offended brother must forgive before even going about the process of confronting the offending person [Lns].

QUESTION—Does ἑβδομηκοντάκις ἑπτά mean 'seventy seven' or 'seventy times seven'?

Whichever number is correct, Jesus' intent was to say that there is no limit to how many times you forgive [BECNT, ICC, Lns, NTC, PNTC, NAC, NIBC, TH, TRT]. Jesus' response alludes to and is in contrast with the vengeful boast of Lamech in Gen 4:24 that he will be avenged seventy-seven times [BECNT, BNTC, EBC, My, NIBC, PNTC, NAC, NICNT, NIGTC, WBC].

1. It means seventy seven times [BAGD, BECNT, BNTC, CC, EBC, My, NAC, NIBC, NICNT, PNTC; CEV, NCV, NET, NIV, NRSV].
2. It means seventy times seven [Lns, NIGTC, NTC, WBC; ESV, GW, KJV, NASB, NLT, REB, TEV].

DISCOURSE UNIT—18:23–35 [NET, NRSV]. The topic is the parable of the unforgiving slave [NET], the parable of the unforgiving servant [NRSV].

18:23 Therefore, the kingdom of heaven has-become-likened-to[a] a-man (who-was) a-king, who wanted to-settle[b] accounts[c] with his servants. **18:24** He having-begun to-settle one debtor of- ten-thousand -talents[d] was-brought to-him.

LEXICON—a. aorist pass. indic. of ὁμοιόω (LN 64.4) (BAGD 1. p. 567): 'to be like' [BAGD, LN], 'to resemble, to be similar to' [LN]. This aorist passive verb is translated 'may/can be compared to' [BECNT, BNTC, NICNT; ESV, NASB, NLT, NRSV], 'is/may be likened unto' [PNTC; KJV], 'should be thought of in this way' [REB], 'is like this' [TEV], 'is like' [NIGTC, NTC; GW, NCV, NET, NIV], 'has become like' [CC], 'is like the situation of' [WBC]. The clause 'the kingdom of heaven has become likened to' is translated 'this story will show you what the kingdom of heaven is like' [CEV]. This verb means to be like or similar to something else [LN].

    b. aorist act. infin. of συναίρω (LN **57.229**) (BAGD p. 783): 'to settle accounts' [BAGD, LN], 'to check on accounts' [**LN**], 'to take account of' [KJV]. The phrase συνᾶραι λόγον 'to settle accounts' [BECNT, BNTC, CC, NICNT, NIGTC, NTC, PNTC; ESV, GW, NASB, NET, NIV, NRSV, REB] is also translated 'to check on accounts' [TEV], 'to ask them to give an account of what they owed him' [CEV], 'to collect the money (his servants) owed him' [NCV], 'to bring his accounts up to date' [NLT]. This verb means to settle or check on accounts with someone [LN].

    c. λόγος (LN **57.228**) (BAGD 2.b. p. 478): 'account' [BAGD, **LN**], 'credit, debit' [LN]. See previous entry. This noun denotes a record of assets and liabilities [LN].

    d. τάλαντον (LN 6.82) (BAGD p. 803): 'talent' [BAGD, BECNT, BNTC, CC, LN, NICNT, NIGTC, NTC, PNTC, WBC; ESV, KJV, NASB, NET, NIV, NRSV, REB]. The phrase 'ten thousand talents' is translated 'fifty million silver coins' [CEV], 'millions of dollars' [GW, NCV, NLT, TEV]. This noun denotes a Greek monetary unit (also a unit of weight) with a value which fluctuated, depending upon the particular monetary system which prevailed at a particular period of time. A silver talent was worth approximately six thousand denarii with gold talents worth at least thirty times that much [LN]. The value of a talent varied considerably from place to place, from one time to another, and also varied depending on the metal involved (whether gold, silver, or copper) [BAGD].

QUESTION—What relationship is indicated by διὰ τοῦτο 'therefore'?

    It indicates a conclusion to be drawn from the premise that disciples must forgive others [BNTC, EBC, My, Lns, NIGTC, NTC, PNTC]. The reign of God establishes certain kinds of personal relationships [EBC], and this parable indicates the reason for what he has just taught about forgiveness [TH, TRT]. It shows that this parable has grown directly out of the question raised in the previous two verses [My, WBC]. Since God requires that our forgiveness be without limit, someone who does not forgive will suffer the

fate of the man in the parable [BNTC]. The kingdom has become the way it
is because of the strong principle of forgiveness [Lns].

QUESTION—How much would ten thousand talents be worth?

The silver talent would have been worth about six thousand denarii
[BECNT, BNTC, CC, ICC, LN, Lns, NICNT, NIGTC, NTC, PNTC]. The
amount was astronomical [EBC, NICNT], over a billion dollars today
[EBC], and would have been impossible to pay [BNTC, CC, NAC, NTC,
TRT, WBC]. It is an almost incalculable amount [My, NICNT, TH, WBC].
It would have been more than the yearly tax revenue from a province
[NIBC], a sum worth ten million dollars or more [BNTC, NIBC]. The talent
was the highest denomination of money known at that time, and μύριοι 'ten
thousand' was the highest number in use [ICC, NAC, NICNT, PNTC, TH,
TRT], and could be used to indicate an unspecified but very large number
[NIGTC]. Jesus may be using hyperbole or extreme exaggeration for effect
[BECNT, CC, EBC, NICNT, WBC]. Whereas a denarius was worth about a
day's wage [BECNT, EBC, CC, ICC, Lns, NICNT, NTC, PNTC, TH,
WBC], ten thousand talents would represent the wages for about sixty
million days [BECNT, CC, Lns].

18:25 **But (since) he did- not -have (the money) to-repay, his master
ordered (that) he-be-sold, along-with his wife and children and everything
he possessed, and repayment-be-made. 18:26 So the servant falling-down,
prostrated-himself-before[a] him saying, 'Be-patient[b] with me and I-will-
repay everything to-you.'**

LEXICON—a. imperf. act. indic. of προσκυνέω (LN 17.21) (BAGD 1. p. 716):
'to prostrate oneself before someone' [BAGD, LN], 'to do/pay obeisance
to' [BAGD]. The words πεσὼν ὁ προσεκύνει αὐτῷ 'falling down,
prostrated himself before him' [WBC] is also translated 'fell to the ground
and prostrated himself before him' [NASB], 'fell down and prostrated
himself' [PNTC], 'fell to the ground and bowed before him' [BECNT],
'fell down and did obeisance to him' [NIGTC], 'threw himself to the
ground before him' [NET], 'fell on his knees before him' [ESV, NIV,
NRSV], 'fell prostrate at his master's feet' [NTC], 'fell prostrate before
him' [BNTC], 'fell down before his master' [NLT], 'fell on his knees
before the king' [TEV], 'fell at his master's feet' [GW, REB], 'fell down
at his feet' [NICNT], 'fell to his knees and begged' [NCV], 'got down on
his knees and began begging' [CEV], 'when he had fallen down…began
to pay obeisance to him' [CC], 'fell down and worshipped him' [KJV].
This verb means to prostrate oneself before someone as an act of
reverence, fear, or supplication [LN].

   b. aorist act. impera. of μακροθυμέω (LN **25.168**) (BAGD 2. p. 488): 'to be
patient' [BAGD, BECNT, BNTC, CC, **LN**, NICNT, NIGTC, WBC; GW,
NET, NIV, NLT, REB, TEV], 'to have patience' [NTC, PNTC; ESV,
NRSV], 'to be forbearing' [BAGD], 'to have pity' [CEV], 'to remain

patient, to wait patiently' [LN]. This verb means to demonstrate patience despite difficulties [LN].

18:27 And[a] the master of that servant having-taken-pity[b] on him, released[c] him and canceled[d] the debt.

LEXICON—a. δέ (LN 89.87, 89.124): 'and' [BECNT, LN (89.87), PNTC, WBC; ESV, NASB, NRSV, REB], 'but' [CC, LN (89.124), NICNT], 'then' [KJV, NLT], 'and then' [LN (89.87)], not explicit [BNTC, NIGTC, NTC; CEV, GW, NCV, NET, NIV, TEV]. This conjunction indicates a sequence of closely related events [LN (89.87], but may also be used to mark contrast [LN (89.124)].

   b. aorist pass. participle of σπλαγχνίζομαι (LN 25.49) (BAGD p. 762): 'to have pity' [BAGD], 'to take pity' [NIV], 'to be filled with pity' [NLT], 'to be moved with pity' [REB], 'to feel compassion' [BECNT, CC, LN; NASB], 'to have compassion' [NIGTC; NET], to be moved by/with compassion' [PNTC, WBC; KJV], 'to be stirred by compassion' [BNTC], 'to feel sorry' [CEV, GW, NCV, TEV], 'to feel sympathy' [BAGD], 'to have great affection for, love' [LN]. This participle is translated as a prepositional phrase: 'out of pity' [ESV, NRSV]. The phrase 'the master of that servant having taken pity on him' is translated 'the heart of that slave's master went out to him' [NICNT], 'the heart of that servant's master was moved with pity' [NTC]. This verb means to experience great affection and compassion for someone [LN].

   c. aorist act. indic. of ἀπολύω (LN 40.8) (BAGD 1. p. 96): 'to release' [BAGD, BECNT, BNTC, CC, NIGTC, PNTC, WBC; ESV, NASB, NET, NLT, NRSV], 'to set free' [BAGD, NICNT], 'to let go free' [NTC; CEV, NCV, NIV], 'to let go' [REB, TEV], 'to free' [GW], 'to loose' [KJV], to pardon' [BAGD, LN], 'to forgive' [LN]. This verb means to remove the guilt resulting from wrongdoing [LN]. He was released from custody [BNTC, Lns, NIBC, TH, TRT], or from any liability to punishment [NTC, PNTC].

   d. aorist act. indic. of ἀφίημι (LN **57.223**) (BAGD 2. p. 125): 'to cancel' [BAGD, WBC; GW, REB], 'to cancel a debt' [**LN**], 'to remit, to pardon' [BAGD], 'to forgive a debt/loan' [BECNT, BNTC, CC, LN, NICNT, NIGTC, NTC, PNTC; ESV, KJV, NASB, NET, NIV, NLT, NRSV, TEV]. 'to tell someone that he does not have to pay back the money' [CEV, similarly NCV]. This verb means to release a person from the obligation of repaying what is owed [LN].

18:28 But that servant having-gone-out found[a] one of-his fellow-servants[b] who owed him one-hundred denarii,[c] and having-seized[d] him was-choking[e] (him) saying, 'Repay whatever you owe (me).'

LEXICON—a. aorist act. indic. of εὑρίσκω (LN 27.27) (BAGD 1.b. p. 325): 'to find' [BAGD, BNTC, CC, LN, NICNT, NIGTC, PNTC, WBC; ESV, GW, KJV, NASB, NCV, NET, NIV], 'to come upon' [BAGD, BECNT, LN, NTC; NRSV], 'to go to' [NLT], 'to meet' [CEV, REB, TEV], 'to

learn the whereabouts of something, to discover, to happen to find' [LN].
This verb means to learn the location of something, either by intentional
searching or by unexpected discovery [LN]. In this context it means to
find something accidentally without seeking [BAGD].

b. σύνδουλος (LN **87.81**) (BAGD 1. p. 785): 'fellow servant' [BNTC,
NTC, PNTC, WBC; ESV, KJV, NLT, REB, TEV], 'fellow slave'
[BAGD, BECNT, CC, **LN**, NICNT, NIGTC; NASB, NET, NRSV],
'servant' [GW], 'another servant' [NCV], 'official' [CEV]. This noun
denotes one who is a fellow slave or a slave alongside another slave [LN].

c. δηνάριον (LN **6.75**) (BAGD p. 179): 'denarius' [BAGD, BECNT,
BNTC, CC, **LN**, NICNT, NIGTC, NTC, PNTC, WBC; ESV, NASB,
NIV, NRSV, REB]. The phrase 'one hundred denarii' is translated 'one
hundred silver coins' [CEV, NET], 'hundreds of dollars' [GW], 'an
hundred pence' [KJV], 'a few dollars' [NCV, TEV], 'a few thousand
dollars' [NLT]. This noun denotes a Roman silver coin equivalent to a
day's wage of a common laborer [BAGD, LN].

d. aorist act. participle of κρατέω (LN 18.6) (BAGD 1.b. p. 448): 'to seize'
[BAGD, BNTC, CC, LN, WBC; ESV, NASB], 'to grab' [BECNT,
NIGTC; GW, NIV, TEV], 'to grab by the throat' [NICNT, NTC; CEV,
NET], 'to seize by the throat' [NRSV], 'to lay hands on' [KJV], 'to grasp'
[BAGD], 'to take hold of' [BAGD, PNTC], 'to hold on to, to retain in the
hand' [LN]. The phrase 'having seized him was choking him' is translated
'took him by the throat' [KJV], 'grabbed him by the throat' NLT],
'grabbed him around the neck' [NCV], 'he took hold of him, seizing him
by the throat' [REB]. This verb means to hold on to an object [LN].

e. imperf. act. indic. of πνίγω (LN **19.53**) (BAGD 1.a. p. 679): 'to choke'
[BAGD, BECNT, BNTC, CC, **LN**, NIGTC, NTC, PNTC, WBC; CEV,
ESV, GW, NASB, NET, NIV, TEV], 'to strangle' [BAGD], not explicit
[NICNT; KJV, NCV, NLT, NRSV, REB]. This verb means to apply
pressure around the neck in order to harm or kill [LN].

QUESTION—How did this servant happen to find his fellow servant?

He encountered him by chance, without searching for him [BAGD, BECNT,
Lns, NTC, TH; CEV, NRSV, REB]. Others think he probably looked for the
man [NIGTC, PNTC].

QUESTION—How much would one hundred denarii be worth today?

This was the equivalent of one hundred days' wages for a laborer [BECNT,
CC, EBC, ICC, NAC, NTC, PNTC, TH, WBC], and a soldier [EBC]. The
huge sum the first servant owed was 600,000 times greater than this [CC,
Lns, NICNT, NTC, TRT, WBC].

QUESTION—What is implied by the imperfect tense of ἔπνιγεν 'was
choking'?

It is translated as having an inceptive sense, meaning that he began to choke
him [BECNT, CC, NIGTC, NTC, PNTC, WBC; CEV, GW, ESV, NASB,
NET, NIV, TEV]. Or, it could have a conative sense, expressing intent,
meaning that he tried to strangle the man [BAGD].

18:29 So having-fallen (to his knees), his fellow-servant was-begging[a] him saying, 'Be-patient with me and I-will-pay you.' **18:30** But he was- not -willing,[b] and-instead he-cast him into prison[c] until he-would-pay what was-owed.

LEXICON—a. imperf. act. indic. of παρακαλέω (LN 33.168) (BAGD 3. p. 617): 'to beg' [NICNT, NTC; CEV, GW, NCV, NET, NIV, NLT, REB, TEV], 'to beg earnestly' [BAGD], 'to plead' [BECNT, WBC; ESV, NASB, NRSV], 'to entreat' [BAGD, BNTC, NIGTC], 'to beseech' [CC, PNTC; KJV], 'to appeal to' [BAGD, LN], 'to request, to implore' [BAGD], 'to plead for' [LN]. This verb means to ask for something earnestly and with propriety [LN].

   b. imperf. act. indic. of θέλω (LN 30.58) (BAGD 2. p. 355): 'to be willing' [BAGD], 'to purpose' [BAGD, LN]. The phrase 'he was not willing' [CC] is also translated 'he was unwilling' [NASB], 'he was and remained unwilling' [NTC], 'he refused' [BECNT, BNTC, NICNT; ESV, GW, NET, NIV, NRSV, REB, TEV], 'he refused to have pity' [CEV], 'he refused to be patient' [NCV], 'he did not want that' [NIGTC], 'he would not' [PNTC; KJV], 'he would not listen' [WBC], 'he would not wait' [NLT]. This verb means to purpose, generally based upon a preference and desire [LN].

   c. φυλακή (LN 7.24) (BAGD 3. p. 867): 'prison' [BAGD, BECNT, BNTC, CC, LN, NICNT, NIGTC, PNTC, WBC; all versions except CEV, REB, TEV], 'jail' [LN, NTC; CEV, REB, TEV]. This noun denotes a place of detention [LN].

QUESTION—What is the meaning of use of the imperfect tense with the verb 'not willing'?

   Since negations normally use an aorist verb, the use of the imperfect here indicates a durative or iterative sense, meaning that he repeatedly refused [EBC]. He remained unwilling, persisting in his refusal [CC, NTC, PNTC]. He made a conscious choice to be hard-hearted [NAC].

18:31 So having-seen what-had-happened, his fellow-servants were-distressed[a] greatly and having-come, they-reported[b] to-their master all that-had-happened.

LEXICON—a. aorist pass. indic. of λυπέομαι (LN 25.274) (BAGD 2.a. p. 481): 'to be or become distressed' [BAGD, LN, NIGTC, WBC; ESV, NIV, NRSV, REB], 'to be upset' [NET, NLT, TEV], 'to be grieved' [BECNT, BNTC; NASB], 'to grieve' [CC], 'to be horrified' [NICNT], 'to feel sad' [NTC; GW], 'to be or become sad' [BAGD, LN], 'to be/feel sorry' [PNTC; CEV, KJV, NCV]. This verb means to be sad or distressed as the result of what has happened or what one has done [LN].

   b. aorist act. indic. of διασαφέω (LN **33.200**) (BAGD 2. p. 188): 'to report' [BAGD, BECNT, BNTC, CC, NICNT; ESV, NASB, NRSV], 'to report in detail' [NTC], 'to explain' [NIGTC], 'to tell' [BAGD, PNTC; all versions except ESV, NASB, NRSV], 'to tell in detail' [BAGD], 'to relate'

[WBC], 'to tell all, to relate fully' [LN], 'to tell everything' [**LN**]. This
verb means to inform in detail and with clarity [LN].

18:32 Then having-called him, his master says to him, '(You) wicked[a] -
servant, I-cancelled for-you all that debt, because you begged me (to).
18:33 Should-you[b] not have-had-mercy-on[c] your fellow-servant, as I-also
had-mercy-on you?'
LEXICON—a. πονηρός (LN 88.110) (BAGD 1.b.α. p. 690): 'wicked' [BAGD,
BECNT, BNTC, LN, NICNT, NIGTC, NTC, PNTC; ESV, KJV, NASB,
NIV, NRSV], 'evil' [BAGD, CC, LN, WBC; CEV, GW, NCV, NET,
NLT], 'worthless' [BAGD; TEV], 'immoral' [LN]. The phrase 'you
wicked servant' is translated 'you scoundrel' [REB]. This adjective
describes what is morally corrupt and evil [LN].
   b. imperf. act. indic. of δεῖ (LN **71.21**) (BAGD 2, 6.b. p. 172): 'should'
   [BAGD 2, 6.b., BECNT, BNTC, **LN**, NIGTC; all versions except REB],
   'ought' [BAGD 2, 6.b., LN, WBC; REB], 'to be necessary' [CC, NIGTC,
   PNTC], 'to have to do' [LN]. The phrase 'should you not have' is
   translated 'wasn't it your duty' [NICNT]. This verb describes something
   which should be done as the result of compulsion, whether internal (as a
   matter of duty) or external (law, custom, and circumstances) [LN].
   c. aorist act. infin. of ἐλεέω (LN 88.76) (BAGD p. 249): 'to have mercy on'
   [BAGD, BECNT, CC, LN, NIGTC, NTC, PNTC; ESV, NASB, NIV,
   NLT, NRSV, TEV], 'to show mercy to/on' [BAGD, BNTC, LN, NICNT;
   NCV, NET, REB], 'to be merciful to/toward' [BAGD, LN, WBC], 'to
   treat mercifully' [GW], 'to have compassion on' [KJV], 'to show pity to'
   [CEV], 'to have pity on' [BAGD]. This verb means to show kindness or
   concern for someone in serious need [LN].

18:34 And having-become-enraged[a] his master handed- him -over[b] to-the
torturers/jailers[c] until he-would-pay-back all that-he-owed. **18:35** Thus
also my heavenly Father will-do to-you(pl), if you(pl)-do- not -forgive each-
one his brother from your(pl) hearts.'
LEXICON—a. aorist pass. participle of ὀργίζομαι (LN 88.174) (BAGD
   p. 579): 'to be enraged' [BECNT], 'to be full of anger' [LN], 'to be
   moved with anger' [NASB], 'to be furious' [LN, NICNT], 'to be angry'
   [BAGD, CC, LN, NIGTC, PNTC, REB, WBC; CEV, GW], 'to be
   angered' [BNTC], 'to be very angry' [NCV, TEV], 'to be filled with
   wrath' [NTC], 'to be wroth' [KJV]. The phrase 'having become enraged'
   is translated as a phrase: 'in anger' [ESV, NET, NIV, NRSV]; as an
   adjective: 'the angry king' [NLT]. This verb means to be relatively angry
   [LN].
   b. aorist act. indic. of παραδίδωμι (LN 37.111) (BAGD 1.b. p. 614): 'to
   hand over' [BAGD, BECNT, BNTC, CC, LN, NICNT, NIGTC, NTC,
   PNTC, WBC; GW, NASB, NRSV], 'to turn over to' [BAGD, LN; NET,
   NIV], 'to deliver to' [ESV, KJV], 'to put (in prison)' [NCV], 'to send (to
   prison/jail)' [NLT, TEV], 'to condemn (to be tortured)' [REB]. This verb

means to deliver a person into the control of someone else, and it involves either the handing over of a presumably guilty person for punishment by authorities or the handing over of an individual to an enemy who will presumably take undue advantage of the victim [LN].

c. βασανιστής (LN **37.126**) (BAGD p. 134): 'torturer' [BAGD, BNTC, CC, LN, NTC, PNTC, WBC; GW, NASB], 'tormentor' [NIGTC; KJV], 'jailer' [BAGD; ESV], 'merciless jailer' [BECNT], 'prison guard' [LN], not explicit [CEV]. The phrase 'to the torturers/jailers' is translated 'to the prison guards to torture him' [NET], 'to the jailers to be tortured' [NIV], 'to be tortured' [NICNT; CEV, NLT, NRSV, REB], '(put) in prison' [NCV], '(sent) to jail to be punished' [TEV]. This noun denotes a person serving as a guard in a prison, whose function was to torture prisoners as a phase of judicial examination. It is difficult to know in the case of Matthew 18:34 if it is to be understood in the specific sense of 'torturer' or only in terms of 'prison guard'. Its use in Matthew 18:34 may simply be an instance of literary hyperbole [LN].

QUESTION—Does βασανιστής mean 'jailer' or 'torturer' in this passage?

It denotes a jailer who tortures or torments [BAGD, BNTC, CC, EBC, ICC, LN, Lns, My, NIBC, NICNT, NIGTC, NTC, PNTC, TH, WBC; CEV, GW, KJV, NASB, NET, NIV, NLT, NRSV, REB]. Such men were appointed by the courts to torture people guilty of terrible crimes [NTC]. In ancient times people with debts might be tortured to force them to reveal sources of money that they had not admitted to before, though torture was forbidden in Jewish law [NIBC]. In this case it would have been punishment only, and not an attempt to force him to divulge other resources [BNTC].

DISCOURSE UNIT—19:1–25:46 [NAC]. The topic is the road to Jerusalem: impending judgment on Israel.

DISCOURSE UNIT—19:1–22:46 [NAC]. The topic is true discipleship versus harsher condemnation for the Jewish leaders.

DISCOURSE UNIT—19:1–20:34 [PNTC, WBC; CEV, REB]. The topic is Jesus' journey to Jerusalem [PNTC], on the way to Jerusalem: increasing confrontation [WBC], on the road to Jerusalem [REB], Jesus goes from Galilee to Jerusalem [CEV].

DISCOURSE UNIT—19:1–20:16 [NIGTC]. The topic is family and possessions in view of the kingdom.

DISCOURSE UNIT—19:1–15 [NIV]. The topic is divorce.

DISCOURSE UNIT—19:1–12 [PNTC; CEV, ESV, GW, NASB, NCV, NET, NLT, NRSV, TEV]. The topic is teaching about divorce [PNTC; CEV, ESV, NRSV], a discussion about divorce and celibacy [GW], discussion about divorce and marriage [NLT], Jesus teaches about divorce [NCV, TEV], questions about divorce [NET], concerning divorce [NASB].

19:1 And it-happened[a] (that) when Jesus had-finished (saying) these words he-departed from Galilee and went into the region of Judea beyond the Jordan. **19:2** And great crowds followed him, and he-healed them there.

LEXICON—a. aorist mid. (deponent = act.) indic. of γίνομαι (LN 13.107) (BAGD I.3.f. p. 159): 'to happen' [BAGD, BNTC, LN, NIGTC], 'to come to pass' [PNTC, WBC; KJV], 'to occur, to come to be' [LN], not explicit [BECNT, CC, NICNT, NTC; all versions except KJV]. This verb means to happen, with the implication that what happens is different from a previous state [LN].

QUESTION—What is the function of the introductory phrase 'and it happened…saying these words'?

It is a transitional formula that normally marks the end of a discourse and it is also used at the end of three other discourses (7:28, 11:1, 13:53) [BECNT, BNTC, CC, EBC, ICC, Lns, NICNT, NIGTC, NTC, PNTC, TH, WBC].

QUESTION—Which side of the Jordan did Jesus go to?

He crossed to the east side of the Jordan River in order to avoid Samaria as he journeyed south, Later he will cross the Jordan again to go west into Judea [BECNT, BNTC, EBC, ICC, Lns, My, NAC, NIBC, NICNT, NIGTC, NTC, PNTC, WBC]. The return to the west side of the Jordan will probably be at Jericho [BECNT, BNTC, My, NICNT, WBC].

DISCOURSE UNIT—19:3–26:5 [EBC]. The topic is opposition and eschatology: the triumph of grace.

DISCOURSE UNIT—19:3–26:2 [BECNT]. The topic is opposition comes to a head in Judea.

DISCOURSE UNIT—19:3–23:39 [BECNT, EBC]. The topic is narrative 5: ministry in Judea [BECNT], narrative [EBC].

DISCOURSE UNIT—19:3–20:28 [NICNT]. The topic is the revolutionary values of the kingdom of heaven: re-education for the disciples.

19:3 And Pharisees came to-him testing[a] him and saying, "Is-it-lawful[b] for-a-man to-divorce his wife for any[c] reason[d]?"

LEXICON—a. pres. act. participle of πειράζω (LN 27.31) (BAGD 2.c. p. 640): 'to test' [BECNT, BNTC, NIGTC, PNTC, WBC; CEV, ESV, GW, NASB, NET, NIV, NRSV, REB], 'to put to the test' [BAGD], 'to trick' [NCV], 'to trap [NLT, TEV], 'to try to trap, to attempt to catch in a mistake' [LN], 'to tempt' [CC, NTC; KJV]. This participle is translated as a phrase: 'with a test question' [NICNT]. It is translated as indicating purpose [BECNT, CC, NIGTC; CEV, GW, NCV, NET, NIV, NLT, NRSV, TEV]. This verb means to obtain information to be used against a person by trying to cause him to make a mistake [LN].

b. pres. act. indic. of ἔξεστι (LN 71.1) (BAGD 1. p. 275): 'to be lawful' [BECNT, CC, NICNT, NTC, PNTC, WBC; ESV, KJV, NASB, NET, NIV, NRSV, REB], 'to be permitted' [BAGD, BNTC, NIGTC], 'to be right' [CEV, NCV], 'can' [GW]. This verb is translated as a phrase: 'should a man be allowed' [NLT], 'does our Law allow' [TEV].

c. πᾶς (LN **59.24**) (BAGD 1.a.γ. p. 631): 'any' [CC, **LN**; ESV, GW, NASB, NET, NRSV], 'any and every' [BAGD, BECNT, BNTC, NIGTC; NIV], 'just any' [BAGD; CEV, NLT], 'any...whatsoever' [NTC, WBC], 'any ...he chooses' [NCV], 'any...he pleases' [REB], 'whatever...he wishes' [TEV], 'every' [BAGD, NICNT, PNTC; KJV], 'anything' [LN]. This adjective describes any one of a totality [LN].

d. αἰτία (LN **89.15**) (BAGD 1. p. 26): 'reason' [BECNT, LN, NTC, WBC; CEV, GW, NASB, NCV, NIV, NLT, TEV], 'cause' [BNTC, LN, NICNT, NIGTC; ESV, KJV, NET, NRSV, REB], 'ground' [PNTC], 'charge' [CC]. This noun denotes the reason or cause for an event or state [LN].

QUESTION—What relationship is indicated by the participle πειράζοντες 'testing'?

It indicates that their purpose for coming to Jesus was to test him [BECNT, CC, BNTC, Lns, NIGTC, PNTC, TRT, WBC; CEV, GW, NCV, NET, NIV, NLT, NRSV, TEV]. They were trying to trap him with their question [CC]. They wanted to discredit Jesus [Lns, TH].

QUESTION—What was the position the questioners held?

They appeared to have held to the view advocated by Rabbi Hillel, who held that there were a wide range of allowable reasons for divorcing one's wife [BECNT, CC, ICC]. Most Jewish men probably held to the view of Hillel [NICNT].

19:4 And answering he-said, "Have-you(pl)- not -read that from (the) beginning the (one) having-created[a] made them male and female? **19:5** And he-said, 'For- this -reason[b] a-man will-leave[c] (his) father and mother and will-be-joined[d] to-his wife, and the two will-be one flesh.[e]'

TEXT—Manuscripts reading ὁ κτίσας 'the one having created' are given a B rating by GNT to indicate it was regarded to be almost certain. Other manuscripts that read ὁ ἐποίησας 'the one having made' are followed by KJV.

LEXICON—a. aorist act. participle of κτίζω (LN 42.35) (BAGD p. 455): 'to create' [BAGD, LN]. The phrase ὁ κτίσας the one having created' is translated 'the One who created' [CC, WBC], 'he who created them' [PNTC; ESV, NASB], 'the one who made them' [NRSV], 'when God made the world' [NCV]. Others translate this as a noun: 'the Creator' [BECNT, BNTC, NICNT, NIGTC, NTC; CEV, GW, NET, NIV, REB, TEV], 'God' [NLT]. This verb means to make or create something which has not existed before, and in the NT it is used exclusively of God's activity in creation [LN].

b. ἕνεκα (LN **89.31**) (BAGD p. 264): 'for (this) reason' [BAGD, BECNT, BNTC, NICNT, NIGTC, NTC, PNTC; NASB, NET, NIV, NRSV, TEV], 'because of (this)' [BAGD, CC, LN, WBC], 'therefore' [ESV], 'for this cause' [KJV], 'so' [NCV], 'on account of' [BAGD, **LN**], 'that is why'

[CEV, GW, REB], 'this explains why' [NLT]. This preposition indicates cause or reason, often with the implication of purpose in the sense of 'for the sake of' [LN].

c. fut. act. indic. of καταλείπω (LN 85.65) (BAGD 1.a. p. 413): 'to leave' [BAGD, LN; all translations], 'to leave behind' [BAGD, LN], 'to abandon' [LN]. This verb means to cause or permit something to remain in a place and to go away, and sometimes the purpose for doing so is implied [LN].

d. fut. pass. indic. of κολλάομαι (LN 34.22) (BAGD 2.b.α. p. 441): 'to be joined' [BECNT, BNTC, CC, LN, NIGTC, PNTC, WBC; NASB, NRSV], 'to join oneself to' [BAGD, LN], 'to be attached' [NICNT], 'to cleave to' [NTC; KJV], 'to hold fast to' [ESV], 'to get married' [CEV], 'to be united with' [NCV, NET], 'to be united to/into' [NIV, NLT, REB], 'to remain united with' [GW, TEV], 'to cling to, to associate oneself with' [BAGD], 'to become a part of' [LN]. This verb means to begin an association with someone whether it be temporary or permanent [LN].

e. σάρξ (LN 8.4) (BAGD 2. p. 743): 'flesh' [BECNT, BNTC, CC, NICNT, NIGTC, NTC, PNTC, WBC; ESV, KJV, NASB, NET, NIV, NRSV, REB], 'body' [BAGD, LN; NCV], 'physical body' [LN]. The phrase ἔσονται...σάρκα μίαν 'will be one flesh' is translated 'he becomes like one person' [CEV], 'will be/become one' [GW, TEV], 'are united into one' [NLT]. This noun denotes a living body [LN].

QUESTION—Who said the words 'For this reason...'?

1. They were spoken by the creator, explaining why a man leaves his parents, etc. [BECNT, BNTC, CC, EBC, ICC, NICNT, NIGTC, NTC, TH, WBC; all versions except CEV].

2. They were part of Jesus' explanation, cited from the Genesis passage, of why a man leaves his parents, etc [PNTC; CEV].

QUESTION—In what sense was the man to 'leave' his parents?

The man's previous loyalty to his parents was to be displaced by a higher loyalty to his wife [CC, Lns, NICNT, NIGTC]. Since in ancient Israel the married couple normally lived in or near where the husband's parents lived, the leaving was not so much a physical leaving as a creating of a new and more important loyalty [NAC, NIGTC]. The couple's previous identity as the children of their parents was to be exchanged for an identity based on their being husband and wife [BECNT]. The man's attachment to his wife should be a more lasting attachment [NTC].

QUESTION—What does it mean that they are one flesh?

It describes the sexual union [Lns, My, NICNT, NIGTC, PNTC, TRT], but much more than that; it is a comprehensive union of their lives that supersedes other family loyalties [NIGTC]. Their union is to be sexual, intellectual, moral, and spiritual [NTC]. It describes an interpersonal intimacy that culminates in sexual relations [NAC]. In addition to sexual union, it describes being united in thoughts and actions [TRT]. It is as though they are one person [CEV], living in an indissoluble union [NIBC].

They are to be considered inseparable from one another [CC]. They are no longer independent individuals, but a new creation that exists only in their union [BNTC]. 'One flesh' shows an indissoluble union, a permanent attachment, such that they are no longer two independent beings who can go their separate ways [NICNT]. Every marriage is a re-enactment of Adam's declaration that Eve was 'bone of my bone and flesh of my flesh' [EBC]. More than an arrangement of convenience, the marriage tie is closer than any other earthly unity and takes precedence over all other relationships [PNTC].

19:6 So[a] they-are no-longer two but one flesh. Therefore[b] what God joined-together[c] let- not man -separate.[d]"

LEXICON—a. ὥστε (LN 89.52) (BAGD 1.a. p. 899): 'so' [BAGD, BECNT, BNTC, CC, NIGTC; ESV, GW, NASB, NCV, NET, NIV, NRSV, TEV], 'so then' [LN, PNTC], 'so that' [LN, WBC], 'then' [CEV], 'therefore' [BAGD, LN], 'wherefore' [KJV], 'for this reason' [BAGD], 'it follows that' [NTC; REB], 'this means that' [NICNT], '(so) accordingly, as a result, and so' [LN], not explicit [NLT]. This conjunction indicates result, often in contexts implying an intended or indirect purpose [LN].

b. οὖν (LN 89.50): 'therefore' [BECNT, BNTC, CC, LN, NTC, PNTC, WBC; ESV, GW, KJV, NASB, NET, NIV, NRSV, REB], 'so' [LN, NICNT; NCV], 'then' [LN, NIGTC; TEV], 'and' [CEV], 'consequently, accordingly, so then' [LN], not explicit [NLT]. This conjunction indicates result, often implying the conclusion of a process of reasoning [LN].

c. aorist act. indic. of συζεύγνυμι (LN **34.73**) (BAGD p. 775): 'to join together' [BAGD, BECNT, BNTC, NICNT, NTC, PNTC; all versions], 'to yoke together' [CC, NIGTC, WBC], 'to join together in marriage' [**LN**], 'to cause to be married, to join in marriage' [LN]. This verb means to join two persons in a marriage relationship [LN].

d. pres. act. (third person) impera. of χωρίζω (LN 34.78) (BAGD 1. p. 890): 'to separate' [BAGD, BECNT, BNTC, CC, LN, NICNT, NIGTC, NTC, WBC; all versions except KJV, NLT], 'to put apart' [PNTC], 'to put asunder' [KJV], 'to split apart' [NLT], 'to divide' [BAGD], 'to divorce' [LN]. This verb means to dissolve the marriage bond [LN].

QUESTION—What relationship is indicated by ὥστε 'so'?

It indicates a conclusion to be drawn from what has just been said [CC, EBC, PNTC, WBC]. It also emphasizes what was said at the end of the previous verse [WBC].

19:7 They-say to-him, "Why then did- Moses -command[a] to-give a-certificate[b] of-divorce[c] and send- her -away?[d]"

LEXICON—a. aorist mid. (deponent = act.) indic. of ἐντέλλομαι (LN 33.329) (BAGD p. 268): 'to command' [BAGD, BECNT, BNTC, CC, LN, NIGTC, NTC, PNTC, WBC; ESV, KJV, NASB, NET, NIV, NRSV], 'to give a command' [NCV], 'to give a commandment' [NICNT], 'to give a law' [TEV], 'to say' [CEV, NLT], 'to order' [GW], 'to give order'

[BAGD], 'to lay it down' [REB]. This verb means to give definite orders, implying authority or official sanction [LN].

b. βιβλίον (LN 6.64) (BAGD 2. p. 141): 'certificate' [BAGD, BECNT, BNTC, CC, NICNT, NTC, PNTC, WBC; ESV, NASB, NET, NIV, NRSV, REB], 'document' [BAGD, NIGTC], 'papers' [CEV, NCV], 'notice' [TEV], 'written notice' [GW, NLT], 'writing' [KJV], 'scroll, roll, book' [LN]. This noun denotes a document consisting of a scroll or book [LN].

c. ἀποστάσιον (LN 33.41) (BAGD p. 98): 'divorce' [BAGD, BECNT, BNTC, CC, NICNT, NTC, PNTC, WBC; CEV, ESV, NASB, NCV, NIV, NLT, TEV], 'dismissal' [NET, NRSV, REB], 'divorcement' [KJV], 'release' [NIGTC], 'written notice of divorce' [LN], not explicit [GW]. This noun denotes a written statement prepared by a husband and given to a wife as evidence of a legal divorce [LN].

d. aorist act. infin. of ἀπολύω (LN 34.78) (BAGD 2.a. p. 96): 'to send away' [BAGD, BECNT, CC, PNTC; CEV, ESV, NASB, NIV, NLT, TEV], 'to divorce' [BAGD, LN, NICNT, NIGTC, NTC, WBC; GW, NCV, NET, NRSV, REB], 'to dismiss' [BAGD, BNTC], 'to put away' [KJV], 'to separate' [LN]. This verb means to dissolve the marriage bond [LN].

QUESTION—What is the certificate of divorce?

It is a written document that gives the wife permission to remarry [CC, NICNT, PNTC, WBC], which was intended as a protection for the woman [BNTC, My, NTC, TRT]. It also documented the separation and stated the reasons for it [WBC].

19:8 He says to-them "Because-of[a] your hardness-of-heart[b] Moses permitted[c] you to-divorce your wives, but from (the) beginning it-was not this-way. **19:9** And[d] I-say to-you that whoever divorces his wife, except for[e] sexual-immorality[f] and (then) marries another-woman commits adultery.

TEXT—Some manuscripts add καί ὁ ἀπολελυμένην γαμήσας μοιχᾶται 'and whoever marries the divorced woman commits adultery'. Only KJV follows this variant. There are also several other variants. Those manuscripts that omit this reading are given a B rating by GNT to indicate it was regarded to be almost certain.

LEXICON—a. πρός with accusative (BAGD III.5.a. p. 710): 'because of' [BAGD, BECNT, BNTC, NIGTC, NTC, PNTC, WBC; ESV, KJV, NASB, NET, REB], 'with a view to' [CC], 'in response to' [NICNT], 'as a concession to' [NLT].

b. σκληροκαρδία (LN 88.224) (BAGD p. 756): 'hardness of heart' [BAGD, BECNT, BNTC, CC, NIGTC, NTC, PNTC; ESV, KJV, NASB], 'hard-heartedness' [WBC], 'hard hearts' [NET, NLT], 'disobedience' [NICNT], 'stubbornness' [BAGD; REB], 'obstinacy' [BAGD], '(being) obstinate' [LN], '(being) stubborn, completely unyielding' [LN]. The phrase 'because of your hardness of heart' is translated 'because you are so hard-hearted' [NRSV], 'because your hearts were hard' [NIV], 'because you are heartless' [GW], 'you are so heartless! That's why...' [CEV], 'because you refused to accept God's teaching' [NCV], 'because you are so hard to teach' [TEV]. This noun denotes being obdurate and obstinate.

c. aorist act. indic. of ἐπιτρέπω (LN 13.138) (BAGD 1. p. 303): 'to permit' [BAGD, BECNT, LN, BNTC, CC, WBC; NASB, NET, NIV, NLT], 'to give permission' [NICNT; REB, TEV], 'to allow' [BAGD, LN, NIGTC, NTC, PNTC; CEV, ESV, GW, NCV, NRSV], 'to suffer' [KJV], 'to let' [LN]. This verb means to allow someone to do something [LN].

d. δέ (LN 89.124, 89.94): 'and' BECNT, CC, LN (89.94), NIGTC; ESV, KJV, NASB, NLT, NRSV], 'but' [LN, (89.124), NTC, PNTC], 'rather' [NICNT], 'now' [NET], not explicit [BNTC, WBC; CEV, GW, NCV, NIV, REB, TEV].

e. ἐπί with dative (LN 89.27) (BAGD II.1.b.γ. p. 287): because of' [LN], 'on the basis of' [BAGD, LN]. The phrase μὴ ἐπί 'except for' [BECNT, BNTC, NICNT, NIGTC, PNTC, WBC; ESV, NASB, NET, NIV, NRSV] is also translated 'except it be for' [KJV], 'except on the ground of' [NTC], 'not on the basis of' [CC], 'for any reason/cause other than' [GW, REB, TEV], 'if (your wife) has not...you must not' [CEV], 'unless (his wife has been unfaithful)' [NLT], 'the only reason is if' [NCV]. This preposition indicates cause or reason as the basis for a subsequent event or state [LN].

f. πορνεία (LN 88.271) (BAGD 1. p. 693): 'sexual immorality' [LN, WBC; ESV], 'immorality' [CC; NASB, NET], 'sexual infidelity' [BECNT], 'infidelity' [NTC], 'sexual unfaithfulness' [NICNT], 'unfaithfulness' [GW, TEV], 'sexual impurity' [NIGTC], 'marital unfaithfulness' [NIV], 'unchastity' [BAGD, BNTC; NRSV, REB], 'fornication' [BAGD, LN, PNTC; KJV], 'has committed some terrible sexual sin' [CEV], 'has sexual relations with another man' [NCV], 'has been unfaithful' [NLT], 'prostitution' [BAGD, LN]. This noun denotes sexual immorality of any kind, often with the implication of prostitution [LN].

QUESTION—Did 'except for sexual immorality' refer both to divorce as well as remarriage, or only to divorce?

1. Sexual immorality is the only allowable reason for divorce and subsequent remarriage, and if a divorce occurs for any other reason, a subsequent remarriage would be adulterous [BECNT, CC, EBC, Lns, ICC, NAC, NICNT, NTC, TH, TRT].

2. Sexual immorality is the only allowable reason for divorce, but even in the case of such a divorce any subsequent remarriage would be adulterous [NIBC, WBC].

QUESTION—Why did Moses make an allowance for divorce because of the hardness of the people's hearts?

God gave laws through Moses to deal with problems such as divorce that come up in a fallen world because of human failure and rebellion against God's purposes [NICNT]. Moses did not command divorce, though he did permit and regulate it [BECNT, Lns, ICC, PNTC]. Moses' legislation was not normative [EBC, WBC], but was necessary to deal with sin and to limit abuse and excess [WBC], to limit further evil [My]. Divorce could never be more than the lesser of two evils [EBC, NAC, NICNT], a second-best situation [NIGTC]. Whereas the Pharisees used the term 'commanded' to describe what Moses wrote, Jesus used the term 'permitted' to contrast between what Moses allowed and what the creation pattern intended [CC, NIGTC]. Whereas the Genesis passage indicates God's perfect will, the divorce provision is his response to human sin [ICC].

19:10 His disciples say to-him "If that is the case[a] of a-man with his wife, it-is-better[b] not to-marry." **19:11** But he-said to-them, "Not everyone is-able-to-accept[c] this word[d] but (only those) to-whom it-has-been-given.

TEXT—Manuscripts reading οἱ μαθηταὶ αὐτοῦ 'the disciples of him, his disciples' are given a C rating by GNT to indicate that choosing it over a variant text was difficult. The translation 'his disciples' is followed by BECNT, CC, NIGTC, NTC, PNTC, WBC; KJV, NRSV, TEV. Other manuscripts omit the possessive adjective αὐτοῦ 'of-him' and they are followed by BNTC, NICNT; CEV, ESV, GW, NASB, NCV, NET, NIV, REB.

LEXICON—a. αἰτία (LN 89.1) (BAGD 1. p. 26): 'case' [BAGD, NTC, PNTC; ESV, KJV, NET, NLT, NRSV], 'relationship' [BAGD, BECNT, BNTC, WBC; NASB], 'situation' [NIGTC; NIV], 'charge' [CC], '(the) way it is' [NICNT], 'how it is' [CEV, TEV], 'how things stand' [REB], 'relation' [**LN**]. The phrase 'the case with a man and his wife' is translated 'the only reason a man can use to divorce/can divorce his wife' [GW, NCV]. This noun denotes a relation existing between two or more objects or events [LN].

    b. pres. act. indic. of συμφέρω (LN 65.44) (BAGD 2.a. p. 780): 'to be better' [BAGD, BECNT, BNTC, NICNT, NIGTC, NTC, WBC; all versions except KJV], 'to be profitable' [CC], 'to be advantageous' [BAGD, LN], 'to be advisable' [PNTC], 'to be good' [KJV], 'to be better off, to be to someone's advantage' [LN]. This verb means to be of an advantage to someone [LN].

    c. pres. act. indic. of χωρέω (LN 31.57) (BAGD p. 890): 'to be able to accept' [BECNT, CC, **LN**, NICNT, NTC; CEV, NASB, NCV, NET, NIV, NLT, NRSV, REB], 'to accept' [BAGD, WBC], 'to be able to receive' [BNTC; ESV, KJV], 'to comprehend, to understand' 'BAGD], 'to grasp' [BAGD, NIGTC], 'to have the capacity' [PNTC], 'to receive' [LN], 'to be able to understand' [**LN**]. The clause 'Not everyone is able to accept this word' is translated 'Not everyone is able to do what you suggest' [GW], 'This teaching does not apply to everyone' [TEV]. This verb means to be able to accept a message and respond accordingly [LN].

    d. λόγος (LN 33.98) (BAGD 1.a.γ. p. 477): 'word' [BECNT, CC, LN, NIGTC; NIV], 'statement' [BAGD, LN, NTC; NASB, NET, NLT], 'saying' [BNTC, LN, NICNT, PNTC; ESV, KJV], 'matter' [WBC], 'teaching' [NCV, NRSV, TEV], 'course' [REB], 'what you suggest' [GW], 'assertion, declaration' [BAGD], 'message' [LN], not explicit [CEV]. This noun denotes that which has been stated or said, with primary focus upon the content of the communication [LN].

QUESTION—What is it that not everyone could accept?

1. Not everyone could accept what the disciples said about it being better to remain unmarried [BECNT, BNTC, CC, EBC, ICC, My, NAC, NICNT, NIGTC, WBC; CEV, GW, REB; probably NASB, NET, NLT].

2. Not everyone could accept Jesus' teaching on marriage as expressed in vv.4–9 [Lns, NIBC, NTC, PNTC, TH; probably NCV, NRSV, TEV], and not everyone could accept what he says about refraining from marriage in v.12 [NTC].

19:12 For there-are eunuchs[a] who were-born this-way from (their) mother's womb, and there-are eunuchs who were-made-eunuchs[b] by men, and there-are eunuchs who made- themselves -eunuchs[c] for-the-sake-of[d] the kingdom of-the heavens. Let- the-one being-able to-accept (this) accept (it).

LEXICON—a. εὐνοῦχος (LN 9.29) (BAGD 2. p. 323): 'eunuch' [BECNT, BNTC, CC, NICNT, NIGTC, NTC, PNTC, WBC; ESV, KJV, NASB, NET, NIV, NLT, NRSV], 'impotent male' [**LN**]. The clause 'there are eunuchs' is translated 'some people are unable to marry' [CEV], 'some are incapable of marriage' [REB], 'some men cannot marry' [NCV], 'there are different reasons why men cannot marry' [TEV], 'some men are celibate' [GW]. This noun denotes a human male who without being castrated is by nature incapable of sexual intercourse [LN]. They are by nature incapable of marrying and begetting children [BAGD].

b. aorist pass. indic. of εὐνουχίζω (**LN 9.26**) (BAGD p. 323): 'to be made a eunuch' [BAGD, BECNT, BNTC, CC, **LN**, NICNT, NIGTC, NTC, PNTC, WBC; ESV, KJV, NASB, NET, NLT, NRSV], 'to be made that way' [NCV, NIV, TEV], 'to be made so' [REB], 'to be castrated' [BAGD, **LN**; GW], 'to be emasculated' [BAGD]. The phrase 'eunuchs who were made eunuchs by men' is translated 'some people are unable to marry…because of what someone has done to their bodies' [CEV]. This verb means to cause a person to be a eunuch [LN].

c. aorist act. indic. of εὐνουχίζω (LN **9.27**): 'to make oneself a eunuch' [BNTC, CC, NICNT, NIGTC, NTC, PNTC, WBC; ESV, KJV, NASB, NRSV, similarly BECNT], 'to become a eunuch' [NET], 'to stay single' [CEV], 'to not marry' [**LN**; TEV], 'to give up marriage' [NCV], 'to renounce marriage' [NIV, REB], 'to choose not to marry' [NLT], 'to decide to be celibate' [GW], 'to be celibate, to live without marrying' LN]. This verb, when used with a reflexive pronoun, means to live without engaging in sexual relations [LN].

d. διά with accusative (LN 89.26): 'for the sake of' [BECNT, BNTC, NIGTC, PNTC, WBC; ESV, KJV, NASB, NET, NLT, NRSV, REB, TEV], 'on account of' [CC, LN], 'because of' [LN, NICNT; GW, NCV, NIV], 'in the interest of' [NTC], 'by reason of' [LN]. The phrase 'for the sake of the kingdom of the heaven' is translated 'in order to serve God better' [CEV]. This preposition indicates cause or reason, with focus upon instrumentality [LN].

QUESTION—In what sense do some men make themselves eunuchs?

It is not to be understood literally, as though referring to actual castration [BECNT, BNTC, CC, EBC, ICC, My, NICNT, NIGTC, NTC, TH, WBC]. This is a reference to a voluntarily chosen life of celibacy [BECNT, BNTC, CC, EBC, ICC, My, NAC, NIBC, NICNT, NTC, PNTC, TH].

QUESTION—Does Jesus' statement imply that celibacy is a morally superior state, or is to be preferred over marriage?

Jesus is not teaching that celibacy is morally superior to marriage [BECNT, EBC, Lns, My, NICNT, NTC, PNTC], nor does he teach asceticism as an ideal [BECNT].

DISCOURSE UNIT—19:13–15 [PNTC; CEV, ESV, GW, NASB, NCV, NET, NLT, NRSV, TEV]. The topic is Jesus and the children [PNTC], Jesus and little children [NET], Jesus blesses children [GW], Jesus blesses the children [NLT], Jesus welcomes children [NCV], Jesus blesses little children [CEV, NASB, NRSV, TEV], let the children come to me [ESV].

19:13 Then children were-brought to-him so-that he-might-lay- (his) hands -on[a] them and pray; but the disciples rebuked[b] them. **19:14** But Jesus said, "Allow the children to-come to me and do- not -prevent[c] them, for of-such-as-these[d] is the kingdom of the heavens." **19:15** And having-laid- (his) hands -on them he-departed from-there.

LEXICON—a. aorist act. subj. of ἐπιτίθημι (LN 85.51) (BAGD 1.a.α. p. 303): 'to lay on' [BAGD, BECNT, BNTC, LN, NICNT, NIGTC, NTC, PNTC, WBC; ESV, NASB, NET, NLT, NRSV, REB], 'to place on' [BAGD, LN; CEV, NIV, TEV], 'to put on' [BAGD, CC, LN; KJV, NCV]. The phrase 'that he might lay his hands on them' is translated 'to have him bless them' [GW]. This verb means to place something on something [LN].

b. aorist act. indic. of ἐπιτιμάω (LN 33.419) (BAGD 1. p. 303): 'to rebuke' [BAGD, BECNT, BNTC, CC, LN, NICNT, NIGTC, NTC, PNTC, WBC; ESV, KJV, NASB, NIV, REB], 'to scold' [NET, TEV], 'to tell (someone) to stop' [NCV], 'to speak sternly to' [NRSV], 'to reprove, to censure' [BAGD]. The phrase 'the disciples rebuked them' is translated 'the disciples told the people not to do that' [GW], 'the disciples scolded the parents for bothering him' [NLT], 'his disciples told the people to stop bothering him' [CEV]. This verb means to express strong disapproval of someone [LN].

c. pres. act. impera. of κωλύω (LN 13.146) (BAGD 1. p. 461): 'to prevent' [BAGD, **LN**], 'to hinder' [BAGD, BECNT, CC, LN, NTC; ESV, NASB,

NIV], 'to forbid' [BAGD, BNTC, PNTC, WBC; KJV], 'to stop (someone)' [NICNT, NIGTC; GW, NCV, NLT, NRSV, TEV], 'to try to stop (someone)' [CEV, NET, REB]. This verb means to cause something not to happen [LN].

d. τοιοῦτος (LN 92.31) (BAGD 3.a.α. p. 821): 'of such a kind, of a kind such as this' [BAGD, LN], 'of such a person' [BAGD]. This genitive plural adjective is translated 'of such' [PNTC, WBC; KJV], 'of such ones' [CC], 'for such as they are' [BNTC], 'to such belongs' [ESV], 'for those who are like these' [NIGTC], 'to such belongs' [NTC], 'to such as these …belongs' [NRSV], 'belongs to such as these' [BECNT; NASB, NET, NIV, REB, TEV], 'belongs to such people' [NICNT], 'belongs to people who are like these children' [NCV, similarly NLT], 'people who are like these children belong to (God's kingdom)' [CEV], 'children like these are part of (the kingdom of God' [GW]. This pronominal adjective describes that which is of such a kind as is identified in the context [LN].

QUESTION—How precise is τότε 'then' in this verse?

It does not indicate a very specific point in time [EBC, WBC]. It is a general term of transition [WBC]. This conversation is grouped with the previous one because of similarity of topic, so the actual time interval between the two events is not known [NAC]. This conversation probably happened very soon after the discussion about marriage [NTC, PNTC], but we cannot be certain of this since Matthew uses the word so often [PNTC]. This is a transition marker [NIGTC, TH].

QUESTION—What was the reason for the laying on of hands?

It was done as a means of communicating the blessing being prayed for [BNTC, Lns, My]. In the Bible prayer with laying on of hands is associated with healings, ordinations, and other blessings [BECNT, NIGTC, WBC], and it was a typical Jewish way of blessing someone [NAC]. It was customary for rabbis and elders to bless children by laying hands on them [EBC, My], particularly on the day of Atonement [NICNT, PNTC].

QUESTION—Who did the disciples rebuke?

They rebuked those who brought the children [CC, EBC, Lns, My, NIGTC, NTC, PNTC, TH, WBC; CEV, NCV, NET, NIV, NLT, NRSV, TEV].

QUESTION—What relationship is indicated by the genitive construction 'of such as these'?

It is possessive, just like the similar genitive construction in 5:3: the kingdom belongs to them [BECNT, CC, EBC, NICNT, NTC, TH; ESV, NASB, NCV, NET, NIV, NLT, REB, TEV]. The kingdom is made up of such as these [PNTC]. They are the kind of people who belong in the kingdom [BNTC, WBC].

QUESTION—What was Jesus' main point about children and the values of the kingdom?

Children exemplify the values of the kingdom, which are humility [BECNT, BNTC, CC, NIGTC, NTC, PNTC], trust [BNTC, NTC, PNTC], a sense of utter dependence [CC, NAC, NICNT, WBC], openness [Lns, WBC], simplicity [BNTC, My]. They are unimportant and vulnerable [NICNT]. The children embodied exactly the opposite of all that the young man in the following section represented with his wealth and self-sufficiency [CC].

DISCOURSE UNIT—19:16–20:34 [PNTC]. The topic is teaching and traveling.

DISCOURSE UNIT—19:16–30 [CEV, ESV, GW, NET, NIV, NLT, NRSV, TEV]. The topic is eternal life in the kingdom [GW], the rich young man [ESV, NET, NIV, NRSV, TEV], a rich young man [CEV], the rich man [NLT].

DISCOURSE UNIT—19:16–26 [NASB]. The topic is the rich young ruler.

19:16 And behold one having-approached him said, "Teacher, what good-thing must-I-do[a] so-that I-may-have[b] eternal life?" **19:17** And he said to-him, "Why do- you -ask me about the good? One is good;[c] but if you-wish to-enter into life, keep the commandments."

TEXT—Manuscripts reading διδάσκαλε 'teacher' are given an A rating by GNT to indicate it was regarded to be certain. Manuscripts that read διδάσκαλε ἀγαθέ 'good teacher' are followed by KJV.

TEXT—Manuscripts reading Τί με ἐρωτᾷς περὶ τοῦ ἀγαθοῦ; εἷς ἐστιν ὁ ἀγαθός 'Why do you ask me about the good? One is good' are given an A rating by GNT to indicate it was regarded to be certain. Some manuscripts read 'Why do you call me good? There is none good but one, (that is) God' and they are followed by KJV.

LEXICON—a. aorist act. subj. of ποιέω (LN 42.7) (BAGD I.1.b.ε. p. 681): 'to do' [BAGD, LN, all translations], 'to act, to carry out, to accomplish, to perform' [LN]. The subjunctive verb 'must I do' [NIGTC, WBC; all versions except GW, KJV, NASB], is also translated 'shall I do' [BNTC, CC, NICNT, NTC, PNTC; KJV, NASB], 'should I do' [BECNT; GW]. This verb means to do or perform, and is highly generic for almost any type of activity [LN].

b. aorist act. subj. of ἔχω (LN 90.65): 'to have' [BNTC, LN, NICNT, NIGTC, PNTC; CEV, ESV, KJV, NCV, NLT, NRSV], 'to gain' [WBC; GW, NET, REB], 'to obtain' [BECNT, BNTC; NASB], 'to get' [NIV], 'to possess' [NTC], 'to receive' [TEV], 'to experience' [LN]. This verb means to experience a state or condition, generally involving duration [LN].

c. ἀγαθός (LN 88.1) (BAGD 1.b.α. p. 3): 'good' [BAGD, LN; all translations]. This adjective describes positive moral qualities of the most general nature [LN]. The phrase εἷς ἐστιν ὁ ἀγαθός 'One is good' is translated 'there is only one who is good' [BECNT; ESV, GW, NASB, NET, NIV, NLT, NRSV, TEV], 'there is one-person/one who is good' [NICNT, WBC], 'one there is who is good' [NTC, PNTC], 'one alone is good' [REB], 'there is one who is the Good One' [BNTC], 'the Good is One' [CC, NIGTC], 'only God is good' [CEV, NCV], 'there is none good but one, that is, God' [KJV].

QUESTION—What does the man's calling Jesus 'teacher' reveal about the man?

He has an inadequate grasp of who Jesus really is [BECNT, CC, NAC]. It indicates that he is not yet a disciple [CC, NAC, NIGTC]. In Matthew's gospel all those who call him 'teacher' are rebuffed or are hostile toward Jesus [CC]. The man shows respect for Jesus, but no commitment [NICNT, WBC]. He intended to learn from Jesus [Lns].

QUESTION—Why did the man ask what good thing (singular) he should do to have eternal life?

He apparently believed or hoped that some great deed would gain him favor with God [EBC, ICC, My, NIBC, NICNT, PNTC, TH]. He believed that there was some unknown good thing that Jesus had discovered that would gain him eternal life [Lns].

QUESTION—What is the point behind Jesus' statement that only God is good?

He turns the man's focus back to God's standard of goodness [NAC], and to doing the will of God, who is himself the only truly good One [My]. God has expressed what is good in his law [BECNT, CC, EBC, ICC, Lns, NAC, NIBC, NTC, PNTC, WBC]. The young man misunderstands the absoluteness of God's goodness, thinking that he is somehow able to do enough good to merit being in the kingdom [EBC]. Jesus shifts the focus of the conversation from presumed human goodness to the goodness of God [BECNT, NAC]. Jesus is challenging the man's ideas about what is good, since he has evidently not thought deeply enough about what constitutes goodness [PNTC]. Even the best of human efforts are insufficient [NICNT]. Jesus responds as an Israelite teacher would and gives him the shallow answer that he should keep the law, but Jesus' real answer to the question in the next exchange is that a person must believe in him and follow him [CC].

19:18 **He says to-him, "Which (ones)?" And Jesus said, "Do-not -murder,[a] do- not -commit-adultery, do- not -steal, do- not -bear-false-witness,[b] 19:19 honor (your) father and (your) mother, and love your neighbor[c] as[d] yourself."**

LEXICON—a. fut. act. indic. of φονεύω (LN 20.82) (BAGD p. 864): 'to murder' [BAGD, BECNT, CC, LN, NICNT, NIGTC, PNTC, WBC; all versions except KJV, NASB, TEV], 'to kill' [BAGD, BNTC, NTC; KJV], 'to commit murder' [BAGD, LN; NASB, TEV]. This future tense form with the negative particle οὐ is translated 'you shall not' [BECNT, BNTC, CC, NICNT, NIGTC, NTC, PNTC, WBC; ESV, NASB, NRSV, similarly KJV], 'you must not' [NCV, NLT], 'do not' [CEV, NET, NIV, REB, TEV], 'never' [GW]. This verb means to deprive a person of life by illegal, intentional killing [LN].

   b. fut. act. indic. of ψευδομαρτυρέω (LN 33.271) (BAGD p. 892): 'to bear false witness' [BAGD, BNTC, CC, NICNT, NIGTC, NTC, PNTC, WBC; ESV, KJV, NASB, NRSV], 'to give false witness' [LN; REB], 'to give false testimony' [BAGD, BECNT; CEV, NET, NIV], 'to testify falsely'

[NLT], 'to accuse anyone falsely' [TEV], 'to tell lies about others/your neighbor' [CEV, NCV], 'to testify falsely' [LN]. This verb means to provide a false or untrue witness [LN].

c. πλησίον (LN 11.89) (BAGD 1.b. p. 672): 'neighbor' [BAGD, LN, all translations except CEV], 'others' [CEV], 'fellow man' [BAGD]. This noun denotes a person who lives close beside others and who by implication is a part of a so-called 'in-group,' that is, the group with which an individual identifies both ethnically and culturally [LN].

d. ὡς (LN 64.12): 'as' [BECNT, BNTC, CC, LN, NICNT, NIGTC, NTC, PNTC, WBC; ESV, KJV, NASB, NET, NIV, NLT, NRSV, REB], 'like' [LN]. The phrase 'as yourself' is translated 'as much as you love yourself' [CEV], 'as you love yourself' [GW, NCV, TEV]. This conjunction indicates a relationship between events or states [LN].

19:20 The young-man[a] says to-him, "All these I-have-kept;[b] what do-I- still -lack[c]?"

TEXT—Manuscripts reading ἐφύλαξα 'I have kept' are given an A rating by GNT to indicate it was regarded to be certain. Other manuscripts read 'I have kept from my youth' and they are followed by KJV.

LEXICON—a. νεανίσκος (LN 9.32) (BAGD 1. p. 534): 'young man' [BAGD, LN, all translations], 'youth' [BAGD]. This noun denotes a young man beyond the age of puberty, but normally before marriage [LN].

b. aorist act. indic. of φυλάσσω (LN **36.19**) (BAGD 1.f., 2.b.p.868): 'to keep' [BAGD, BECNT, BNTC, LN, NICNT, NIGTC, PNTC, WBC; ESV, KJV, NASB, NIV, NRSV, REB], 'to guard' [CC], 'to observe' [BAGD, NTC], 'to obey' [LN; CEV, GW, NCV, NLT, TEV], 'to continue to obey' [**LN**], 'to obey wholeheartedly' [NET]. This aorist verb is translated as a perfect tense: 'I have (kept, etc)' [all translations]. This verb means to continue to obey orders or commandments [LN].

c. pres. act. indic. of ὑστερέω (LN 13.21) (BAGD 1.c. p. 849): 'to lack' [BAGD, BECNT, BNTC, NTC, PNTC, WBC; ESV, KJV NET, NIV, NRSV, REB], 'to be lacking' [CC; NASB], 'to fall short' [NICNT], 'to be deficient' [NIGTC], 'to be inferior' [BAGD], 'to fail to attain, to not attain' [LN]. The question 'What do I still lack?' is translated 'What else must I do?' [CEV, NLT], 'What else do I need to do?' [GW, NCV, TEV]. This verb means to fail in some measure to attain some state or condition [LN].

QUESTION—How old was the 'young man'?

The term itself denotes a man between the ages of about twenty and about forty [NAC, TRT], or twenty four and forty [Lns]. He would not have been older than forty, but was probably much younger [NTC].

19:21 Jesus told him, "If you-wish to-be perfect,[a] go (and) sell your possessions[b] and give to-the-poor, and you-will-have treasure[c] in (the)

heavens, and[d] **come**[e] **follow me.** **19:22** **But the young-man having-heard the statement went-away grieving,**[f] **for he-was (one) having many possessions.**[g]

LEXICON—a. τέλειος (LN 88.36) (BAGD 2.d. p. 809): 'perfect' [BAGD, BNTC, LN, NICNT, NTC, PNTC, WBC; all versions except NASB], 'complete' [BECNT, CC; NASB], 'fully developed' [BAGD]. This adjective describes being perfect in the sense of not lacking any moral quality [LN].

b. pres. act. participle of ὑπάρχω, used here as a noun (LN 57.16) (BAGD 1. p. 838): 'possessions' [BAGD, BECNT, BNTC, LN; NASB, NCV, NET, NIV, NLT, NRSV, REB], 'property' [BAGD, LN], 'belongings' [CC], 'all you have' [NICNT; TEV], 'everything you own' [CEV], 'what you own' [GW], 'what you possess' [ESV], 'that thou hast' [KJV]. This neuter plural participle is used to denote that which constitutes someone's possession [LN].

c. θησαυρός (LN 65.10) (BAGD 2.b.α. p. 361): 'treasure' [BAGD, LN; all translations except CEV, TEV], 'riches' [LN; CEV, TEV], 'wealth' [LN], 'that which is stored up' [BAGD]. This noun denotes that which is of exceptional value and kept safe [LN].

d. καί (LN 89.87): 'and' [BNTC, CC, LN, NIGTC, NTC, PNTC, WBC; ESV, KJV, NASB], 'then' [BECNT, NICNT; all versions except ESV, KJV, NASB], 'and then' [LN]. This conjunction indicates a sequence of closely related events [LN].

e. δεῦρο (LN **84.24**) (BAGD 1. p. 176). This adverb, which is used here as an aorist active imperative, describes extension toward a goal at or near the speaker and implying movement. It is translated 'come' [BAGD; all translations except GW], 'come here' [BAGD, **LN**], not explicit [GW].

f. pres. pass. participle of λυπέομαι (LN 25.274) (BAGD 2.b. p. 481): 'to be sad, to be distressed' [BAGD, LN], 'to be sorrowful' [BAGD]. This participial form is translated as an adjective: 'sad' [BECNT; CEV, GW, NIV, NLT, TEV], 'sorrowful' [NTC; ESV, KJV, NET], 'grieved' [PNTC]; as an adverb: 'sorrowfully' [NCV]; as a participle: 'sorrowing' [BNTC], 'grieving' [CC, NIGTC; NASB, NRSV]; as a phrase: 'in sorrow' [BECNT, WBC], 'in distress' [NICNT], 'with a heavy heart' [REB]. This verb means to be sad as the result of what has happened or what one has done [LN].

g. κτῆμα (LN 57.15) (BAGD 1. p. 455): 'possession' [BAGD, BECNT, BNTC, CC, **LN**, NIGTC, PNTC, WBC; ESV, KJV, NLT, NRSV], 'property' [BAGD, LN, NICNT, NTC; GW, NASB], 'wealth' [NIV, REB]. The phrase 'he was one having many possessions' is translated 'he was rich' [NCV], 'he was very rich' [CEV, NET, TEV]. This noun denotes that which is owned or possessed [LN].

QUESTION—What does τέλειος 'perfect' mean here?

It is to be wholehearted in service to God [PNTC]. It describes whole-hearted obedience [EBC, ICC], and undivided loyalty to God, which would be expressed in absolute self-surrender [EBC]. It means to have a level of spiritual maturity and development that makes and keeps a total commitment to the kingdom [BECNT]. It means to be fully mature [BNTC, NAC, NICNT, NTC], to be complete [CC, Lns, NICNT], to be completely whole [NAC]. Being complete is the opposite of 'lacking' [CC, Lns, NIGTC], and recalls what Jesus said in 5:48 about being perfect or complete [NIGTC]. It refers to being completely the way God wants people to be [TH]. 'Perfect' does *not* indicate two tiers of discipleship, one for the average person and one for the especially holy, who can be perfect [EBC, ICC, NICNT, NIGTC, PNTC, TH, TRT, WBC].

QUESTION—How broadly should Jesus' command to sell all one's possessions be taken?

Though all disciples are called to wholeheartedness and undivided loyalty [PNTC], to an absolute commitment [WBC], this command was particular to this man, and not intended as a general principle for all disciples [BNTC, CC, Lns, ICC, NAC, NIBC, NIGTC, NTC]. Though not all are called to sell everything, all disciples should use all their possessions for the priorities of the kingdom [NAC]. For this particular young man, his wealth was his God [CC, PNTC], and he was unable to part with it [PNTC]. All are called to obey whatever divine command comes to them [ICC]. Jesus was calling him primarily to discipleship, not to disinvestment [NICNT].

19:23 And Jesus said to- his -disciples, "Truly I-say to-you that with-difficulty[a] a-rich-man will-enter into the kingdom of-the heavens. **19:24** And again I-say to-you, it-is easier (for) a-camel to-go-through (the) eye[b] of-a-needle[c] than (for) a-rich-man to-enter-into the kingdom of God." **19:25** And the disciples having-heard were- greatly -astonished[d] saying, "Then who is-able to-be-saved?" **19:26** And Jesus looking-directly[e] (at-them) said to-them, "With man this is-impossible, but with God all-things (are) possible.

LEXICON—a. δύσκολος (LN **22.32**) (BAGD p. 209): 'with difficulty' [BAGD. BNTC, CC, **LN**, NIGTC, PNTC, WBC; ESV], 'hardly' [KJV], 'difficult, hard' [LN]. The phrase 'with difficulty' is translated 'it-is/will-be hard' [BECNT, NICNT, NTC; GW, NASB, NCV, NET, NIV, NRSV], 'it is terribly hard' [CEV], 'it-is/will-be very hard' [NLT, TEV], '(a rich man) will find it hard' [REB]. This adverb describes that which is difficult to accomplish or do [LN].

   b. τρύπημα (LN **6.216**) (BAGD p. 828): 'eye (of a needle)' [BAGD, **LN**; all translations], 'hole' [LN], 'that which is bored' [BAGD]. The hole in a needle is variously referred to in different languages, for example, 'the nostril of the needle,' 'the ear of the needle,' 'the mouth of the needle' [LN].

   c. ῥαφίς (LN **6.215**) (BAGD p. 734): 'needle' [BAGD, **LN**; all transla-tions]. This noun denotes a small, slender instrument, pointed on one end and with a hole at the other end, used in passing thread through cloth in sewing [LN].

d. imperf. pass. indic. of ἐκπλήσσομαι (LN 25.219) (BAGD 2. p. 244): 'to be astonished' [CC, NIGTC, PNTC, WBC; ESV, NASB, NET, NIV, REB], 'to be amazed' [BAGD, BECNT, BNTC; KJV, TEV], 'to be astounded' [NLT, NRSV], 'to be flabbergasted' [NICNT], 'to be shocked' [NTC], 'to be surprised' [CEV, NCV], 'to be overwhelmed' [BAGD], 'to be greatly astounded' [LN]. This passive verb is translated by an active verb form: 'He amazed his disciples' [GW]. This verb means to be so amazed as to be practically overwhelmed [LN].

e. aorist act. participle of ἐμβλέπω (LN 24.9) (BAGD 1. p. 254): 'to look directly at' [LN], 'to look at' [BAGD, BECNT, BNTC, WBC; ESV, GW, NASB, NCV, NET, NIV, NRSV, REB], 'to look straight at' [LN; CEV, TEV], 'to look intently at' [NICNT; NLT], 'to gaze' [CC], 'to fasten one's eyes upon' [NTC], 'to behold' [KJV], 'to fix one's gaze upon' [BAGD, PNTC], not explicit [NIGTC]. This verb means to direct one's vision and attention to a particular object [LN].

QUESTION—Is there any difference between Jesus' use of the phrase 'kingdom of the heavens' and the phrase 'kingdom of God'?

Both terms have the same meaning [CC, ICC, NAC, NICNT, NIGTC, NTC, PNTC, TH, WBC].

QUESTION—Why did Jesus use the illustration of a camel and the eye of a needle?

Jesus is using hyperbole here [BECNT, BNTC, CC, EBC, NIB, NICNT, WBC]. He exaggerates for the sake of interest and emphasis [TH]. He is using humor to make his point [PNTC]. The camel was the largest animal in Palestine and the eye of a needle was the smallest opening currently being used [EBC, ICC, NAC, NIBC, PNTC].

QUESTION—Why were the apostles so astonished at what Jesus said?

They assumed, as did many of their contemporaries, that wealth was an indication of God's favor [BECNT, CC, EBC, ICC, NAC, NIBC, NICNT, NIGTC, PNTC, TH]. They may have reasoned that, even though not all men are rich, all desire to be, and consequently they all trust in riches [Lns, NTC].

QUESTION—What does the expression 'saved' mean here?

It is equivalent to entering the kingdom [BECNT, BNTC, CC, EBC, ICC, NAC, NICNT, NTC, TRT, WBC], and having eternal life [BNTC, CC, NAC, NTC, TH, TRT, WBC]. It is used in parallel with being perfect [BNTC], and having treasure in heaven [BECNT, CC, BNTC]. It means to be rescued from mortal danger [Lns].

DISCOURSE UNIT—19:27–30 [NASB]. The topic is the disciples' reward.

19:27 Then Peter having-answered said to-him, "Behold, we left[a] everything[b] and followed you; what then will-there-be for-us?" **19:28** And Jesus said to-them, "Truly I-say to-you(pl) that you, the ones-having-followed me, in the renewal,[c] when the Son of-Man sits on his glorious

throne,[d] you also will-sit on twelve thrones judging[e] the twelve tribes of Israel.

LEXICON—a. aorist act. indic. of ἀφίημι (LN 85.45) (BAGD 3.a. p. 126): 'to leave' [BAGD, LN; all translations except GW, KJV, NLT], 'to give up' [GW, NLT], 'to forsake' [KJV], 'to abandon' [BAGD], 'to leave behind' [LN]. This verb means to let something be put behind in a place [LN].

    b. πᾶς (LN 59.23): 'everything' [BECNT, BNTC, NICNT, NIGTC, NTC, PNTC, WBC; all versions except KJV], 'all' [LN; KJV], 'all things' [CC]. This adjective describes the totality of any object, mass, collective, or extension [LN].

    c. παλιγγενεσία (LN **67.147**) (BAGD 1.b. p. 606): 'renewal' [NIGTC, PNTC], 'renewal of all things' [NIV], 'new age' [BAGD, **LN**, NICNT; TEV], 'Messianic age' [BAGD, LN], 'age to come' [NCV], 'age of the renewing of the world' [WBC], 'age when all things are renewed' [NET], 'new world' [BAGD; ESV], 'world of renewal' [BNTC], 'future world' [CEV], 'the world that is to be' [REB], 'world to come' [GW], 'restored universe' [NTC], 'regeneration' [CC; KJV, NASB]. The phrase 'in the renewal' is translated 'when the world is-renewed/made-new' [BECNT; NLT]. This noun denotes an era involving the renewal of the world (with special reference to the time of the Messiah) [LN].

    d. δόξα (LN 14.49) (BAGD 1.a. p. 203): 'glory' [BAGD], 'majesty' [BAGD], 'brightness, shining, radiance' [LN]. The genitive phrase 'his glorious throne' [BECNT, BNTC, NICNT; all versions except KJV, NCV, NRSV] is also translated 'throne of his glory' [CC, NIGTC, NTC, PNTC; KJV, NRSV], 'his great throne' [NCV]. This noun denotes the state of brightness or shining [LN].

    e. κρίνω (LN 37.49) (BAGD 4.b.β. p. 452): 'to judge' [BAGD, LN; all translations except TEV], 'to rule' [LN; TEV], 'to govern' [LN]. This verb means to rule over people [LN]. Though it would be possible to understand κρίνω as meaning 'to judge' (see 56.30), the function of the twelve disciples seems to be far greater than that. Furthermore, there seems to be a significant Semitic influence in the meaning of κρίνω, since the corresponding Hebrew term likewise involved far more than merely making judicial decisions [LN].

QUESTION—What prompted Peter's question?

    Jesus' statement that it was impossible even for the wealthy to get into the kingdom worried Peter, who apparently believed that he and the other disciples had merited at least something by what they have given up [EBC]. Even though he and the other disciples had done what Jesus told the young man to do, Peter was unsure due to the fact that Jesus had said that with men it is impossible to be saved [NTC, PNTC]. The use of the personal pronoun 'we' in Peter's statement is emphatic [CC, Lns, My, NICNT, WBC].

QUESTION—What is the παλιγγενεσία 'renewal'?

    It is the consummation of the kingdom [EBC], the renewal of the created order [BECNT], the new heaven and earth [NAC, NICNT, NTC], the renewal of all things in the messianic age [My, PNTC, WBC], the new age in which Christ will rule [ICC]. Jewish people thought of it as the renewal of Israel that would occur when God's kingdom is established on earth [NIBC]. It is the last day, when the kingdom of God will finally break in fully, Jesus will rule, evil will be destroyed, and everything will be restored to its proper order [CC].

QUESTION—What is meant by the disciples judging the twelve tribes of Israel?

This promise did not include Judas [Lns, My, NIBC, NTC], who would have no place in the new age [NIBC].

1. They will judge Israel for their unbelief [My] and for their rejection of the Messiah [EBC]. They will judge all the people of Israel of all times [Lns]. They as the new Israel will judge the old Israel that has failed [NICNT]. The future kingdom is described in terms of the twelve tribes of Israel [BECNT], which in the NT is taken to represent the Church [NIBC]. The twelve disciples represent all believers, who will likewise judge the world and even angels, and Israel represents lost humanity in general [NAC]. They will have some role in the coming universal judgment, but what Jesus says in v.30 indicates that there will be no great distinction between one believer and another at that time [CC].

2. 'Judging' should be understood here as 'ruling' [ICC, NIBC, NTC, TH, WBC; TEV]. They will not only judge Israel, they will assist in ruling the world to come [BECNT]. They will rule over the restored new Israel [NTC]. The twelve disciples represent the true Israel and will judge unbelieving Israel and exercise authority over them [WBC].

19:29 And everyone who left houses[a] or brothers or sisters or father or mother or children or fields[b] for-the-sake of-my name, will-receive one-hundredfold and will-inherit[c] eternal life. **19:30** But many (who are) first will-be last and (the) last (will-be) first.

TEXT—Manuscripts reading ἢ πατέρα ἢ μητέρα 'or father or mother' are given a C rating by GNT to indicate that choosing it over a variant manuscript was difficult. The variant manuscript that includes ἢ γυναῖκα 'or wife' is followed by KJV.

TEXT—Manuscripts reading ἑκατονταπλασίονα 'one hundred fold' are given a B rating by GNT to indicate it was regarded to be almost certain. This reading is followed by CC, NICNT, NIGTC, NTC, PNTC, WBC; NET, NIV, NLT, NRSV, TEV. Other manuscripts that read πολλαπλασίονα 'many times' are followed by BECNT, BNTC; NASB, NCV, REB.

LEXICON—a. οἰκία (LN 7.3) (BAGD 1.a. p. 557): 'house' [BAGD, LN; all translations except CEV, GW], 'home' [LN; CEV, GW], 'dwelling, residence' [LN]. This noun denotes a building or place where one dwells [LN].

b. ἀγρός (LN 1.95) (BAGD 1. p. 14): 'field' [BAGD, BNTC, CC, LN, NIGTC, NTC, WBC; GW, NET, NIV, NRSV, TEV], 'farm' [BECNT;

NASB, NCV], 'land' [LN, NICNT, PNTC; CEV, ESV, KJV, REB], 'property' [NLT]. This noun denotes land under cultivation or used for pasture [LN].

c. fut. act. indic. of κληρονομέω (LN 57.131) (BAGD 2. p. 434): 'to inherit' [BECNT, BNTC, CC, NICNT, NIGTC, NTC, PNTC, WBC; ESV, GW, KJV, NASB, NET, NIV, NLT, NRSV], 'to receive' [BAGD, LN], 'to have' [CEV, NCV], 'to gain' [REB], 'to be given' [LN; TEV], 'to gain possession of' [LN], 'to share in, to obtain' [BAGD]. This verb means to receive something of considerable value which has not been earned [LN].

QUESTION—In what sense would they 'inherit' eternal life?

'Inherit' means that it is a blessing that will be freely given to them, not earned by them [Lns, NTC]. It is a gift [PNTC, WBC]. It is granted not for meritorious works, but for obedience to Christ [My].

QUESTION—What is meant by 'the first will be last and the last, first'?

There will be a great reversal in which those who have childlike trust in God will enter into and advance in the kingdom, as opposed to those who enjoy worldly prominence now [EBC]. Some who are held in high esteem by people will not fare well when the judgment comes, and others who were not regarded as important shall be highly rewarded [NTC]. Those who are highly esteemed now have put all their hope and effort into success in the temporal things of this world, and will rank last [PNTC]. Many who are wealthy, powerful, and influential will find themselves condemned, while the dispossessed and powerless who were Christ's disciples will be honored [NAC]. Those who push themselves up to the top to be rich will find themselves impoverished in the end [WBC]. Since salvation is by grace, no human prestige or position will matter when the end time comes [CC]. It is also a warning to the disciples not to presume too much on their position [NICNT, WBC]. Jesus said this to encourage and assure the disciples that they do have eternal life [TRT]. 'First' means to be included in the kingdom, and 'last' means to be excluded from the kingdom, and some who think they are in the kingdom will find that they are not [Lns]. 'First' and 'last' refer to being greatest or least, not to time [TH].

DISCOURSE UNIT—20:1–16 [CEV, ESV, GW, NASB, NCV, NET, NIV, NLT, NRSV, TEV]. The topic is a story about vineyard workers [GW], a story about workers [NCV], the workers in the vineyard [NET, TEV], workers in a vineyard [CEV], laborers in the vineyard [ESV], the laborers in the vineyard [NRSV], laborers in the vineyard [NASB], the parable of the workers in the vineyard [NIV], parable of the vineyard workers [NLT].

20:1 "For the kingdom of the heavens is like a-man (who is) a-landowner,[a] who went-out early in-the-morning to-hire workers[b] for his vineyard. **20:2** And having-agreed with the workers for a-denarius[c] (for) the day he-sent them into his vineyard.

LEXICON—a. οἰκοδεσπότης (LN 57.14) (BAGD p. 558): 'landowner' [BECNT, LN, NICNT, NIGTC; GW, NASB, NET, NIV, NLT, NRSV,

REB], 'farm owner' [BNTC], 'householder' [CC, PNTC; KJV], 'owner of an estate' [NTC], 'master of the household' [LN, WBC], 'master of the house' [BAGD; ESV], 'a person who owned some land' [NCV], not explicit [CEV, TEV]. This noun denotes one who owns and manages a household, including family, servants, and slaves [LN].

b. ἐργάτης (LN 42.43) (BAGD 1.a. p. 307): 'worker' [BNTC, CC, LN, NICNT, NIGTC, WBC; CEV, GW, NET, NLT], 'workmen' [BAGD, NTC, PNTC], 'men to work' [NIV, TEV], 'laborer' [BAGD, BECNT; ESV, KJV, NASB, NRSV, REB], 'people to work' [NCV]. This noun denotes one who works [LN].

c. δηνάριον (LN 6.75) (BAGD p. 179): 'denarius' [BAGD, BECNT, BNTC, CC, LN, NICNT, NIGTC, NTC, PNTC, WBC; ESV, NASB, NIV], 'coin' [NCV], 'penny' [KJV]. The phrase δηναρίου τὴν ἡμέραν 'a denarius for the day' is translated 'the usual amount for a day's work' [CEV], 'the usual day's wages' [GW, REB], 'the usual daily wage' [NRSV], 'the normal daily wage' [NLT], 'the standard wage' [NET], 'the regular wage, a silver coin' [TEV]. This noun denotes a Roman silver coin equivalent to a day's wage of a common laborer [LN].

QUESTION—What relationship is indicated by γάρ 'for'?

It indicates the parable in 20:1–16 as explanation for the principle stated in the preceding passage, and particularly for Jesus' statement in 19:30 about the first being last and the last first [BNTC, CC, ICC, My, NAC, NIBC, NICNT, NTC, TH, TRT, WBC]. The parable is prompted by Peter's question in 19:27 [BNTC, NICNT, PNTC, WBC]. In 19:27 Peter asked what reward there would be for the twelve disciples, and Jesus answers through this parable that they should not have too high an estimation of their own merit or achievement [PNTC] or think that they deserve a more favored position [BNTC].

QUESTION—What do the various elements of the parable symbolize, if anything?

In Jewish thinking a vineyard often represented Israel, as in Isaiah 5:1–7 [ICC, NAC, NICNT, WBC]. Here, working in the vineyard signifies sharing in Jesus' mission to Israel [NIGTC]. The owner of the vineyard represents God [NICNT, NTC, TH] or Jesus Christ [TRT]. Collecting wages at the end of the day represents judgment day [ICC, NTC, TRT]. The equal pay for all represents the gift of eternal life, the vineyard workers are Jesus' followers, and the ones hired last are the people like tax collectors and prostitutes who were rejected by the Jewish leaders [TRT].

20:3 And having-gone-out around (the) third hour he-saw others standing idle[a] in the marketplace[b] **20:4** and he-said to-them, 'You go into the vineyard, and whatever is right[c] I-will-give you.' **20:5** And they went. And again having-gone-out about (the) sixth and (the) ninth hour he-did likewise. **20:6** And having-gone-out about the eleventh (hour) he-found others standing (there) and he-says to-them, 'Why have-you-stood here idle the whole day?' **20:7** And they-say to-him, 'Because no-one hired us.' He-says to-them, 'You also go into the vineyard.'

LEXICON—a. ἀργός (LN **42.46**) (BAGD 1. p. 104): 'idle' [BAGD, BECNT, BNTC, CC, LN, NIGTC, PNTC, WBC; ESV, KJV, NASB, NRSV, REB], 'not working' [**LN**], 'without work' [GW, NET], 'with no work to do' [NICNT], 'with nothing to do' [BAGD, NTC; CEV], 'doing nothing' [NIV], 'standing there doing nothing' [NCV, TEV, similarly NLT], 'unemployed' [BAGD]. This adjective pertains to not working [LN].

   b. ἀγορά (LN 57.207) (BAGD p. 12): 'marketplace' [BAGD, BECNT, BNTC, CC, LN, NICNT, NTC, PNTC, WBC; all versions except CEV], 'public square' [NIGTC], 'market' [LN; CEV], 'business center' [LN]. This noun denotes a commercial center with a number of places for doing business [LN].

   c. δίκαιος (LN 66.5) (BAGD 5. p. 196): 'right' [BAGD, BNTC, LN, NIGTC, NTC, PNTC; ESV, GW, KJV, NASB, NET, NIV, NLT, NRSV], 'fair' [BECNT, NICNT; CEV], 'a fair wage' [REB, TEV], 'just' [CC, WBC], 'proper' [LN], 'what your work is worth' [NCV]. This adjective describes what is proper or right in the sense of being fully justified [LN].

QUESTION—What do the third, sixth, ninth, and eleventh hours correspond to today?

   They correspond respectively to nine o'clock in the morning, twelve noon, three o'clock in the afternoon, and five o'clock [BNTC, CC, EBC, ICC, My, NAC, NIBC, NTC, TH, WBC]. These refer to the number of hours after sunrise [NIGTC, PNTC], though it was imprecise and varied from season to season [NIGTC].

20:8 And evening having-come the owner of-the vineyard says to his foreman,[a] 'Call the workers and give them (the) pay,[b] having-begun with the last (ones) to the first (ones).' **20:9** And having-come those (hired) around the eleventh hour each received a-denarius.

LEXICON—a. ἐπίτροπος (LN **37.86**) (BAGD 1. p. 303): 'foreman' [BAGD, **LN**, NICNT, NTC, WBC; ESV, NASB, NIV, NLT, TEV], 'manager' [BAGD, BECNT, PNTC; NET, NRSV], 'steward' [BAGD, BNTC, CC, NIGTC; KJV], 'supervisor' [GW], 'overseer' [REB], 'the man in charge of the workers' [CEV], 'boss of all the workers' [NCV]. This noun denotes a person in charge of supervising workers [LN].

   b. μισθός (LN 57.173) (BAGD 1. p. 523): 'pay' [LN, WBC; NET, NRSV, REB], 'wages' [BECNT, BNTC, LN, NICNT, NTC; ESV, GW, NASB, NIV, TEV], 'wage' [CC, PNTC], 'hire' [NIGTC; KJV], 'money' [CEV]. The phrase ἀπόδος αὐτοῖς τὸν μισθόν 'give them the pay' is translated 'pay them' [NCV, NLT]. This noun denotes the amount offered for services or paid for work done [LN].

20:10 And (when) the first (ones) (hired) having-come thought[a] they-would-receive more; and they each received a-denarius also. **20:11** And having-received (it) they-grumbled[b] against the landowner **20:12** saying,

'These last (ones) worked a-single hour, and you-made them equal[c] to-us the-ones having-born the burden[d] of-the day and the scorching-heat.[e]'

LEXICON—a. aorist act. indic. of νομίζω (LN 31.29) (BAGD 2. p.541): 'to think' [BAGD, BECNT, CC, LN, PNTC, WBC; CEV, ESV, NASB, NCV, NET, NRSV, TEV], 'to suppose' [BAGD, BNTC, LN; KJV], 'to assume' [LN, NICNT; NLT], 'to expect' [NIGTC, NTC; GW, NIV, REB], 'to presume, to imagine, to believe' [LN]. This verb means to regard something as presumably true, but without particular certainty [LN].

b. imperf. act. indic. of γογγύζω (LN 33.382) (BAGD 1. p. 164): 'to grumble' [BAGD, BECNT, BNTC, CC, LN, NICNT, NIGTC, NTC, PNTC; ESV, NASB, NIV, NRSV, REB, TEV], 'to complain' [LN; CEV, NCV, NET], 'to speak complainingly' [BAGD], 'to murmur' [WBC; KJV], 'to protest' [GW, NLT]. This verb means to express one's discontent [LN].

c. ἴσος (LN 58.33) (BAGD p. 381): 'equal' [BAGD, BNTC, CC, LN, NICNT, NIGTC, PNTC, WBC; ESV, KJV, NASB, NET, NIV, NRSV], 'the same' [BAGD, BECNT, LN; GW], 'on a par' [NTC], 'on a level' [REB]. The phrase ἴσους ἡμῖν αὐτοὺς ἐποίησας 'you made them equal to us' is translated 'you paid them the same that you did us' [CEV, similarly NCV, NLT, TEV]. This adjective describes that which is equal, either in number, size, quality, or characteristics [LN].

d. βάρος (LN 22.4) (BAGD 1. p. 134): 'burden' [BAGD, BECNT, BNTC, CC, LN, NIGTC, PNTC, WBC; ESV, KJV, NASB, NRSV], 'arduous toil' [NTC], 'hardship' [LN; NET]. The phrase 'burden of the day' is translated 'burden of the work' [NIV], 'a whole day's work' [NICNT; TEV], 'we worked...all day long' [CEV, similarly NCV], 'we worked hard all day' [GW], 'who worked all day' [NLT], 'who have sweated the whole day long' [REB]. This noun denotes hardship which is regarded as particularly burdensome and exhausting [LN]. In Matthew 20:12, βάρος refers not to difficulties in general but to the specific hardship of working for the entire day [LN, NICNT; CEV, GW, NCV, NIV].

e. καύσων (LN 14.67) (BAGD p. 425): 'heat' [BAGD, CC, LN, WBC; KJV, NIV], 'scorching heat' [BAGD, BECNT, LN; ESV, NASB, NLT, NRSV], 'burning heat' [BNTC, NIGTC, PNTC; NET], 'sweltering heat' [NTC], 'heat of the sun' [NICNT], 'hot sun' [CEV, NCV, TEV], 'blazing sun' [REB]. This noun denotes heat sufficiently intense to cause suffering or burning [LN].

20:13 And answering he-said to-one of them, 'Friend,[a] I-am- not -doing-wrong[b] to-you. Did-you- not -agree with-me for-one denarius? **20:14** Take what-is-yours and go. But I-wish to-give to-this last (one) as also (I-gave) to-you. **20:15** Or is-it- not -permissible[c] to-me to-do what I-wish with what (is) mine? Or is your eye evil[d] because I am good[e]?'

TEXT—Manuscripts reading ἤ 'or' at the beginning of verse 15 are given a C rating by GNT to indicate that choosing it over a variant manuscript that omits it was difficult. It is included by NICNT and it is included in brackets by BECNT, GNT, WBC. It is omitted by BNTC, CC, NIGTC, NTC, PNTC; CEV, ESV, GW, KJV, NASB, NCV, NET, NIV, NLT, NRSV, REB, TEV.

LEXICON—a. ἑταῖρος (LN **34.16**) (BAGD p. 314): 'friend' [BAGD, BECNT, CC, **LN**, NICNT, NTC, PNTC, WBC; all versions], 'comrade' [BAGD, BNTC, NIGTC], 'companion' [BAGD, LN]. This noun denotes a person who is associated with someone else, though not necessarily involving personal affection [LN].

 b. pres. act. indic. of ἀδικέω (LN **88.128**, 88.22) (BAGD 2.a. p. 17): 'to do wrong to (someone)' [BAGD, PNTC; ESV, KJV, NASB, NRSV], 'to wrong (someone)' [NIGTC], 'to do injustice to' [BNTC, NTC, WBC], 'to cheat' [BECNT, NICNT; CEV, TEV], 'to treat someone unjustly' [BAGD, CC], 'to treat someone unfairly' [GW, NET], 'to be unfair toward (someone)' [NIV, REB], 'to be unfair' [NLT], 'to act unjustly toward' [LN (88.128)], 'to mistreat' [**LN** (88.128)], 'to act unjustly, to do what is wrong' [LN (88.22)]. The phrase οὐκ ἀδικῶ σε 'I am not doing wrong to you' is translated 'I am being fair to you' [NCV]. This verb means to mistreat by acting unjustly toward someone [LN (88.128)], or to do that which is unjust or unrighteous [LN (88.22)].

 c. pres. act. indic. of ἔξεστι (LN 71.1) (BAGD 2. p. 275): 'to be permitted' [BAGD, BECNT, BNTC, NIGTC; NET], 'to be lawful' [CC, PNTC; KJV, NASB], 'to have the right' [NICNT, NTC; NIV, TEV], 'to be allowed' [ESV, NRSV], 'can't I' [GW], 'to be proper' [BAGD, WBC], 'to be possible' [BAGD, LN]. The phrase οὐκ ἔξεστίν μοι 'is it not permissible to me' is translated 'I can do what I want' [NCV], 'is it against the law' [NLT], 'surely I am free to do (what I like)' [REB]. This verb means to mark an event as being possible' [LN].

 d. πονηρός (LN 88.165, **57.108**) (BAGD 1.b.β. p. 691): 'evil' [BAGD, BNTC, CC, NIGTC, PNTC; KJV], 'bad' [BAGD], 'jealous' [LN (88.165), WBC], 'envious' [NASB], 'stingy' [**LN** (57.108)], 'miserly' [LN (57.108)]. The phrase ὁ ὀφθαλμός σου πονηρός ἐστιν 'is your eye evil' is translated 'are you envious' [BECNT, NTC; NET, NIV, NRSV], 'are you jealous' [NICNT; NCV, TEV], 'why should you be jealous' [CEV, similarly NLT, REB], 'do you begrudge (my generosity)' [ESV], 'do you resent (my generosity)' [GW]. This adjective describes being stingy [LN (57.108)], or having a feeling of jealousy and resentment because of what someone else has or does [LN (88.165)].

e. ἀγαθός (LN **57.110**) (BAGD 1.b.α. p. 3): 'generous' [BAGD, BECNT, **LN**, NICNT, NTC; CEV, NASB, NET, NIV, NRSV, REB, TEV], 'good' [BNTC, CC, NIGTC, PNTC, WBC; KJV, NCV], 'kind' [BAGD; NLT]. The phrase ὅτι ἐγὼ ἀγαθός εἰμι 'because I am good' is translated 'my generosity' [ESV, GW]. This adjective describes being generous, with the implication of its relationship to goodness [LN].

QUESTION—What is implied by the use of Ἑταῖρε 'friend'?

It indicates a mild reproach [EBC, My, NAC, NIBC, PNTC], though with a friendly tone [ICC, NIBC, PNTC, WBC]. It distances the speaker somewhat from the person addressed [NAC]. It is a friendly way to address someone whose name is not known to the speaker [ICC, NIGTC, TH]. The three times in the NT that this noun is used are all in Matthew, and in each case the person addressed is clearly in the wrong [CC, ICC, TH].

QUESTION—How does οὐκ ἔξεστίν 'is it not permissible' function in the larger passage?

It forms an inclusio or 'bookend' with 'is it lawful' in 19:3, which questions what God requires people to do, and ends with this very similar statement in this verse concerning what humans want to require God to do [NAC].

QUESTION—What does it mean for someone's eye to be 'evil'?

It means being miserly [ICC, NICNT, PNTC], jealous [BNTC, EBC, PNTC, TRT; CEV, NLT, REB], resentful [BNTC, NIGTC; GW], or envious [ICC, NIBC, NTC, WBC; NET, NIV, NRSV TRT]. Here it means that their resentment toward the landowner is visible in their eyes [NIGTC]. It means to have a bad heart or character [NAC].

20:16 So[a] the last shall-be first, and the first last."

TEXT—Some manuscripts add 'Thus the last shall be first, and the first last'. GNT omits this with an A rating, indicating that the text is certain. Only KJV follows this variant reading.

LEXICON—a. οὕτως (LN 61.9) (BAGD 1.b. p. 597): 'so' [BAGD, BECNT, BNTC, LN, NICNT, NIGTC, NTC; all versions except CEV, GW], 'thus' [BAGD, LN, WBC], 'even so' [PNTC], 'so it is' [CEV], 'in this way' [CC, LN; GW], 'in this manner' [BAGD]. This adverb refers to that which precedes [LN].

QUESTION—How does this statement function in the larger discourse?

It relates this parable to what was said in 19:30 [BNTC, CC, ICC, NAC, NICNT, NIGTC, PNTC, WBC]. Verses 1–15 are marked or 'bookended' by this statement, which repeats 19:30 [BNTC, CC, WBC]. It shows that 19:27–20:16 are a single unit [CC].

QUESTION—Who are the ones who will be 'first' and 'last' in this verse?

1. Both groups represent believers [BNTC, CC, NAC, NIBC, NICNT, NIGTC, PNTC, WBC]. In 19:30 the ones who are currently last but will become first are believers, and the ones who are currently first but will become last are unbelievers, but here the terms 'first' and 'last' both refer to believers. This is not about different rewards as in 19:30, but rather the

sequence of their being rewarded [NAC]. 'First' represents those who
were involved early on in the ministry, as opposed to those who would
come to it later [BNTC]. Both in 19:30 as well as here the people who are
considered first in this life are those who are seen as important by worldly
standards, and those who are considered last now are the ones seen as
unimportant by those standards [TRT]. 'First' and 'last' refer to rankings
made by human estimation [CC, PNTC, TH], but which do not count with
God [CC, PNTC]. The last are those such as tax collectors and others who
were religious outcasts [NIBC, WBC]. Just as the vineyard workers hired
last had been rejected by other employers, so also the 'last', who are
people of low regard or status such as tax collectors and prostitutes, are
given an open invitation to come into the kingdom [WBC]. For Jesus the
'first' were those who had remained faithful to God, as opposed to the last
who were sinners responding to his ministry, but for Matthew the 'first'
would have been those from the earliest circles of disciples, as opposed to
others who came later and did not have longstanding status as disciples
[NIGTC].

2. In both 19:30 as well as here, those who will come to be 'first' are the
elect whose destiny is heaven, and those who will come to be 'last' are
those who resisted and rejected grace, and whose destiny is hell [Lns].

QUESTION—What was Jesus' point in telling this parable?

This parable answers the question Peter raised in 19:27 about how he and the
other disciples would be rewarded [ICC, NAC, NIGTC, WBC]. They should
not think they will have a greater reward simply because they were the first
to follow Christ [NIGTC, PNTC]. Those converted late in life are not at a
disadvantage when it comes to rewards [ICC], because God's rewards are
given on the basis of his goodness, not merits or achievements [ICC, NIBC].
Within the kingdom of God, comparisons of rank and status are out of place
[CC, WBC]. All will receive the same reward to be given the disciples and in
this sense the last will be first and the first last [WBC]. He is saying that
there are no differences of reward in heaven [CC, NAC]. God's gifts are
richly shared by all, regardless of how much or little time they have been
involved in ministry [BNTC, CC, My], or how much or little they have
sacrificed [BNTC, CC], or what they have achieved [CC]. All who are saved
are equally rewarded with eternal happiness [NAC]. Jesus' point was to
teach that God acts in grace toward all believers, and salvation is always a
result of God's grace [PNTC, WBC]. Some think that not all receive the
same reward, and those rewards in God's kingdom are entirely dependent on
his grace [EBC]. Although some may be rewarded more than others, no one
can claim the right to a greater reward because of what he has done [ICC,
My].

DISCOURSE UNIT—20:17–21:11 [NIGTC]. The topic is redefining
greatness, Jesus goes to Jerusalem to die: Jericho, Bethphage, entry into
Jerusalem.

DISCOURSE UNIT—20:17-19 [CEV, ESV, NASB, NCV, NET, NIV, NLT, NRSV]. The topic is Jesus talks about his own death [NCV], Jesus foretells his death a third time [ESV], a third time Jesus foretells his death and resurrection [NRSV], third prediction of Jesus' death and resurrection [NET], Jesus again predicts his death [NIV, NLT], Jesus again tells about his death [CEV], death and resurrection foretold [NASB].

20:17 And (as) Jesus (was) going-up to Jerusalem he-took the twelve disciples aside-privately[a] and on the way he-said to-them, **20:18** "Behold,[b] we-are-going-up to Jerusalem, and the Son of Man will-be-handed-over[c] to-the chief-priests and scribes, and they-will-condemn him to-death, **20:19** and they-will-hand- him -over to-the Gentiles to-be-mocked[d] and scourged[e] and crucified, and on-the third day he-will-be-raised.[f]

TEXT—In verse 17, manuscripts reading τοὺς δώδεκα μαθητάς 'the twelve disciples' are given a C rating by GNT to indicate that choosing it over a variant text that omits μαθητάς was difficult. Μαθητάς 'disciples' is included by NICNT, NTC, PNTC; CEV, ESV, GNT, GW, KJV, NIV, NLT, NRSV, TEV. It is included in brackets by BECNT, CC, WBC; NASB. It is omitted by BNTC, NIGTC; NET, REB.

LEXICON—a. κατ' ἰδίαν (LN 28.67) (BAGD 4. p. 370): The phrase 'aside privately' [NICNT, NIGTC, WBC; GW, NCV, NET, NLT, TEV], is also translated 'aside' [BNTC, NTC; ESV, NIV, REB], 'aside by themselves' [BECNT; NASB, NRSV], 'aside in private' [CEV], 'privately' [BAGD, CC, LN], 'apart privately' [PNTC], 'apart' [KJV]. This idiomatic expression describes what occurs in a private context or setting in the sense of not being made known publicly [LN].

b. ἰδού (LN 91.13) (BAGD 1.b.ε. p. 371): 'behold' [BAGD, BNTC, WBC; KJV, NASB], 'look' [BAGD, BECNT, CC, LN, NICNT, NIGTC; NCV, NET], 'see' [BAGD; ESV, NRSV], 'listen' [LN, NTC, PNTC; NLT, TEV], 'pay attention, come now, then' [LN], not explicit [CEV, GW, NIV, REB]. This particle is a prompter of attention, which serves also to emphasize the following statement [LN].

c. fut. pass. indic. of παραδίδωμι (LN 37.111) (BAGD 1.b. p. 614): 'to be handed over' [BAGD, BECNT, BNTC, CC, LN, NIGTC, NTC, WBC; CEV, NET, NRSV, REB, TEV], 'to be turned over' [NCV], 'to be delivered up' [PNTC], 'to be delivered to' [NASB], 'to be given up' [BAGD], 'to be betrayed' [NICNT, LN; GW, KJV, NIV, NLT], 'to be turned over to' [BAGD, LN]. This verb means to deliver a person into the control of someone else, involving either the handing over of a presumably guilty person for punishment by authorities or the handing over of an individual to an enemy who will presumably take undue advantage of the victim [LN].

d. aorist act. infin. of ἐμπαίζω (LN 33.406) (BAGD 1. p. 255): 'to mock' [BAGD, BECNT, BNTC, CC, LN, NICNT, NIGTC, NTC, PNTC, WBC; ESV, KJV, NASB, NET, NIV, NLT, NRSV, REB], 'to make fun of'

[BAGD; CEV, GW, TEV], 'to laugh at' [NCV], 'to ridicule' [BAGD, LN]. This active voice infinitive in this verse is translated as being passive: 'to be mocked' etc. [BECNT, NICNT; ESV, NET, NIV, NLT, NRSV, REB]. This verb means to make fun of someone by pretending that he is not what he is or by imitating him in a distorted manner [LN].

e. aorist act. infin. of μαστιγόω (LN 19.9) (BAGD 1. p. 495): 'to scourge' [BAGD, BNTC, CC, NTC, WBC; KJV, NASB], 'to flog' [BAGD, BECNT, NICNT, NIGTC, PNTC; ESV, NIV, NRSV, REB], 'to flog with a whip' [NLT], 'to flog severely' [NET], 'to whip' [BAGD, LN; GW, TEV], 'to beat' [CEV], 'to beat with a whip' [LN; NCV]. This verb means to beat severely with a whip [LN].

f. fut. pass. indic. of ἐγείρω (LN 23.94): 'to be raised' [CC, NICNT, NIGTC, PNTC, WBC; ESV, NET, NRSV], 'to be raised up' [BECNT, NTC; NASB], 'to be raised to life' [LN; NIV, TEV], 'to be raised to life again' [NCV, REB], 'to be raised from the dead' [NLT], 'to be brought back to life' [GW], 'to rise' [BNTC], 'to rise again' [KJV], 'to rise from death' [CEV], 'to be made to live again' [LN]. This verb means to cause someone to live again after having once died [LN].

QUESTION—What is implied by the use of the term 'privately'?

There are other disciples and travelers going to Jerusalem with Jesus, and he takes the twelve aside to tell them what will happen to him [CC, Lns, NTC]. There would normally be many pilgrims on the road to Jerusalem for the Passover, and he wanted to avoid having those people hear what he was going to tell the disciples [EBC, NICNT, PNTC]. Others were traveling along with them [My].

QUESTION—Is there any distinction between "the chief-priests and scribes" here, and "the elders, the chief-priests and scribes" in16:21?

Both phrases describe the Jewish Sanhedrin or supreme court [Lns, NICNT, NTC, PNTC].

DISCOURSE UNIT—20:20–28 [CEV, ESV, GW, NASB, NCV, NET, NIV, NLT, NRSV, TEV]. The topic is a mother makes a request [GW], a mother asks Jesus for a favor [NCV], a mother's request [CEV, ESV, NIV, TEV], a request for James and John [NET], the request of the mother of James and John [NRSV], preferment asked [NASB], Jesus teaches about serving others [NLT].

20:20 Then the mother of-the sons of-Zebedee approached him with her two sons bowing-down[a] and requesting[b] something from him. **20:21** And he-said to-her, "What do-you(sg)-want?" She-says to-him, "Say[c] that these two sons of-mine may-sit one at your right and one at your left in your kingdom."

LEXICON—a. pres. act. participle of προσκυνέω (LN 53.56, 17.21) (BAGD 5. p. 717): 'to bow down' [BECNT; NASB], 'to bow before' [NICNT; NCV, REB, TEV], 'to bow down in front of' [GW], 'to kneel before' [NTC; ESV, NRSV], 'to kneel' [PNTC], 'to kneel down' [CEV, NET, NIV], 'to kneel respectfully' [NLT], 'to pay homage' [CC], 'to fall reverently before' [BNTC], 'to fall down before' [WBC], 'to worship' [BAGD, LN (53.56); KJV], 'to prostrate oneself before' [BAGD], 'to do obeisance to' [LN, NIGTC], 'to do reverence to' [BAGD], 'to prostrate oneself in worship, to bow down and worship' [LN (53.56)], 'to prostrate oneself before' [LN (17.21)]. This verb means to express by attitude and possibly by position one's allegiance to and regard for deity [LN (53.56)] or to prostrate oneself before someone as an act of reverence, fear, or supplication [LN (17.21)].

b. pres. act. participle of αἰτέω (LN 33.163) (BAGD p. 26): 'to request something' [BAGD], 'to make a request' [BNTC, PNTC; NASB], 'to ask for something' [BAGD, BECNT, CC, LN, NIGTC, WBC; ESV], 'to ask someone to do something' [NCV], 'to ask a favor' [NICNT, NTC; GW, NET, NIV, NLT, NRSV, TEV], 'to beg a favor' [REB], 'to beg someone to do something' [CEV], 'to desire something of someone' [KJV], 'to plead for' [LN]. This verb means to ask for with urgency, even to the point of demanding [LN].

c. aorist act. impera. of λέγω (LN 33.69): 'to say' [CC, LN, NIGTC, NTC, PNTC, WBC; ESV], 'to grant' [KJV, NIV], 'to command' [BECNT, BNTC; NASB], 'to give orders' [REB], 'to declare' [NRSV], 'to promise' [GW, NCV, TEV], 'to give someone your word'[NICNT]. The phrase Εἰπὲ ἵνα 'say that' is translated 'please let' [CEV, NLT], 'permit' [NET]. This verb means to speak or talk, with apparent focus upon the content of what is said [LN].

QUESTION—Who was this woman?

There is a good possibility that the wife of Zebedee was Salome, the sister of Jesus' mother, and hence Jesus' aunt, and if so, James and John were Jesus' cousins [BNTC, EBC, Lns, My, NAC, NIBC, NTC, PNTC, WBC]. This relationship may explain why she expected Jesus to give James and John a special favor [NAC].

QUESTION—When did this incident occur?

It occurred sometime after Jesus' prediction of his passion, while they were journeying to Jerusalem [EBC, ICC, My, NICNT, NIGTC, NTC, PNTC, TH, WBC]. 'Then' does not necessarily mean that it happened immediately afterward, just sometime later [PNTC].

20:22 **But answering Jesus said, "You(pl)-do- not -know what you-are-asking. Are-you-able to-drink the cup[a] which I am- about[b] -to-drink?" They-say to him, "We-are-able."** **20:23** **He-says to-them, "You-will-drink my cup, but to-sit at my right and at my left is-not mine to-give, but (is) for-those (for whom) it-has-been-prepared by my father.**

TEXT—In 20:22 another manuscript adds to Jesus' question 'or to be baptized with the baptism which I will be baptized with'. GNT omits this with an A rating, indicating that the text is certain. Only KJV follows the variant manuscript.

TEXT—In verse 20:23 another manuscript adds to Jesus' answer 'and you will be baptized with the baptism which I will be baptized with'. GNT omits this with an A rating, indicating that the text is certain. Only KJV follows the variant manuscript.

LEXICON—a. ποτήριον (LN 24.81) (BAGD 2. p. 695): 'cup' [BAGD, all translations except NLT, TEV], 'the cup of suffering' [TEV], 'the bitter cup of suffering' [NLT]. The idiom 'to drink a cup' means to undergo a trying, difficult experience [LN].

    b. pres. act. indic. of μέλλω (LN **67.62**) (BAGD 1.c.δ. p. 501): 'to be about to' [BECNT, BNTC, CC, **LN**, NIGTC, NTC, WBC; NASB, NCV, NET, NLT, NRSV, TEV], 'to be going to (do)' [PNTC; GW, NIV], 'must, to be destined' [BAGD]. The phrase 'I am about to drink' is translated 'I am to drink' [ESV, REB], 'I am soon to drink' [NICNT], 'I must soon drink' [CEV], 'that I shall drink of' [KJV]. This verb means to occur at a point of time in the future which is subsequent to another event and closely related to it [LN].

QUESTION—Who is Jesus speaking to?

He is speaking to James and John, and not their mother [BECNT, BNTC, CC, My, NIBC, NIGTC, NTC, PNTC, WBC]. He primarily addresses the sons, but also includes their mother in what he says [NAC]. After he says 'you do not know what you are asking' he is speaking only to James and John [NICNT].

QUESTION—What does the cup represent?

The cup represents suffering [BECNT, ICC, Lns, My, NICNT, NIBC, PNTC, TH, TRT, WBC]. It is drawn from OT imagery representing the wrath or judgment of God [CC, EBC, ICC, NICNT, NIGTC, PNTC]. It represents eschatological sorrow [ICC]. Jesus foresaw that he would experience the wrath of God vicariously for sinners [CC].

20:24 And having-heard (this) the ten were-indignant[a] with the two brothers. **20:25** And Jesus having-called- them -to-himself said, "You know that the rulers of-the Gentiles lord-it-over[b] them and the great-ones[c] exert-authority-over[d] them.

LEXICON—a. aorist act. indic. of ἀγανακτέω (LN 88.187) (BAGD p. 4): 'to be indignant' [BAGD, BNTC, CC, LN, PNTC; ESV, NASB, NIV, NLT, REB], 'to-be/become angry with' [BAGD, BECNT, LN, NICNT, NIGTC, NTC, WBC; CEV, NCV, NET, NRSV, TEV], 'to be moved with indignation' [KJV], 'to be irritated with' [GW]. This verb means to be indignant against what is judged to be wrong [LN].

    b. pres. act. indic. of κατακυριεύω (LN 37.50) (BAGD 2. p. 412): 'lord it over' [BAGD, BECNT, BNTC, CC, NICNT, NTC; ESV, NASB, NET, NIV, NLT, NRSV, REB], 'to exercise lordship over' [PNTC], 'to reign over' [**LN**], 'to rule over' [BAGD, WBC], 'to have power over' [TEV], 'to rule, to govern' [LN], 'to have dominion over' [NIGTC], 'to exercise dominion over' [KJV], 'to have absolute power over' [GW], 'to love to

show one's power over' [NCV], 'to order people around' [CEV]. This
verb means to rule or reign over, with the implication in some contexts of
'lording it over' [LN].

c. μεγάλοι (LN 87.40) (BAGD 2.b.a. p. 498): 'great ones' [NIGTC; ESV,
NRSV], 'great men' [BAGD, BECNT, BNTC, CC, LN, NICNT, NTC,
PNTC; NASB], 'great leaders' [WBC; CEV], 'the great' [REB], 'those
that are great' [KJV], 'leaders' [TEV], 'important leaders' [NCV],
'important persons' [LN], 'officials' [GW, NLT], 'high officials' [NIV],
'those in high position' [BAGD; NET]. This noun occurs only in the
plural in the NT and it denotes persons of important or high status [LN].

d. pres. act. indic. of κατεξουσιάζω (LN 37.48) (BAGD p. 421): 'to
exercise authority over' [BAGD, BECNT, NIGTC, PNTC, WBC; ESV,
NASB, NIV, similarly KJV], 'to use authority over' [NASB], 'to flaunt
one's authority over' [NLT], 'to make one's authority felt' [REB], 'to
have complete authority' [TEV], 'to rule' [LN], 'to tyrannize' [BAGD,
BNTC], 'to be a tyrant over' [NRSV], 'to act as tyrant over' [CC], 'to
keep under despotic power' [NTC], 'to have full power over those ruled'
[CEV], 'to have absolute authority over' [GW], 'to impose authority on'
[NICNT], 'to love to use all one's authority [NCV], 'to reign' [**LN**]. This
verb means to rule or reign by exercising authority over [LN].

QUESTION—Who were the ἄρχοντες τῶν ἐθνῶν 'rulers of the Gentiles'?

1. He is describing the practice of rulers in the non-Jewish world [BECNT,
BNTC, CC, ICC, Lns, My, NAC, NIBC, NIGTC, NTC, TRT, WBC;
CEV, ESV, KJV, NASB, NCV, NET, NIV, NRSV, REB, TEV]. Jewish
leaders were not much better, but that is not what he is focusing on here
[NAC].

2. He is describing what happens in nations, not necessarily just among
Gentiles as opposed to Jews [PNTC; GW].

20:26 It-shall- not -be this-way among you, but whoever wishes to-become
great among you shall-be your servant,[a] **20:27** and whoever wishes to-be
first[b] among you shall be your slave.[c] **20:28** Just-as[d] the Son of-Man did-
not -come to-be-served[e] but to-serve and to-give his life (as) a-ransom[f] for[g]
many.

LEXICON—a. διάκονος (LN 35.20) (BAGD 1.a. p. 184): 'servant' [BAGD,
LN; all translations except KJV, NCV], 'minister' [KJV]. The phrase
ἔσται ὑμῶν διάκονος 'shall be your servant' is translated 'serve…like a
servant' [NCV]. This noun denotes a person who renders service [LN].

b. πρῶτος (LN **87.45**) (BAGD 1.c.β. p. 726): 'first' [BAGD, BECNT,
BNTC, CC, NICNT, NTC, PNTC, WBC; all versions except GW, KJV],
'important' [**LN**], 'most important' [BAGD; GW], 'chief' [KJV], 'having
first rank' [**LN**], 'one who has the first place' [NIGTC], 'great, prominent'
[LN], 'most prominent' [BAGD], 'foremost' [BAGD, LN]. This adjective
describes being of high rank, with the implication of special prominence
and status [LN].

c. δοῦλος (LN 87.76) (BAGD 3. p. 205): 'slave' [BAGD, BECNT, BNTC, CC, LN, NICNT, NIGTC, PNTC, WBC; all versions except KJV, NCV], 'servant' [KJV], 'humble attendant' [NTC], 'bondservant' [LN]. The phrase ἔσται ὑμῶν δοῦλος 'shall be your slave' is translated 'must serve the rest of you like a slave' [NCV]. This noun denotes one who is a slave in the sense of becoming the property of an owner (though in ancient times it was frequently possible for a slave to earn his freedom) [LN].

d. ὥσπερ (LN 64.13) (BAGD 2. p. 899): 'just as' [BAGD, BECNT, BNTC, CC, LN, NICNT, NIGTC, NTC; NASB, NET, NIV, NRSV, REB], 'even as' [PNTC; ESV, KJV], 'as' [LN], 'in the same way' [NCV], 'for even' [NLT], 'it's the same way' [GW], 'like' [TEV], not explicit [CEV]. This conjunction marks similarity between events and states [LN].

e. aorist pass. infin. of διακονέω (LN 35.19) (BAGD 2. p. 184): 'to be served' [BNTC, CC, **LN**, NICNT, NIGTC, NTC, PNTC, WBC; ESV, NASB, NCV, NET, NIV, NLT, NRSV, REB], 'to be a slave master' [CEV], 'to be ministered unto' [KJV], 'to be rendered service' [LN], 'to be helped' [LN]. The verb διακονηθῆναι 'to be served' is translated 'so that others could serve him' [GW]. This verb means to render assistance or help by performing certain duties, often of a humble or menial nature [LN].

f. λύτρον (LN 37.130) (BAGD p. 482): 'ransom' [BAGD, BECNT, BNTC, **LN**, NICNT, NIGTC, NTC, PNTC, WBC; all versions except CEV, TEV], 'ransom payment' [CC], 'means of liberating' [**LN**], 'price of release' [BAGD], 'means of release' [LN]. This noun is translated as an infinitive verb: 'to rescue' [CEV], 'to redeem' [TEV]. This noun denotes the means or instrument by which release or deliverance is made possible [LN].

g. ἀντί with the genitive (LN 90.37) (BAGD 3. p. 73): 'for' [BECNT, BNTC, LN, NIGTC, PNTC, WBC; all versions except CEV, TEV], 'in exchange for' [CC], 'in place of' [NICNT, NTC], 'on behalf of' [LN], 'in behalf of' [BAGD], 'in place of' [BAGD], not explicit [CEV, TEV]. This preposition indicates a participant who is benefited by an event, usually with the implication of some type of exchange or substitution involved [LN].

QUESTION—Is there any distinction between the nouns 'servant' and 'slave' as they are used here?

Δοῦλος 'slave' is a stronger term than διάκονος 'servant' [EBC, Lns, My, NICNT, NIGTC, PNTC], which Jesus uses for emphasis [EBC, My, NIGTC]. They are used synonymously here [NTC].

QUESTION—Does the verb 'come' imply Jesus' pre-existence?

It does imply his pre-existence [CC, EBC, Lns, PNTC, TRT], though it does not require it [EBC, PNTC].

QUESTION—What area of meaning is intended for the preposition ἀντί 'for'?

It means 'in the place of' or 'in exchange for' [CC, EBC, ICC, Lns, My, NAC, NIBC, NTC, PNTC], as in a substitutionary payment [BECNT, CC, EBC, Lns, My, WBC]. It also includes 'for the benefit of' [NTC].

QUESTION—Who are the 'many' for whom the ransom price is given?

The ransom was given for all who are God's elect [NTC, WBC]. It was for the elect eschatological people of God [EBC]. It refers to anyone who accepts the forgiveness Jesus offers and commits his life to him [NAC]. 'Many' indicates the benefits of Jesus' suffering will be widely effective [BNTC]. It refers to all who believe or will come to believe [My]. It refers to all people [ICC, Lns, TRT]. The contrast in focus here is not between 'many' and 'all', but between 'the one' and 'the many' [CC, Lns, NICNT, NIGTC, probably WBC].

DISCOURSE UNIT—20:29–34 [NICNT; CEV, ESV, GW, NASB, NCV, NET, NIV, NLT, NRSV, TEV]. The topic is sight restored [NICNT], Jesus gives two blind men their sight [GW], Jesus heals two blind men [CEV, ESV, NCV, NLT, NRSV, TEV], two blind men healed [NET], two blind men receive sight [NIV], sight for the blind [NASB].

20:29 And (as) they were-going-out from Jericho large crowds followed him. **20:30** And behold two blind-men sitting by the road having-heard that Jesus is-passing-by, cried-out[a] saying, "Have-mercy-on[b] us, Lord, Son of David." **20:31** And the crowd rebuked[c] them that they-might-be-quiet; but they-cried-out more-loudly[d] saying, "Have-mercy-on us, Lord, Son of David."

TEXT—Manuscripts reading κύριε, υἱὸς Δαυίδ 'Lord, son of David' are given a C rating by GNT to indicate that choosing it over a variant text that omits κύριε 'Lord' was difficult. Manuscripts that do not include this word are followed by REB.

LEXICON—a. aorist act. indic. of κράζω (LN 33.83) (BAGD 2.a. p. 447): 'to cry out' [BNTC, CC, NTC, PNTC, WBC; ESV, KJV, NASB], 'to call out' [BAGD, NIGTC], 'to cry' [BAGD], 'to call' [BAGD], 'to say loudly' [BAGD], 'to shout' [BECNT, LN; all versions except ESV, KJV, NASB], 'to shout out' [NICNT], 'to scream' [LN]. This verb means to shout or cry out [LN].

   b. aorist act. impera. of ἐλεάω (LN 88.76) (BAGD p. 249): 'to have mercy on' [BAGD, BECNT, BNTC, CC, LN, NIGTC, WBC; all versions except CEV, REB], 'to show mercy' [BAGD, LN, NICNT], 'to take pity on' [NTC, PNTC], 'to have pity on' [BAGD; CEV, REB], 'to be merciful toward' [BAGD, LN]. This verb means to show kindness or concern for someone in serious need [LN].

   c. aorist act. indic. of ἐπιτιμάω (LN 33.419) (BAGD 1. p. 303): 'to rebuke' [BAGD, CC, LN, NICNT, NIGTC, WBC; ESV, KJV], 'to reprove, to censure' [BAGD], 'to warn sternly' [BECNT], 'to warn' [BAGD, NTC;

NCV], 'to charge sternly' [BNTC], 'to sternly tell' [NASB], 'to sternly order' [NRSV], 'to admonish' [PNTC], 'to scold and tell (to be quiet)' [TEV], 'to tell (to be quiet)' [CEV, GW, NIV, REB]. The phrase ἐπετίμησεν αὐτοῖς ἵνα σιωπήσωσιν 'they rebuked them that they might be quiet' is translated 'they scolded them to get them to be quiet' [NET], 'Be quiet! The crowd yelled at them' [NLT]. This verb means to express strong disapproval of someone [LN].

d. μέγας (LN 78.2) (BAGD 2.a.γ. p. 497): 'greatly' [LN]. This comparative form is translated 'even more loudly' [BECNT, NIGTC; NET, NRSV, TEV], 'even louder' [CEV, GW], 'all the louder' [NTC; NIV], 'still louder' [BNTC], 'louder' [NLT], 'even more' [NICNT; NCV], 'all the more' [BAGD, PNTC, WBC; ESV, NASB, REB], 'the more' [KJV], 'more greatly' [CC]. This adverb describes the upper range of a scale of extent, with the possible implication of importance in relevant contexts [LN].

QUESTION—Why did the crowd rebuke them for calling out to Jesus?

Perhaps they did not want Jesus to be delayed on his journey to Jerusalem [BECNT]. The unsympathetic crowd wanted to see and hear Jesus, and the blind men were a disturbance and a distraction [PNTC]. The people were probably impatient for Jesus to move on and enter Jerusalem triumphantly to assume his place as messianic king [BNTC, NAC]. The crowd saw the blind men as a nuisance [ICC, PNTC] or a distraction from Jesus' more important concerns as he headed toward Jerusalem [WBC].

QUESTION—How far was Jesus from Jerusalem at this point in his journey?

Jericho was about fifteen miles from Jerusalem [BECNT, ICC, NAC, NIGTC, NTC, PNTC, TRT, WBC], and the uphill climb from Jericho to Jerusalem would be over 3,300 feet (over 1,000 meters) [BECNT, NICNT, NTC].

20:32 **And having-stood-still Jesus called[a] them and said, "What do-you-want that-I-should-do for-you?"** **20:33** **They-say to-him, "Lord, that our eyes be-opened.[b]"** **20:34** **And having-been-moved-with-compassion[c] Jesus touched their eyes, and immediately they received-sight[d] and followed him.**

LEXICON—a. aorist act. indic. of φωνέω (LN 33.307) (BAGD 2.b. p. 870): 'to call' [BNTC, LN, NICNT, NIGTC, NTC, PNTC, WBC; all versions except CEV, NCV], 'to call out' [BECNT], 'to address' [CC], 'to say' [NCV], 'to call to oneself' [BAGD], 'to summon' [BAGD, LN]. The phrase ἐφώνησεν αὐτοὺς καὶ εἶπεν 'called them and said' is conflated and translated 'asked' [CEV]. This verb means to communicate directly or indirectly to someone who is presumably at a distance, in order to tell such a person to come [LN].

b. aorist pass. subj. of ἀνοίγω (LN 24..43) (BAGD 1.e.β. p. 71): 'to be opened' [BAGD, BECNT, BNTC, CC, LN, NICNT, NIGTC, NTC, PNTC, WBC; ESV, KJV, NASB, NET, NRSV], 'to be caused to see' [LN]. The phrase ἵνα ἀνοιγῶσιν οἱ ὀφθαλμοὶ ἡμῶν 'that our eyes be opened' is translated 'open our eyes' [REB], 'we want to see' [CEV, NCV, NLT], 'we want our sight' [NIV], 'give us our sight' [TEV], 'give us our eyesight back' [GW]. The idiom ἀνοίγω τοὺς ὀφθαλμούς 'to open the eyes' means to cause someone to be able to see [LN].

c. aorist pass. participle of σπλαγχνίζομαι (LN 25.49) (BAGD p. 762): 'to be moved with compassion' [BECNT, NTC, PNTC, WBC; NASB, NET, NRSV], 'to feel compassion' [CC, LN], 'to have compassion' [NIGTC; KJV, NIV], 'to be deeply moved' [REB], 'to have pity' [BAGD; TEV], 'to feel sympathy' [BAGD], 'to feel sorry for' [CEV, GW, NCV, NLT], 'to have great affection for' [LN]. The participle σπλαγχνισθεὶς 'having been moved with compassion' is translated 'Jesus' heart went out to them' [NICNT], 'in compassion' [BNTC], 'in pity' [ESV]. This verb means to experience great affection and compassion for someone [LN].

d. aorist act. indic. of ἀναβλέπω (LN 24.42) (BAGD 2.a.α. p. 51): 'to receive one's sight' [BNTC, PNTC, WBC; KJV, NET, NIV], 'to gain one's sight' [BAGD, LN, NIGTC], 'to regain one's sight' [BAGD, BECNT, CC, LN, NTC; NASB, NRSV], 'to recover one's sight' [ESV, REB], 'to be able to see again' [NICNT], 'to be able to see' [LN; CEV, NCV, NLT, TEV]. The verb ἀνέβλεψαν 'they received sight' is translated 'their eyesight was restored' [GW]. This verb means to become able to see, whether for the first time or again [LN].

QUESTION—Did Jesus call them to come, or simply address them?

He called them to come to him [Lns, WBC].

QUESTION—If it was apparent that they were blind, why did Jesus ask what they wanted him to do for them?

He wanted to draw out their faith [BECNT, WBC]. He wanted them to state their need in concrete form [ICC]. They could have been asking for alms, so Jesus wants them to state clearly what they want [NTC].

QUESTION—What is meant by the verb ἀνέβλεψαν 'they received sight'?

It means that they recovered the sight that they previously had [BECNT, CC, NTC, ICC, PNTC; ESV, GW, NASB, NRSV, REB].

QUESTION—Does 'followed' mean that they went along with the crowd, or that they became disciples?

They followed him along with the crowd [BECNT, BNTC, CC, EBC, NICNT, NIGTC, NTC, PNTC, WBC; all versions except CEV]. They actually became his followers [PNTC, TH; CEV]. This represents at least some degree of discipleship [My, NAC, NICNT, NIGTC]. They follow as new disciples [WBC].

DISCOURSE UNIT—21:1–27:66 [CEV]. The topic is Jesus' last week: his trial and death.

DISCOURSE UNIT—21:1–25:46 [NICNT]. The topic is Jerusalem: the Messiah in confrontation with the religious authorities.

DISCOURSE UNIT—21:1–25:26 [PNTC]. The topic is Jesus' ministry in Jerusalem.

DISCOURSE UNIT—21:1–23:39 [CC; REB]. The topic is Jesus in the temple [REB], Jesus in Jerusalem [CC].

DISCOURSE UNIT—21:1–22:46 [WBC]. The topic is the last days in Jerusalem.

DISCOURSE UNIT—21:1–27 [NICNT, PNTC]. The topic is the confrontation begins: three symbolic actions [NICNT], beginnings [PNTC].

DISCOURSE UNIT—21:1–11 [CEV, ESV, GW, NASB, NCV, NET, NIV, NLT, NRSV, TEV]. The topic is the king comes to Jerusalem [GW], Jesus enters Jerusalem [CEV], Jesus enters Jerusalem as a king [NCV], Jesus' triumphal entry into Jerusalem [NRSV], the triumphal entry into Jerusalem [TEV], the triumphal entry [ESV, NASB, NET, NIV], Jesus' triumphant entry [NLT].

21:1 **And when they-drew-near to Jerusalem and came to Bethphage, to the Mount of Olives, then Jesus sent two disciples 21:2 saying to them, "Go into the village opposite[a] you, and immediately you-will-find a-donkey[b] tied-up and a-colt with her. Having-untied (them) bring (them) to-me. 21:3 And if anyone says anything to-you, say 'The Lord has need of them;' and immediately he-will-send them."**

LEXICON—a. κατέναντι (LN **83.42**) (BAGD 2.a. p. 421): 'opposite' [BAGD, BNTC, **LN**, NIGTC, NTC, PNTC; NASB, REB], 'ahead of' [BECNT; GW, NET, NIV, NRSV, TEV], 'next' [CEV], 'in front of' [LN; ESV], 'over against' [KJV], 'before, across from, in the presence of' [LN], 'lying before' [BAGD]. The phrase κατέναντι ὑμῶν 'opposite you' is translated 'over there' [NICNT; NLT], 'which lies before you' [WBC], '(town) you can see there' [NCV]. This preposition indicates a position over against an object or other position [LN].

  b. ὄνος (LN 4.31) (BAGD p. 574): 'donkey' [BECNT, LN, NIGTC, NTC; all versions except KJV], 'female donkey' [NICNT], 'ass' [BNTC, LN, PNTC, WBC; KJV].

QUESTION—How did Jesus' know they would find the donkey and colt and be able to bring them to him?

  Jesus knowledge of what would happen was supernatural [BECNT, ICC, Lns, My]. God ordered these events, as is shown by the use of the word 'immediately' and the future tense verb 'you will find' [WBC]. Jesus had pre-arranged with the owners of the animals what he wanted to do, and the statement 'the Lord has need of them' was a pre-arranged password [PNTC]. It appears that the owners of the animals knew Jesus and were his followers [Lns, NIBC, NTC].

QUESTION—Who is 'the Lord' who has need of them?
1. This refers to Jesus himself [EBC, BNTC, ICC, My, NAC, NIBC, NIGTC, NTC].
2. This refers to God [NICNT].
3. It is best to understand it simply as a pre-arranged password, and not as referring to anyone in particular [PNTC].

21:4 This happened[a] so-that what-was-spoken[b] through the prophet might-be-fulfilled saying, **21:5** "Say to the daughter of Zion[c], 'Behold your(sg) king comes to-you(sg) humble[d] and mounted on a-donkey and[e] on a-colt (the) foal[f] of-a-beast-of-burden.[g]'"

LEXICON—a. perf. act. indic. of γίνομαι (LN 13.107): 'to happen' [BNTC, LN, NICNT, NIGTC, NTC, PNTC, WBC; GW, TEV], 'to take place' [BECNT; ESV, NASB, NET, NIV, NLT, NRSV], 'to be done' [KJV], 'to occur, to come to be' [LN], not explicit [CEV, NCV, REB]. This verb means to happen, with the implication that what happens is different from a previous state [LN].

b. aorist pass. participle of λέγω (LN 33.69): 'to be spoken' [BECNT, LN, NIGTC, NTC, PNTC, WBC; ESV, KJV, NASB, NET, NIV, NRSV], 'to be said' [LN], 'to be declared' [NICNT]. This passive participle is translated as a substantive: 'the saying' [BNTC]; as an active verb: '(the prophet) had said' [CEV, GW, NCV, TEV], '(the prophecy) that said/says' [NLT, REB]. This verb means to speak or talk, with apparent focus upon the content of what is said [LN].

c. θυγάτηρ Σιών (LN **11.66**) (BAGD 2.e. p. 365): 'daughter of Zion' [BECNT, BNTC, NTC, PNTC, WBC; ESV, KJV, NASB, NIV, NRSV, REB], 'people of Zion' [**LN**; GW, NET], 'people of Jerusalem' [LN; CEV, NCV], 'city of Zion' [TEV], 'my daughter Zion' [NICNT], 'daughter Zion' [NIGTC]. This phrase denotes the inhabitants of Jerusalem [LN].

d. πραΰς (LN 88.60) (BAGD p. 699): 'humble' [BAGD, BECNT, BNTC, NIGTC; CEV, ESV, NLT, NRSV, TEV], 'gentle' [BAGD, LN; GW, NASB, NCV, NIV], 'in gentleness' [REB], 'meek' [BAGD, LN, NICNT, NTC, PNTC, WBC; KJV], 'unassuming' [NET], 'mild' [LN]. This adjective describes being gentle and mild [LN].

e. καί (LN 89.92) (BAGD 1.3. p. 393): 'and' [BAGD, BNTC, LN, NICNT, NIGTC, PNTC, WBC; ESV, KJV, NET, NRSV, TEV], 'even' [BECNT, NTC; NASB], not explicit [CEV, GW, NCV, NIV, NLT, REB].

f. υἱός (LN **4.9**) (BAGD 1.a.β. p. 833): 'foal' [BECNT, LN, NIGTC, NTC, PNTC, WBC; ESV, KJV, NASB, NET, NIV, NRSV, REB, TEV], 'colt' [BNTC, NICNT; CEV], 'offspring' [BAGD, **LN**], not explicit [GW, NCV, NLT]. This noun denotes the male offspring of an animal [LN].

g. ὑποζύγιον (LN **4.7**) (BAGD p. 844): 'beast of burden' [BAGD, BECNT, BNTC, **LN**, NIGTC, PNTC, WBC; ESV, NASB, REB], 'pack animal' [BAGD, LN, NTC; GW], 'donkey' [BAGD; CEV, NCV, NET, NIV,

NLT, NRSV, TEV], 'ass' [NICNT; KJV], 'riding animal' [LN]. This
noun denotes an animal which can be used to carry a burden or be ridden
[LN].

QUESTION—Why did Jesus choose to enter Jerusalem riding on a donkey?

He wanted to fulfill the messianic passage in Zechariah 9:10, which
describes the Messiah riding on a donkey and coming as the prince of peace,
not as a conquering king [EBC, ICC, Lns, NAC, NICNT, WBC]. He was
enacting a parable, showing by a symbolic act who he was [BECNT, BNTC,
EBC, ICC, My], the Suffering Servant Messiah [BNTC]. The use of the
donkey demonstrated his humility [BECNT]. Jesus saw the nationalistic
enthusiasm of the crowds, and by his coming mounted on a donkey he
wanted to show that he came as Prince of Peace, not as a conquering king
[NTC, PNTC]. Riding a donkey would symbolize humility and peace as
opposed to riding a war horse [My, NIBC, NICNT, TRT, WBC].

QUESTION—Why would they bring the mother as well as its colt?

Since the colt was not accustomed to carrying a rider it would be natural to
bring its mother along as well [BECNT, EBC, NAC, NIBC, NICNT, NTC,
PNTC, TRT]. An animal not accustomed to being ridden would have been
nervous in such a crowd, so the presence of the mother would have had a
calming effect on it [EBC, NICNT, PNTC]. An unbroken colt would
normally be introduced to being ridden with its mother nearby [WBC].

QUESTION—What is the function of καί 'and'?

1. It is additive, indicating there were two animals [BNTC, ICC, NICNT,
   TH, WBC].
2. It is explicative, indicating that the second clause expands on or explains
   the first, such as with 'that is' or 'even' [BAGD, BECNT, My, NTC,
   PNTC; NASB]: on a donkey, that is, on a donkey's colt.

21:6 **And the disciples having-gone and having-done as Jesus commanded
them, 21:7 they-brought the donkey and the colt and put their garments[a]
upon them, and he-sat upon them. 21:8 And a-great crowd spread-out
their garments in the road, and others cut branches[b] from the trees and
were-spreading- (them) -out in the road.**

LEXICON—a. ἱμάτιον (LN 6.162) (BAGD 1. p. 376): 'garment' [BAGD,
   BNTC, NIGTC, WBC; NLT], 'outer garment' [NTC], 'coat' [BECNT;
   GW, NASB, NCV], 'cloak' [PNTC; ESV, NET, NIV, NRSV, REB,
   TEV], 'cloths' [NICNT], 'clothes' [CEV, KJV], 'clothing' [LN], 'apparel'
   [LN]. This noun denotes any kind of clothing [LN].

   b. κλάδος (LN **3.49**) (BAGD p. 433): 'branch' [BAGD, **LN**; all
   translations]. Some languages distinguish carefully between two major
   types of branches: those which are essentially leaves (as in the case of
   palms) and those which have a number of buds or potential branches.
   Other languages may make a distinction between branches of a plant
   which is woody (a perennial) and those which are relatively soft and
   flexible, typical of an annual plant [LN].

QUESTION—Does 'he sat upon them' mean that he sat on the garments or on the donkey and her colt?

1. It means that he sat on the garments [BECNT, BNTC, Lns, My, NAC, NIBC, NICNT, NTC, PNTC, TH].
2. It means that he sat on the animals [NIGTC, WBC]. Although he could only sit on one of them, probably the colt with the donkey just beside it, the two are considered conceptually here as a unit [WBC].

QUESTION—Why would they put clothes and branches on the road as Jesus approached?

These actions were typical of a welcome fitting for a king [My, NAC, PNTC, WBC]. They were acknowledging that Jesus was a king [BECNT, EBC, ICC, Lns, NICNT, NTC]. They were showing him honor [TH].

QUESTION—What were the branches like that people were spreading in the road?

They were palm branches [Lns, NAC, PNTC, WBC]. They were very small branches [EBC, TH]. Branches are fitting to a religious procession [ICC].

21:9 **And the crowds going-before him and following (him) cried-out saying, "Hosanna[a] to the Son of-David; blessed[b] (is/be) the one-coming in (the) name of-(the) Lord. Hosanna in the highest.[c]"** **21:10** **And (when) he came into Jerusalem all the city was-stirred-up[d] saying, "Who is this?"** **21:11** **And the crowds were-saying "This is the prophet Jesus from Nazareth of Galilee."**

LEXICON—a. ὡσαννά (LN 33.364) (BAGD p. 899): 'hosanna' [BAGD, BECNT, BNTC, LN, NICNT, NIGTC, NTC, PNTC, WBC; ESV, GW, KJV, NASB, NET, NIV, NRSV, REB]. The phrase 'hosanna to' is translated 'praise to' [NCV, TEV], 'praise God for' [NLT], 'hooray for' [CEV]. This word is a shout of praise [LN] or can be an appeal for help [BAGD].

   b. perf. pass. participle of εὐλογέω (LN 33.470) (BAGD 2.a. p. 322): 'to be blessed' [BAGD, LN]. The participle is translated as a statement: 'blessed is' [BECNT, BNTC, NICNT, NIGTC, NTC, PNTC, WBC; ESV, GW, KJV, NASB, NET, NIV, NRSV, REB]; as a wish or prayer for blessing: 'God bless' [CEV, NCV], 'blessings on' [NLT, TEV]. This verb means to ask God to bestow divine favor on, with the implication that the verbal act itself constitutes a significant benefit [LN].

   c. ὕψιστος (LN 1.13) (BAGD 1. p. 850): 'highest' [BECNT, LN, NICNT, NIGTC, NTC, PNTC, WBC; ESV, KJV, NASB, NET, NIV], 'highest heaven' [BAGD, BNTC; GW, NLT, NRSV], 'heaven above' [CEV], 'heaven' [LN; NCV], 'the heavens' [REB], 'on high' [LN]. The phrase 'hosanna in the highest' is translated 'praise be to God' [TEV]. This noun denotes a location above the earth and is associated with supernatural events or beings [LN].

   d. aorist pass. indic. of σείω (LN **25.233**) (BAGD 2. p. 746): 'to be stirred up' [BAGD, BECNT, LN, NTC, PNTC; ESV], 'to be stirred' [BAGD,

BNTC; NASB, NIV], 'to be in turmoil' [NIGTC; NRSV], 'to be moved' [KJV], 'to be shaken' [WBC], 'to be excited' [CEV], 'to be filled with excitement' [NCV], 'to be wild with excitement' [REB], 'to be in an uproar' [NICNT; GW, NLT], 'to be thrown into an uproar' [LN; NET, TEV], 'to be caused to be in an uproar, to be caused great anxiety' [LN]. This verb means to cause extreme anxiety and apprehension, implying accompanying movement [LN].

QUESTION—What does 'hosanna' mean?

The original, literal meaning of 'hosanna' is 'O save' [BECNT, BNTC, ICC, NICNT, NTC, PNTC, TH, TRT, WBC], but here it is a jubilant expression of praise for Jesus as the messianic Son of David [BECNT, BNTC, Lns, PNTC, NICNT, WBC]. It expresses honor and exultation [PNTC] and praise [ICC, NAC, NIBC, NTC, TH, TRT]. It is a greeting, along with a wish that God would prosper his purposes [NIGTC].

QUESTION—What does 'in the highest' mean?

'Hosanna in the highest' indicates that they saw Jesus to be the Messiah given by God, who is in the highest heaven [NTC]. It is a prayer to God in the highest heaven to grant his blessing [My]. It means that angels in the highest heaven should praise him [BNTC, NIBC, TH]. The hosanna is to be heard in heaven itself [Lns, NIGTC], and regarded by God as a prayer [NIGTC]. It is a way of referring to God himself without mentioning his name; that is, praise be to God who dwells on high [NICNT, TH].

QUESTION—What does it mean to 'come in the name of the Lord'?

Their words 'Blessed is the one who comes in the name of the Lord' is from the Greek version of Psalm 118:25 [NAC, NICNT, NTC, WBC], which was sung at Passover time [WBC]. This shows that they believe Jesus is the Messiah [Lns, NAC, BNTC, NIBC, NICNT, NTC], and deserves all honor and praise [BNTC]. They believed that Jesus had come as God's representative [My, NIBC, NIGTC, PNTC, TH]. He came at God's command and as God's voice to his people [NTC].

QUESTION—Why did the people say that Jesus was 'the prophet'?

1. It simply means that they saw him as a prophet [BECNT, EBC, Lns, NAC, NIGTC, PNTC, WBC]. It was a way to show respect to Jesus as a prophet, though without necessarily designating him as the prophet promised in Deut 18:18 [WBC].

2. It means they believed he was the promised prophet mentioned in Deut. 18:18 [BNTC, ICC, NIBC, NICNT, TH].

DISCOURSE UNIT—21:12–46 [NIGTC]. The topic is a provocative ministry in Jerusalem.

DISCOURSE UNIT—21:12–17 [CEV, ESV, GW, NASB, NCV, NET, NIV, NLT, NRSV, TEV]. The topic is Jesus throws out the moneychangers [GW], Jesus goes to the temple [NCV, TEV], Jesus in the temple [CEV], Jesus at the temple [NIV], Jesus clears the temple [NLT], Jesus cleanses the temple [ESV, NRSV], cleansing the temple [NASB, NET].

21:12 And Jesus went-into the temple and drove-out[a] all those-selling and those-buying in the temple, and he-overturned[b] the tables of-the money-changers[c] and the seats of-those-selling the doves.[d]

TEXT—Manuscripts reading τὸ ἱερόν 'the temple' are given a B rating by GNT to indicate it was regarded to be almost certain. Manuscripts that read τὸ ἱερόν τοῦ θεοῦ 'the temple of God' are followed by KJV.

LEXICON—a. aorist act. indic. of ἐκβάλλω (LN 15.44) (BAGD 1. p. 237): 'to drive out' [BAGD, BECNT, BNTC, LN, NIGTC, NTC; ESV, NASB, NET, NIV, NLT, NRSV, REB, TEV], 'to throw out' [BAGD, NICNT, PNTC, WBC; GW, NCV], 'to chase out' [CEV], 'to cast out' [KJV], 'to expel' [BAGD, LN], 'to send away' [LN]. This verb means to cause to go out or leave, and it often involves force [LN].

b. aorist act. indic. of καταστρέφω (LN **16.18**) (BAGD 1. p. 419): 'to overturn' [BAGD, BECNT, BNTC, **LN**, NICNT, NIGTC, PNTC, WBC; ESV, GW, NASB, NIV, NRSV, TEV], 'to turn over' [LN; CEV, NCV, NET], 'to knock over' [NLT], 'to turn upside down' [NTC], 'to overthrow' [KJV], 'to upset' [BAGD, LN; REB]. This verb means to cause something to be completely overturned [LN].

c. κολλυβιστής (LN 57.205) (BAGD p. 442): 'money changer' [BAGD, LN; all translations except NCV], 'those who were exchanging different kinds of money' [NCV]. This noun denotes one who exchanges currency, either in terms of different types of currency or different values of the same currency [LN].

d. περιστερά (LN 4.44) (BAGD p. 651): 'dove' [BAGD, BECNT, BNTC, LN, NICNT, NIGTC, NTC, PNTC; CEV, KJV, NASB, NCV, NET, NIV, NLT, NRSV], 'pigeon' [BAGD, LN, WBC; ESV, GW, REB, TEV]. Though in English a relatively clear distinction is made between 'doves' (which have pointed tails) and 'pigeons' (which have squared off tails), there seems to be no such distinction in the use of περιστερά and τρυγών in the Greek of the New Testament [LN].

QUESTION—In what part of the temple did this occur?

This was in the Court of the Gentiles, which is part of the temple area [BECNT, BNTC, EBC, ICC, Lns, NAC, NIBC, NICNT, NTC, PNTC, TH, TRT, WBC], and which was known as the courtyard [GW, NET, TRT] or the outer court [BNTC, ICC, NIBC, NIGTC, NTC]. The noun ἱερόν 'temple' refers to the entire complex [BECNT, EBC, ICC, Lns, NIBC, TH, TRT].

QUESTION—Why would moneychangers have been needed?

Only coins from Tyre could be used for offerings or to pay the temple tax, so any other coins had to be exchanged [ICC, NICNT, NIGTC, PNTC, WBC]. Coins from Tyre were more likely to be precise with regard to having the proper weight of gold and silver [PNTC], and were considered to be of high quality [NIBC]. Roman and Greek coins were not accepted [EBC, ICC, NTC, TH], since coins with pagan inscriptions could not be used to pay the temple tax [BECNT, ICC, NIBC].

21:13 and he-says to-them, "It-is-written, 'My house shall-be-called a-house of-prayer, but you(pl) made it a-den^a of-robbers.^b'" **21:14** And (the) blind and lame^c came to-him in the temple, and he-healed them.

LEXICON—a. σπήλαιον (LN **1.57**) (BAGD p. 762): 'den' [BAGD, BECNT, BNTC, **LN**, NIGTC, NTC, WBC; ESV, KJV, NASB, NET, NIV, NLT, NRSV], 'cave' [BAGD, LN, NICNT, PNTC; REB], 'gathering place' [GW], 'hideout' [LN; NCV, TEV], 'place where (robbers) hide' [CEV]. This noun denotes a cave or den generally large enough for at least temporary occupation by persons; since such places were often used for habitation or refuge by those who were refugees or thieves, and in certain contexts it has the connotation of a 'hideout' [LN].

    b. ληστής (LN 57.240) (BAGD 1. p. 473): 'robber' [BAGD, BECNT, BNTC, LN, NTC, PNTC; CEV, ESV, NASB, NCV, NET, NIV, NRSV], 'bandit' [BAGD, NICNT, NIGTC; REB], 'thief' [WBC; GW, KJV, NLT, TEV], 'highwayman' [BAGD, LN]. This noun denotes one who robs by force and violence [LN].

    c. χωλός (LN 23.175) (BAGD p. 889): 'lame' [BAGD, LN; all translations except NCV, REB, TEV], 'crippled' [BAGD, NCV, REB, TEV], 'one who is lame' [LN]. This adjective describes a disability that involves the imperfect function of the lower limbs [LN].

QUESTION—Does the charge of making the temple a den of robbers imply that the vendors and moneychangers were cheating people?

They were overcharging people [BNTC, ICC, My, NAC, NIBC, NTC, TRT] and trading dishonestly [PNTC], and they were also robbing God of worship [TRT]. The priests were probably profiting from the commerce in the temple [BNTC, NIBC, NTC], and some of the money would have even gone to Caiaphas himself [NTC]. The noun ληστής 'robber' can also mean 'insurrectionist', in which case Jesus' criticism could be directed toward their making the temple a center for nationalism [BECNT, EBC, NAC, WBC]. The violence implied in the noun ληστής may simply refer to the extortion involved in their business dealings [ICC]. He was deliberately quoting the wording of the Greek version of Jeremiah 7:11 to describe their lack of respect for the temple as a place of God's presence [NICNT]. His citing Jeremiah 7:11 shows that he views the people as being wicked, yet he still views the temple and its worship as representing refuge for them despite their many sins [Lns].

QUESTION—What is the significance of Jesus' healing the blind and lame in the temple area?

This is the only healing done in Jerusalem that is recorded by the synoptic gospels [NICNT, NIGTC, TH, WBC]. It shifts the focus of the temple from being a commercial center to a place for healing [WBC]. Along with the cleansing of the temple, it shows Jesus' superiority over the temple, since Jewish authorities generally banned the blind and the lame from the temple, whereas Jesus healed them in the temple [EBC]. Jewish oral law prohibited the blind and lame from coming to the temple to offer sacrifice [NIBC].

Jesus' healing the blind and lame removed the barrier to their being able to participate fully in the worship at the temple, so when Jesus drives out the moneychangers and merchants and then heals the others, he is casting out the insiders and welcoming the outsiders [BECNT]. He is demonstrating the priority of mercy over sacrifice [NAC].

21:15 But the chief-priests and the scribes having-seen the wonders[a] that he-did and the children crying-out in the temple and saying "Hosanna to-the Son of-David" were-indignant[b] **21:16** and said to-him, "Do-you-hear what these are-saying?" And Jesus said to-them, "Yes. Have-you- never - read that 'From (the) mouths of-babies and those-nursing[c] I-prepared[d] praise[e]'?" **21:17** And having-left them he-went-out of-the city to Bethany and spent-the-night there.

LEXICON—a. θαυμάσιος (LN **25.215**) (BAGD 1. p. 352): 'wonder' [BAGD, BNTC, WBC], 'wonderful thing' [BAGD, BECNT, **LN**, NICNT, NTC, PNTC; ESV, KJV, NASB, NCV, NET, NIV, REB, TEV], 'marvelous thing' [NIGTC], 'miracle' [CEV], 'amazing miracle' [GW], 'wonderful miracle' [NLT], 'amazing thing' [NRSV], 'wonderful, remarkable, marvelous' [LN]. This adjective describes that which causes or is worthy of amazement and wonder [LN].

   b. aorist act. indic. of ἀγανακτέω (LN **88.187**) (BAGD p. 4): 'to be indignant' [BAGD, BNTC, LN, PNTC, WBC; ESV, NIV, NLT, REB], 'to become indignant' [NASB, NET], 'to become angry' [BECNT, NIGTC, NTC; NRSV, TEV], 'to be angry' [BAGD, LN, NICNT; CEV], 'to be made very angry' [NCV], 'to be irritated' [GW], 'to be sore displeased' [KJV]. This verb means to be indignant against what is judged to be wrong [LN].

   c. pres. act. participle of θηλάζω (LN 23.7, 23.8) (BAGD 2. p. 360): 'to nurse (of a baby), to feed on' [LN (23.7)], 'to suck' [BAGD], 'to nurse a baby' [LN (23.8)]. This plural participle is translated 'nursing babies' [BECNT, NIGTC; ESV, NASB, NRSV], 'babies' [NCV, TEV], 'babes at the breast' [REB], 'nursing infants' [NET], 'infants' [NICNT; CEV, GW, NIV, NLT], 'sucklings' [BNTC, NTC; KJV], 'those who suckle' [WBC]. It is also translated as referring to the nursing mothers: 'those giving suck' [PNTC]. This verb denotes the activity of a baby feeding at the breast [LN (23.7)], but can also denote the action of causing a baby to feed at the breast [LN (23.8)].

   d. aorist mid. indic. of καταρτίζω (LN **13.130**) (BAGD 2.b. p. 418): 'to prepare' [BAGD, BECNT, BNTC, NTC; ESV, NASB, NET, NRSV], 'to ordain' [NIV], 'to create' [GW], 'to perfect' [KJV], 'to bring (perfect)' [PNTC], 'to bring forth' [WBC], 'to cause to come' [NICNT], 'to arrange' [NIGTC], 'to produce' [**LN**], to arrange for, to cause to happen' [LN]. The phrase 'from the mouths of babies and those nursing I ordained praise' is translated 'you have taught children and babies to sing praises' [NCV, similarly NLT], 'you have trained children and babies to offer

perfect praise' [TEV], 'you have made children and babes at the breast
sound your praise aloud' [REB], 'children and infants will sing praises'
[CEV]. This verb means to cause to happen by means of some
arrangement [LN].

   e. αἶνος (LN 33.354) (BAGD p. 23): 'praise' [BAGD, LN; all translations].
   This noun denotes speaking of the excellence of a person, object, or event
   [LN].

QUESTION—What is implied by Jesus citing the words of Psalm 8?

   Jesus is applying to himself something that was said originally of God [EBC,
   Lns, NAC, NICNT]. He is affirming that his actions are approved by God
   himself [TH].

DISCOURSE UNIT—21:18–22 [CEV, ESV, GW, NASB, NCV, NET, NIV,
NLT, NRSV, TEV]. The topic is Jesus curses the fig tree [ESV, GW, NLT,
NRSV, TEV], the power of faith [NCV], the withered fig tree [NET], the fig tree
withers [NIV], the barren fig tree [NASB], Jesus puts a curse on a fig tree
[CEV].

21:18 And (in the) morning returning to the city he-became-hungry. **21:19**
And having-seen one[a] fig-tree by the road he-went to it and found nothing
on it except leaves only, and he-says to-it, "Never[b] may-there-be fruit from
you ever." And at-once[c] the fig-tree withered.[d] **21:20** And having-seen
(this) the disciples were-amazed[e] saying, "How (did) the fig-tree wither
instantly?"

LEXICON—a. μία (LN 92.22) (BAGD 3.b. p. 231): 'one' [LN, WBC], 'a'
    [BAGD, BNTC, LN, NTC, PNTC; all versions except NASB], 'a lone'
    [NASB], 'a single' [BECNT, NICNT], 'a certain' [NIGTC]. This
    adjective describes a single, indefinite person or thing [LN].

   b. μηκέτι (LN 67.130) (BAGD 6.a. p. 518): 'no longer' [BAGD, LN]. The
    phrase μηκέτι...τὸν αἰῶνα 'never...ever' is translated 'no longer'
    [BECNT], 'no longer...ever' [PNTC], 'no longer...any' [NASB], 'no
    (fruit)...ever...again' [BNTC, WBC; NRSV], 'never...forever' [NICNT],
    'from now on...not (come)...forever' [NIGTC], 'never again' [NTC; GW,
    NCV, NET, NIV, NLT, REB, TEV], 'never again...any' [CEV], 'no
    (fruit) ever...again' [ESV], 'no (fruit)...henceforward forever' [KJV].
    This adverb describes the extension of time up to a point but not beyond
    [LN].

   c. παραχρῆμα (LN 67.113) (BAGD p. 623): 'at once' [BAGD, BECNT,
    LN, NIGTC, NTC, PNTC; ESV, GW, NASB, NET, NRSV, REB, TEV],
    'immediately' [BAGD, BNTC, LN, NICNT, WBC; NCV, NIV, NLT],
    'right then' [CEV], 'presently' [KJV], 'suddenly' [LN]. This adverb
    describes an extremely short period of time between a previous state or
    event and a subsequent state or event [LN].

   d. aorist pass. indic. of ξηραίνω (LN 79.82) (BAGD 2.a. p. 548): 'to wither'
    [BAGD, BECNT, BNTC, LN, NICNT, NIGTC, NTC, WBC; ESV,
    NASB, NET, NIV, NRSV], 'to wither away' [PNTC; KJV, REB], 'to

wither up' [NLT], 'to dry up' [BAGD, LN; CEV, GW, NCV, TEV], 'to
dry out' [LN]. This verb means to cause something to become dry [LN].

e. aorist act. indic. of θαυμάζω (LN 25.213) (BAGD 1.a.α. p. 352): 'to be
amazed' [BECNT, LN, NICNT, NIGTC; NASB, NCV, NET, NIV, NLT,
NRSV, REB], 'to be astonished' [BAGD, NTC, PNTC], 'to be astounded'
[TEV], 'to marvel' [BAGD, BNTC, LN, WBC; ESV, KJV], 'to be
shocked' [CEV], 'to be surprised' [GW], 'to wonder' [BAGD, LN]. This
verb means to wonder or marvel at some event or object [LN].

QUESTION—Why did Jesus curse the fig tree?

The action of cursing the fig tree is a prophetic and symbolic action against
Israel itself, which had outward signs of vitality (corresponding to the
leaves) but was still spiritually barren and without the proper fruit [BECNT,
EBC, My, NICNT, PNTC, WBC], which in this case would be the kind of
righteous life God requires [NICNT]. This action was symbolic of how God
was judging Jewish religious practice, which did not produce the kind of
fruit God wanted [NIBC, NICNT, TH]. It symbolized the judgment of God
on Israel for its failure [Lns, NICNT, NIGTC, WBC]. The fruitless fig tree
represented centuries of failure on the part of God's people, which had now
reached a point of no return and with judgment now being unavoidable
[NICNT]. It foreshadows the destruction of the Jewish sacrificial system
[NAC]. This was an acted parable [BECNT, ICC, NAC, NICNT, PNTC],
along with the triumphant entry on the donkey and the cleansing of the
temple [BECNT, NICNT]. In the Old Testament prophets the fig tree
symbolically represents Israel [ICC, NICNT]. Here the fig tree represents
God's judgment against Jerusalem and the priestly hierarchy [ICC]. Leaves
normally would have come after the fruit, so the presence of leaves would
have meant that fruit would be present [EBC, ICC, Lns, My, NIBC, NICNT,
NTC, WBC]. Even though it was too early in the year for figs, the fact that
the tree had leaves on it would normally have indicated that it also had fruit
[NTC].

21:21 **And Jesus answering said to-them, "Truly I-say to-you, if you-have
faith and do- not -doubt,[a] not only will-you-do that to-the fig-tree, but even-
if you-say to this mountain 'Be-lifted-up[b] and be-thrown into the sea,' it-
will-happen; 21:22 and all-things as-much-as you-ask in prayer believing
you-will-receive."**

LEXICON—a. aorist pass. subj. of διακρίνομαι (LN 31.37) (BAGD 2.b.
p. 185): 'to doubt' [BAGD, LN; all translations except REB], 'to have
doubts' [REB], 'to be uncertain about' [LN], 'to waver' [BAGD]. This
verb means to think that something may not be true or certain [LN].

b. aorist pass. impera. of αἴρω (LN 15.203) (BAGD 1.a. p. 24): 'to be lifted
up' [BAGD, NIGTC, NTC; NET, NLT, NRSV], 'to be lifted from (your
place)' [REB], 'to be taken up' [BAGD, BECNT, PNTC; ESV, NASB],
'to be picked up' [BAGD, BNTC], 'to be raised up' [WBC], 'to be
uprooted' [GW], 'to get up' [CEV, TEV], 'to be removed' [LN; KJV], 'to

be carried (away), to be carried off, to be taken (away)' [LN], 'to arise' [BAGD]. This imperative is translated 'Up with you!' [NICNT], 'Go' [NCV, NIV]. This verb means to lift up and carry (away) [LN].

QUESTION—What is the nature of the doubt they were to avoid?

They should not waver in doubt about what God can do by his power [NICNT, TH]. He was talking about a lack of practical trust in God, as opposed to faith that is a practical confidence in God's power along with the willingness to respond appropriately to it [NICNT].

QUESTION—What mountain does 'this' refer to?

1. He is referring to the Mount of Olives [Lns, NICNT, NIGTC, NTC, PNTC].

2. He is referring to the temple mount, which was visible just across the ravine from the Mount of Olives, and toward which they were heading [NAC].

3. This is a stereotyped expression that is hyperbolic and does not refer to any specific mountain [WBC]. It is a hyperbolic expression describing a miraculous occurrence [EBC].

QUESTION—What limitations, if any, does he put upon the power they have to receive whatever they ask for?

The plural verbs here indicate that it is addressed to the community united in prayer, not to an individual's personal concerns [NICNT]. This statement is hyperbole and the focus is on a genuine trust in God and on discerning and obeying the will of God [EBC]. The fact that he is talking about asking 'in prayer' limits it to what is within the purposes of God [WBC]. He is saying that the disciples would also be able to perform symbolic prophetic actions that warn of judgment to come, but not just anything they wanted to do. Also the focus of their prayer should be on the priorities of the coming kingdom; that is, they exercise their faith to contribute in a miraculous way to the proclaiming of God's judgment and the restoration that represents his purposes being fulfilled [NIGTC]. The qualifier 'if you believe' excludes purely selfish requests [NAC, PNTC], which are not related to the outworking of faith [PNTC], since they assume that we will allow God's will to prevail over our own wills [NAC]. No task that is in harmony with God's will would be impossible for those who believe [NTC].

DISCOURSE UNIT—21:23–27 [CEV, ESV, GW, NASB, NCV, NET, NLT, NRSV, TEV]. The topic is Jesus' authority challenged [GW], leaders doubt Jesus' authority [NCV], a question about Jesus' authority [CEV], the question about Jesus' authority [TEV], the authority of Jesus challenged [ESV, NLT], authority challenged [NASB], the authority of Jesus questioned [NRSV], the authority of Jesus [NET].

21:23 **And (after) he had-gone-into the temple, the chief-priests and the elders of the people approached him while-he-was-teaching saying, "By what authority[a] do-you-do these-(things)? And who gave you this authority?" 21:24 And answering Jesus said to-them, "I-also will-ask you**

one[b] **question, which if you answer me I-will- also -tell you by what authority I-do these-(things).**

LEXICON—a. ἐξουσία (LN 37.35) (BAGD 3. p. 278): 'authority' [BAGD; all translations except CEV, GW, TEV], 'warrant' [BAGD], 'authority to rule, right to control' [LN]. The question 'By what authority do you do these things?' is translated 'What right do you have to do these things?' [CEV, TEV], 'What gives you the right to do these things?' [GW]. This noun denotes the right to control or govern over [LN].

  b. εἷς (LN 60.10, 92.22) (BAGD 2.b. p. 231): 'one' [LN (60.10, 92.22), NIGTC, PNTC, WBC; ESV, KJV, NASB, NET, NIV, NLT, NRSV], 'just one' [NICNT; CEV, TEV], 'only one, single' [BAGD], 'a' [BECNT, BNTC, LN (92.22), NTC; GW, NCV, REB]. This adjective describes one, in contrast to more than one [LN (60.10)], but may also serve as a reference to a single, indefinite person or thing [LN (92.22)].

QUESTION—What is the antecedent of 'these things'?

  It refers to his cleansing the temple [BNTC, EBC, ICC, Lns, My, NAC, NIBC, NICNT, NTC, PNTC, TRT, WBC], and also to the healings [BNTC, EBC, Lns, My, NTC, PNTC, WBC], his triumphal entry [BNTC, ICC, Lns, My, NIBC, NICNT, NTC, PNTC, WBC], and even his teaching there in the temple [BNTC, EBC, ICC, My, NTC, WBC]. It is fairly general, but probably includes his teaching in the temple [NIGTC]. All these things taken together indicated to them that he was a messianic pretender [My].

21:25 **The baptism of John, where- was-(it) -from[a]? From heaven or from men?" But they-discussed[b] among themselves saying, "If we-say, 'From heaven' he will-say to-us, 'Why then did-you- not -believe him?'** **21:26** **But if we-say, 'From men,' we-fear the crowd, for (they)-all regard[c] John as a-prophet."** **21:27** **And answering they-said to Jesus, "We-do- not -know."** **He also said to-them, "Neither do- I -tell you by what authority I-do these-(things).**

LEXICON—a. πόθεν (LN 84.6) (BAGD 2. p. 680): 'from where?' [LN, NIGTC, NTC, PNTC; ESV, NIV], 'from what source' [BAGD, BECNT, BNTC; NASB], 'from whence' [WBC], 'whence?' [LN; KJV], 'where?' [LN], 'the origin' [NICNT]. The phrase πόθεν ἦν 'where was it from' is translated 'was it from' [REB], 'did (it) come from' [GW, NCV, NLT, NRSV, TEV]. The question τὸ Ἰωάννου πόθεν ἦν 'The baptism of John, where was it from?' is translated 'Who gave John the right to baptize?' [CEV]. This adverb describes extension from a source, with an incorporated interrogative point of reference [LN].

  b. imperf. mid. or pass. (deponent = act.) indic. of διαλογίζομαι (LN 33.158) (BAGD 1. p. 186): 'to discuss' [LN, NICNT, NIGTC; ESV, GW, NIV], 'to reason' [BAGD, BECNT, BNTC, NTC, PNTC, WBC; KJV, NASB], 'to argue' [NCV, NRSV, REB, TEV], 'to think (it) over' [CEV], 'to talk (it) over' [NLT], 'to consider, to ponder' [BAGD], 'to converse'

[LN]. This verb means to engage in some relatively detailed discussion of a matter [LN].

    c. pres. act. indic. of ἔχω (LN 31.1) (BAGD I.5. p. 333): 'to regard' [BECNT, BNTC, LN, NICNT, WBC; NASB, NRSV], 'to consider' [BAGD, LN, NIGTC, NTC], 'to hold' [PNTC; ESV, KJV, NIV], 'to think of' [GW], 'to believe' [NET, NLT], 'to take...(as)' [REB], 'to be convinced that' [TEV], 'to look upon' [BAGD], 'to hold a view, to have an opinion' [LN]. This verb means to hold a view or have an opinion with regard to something [LN].

QUESTION—What is Jesus referring to when he says 'the baptism of John'?

The phrase 'the baptism of John' refers to the entire ministry and message of John the Baptist [BECNT, EBC, Lns, NAC, NIGTC]. It refers to John's ministry as a prophet of God [ICC, PNTC], to his message of repentance [BNTC]. It refers to John's ministry [NICNT, WBC], but focuses specifically on baptism, which is the one aspect of it that would be most likely to be offensive to the Jewish leaders [NICNT]. He was asking about who gave John the authority to baptize [NIBC, TH, TRT].

DISCOURSE UNIT—21:28–22:14 [NICNT, PNTC]. The topic is three polemical parables [NICNT], teaching in parables [PNTC].

DISCOURSE UNIT—21:28–32 [CEV, ESV, GW, NASB, NCV, NET, NIV, NLT, NRSV, TEV]. The topic is a story about two sons [CEV, GW, NCV], the parable of the two sons [ESV, NET, NIV, NLT, NRSV, TEV], parable of two sons [NASB].

21:28 But what do-you-think? A man had two sons. And going to-the first he-said, 'Son, go work in the vineyard today.' **21:29** But answering he-said, 'I-will not,[a] but later having-changed-(his)-mind[b] he went. **21:30** And going-to the other he-said the-same. And answering he-said 'I (will go)[c] sir,[d] but he-did- not -go.

TEXT—Some manuscripts reverse the order of the response of the two sons. All translations except REB follow those manuscripts that show the first son as refusing to go, but later going. GNT follows those manuscripts also, and rates that choice with a C rating to indicate that choosing it over a variant text was difficult. Only REB follows those manuscripts that show the first son as agreeing to go, but not doing so.

LEXICON—a. pres. act. indic. of θέλω (LN 25.1, 30.58): 'to want, to desire, to wish' [LN (25.1)], 'to purpose' [LN (30.58)]. The phrase Οὐ θέλω 'I do not want to' is translated as indicating purpose or intent: 'I will not' [BECNT, BNTC, NTC, WBC; ESV, KJV, NASB, NCV, NET, NIV, NRSV, REB], 'I won't' [NICNT, PNTC], 'I won't go' [NLT], 'told him that he would not do it' [CEV]. It is translated as indicating a lack of willingness: 'I don't want to' [NIGTC; GW, TEV]. This verb means to desire to have or experience something [LN (25.1)], or it may mean to purpose, generally based upon a preference and desire [LN (30.58)].

b. aorist pass. (deponent = act.) participle of μεταμέλομαι (LN 25.270 or
31.59) (BAGD p. 511): 'to change one's mind' [BAGD, BECNT, BNTC,
LN (31.59), NICNT, NIGTC, PNTC, WBC; all translations except KJV,
NASB, NET], 'to think differently' [LN (31.59)], 'to regret' [BAGD, LN
(25.270); NASB], 'to repent' [BAGD, NTC; KJV], 'to have a change of
heart' [NET], 'to feel sad about, to feel sorry because of' [LN (25.270)].
This verb means to change one's mind about something, with the probable
implication of regret [LN (31.59)], or it can mean to feel regret as the
result of what one has done [LN (25.270)].

c. ἐγώ (LN 92.1) (BAGD p. 217): 'I' [BAGD, LN], 'I indeed' [LN]. This
pronoun is translated as though implying intent for an action by the
speaker: 'I will' [BECNT, NIGTC, NTC, PNTC; GW, NASB, NET, NIV,
REB], 'I will go' [WBC], 'I go' [BNTC; ESV, KJV, NRSV], '(said) he
would' [CEV]. The phrase Ἐγώ, κύριε 'I will go sir' is translated 'yes
sir' [NICNT; TEV], 'yes sir, I will' [NCV, NLT]. This pronoun is a
reference to the speaker [LN].

d. κύριος (LN 87.53) (BAGD 1.b. p. 459): 'sir' [BAGD, LN; all translations
except CEV], 'mister' [LN], not explicit [CEV]. This noun is a title of
respect used in addressing or speaking to a man [LN].

QUESTION—Does 'first' mean that he was the oldest, or that he was the one
whom the father approached first?

He was most likely the oldest [EBC, WBC]. He is often taken to be the
oldest [ICC, NIBC, PNTC]. He was the first one approached [NICNT] or at
least the first mentioned in the parable [My].

QUESTION—Does Οὐ θέλω 'I do not want to' indicate a refusal or a lack of
desire to do what was asked of him?

It was a refusal [BECNT, BNTC, ICC, Lns, My, NAC, NIBC, NICNT,
NIGTC, NTC, PNTC, TH, WBC; ESV, KJV, NASB, NCV, NET, NIV,
NLT, NRSV, REB]. It expressed an unwillingness to go [GW, TEV].

QUESTION—Who do the two sons in the parable represent?

The son who agreed to go but did not do so represents the unrepentant
Jewish establishment, and the son who refused but later went anyway
represents openly sinful Jewish people who truly repent [BECNT, BNTC,
Lns, My, NAC, NIBC, NICNT, NTC, PNTC, TH, WBC]. The second son
represents the Sanhedrin [My].

21:31 **Which of the two did the will[a] of-the father?" They-said, "The first."
Jesus says to-them, "Truly I-say to you that the tax-collectors and the
prostitutes are-going-ahead[b] of-you into the kingdom of God. 21:32 For
John came to you in the-way[c] of-righteousness, and you-did- not -believe
him, but the tax-collectors and the prostitutes did-believe him. But you
having-seen (this) did- not -change-your-minds[d] afterward (and) believe
him.**

LEXICON—a. θέλημα (LN 30.59) (BAGD 1.c.α. p. 354): 'will' [BAGD,
BECNT, BNTC, LN, NICNT, NIGTC, PNTC, WBC; ESV, KJV, NASB,

NET, NRSV], 'intent, purpose, plan' [LN]. The phrase ἐποίησεν τὸ θέλημα τοῦ πατρός 'did the will of the father' is translated 'did what the/his father wanted' [NTC; GW, NIV, REB, TEV], 'obeyed his father' [CEV, NCV, NLT]. This noun denotes that which is purposed, intended, or willed [LN].

b. pres. act. indic. of προάγω (LN 15.142) (BAGD 2.b. p. 702): 'to go ahead of (into)' [NIGTC; GW, NET], 'to go (into) before' [BAGD, BNTC, NICNT, PNTC, WBC; ESV, KJV], 'to get into ahead of' [NTC; NRSV, TEV], 'to get into before' [BAGD, BECNT; CEV, NASB, NLT], 'to enter ahead of' [NIV, REB], 'to enter before' [NCV], 'to go prior to, to go away beforehand' [LN]. This verb means to go prior to someone else's going [LN].

c. ὁδός (LN **41.16**) (BAGD 2.b. p. 554): 'way' [BECNT, BNTC, **LN**, NIGTC, NTC, WBC; ESV, KJV, NASB, NET, NIV, NRSV], 'path' [PNTC], 'way of life' [BAGD, LN], 'way to live' [LN], 'way of acting, conduct' [BAGD]. The phrase ἦλθεν...πρὸς ὑμᾶς ἐν ὁδῷ δικαιοσύνης 'came to you in the way of righteousness' is translated 'came to you as a preacher of righteousness' [NICNT], 'showed you the way God wants you to live' [GW], 'to show you the right way to live' [NCV, REB, similarly NLT], 'showing you the right path to take' [TEV], 'showed you how to do right' [CEV]. This noun denotes a customary manner of life or behavior, with probably some implication of goal or purpose [LN].

d. aorist pass. (deponent = act.) indic. of μεταμέλομαι (LN **31.59**, 25.270) (BAGD p. 511): 'to change one's mind' [BAGD, BECNT, **LN** (31.59), NICNT, NIGTC, WBC; CEV, ESV, GW, NET, NRSV, REB, TEV], 'to repent' [BAGD, BNTC, NTC, PNTC; KJV, NIV], 'to repent of one's sins' [NLT], 'to think differently' [LN], 'to feel remorse' [NASB], 'to change one's ways' [NCV], 'to feel regret' [BAGD], 'to regret' [LN (25.270)]. This verb means to change one's mind about something, with the probable implication of regret [LN].

QUESTION—Does προάγω 'to go ahead' imply that the tax collectors and prostitutes are going into the kingdom ahead of the religious leaders, or that they are going into it and the religious leaders are not going in at all?

1. They will get in instead of the religious leaders, who do not go in [EBC, ICC, Lns, NIBC, NICNT, NTC, PNTC, TH, TRT]. They are entering but the religious leaders are being excluded by their own choice [NTC].

2. They will get there before the religious leaders [BECNT, NIGTC]. There is still room for the religious leaders to repent and enter the kingdom [BECNT].

QUESTION—What does it mean that John came 'in the way of righteousness'?

John showed them the way to be righteous [EBC, ICC, Lns, NIBC, TH, TRT; CEV, GW, NCV, NLT, REB, TEV], and demanded ethical transformation of those who hoped to enter the kingdom [EBC]. It primarily refers to the message John preached [NICNT, TH], but it also includes the godly life that John lived [ICC, Lns, My, NICNT]. John himself was righteous, and as God's prophet he also demanded righteous conduct from people [NTC]. In the Old Testament this expression describes a life lived in obedience to God's command, and here it implies God's affirmation of John's life as well as his testimony about Jesus [BECNT]. John's message was about how the kingdom of God meant a state of things in which all is right in the relation between God and his world [NIGTC]. It refers to how God used John to help bring about the accomplishment of salvation in human history through proclaiming Jesus and the imminence of the kingdom of God [WBC].

QUESTION—What is meant by οὐδὲ μετεμελήθητε 'you did not change your minds'?

They did not change their thinking [BAGD, BECNT, EBC, **LN** (31.59), NIBC, NICNT, NIGTC, WBC; CEV, ESV, GW, NET, NRSV, REB, TEV]. They did not repent or change their ways [BAGD, BNTC, ICC, NIGTC, NTC, PNTC; KJV, NCV, NIV, NLT]. A change of thinking about John would have resulted in a genuine change of heart [NIGTC].

DISCOURSE UNIT—21:33–46 [CEV, ESV, GW, NASB, NCV, NET, NIV, NLT, NRSV, TEV]. The topic is a story about a vineyard [GW], a story about God's son [NCV], the parable of the tenants in the vineyard [TEV], the parable of the tenants [ESV, NET, NIV], the parable of the wicked tenants [NRSV], parable of the landowner [NASB], parable of the evil farmers [NLT], renters of a vineyard [CEV].

21:33 Listen-to another parable. There-was a-man (who was) a-landowner who planted a vineyard and put- a-wall[a] -around[b] (it) and dug a-winepress[c] in it and built a-watchtower[d] and leased[e] it to-tenant-farmers[f] and traveled-abroad.[g]

LEXICON—a. φραγμός (LN **7.59**) (BAGD 1. p. 865): 'wall' [BAGD, BECNT, LN, NIGTC; CEV, GW, NASB, NCV, NIV, NLT, REB], 'fence' [BAGD, LN, NICNT, NTC, PNTC, WBC; ESV, NET, NRSV, TEV], 'hedge' [BAGD, BNTC], not explicit [KJV]. This noun denotes a structure for enclosing an open area [LN].

    b. aorist act. indic. of περιτίθημι (LN **85.39**) (BAGD 1. p. 652): 'to put around' [BAGD, BECNT, BNTC, LN, NICNT, NIGTC, PNTC, WBC; all versions except CEV, KJV, NLT], 'to build around' [CEV, NLT], 'to set around' [NTC], 'to place around' [BAGD], 'to surround' [LN]. The phrase φραγμὸν αὐτῷ περιέθηκεν 'built a wall around it' is translated 'hedged it round about' [KJV]. This verb means to place something around an object or area [LN].

    c. ληνός (LN **7.66**) (BAGD p. 473): 'wine press' [BAGD, LN; all translations except CEV, NLT], 'a pit to crush the grapes' [CEV], 'a pit for pressing out the grape juice' [NLT]. This noun denotes an instrument for pressing out the juice of grapes for the making of wine [LN].

    d. πύργος (LN **7.23**) (BAGD 1. p. 730): 'watchtower' [BECNT, BNTC, LN, NICNT, NIGTC, NTC; GW, NET, NIV, NRSV, REB, TEV], 'tower'

[BAGD, LN, PNTC; ESV, KJV, NASB, NCV], 'lookout tower' [CEV, NLT]. This noun denotes a tall structure with a lookout at the top [LN].

e. aorist mid. indic. of ἐκδίδομαι (LN 57.177) (BAGD p. 238): 'to lease' [BAGD, BECNT, BNTC, LN, NTC, WBC; ESV, GW, NCV, NET, NLT, NRSV], 'to lease out' [NIGTC], 'to rent out' [LN; CEV, NASB], 'to rent' [NIV, TEV], 'to let out' [LN, NICNT, PNTC; KJV, REB], 'to let out for hire' [BAGD]. This verb means to permit the use of property or assets in exchange for remuneration [LN].

f. γεωργός (LN **43.2**) (BAGD 2. p. 157): 'tenant farmer' [BAGD, BECNT, BNTC, NICNT, NIGTC, WBC; NET, NLT], 'tenant' [ESV, NRSV, TEV], 'farmer' [**LN**; NCV, NIV], 'sharecropper' [NTC], 'vine grower' [PNTC; NASB, REB], 'vineyard worker' [GW], 'husbandman' [KJV], 'vinedresser' [BAGD], 'gardener' [LN], not explicit [CEV]. This noun denotes one who engages in agriculture or gardening [LN].

g. aorist act. indic. of ἀποδημέω (LN 15.47) (BAGD 1. p. 90): 'to go on a journey' [BAGD, BNTC; NASB, NET], 'to go off on a journey' [WBC], 'to go away on a journey' [BECNT; NIV], 'to go on a trip' [GW], 'to leave/leave home on a trip' [NCV, TEV], 'to go away from the district' [NIGTC], 'to travel away' [NICNT], 'to go abroad' [NTC, PNTC; REB], 'to leave the country' [CEV], 'to go into/to another country' [ESV, NRSV], 'to go into a far country' [KJV], 'to move to another country' [NLT], 'to leave home on a journey, to be away from home on a journey' [LN]. This verb means to journey away from one's home or home country, implying for a considerable period of time and at quite a distance [LN].

21:34 And when the time of-harvest[a] drew-near, he-sent his servants to the tenant-farmers to-collect[b] his[c] fruit.[d]

LEXICON—a. καρπός (LN 43.15) (BAGD 1.a. p. 404): 'harvest' [BECNT, LN; NASB, NET, NIV, NRSV, REB], 'grape harvest' [NLT], 'fruit' [BAGD, BNTC, LN, NIGTC, WBC; CEV, ESV, KJV], 'vintage' [NICNT], 'crop, grain' [LN]. The phrase ὁ καιρὸς τῶν καρπῶν 'the time of harvest' is translated 'the time of fruit bearing' [PNTC], 'the time to harvest the grapes' [NTC], 'time to gather the grapes' [TEV], 'time for the grapes to be picked' [NCV], 'when the grapes were getting ripe' [GW]. This noun denotes that which is harvested [LN].

b. aorist act. infin. of λαμβάνω (LN 57.65) (BAGD 1.d. p. 464): 'to collect' [BAGD, LN, NICNT, NTC; GW, NET, NIV, NLT, NRSV, REB], 'to get' [BECNT; CEV, ESV, NCV], 'to receive' [BAGD, BNTC, LN, NIGTC, PNTC, WBC; KJV, NASB, TEV], 'to accept' [BAGD]. This verb means to collect what is due [LN].

c. αὐτοῦ (possessive genitive of αὐτός): 'his' [BECNT, BNTC, NICNT, NIGTC, PNTC, WBC; ESV, NASB, NIV, NRSV], 'his share' [NTC; CEV, GW, NCV, NLT, TEV], 'his portion' [NET], 'due to him' [REB], 'of it' [KJV].

d. καρπός (LN 3.33) (BAGD 1.a. p. 404): 'fruit' [BAGD, BECNT, BNTC, LN, NICNT, NIGTC, NTC, PNTC, WBC; ESV, KJV, NIV], 'grapes' [CEV, NCV], 'produce' [GW, NASB, NRSV, REB], 'crop' [NET, NLT], 'harvest' [TEV]. This noun denotes any fruit part of plants, including grain as well as pulpy fruit [LN].

QUESTION—What do the various elements of the parable represent?

God is the owner of the vineyard, Israel is the vineyard, the tenants were Israel's leaders, the slaves were the prophets, and the son is Jesus himself [BECNT, BNTC, EBC, ICC, Lns, My, NAC, NICNT, NIGTC, NTC, PNTC, WBC]. The fruit represents right living [BECNT, NAC, PNTC]. The fruits would be such things as faith, contrition, and obedience [Lns]. The other details, such as the winepress, tower or wall don't represent anything in particular [NAC, NICNT], other than perhaps to express the care God gives to his people [NAC].

21:35 And having-seized[a] his servants, the farmers beat[b] one, they-killed another, and they-stoned[c] another. **21:36** Again he-sent other servants more-than[d] the first-ones, and they-did the-same to them.

LEXICON—a. aorist act. participle of λαμβάνω (LN 18.1) (BAGD 1.c. p. 464): 'to seize' [BAGD, BECNT, NIGTC; NET, NIV, NRSV, REB], 'to lay hands on' [BAGD], 'to take' [BAGD, BNTC, NICNT, NTC, PNTC, WBC; ESV, GW, KJV, NASB], 'to grab' [LN; CEV, NCV, NLT, TEV], 'to take hold of, to grasp' [LN]. This verb means to take hold of something or someone, with or without force [LN].

b. aorist act. indic. of δέρω (LN 19.2) (BAGD p. 175): 'to beat' [BAGD, BECNT, BNTC, NIGTC, PNTC, WBC; ESV, GW, KJV, NASB, NCV, NET, NIV, NLT, NRSV, TEV], 'to beat up' [NICNT, NTC; CEV], 'to thrash' [REB], 'to strike, to whip' [LN]. This verb means to strike or beat repeatedly [LN].

c. aorist act. indic. of λιθοβολέω (LN 20.79) (BAGD 1. p. 474): 'to stone' [all translations except CEV, GW, NCV], 'to stone to death' [LN; CEV, GW], 'to kill with stones' [NCV], 'to throw stones at' [BAGD]. This verb means to kill or attempt to kill by means of hurling stones, normally carried out by angry mobs [LN].

d. πλείονας (comparative of πολύς) (LN 59.1) (BAGD II.1.a. p. 689): 'more than' [BAGD, BECNT, BNTC, NICNT, NIGTC, PNTC, WBC; CEV, ESV, KJV, NET, NIV, NRSV, TEV], 'even more than' [NCV], 'more in number' [NTC], 'more' [GW], 'a larger number' [REB], 'larger (group of slaves)' [NASB, NLT].

QUESTION—Would the servants who were stoned have been killed by the stoning?

1. They were killed by the stoning [ICC, Lns, My, NIBC, NIGTC, NTC, PNTC; CEV, GW, NCV].

2. The verb might mean they were killed or might only mean that they had stones thrown at them [BAGD, TH, TRT].

21:37 But finally[a] he-sent his son to them saying, 'They-will-respect[b] my son.' **21:38** But the farmers having-seen the son said among themselves, 'This is the heir; come, let-us-kill him and let-us-take[c] his inheritance,' **21:39** and having-seized him they-cast (him) out of the vineyard and killed (him).

LEXICON—a. ὕστερον (LN **61.16**) (BAGD 2.b. p. 849): 'finally' [BAGD, BECNT, BNTC, **LN**, NIGTC, NTC, WBC; CEV, ESV, GW, NET, NLT, NRSV, REB], 'in the end' [NICNT], 'last of all' [PNTC; KJV, NIV, TEV], 'afterward' [NASB], 'last' [LN], not explicit [NCV]. This adverb describes being final in a series [LN].

 b. fut. pass. indic. of ἐντρέπομαι (LN 87.11) (BAGD 2.b. p. 269): 'to respect' [BAGD, BECNT, BNTC, LN, NICNT, NIGTC, PNTC; all versions except KJV], 'to have regard for' [BAGD, NTC, WBC], 'to reverence' [KJV], 'to show respect' [LN]. This verb means to show respect to a person on the basis of his high status [LN].

 c. aorist act. subj. of ἔχω (LN 57.1): 'to take' [BNTC, PNTC; NIV], 'to get' [GW, NET, NLT, NRSV, REB, TEV], 'to get hold of' [NICNT], 'to get possession' [NTC], 'to seize' [NASB], 'to seize on' [KJV], 'to have' [BECNT, LN, NIGTC, WBC; ESV], 'to own, to possess' [LN]. The phrase καὶ σχῶμεν 'and let us take possession' is translated 'we can have it all for ourselves' [CEV], 'it will be ours' [NCV]. This verb means to have or possess objects or property [LN].

21:40 So when the owner of-the vineyard comes, what will-he-do to-those farmers?" **21:41** They say to-him, "He-will-bring-to-a- miserable[a] -end[b] (those) wicked[c] (men) and he-will-lease the vineyard to-other farmers, who will-give[d] to-him the fruits in their seasons."

LEXICON—a. κακῶς (LN 78.17): 'seriously, severely, grievously, danger-ously' [LN]. This word is translated as an adverb describing the action of the owner of the vineyard: 'mercilessly' [WBC], 'in an evil manner' [NIGTC], 'in some horrible way' [CEV], 'miserably' [KJV], 'utterly' [BECNT; NET], 'surely' [NCV], 'certainly' [TEV]. It is translated as an adjective describing the death of the farmers: 'miserable' [BNTC; ESV, NRSV], 'wretched' [NASB, NIV], 'bad' [NICNT, PNTC; REB], 'dreadful' [NTC], 'horrible' [NLT], not explicit [GW]. It describes a high point on a scale of extent and implying harm and seriousness of the state [LN].

 b. fut. act. indic. of ἀπόλλυμι (LN 20.31) (BAGD 1.a.α. p. 95): 'to bring to an end' [NICNT, NTC, PNTC; NASB, NIV, REB], 'to destroy' [BECNT, LN, NIGTC, WBC; GW, KJV, NET], 'to kill' [CEV, NCV, CEV], 'to put to death' [ESV, NLT, NRSV], 'to inflict death' [BNTC], 'to ruin' [LN]. This verb means to destroy or to cause the destruction of persons, objects, or institutions [LN].

 c. κακός (LN **88.106**) (BAGD 1.a. p. 397): 'wicked' [BECNT; KJV, NLT], 'bad' [BAGD, **LN**, NICNT, PNTC; REB], 'miserable' [BNTC], 'evil'

[BAGD, LN, NIGTC, WBC; GW, NCV, NET, TEV], 'dreadful scoundrel' [NTC], 'wretch' [ESV, NASB, NIV, NRSV], not explicit [CEV]. This adjective describes being bad, with the implication of harmful and damaging [LN].

d. fut. act. indic. of ἀποδίδωμι (LN **57.153**) (BAGD 1. p. 90): 'to give' [BAGD, BECNT, NIGTC, NTC; all versions except KJV, NASB], 'to give over' [WBC], 'to render' [LN; KJV], 'to return' [NICNT], 'to deliver' [BNTC], 'to pay' [**LN**, PNTC; NASB]. This verb means to make a payment, with the implication of such a payment being in response to an incurred obligation [LN].

21:42 Jesus says to-them, "Have-you- never -read in the scriptures, "(The) stone which the builders rejected,[a] this became (the) head of-(the)-corner;[b] this happened[c] from (the) Lord and it-is marvelous[d] in our eyes. **21:43** Therefore I-say to-you that the kingdom of-God will-be-taken from you and it-will-be-given to-a-people[e] producing its fruit.

LEXICON—a. aorist act. indic. of ἀποδοκιμάζω (LN 30.117) (BAGD 1. p. 90): 'to reject' [BAGD, BECNT, LN, NICNT, NIGTC, NTC, PNTC, WBC; all versions except CEV, TEV], 'to reject as worthless' [TEV], 'to discard' [BNTC], 'to toss aside' [CEV], 'to declare useless' [BAGD], 'to regard as not worthy' [LN]. This verb means to judge someone or something as not being worthy or genuine and thus something to be rejected [LN].

b. κεφαλὴ γωνίας (LN 7.44) (BAGD p. 168): This phrase is translated 'head of the corner' [NICNT, NIGTC, PNTC; KJV], 'cornerstone' [BAGD, LN, NTC, WBC; ESV, GW, NCV, NET, NLT, NRSV], 'chief cornerstone' [NASB], 'main cornerstone' [REB], 'capstone' [BNTC; NIV], 'the most important stone of all' [CEV, similarly TEV], 'important stone' [LN]. The phrase κεφαλὴ γωνίας 'head of the corner' denotes the cornerstone or capstone of a building, essential to its construction [LN].

c. aorist mid. (deponent = act.) indic. of γίνομαι (LN 13.107): 'to happen' [LN], 'to come about' [BECNT, PNTC; NASB], 'to come (from)' [BNTC], 'to come to be' [LN, NIGTC], 'to occur' [LN], 'to be done' [NTC; TEV]. The phrase παρὰ κυρίου ἐγένετο αὕτη 'this happened from the Lord' is translated 'this is from the Lord' [WBC; NET], 'this is what the Lord has done' [NICNT; similarly CEV], 'the Lord did this' [NCV], 'the Lord has done this' [NIV], 'this was/is the Lord's doing' [ESV, KJV, NLT, NRSV, REB], 'the Lord is responsible for this' [GW]. This verb means to happen, with the implication that what happens is different from a previous state [LN].

d. θαυμαστός (LN 25.215) (BAGD 2. p. 352): 'marvelous' [BAGD, BNTC, LN, NIGTC, WBC; ESV, KJV, NASB, NET, NIV], 'amazing' [BECNT, NICNT; CEV, GW, NRSV], 'wonderful' [LN, NTC; NCV, NLT, REB, TEV], 'astonishing' [PNTC], 'remarkable' [BAGD, LN]. This adjective describes that which causes or is worthy of amazement and wonder [LN].

e. ἔθνος (LN 11.55): 'people' [BECNT, LN, NIGTC, WBC; all versions
except KJV, NLT, REB], 'nation' [BNTC, LN, NICNT, NTC, PNTC;
KJV, NLT, REB]. This noun denotes the largest unit into which the
people of the world are divided on the basis of their constituting a socio-
political community [LN].

QUESTION—What is the head of the corner?

It is the top stone of a roof parapet, a staircase, or a city wall [EBC]. It could
be the capstone of an arch [BECNT, NIGTC, WBC] or the capstone at the
top of a building corner [BECNT, ICC, NICNT]. Since the stone in the
citation was found to be of use later in the construction process it may be
referring to a capstone rather than a foundation stone [BNTC]. It could be
that large stone in the foundation joining two walls [NIGTC]. It probably
was a large stone set in the corner of the foundation [My, NTC, PNTC; ESV,
GW, NASB, NCV, NET, NLT, NRSV, REB]. A stone that could be
stumbled over would more naturally be understood as a foundation
cornerstone, but one that could fall on someone would more naturally be
understood as an overhead capstone [NAC]. Whether it was the foundation
stone or a capstone is unclear, but whichever it was, it is the most important
stone of all [TH; CEV, TEV].

QUESTION—What 'marvelous' thing might Jesus have in mind for the
application of this scripture passage?

In the Old Testament passage cited, the marvel is that the rejected stone
became the most important one [TH, TRT; CEV, TEV]. In Jesus' application
of that passage, the marvelous thing was the reversal of events in which
Jesus would be rejected by men but then be exalted [EBC, NAC, NICNT,
NIGTC, NTC, PNTC, WBC], particularly by his resurrection [NAC,
NICNT, NTC].

QUESTION—Who are the 'people' who will produce the fruit of the kingdom
of God?

The term 'people' or 'nation' refers to a reconstitution of the people of God.
It does not specifically refer to the Gentiles, although it certainly does
include Gentiles as well as Jews [BNTC, Lns, My, NICNT, NIGTC]. The
parable is not about ethnicity, but about ethics; Jesus is saying that the
kingdom will be taken away from the disobedient religious leaders and given
to the disciples of Jesus [BECNT]. The kingdom will be taken away from the
Jewish hierarchy and given to the Christian church [PNTC, WBC], which
will include both Gentiles and Jews [WBC]. It will be taken away from the
Jewish people and given to the church [NAC, NTC], which will become
predominantly Gentile [NTC]. It will be taken from the Jews and given to
the Gentiles [NIBC].

21:44 And the-one-having-fallen on this stone will-be-broken-to-pieces;[a]
but (the one) on whomever it-falls it-will-crush him.[b]" **21:45** And the
priests and Pharisees having-heard his parables knew that he-is-speaking

about them. `21:46` **And seeking to-arrest him they-feared the crowds, because they-considered him a-prophet.**

TEXT—Manuscripts that include verse 44 are given a C rating by GNT to indicate that choosing it over a variant text was difficult. It is included by BECNT, BNTC, NICNT, PNTC. It is omitted by NIGTC; REB, TEV. It is included in brackets by WBC indicating doubt about its authenticity, and also by NTC along with a note that it was probably not original in Matthew's gospel.

LEXICON—a. fut. pass. indic. of συνθλάω (LN **19.39**) (BAGD p. 790): 'to be broken into/to pieces' [BECNT, **LN**; ESV, NASB, NET, NIV, NLT, NRSV], 'to be broken' [GW, KJV, NCV], 'to be dashed to pieces' [BAGD, BNTC, NTC, WBC], 'to be crushed' [BAGD, PNTC; CEV], 'to be shattered' [LN]. This verb means to break or shatter a solid object into pieces, with the implication of destruction [LN].

    b. fut. act. indic. of λικμάω: (LN 19.47) (BAGD p. 474): 'to crush' [BAGD, BNTC, LN, NTC, WBC; ESV, GW, NLT, NRSV], 'to pulverize' [PNTC], 'to grind to powder' [KJV], 'to scatter like dust' [NASB]. This active voice verb is translated as passive: 'to be crushed' [NCV, NET, NIV], 'to be scattered like chaff' [BECNT], 'to be smashed to pieces' [CEV]. This verb means to crush by a destructive amount of vertical pressure [LN].

QUESTION—What is the nature of the falling or tripping described here?

It describes falling from a height onto the stone, or having the stone fall from a height onto the person [NIGTC]. It describes someone who falls over a roof parapet stone that is too low and would then fall from the roof, or the possibility that such a stone were to be knocked loose and would then fall on someone and crush them [EBC]. Those who reject Jesus will be like someone tripping over a stone, and they will suffer a judgment that will be similar to having such a stone fall on them [BECNT]. Falling on the stone produces brokenness, which may possibly be healed, but there is no healing possible for one whom the stone crushes [PNTC].

DISCOURSE UNIT—22:1–46 [NIGTC]. The topic is Jesus silences the leaders who are his opponents.

DISCOURSE UNIT—22:1–14 [CEV, ESV, GW, NASB, NCV, NET, NIV, NLT, NRSV, TEV]. The topic is a story about a wedding reception [GW], a story about a wedding feast [NCV], the parable of the wedding feast [ESV, TEV], the parable of the wedding banquet [NET, NIV, NRSV], parable of the marriage feast [NASB], parable of the great feast NLT], the great banquet [CEV].

22:1 And answering Jesus again spoke to-them in parables saying, **22:2** "The kingdom of the heavens is-like a-man, a-king, who prepared[a] a-wedding-feast[b] for-his son. **22:3** And he-sent his servants to-call those who-had-been-invited to the feast, and they-were- not -willing[c] to-come.

LEXICON—a. aorist act. indic. of ποιέω (LN 90.45) (BAGD I.1.b.ζ. p. 681): 'to prepare' [BECNT, NCV, NIV, NLT, TEV], 'to make' [BNTC, LN, NICNT, PNTC; KJV], 'to make arrangements for' [NIGTC], 'to arrange' [REB], 'to plan' [GW], 'to give' [BAGD, NTC; CEV, ESV, NASB, NET, NRSV], 'to hold' [WBC], 'to do, to perform, to practice' [LN]. This verb indicates an agent relation [LN].

    b. γάμος (LN **34.68**) (BAGD 1.a. p. 151): 'wedding feast' [BECNT, BNTC, NICNT, PNTC; ESV, NASB, NCV, TEV], 'great wedding feast' [NLT], 'marriage feast' [NTC], 'wedding banquet' [NIGTC, WBC; CEV, NET, NIV, NRSV], 'banquet for a wedding' [REB], 'wedding celebration' [BAGD], 'wedding' [**LN**; GW], 'marriage' [KJV]. This noun denotes the ceremony associated with becoming married [LN].

    c. imperf. act. indic. of θέλω (LN 30.58) (BAGD 2. p. 355): 'to be willing' [BAGD, BECNT, NICNT, NTC; NASB], 'to want' [BAGD, NIGTC, WBC; TEV], 'to purpose' [LN]. The phrase οὐκ ἤθελον 'were not willing' is translated 'refused' [BNTC; CEV, GW, NCV, NIV, REB], 'would not' [PNTC; ESV, KJV, NET, NRSV]. This verb means to purpose, generally based upon a preference and desire [LN].

QUESTION—Does 'answering' refer to a response to a specific question?

It is an introductory formula [EBC, NICNT, WBC], that does not necessarily mean that Jesus is addressing any specific question [WBC], and this verb is not even included in many translations [omitted in all versions except KJV]. However, it may indicate how Jesus was responding to the hostility of the chief priests and Pharisees [Lns, My, NIGTC, NTC, PNTC].

QUESTION—What does the wedding feast in the parable represent?

It represents the glad privilege of sharing in the kingdom [BNTC]. It symbolizes the dawning of the kingdom of heaven that was being brought about by Jesus' ministry [WBC]. It may not have any specific symbolic meaning, but may be simply understood as a warning that those who refuse to answer God's call will be excluded and someone else brought in to replace them [NICNT]. A wedding banquet depicts the blessings of the age to come [NIBC], and the fellowship that the Messiah will have with his own people at the end of time [NAC]. It represents the setting up of the messianic kingdom [My].

QUESTION—What does the imperfect tense of the verb (οὐκ) ἤθελον 'were (not) willing' reflect?

It indicates a persistent refusal to come [EBC], a repeated unwillingness [Lns, WBC]. Their wills were set against going [PNTC].

22:4 Again he-sent other servants saying, 'Say to-those invited, "Behold[a] I-have-prepared my banquet,[b] my oxen[c] and the fattened-cattle[d] have-been-

slaughtered and everything (is) ready. Come to the wedding-feast.'" 22:5
But having-paid-(them)-no-attention[e] they-went-off, one to his-own field,
another to his business.[f]

LEXICON—a. ἰδού (LN 91.13) (BAGD 1.c. p. 371): 'behold' [BAGD, BNTC; KJV, NASB], 'look' [BAGD, BECNT, LN, NICNT, NIGTC, NTC, PNTC, WBC; NET, NRSV, REB], 'see' [BAGD; ESV], 'listen, pay attention' [LN], not explicit [CEV, GW, NCV, NIV, NLT, TEV]. This participle is a prompter of attention that serves to emphasize the following statement [LN].

b. ἄριστον (LN **23.22**) (BAGD 2. p. 106): 'banquet' [LN, NTC, PNTC; CEV, REB], 'feast' [**LN**; NCV, NET, NLT], 'dinner' [BECNT, BNTC; GW, ESV, KJV, NASB, NIV, NRSV], 'meal' [BAGD, LN, NICNT, NIGTC], 'food' [WBC]. This noun denotes a meal, whether simple or elaborate [LN].

c. ταῦρος (LN 4.16) (BAGD p. 806): 'ox' [BAGD, BECNT, BNTC, NIGTC, PNTC, WBC; ESV, KJV, NASB, NET, NIV, NRSV], 'bull' [BAGD, LN, NICNT; GW, NLT], 'bullock' [REB], 'best bull' [NCV], 'steer' [NTC; TEV]. The phrase 'my oxen' is translated 'my cattle' [CEV].

d. σιτιστός (LN **44.2**) (BAGD p. 752): 'fattened' [BAGD, LN], 'fat, grain-fattened' [LN], 'grain-fed' [**LN**]. This plural adjective is translated as a noun phrase: 'fattened cattle' [BECNT, BNTC, NICNT, NTC; NET, NIV, NLT], 'fatted cattle' [WBC], 'fattened calves' [GW], 'fat calves' [NIGTC; ESV, NRSV], 'prize calves' [CEV, TEV], 'best calves' [NCV], 'fattened beasts' [PNTC], 'fatted beast' [REB], 'fattened livestock' [NASB], 'fatlings' [KJV]. This adjective, used here as a substantive, describes being well fed on grain and hence fattened [LN].

e. aorist act. participle of ἀμελέω (LN **30.50**) (BAGD p. 45): 'to pay no attention' [BAGD, BECNT, BNTC, **LN**, NTC, WBC; GW, ESV, NASB, NIV, TEV], 'to not pay attention' [CEV], 'to refuse to listen' [NCV], 'to take no notice' [NICNT; REB], 'to ignore' [NLT], 'to be a matter of no concern' [NIGTC], 'to not care' [PNTC], 'to be indifferent to' [NET], 'to make light of' [KJV, NRSV], 'to neglect, to disregard' [BAGD, LN]. This verb means to not think about something and thus not respond appropriately [LN].

f. ἐμπορία (LN **57.196**) (BAGD p. 256): 'business' [BAGD, BECNT, BNTC, **LN**, NICNT, NIGTC, PNTC, WBC; all versions except CEV, KJV, TEV], 'place of business' [NTC; CEV], 'store' [TEV], 'merchandise' [KJV]. This verb means to carry on a business involving buying and selling [LN].

QUESTION—What is the nature of the ἄριστον 'banquet'?

It was the beginning of festivities that would go on for several days [EBC], the first of the various meals that would follow [Lns, My]. Such a wedding banquet would have been magnificent [PNTC] and sumptuous [NAC].

22:6 And the rest, having-seized[a] his servants, mistreated[b] and killed (them). **22:7** But the king was-enraged[c] and having-sent his soldiers he-destroyed[d] those murderers and burned their city. **22:8** Then he-says to-his -servants, 'The wedding-feast is ready, but those called were not worthy;[e]

LEXICON—a. aorist act. participle of κρατέω (LN 18.6) (BAGD 1.b. p. 448): 'to seize' [BAGD, BECNT, BNTC, LN, NIGTC, WBC; ESV, NASB, NET, NIV, NLT, NRSV, REB], 'to grab' [NICNT, NTC; CEV, GW, NCV, TEV], 'to lay hands on' [PNTC], 'to take' [KJV], 'to grasp, to take hold of' [BAGD], 'to hold on to' [LN]. This verb means to hold on to an object [LN].

    b. aorist act. indic. of ὑβρίζω (LN **88.130**) (BAGD p. 831): 'to mistreat' [BAGD, BECNT, **LN**; GW, NASB, NIV, NRSV], 'to mistreat insolently' [NET], 'to mistreat with insolence' [LN], 'to treat shamefully' [NIGTC, NTC, WBC; ESV], 'to ill-treat' [PNTC], 'to abuse' [NICNT], 'to attack brutally' [REB], 'to beat up' [CEV], 'to beat' [NCV, TEV], 'to maltreat' [LN], 'to treat spitefully' [KJV], 'to insult' [BNTC; NLT], 'to treat in an arrogant or spiteful manner' [LN]. This verb means to maltreat in an insolent manner [LN].

    c. aorist pass. (deponent = act.) indic. of ὀργίζομαι (LN 88.174) (BAGD p. 579): 'to be enraged' [BECNT, NIGTC; NASB, NIV, NRSV], 'to be angry' [BAGD, LN, PNTC; ESV], 'to be very angry' [TEV], 'to become angry' [WBC; GW], 'to be angered' [BNTC], 'to be furious' [LN, NICNT; NCV, NET, NLT, REB], 'to be wroth' [KJV], 'to be full of anger' [LN]. The phrase ὁ βασιλεὺς ὠργίσθη 'the king was enraged' is translated 'the king's wrath was kindled' [NTC], 'this made the king furious' [CEV]. This verb means to be relatively angry [LN].

    d. aorist act. indic. of ἀπόλλυμι (LN 20.31) (BAGD 1.a.α. p. 95): 'to destroy' [BAGD, BECNT, LN, NICNT, NIGTC, NTC, PNTC, WBC; ESV, KJV, NASB, NIV, NLT, NRSV], 'to kill' [BNTC; CEV, GW, NCV, TEV], 'to put to death' [NET, REB]. This verb means to destroy or to cause the destruction of persons, objects, or institutions [LN].

    e. ἄξιος (LN 65.17) (BAGD 2.a. p. 78): 'worthy' [BAGD, BECNT, BNTC, LN, NIGTC, PNTC, WBC; ESV, KJV, NASB, NET, NRSV], 'worthy to come' [NCV], 'worthy of the honor' [NLT], 'fit' [BAGD]. The phrase οὐκ ἦσαν ἄξιοι 'were not worthy' is translated 'did not deserve it' [NICNT; TEV], 'did not/don't deserve the honor' [NTC; GW, REB], 'don't/did not deserve to come' [CEV, NIV]. This adjective describes having a relatively high degree of comparable merit or worth [LN].

22:9 So go to the intersections[a] of the roads and call whomever you find to the wedding-feast.' **22:10** And those servants having-gone-out to the roadways gathered-together all they found, both bad[b] and good;[c] and the wedding-feast was-filled with-guests. **22:11** And the king having-entered

to-see[d] **the guests, saw there a-man not having-been-clothed (with) a-wedding garment.**[e]

LEXICON—a. διέξοδος (LN **1.102**) (BAGD p. 194): 'intersection' [PNTC]. The phrase διεξόδους τῶν ὁδῶν 'intersections of the roads' is translated 'main streets' [BECNT; NET, NRSV, TEV], 'main roads' [ESV], 'main thoroughfares' [REB], 'main highways' [NASB], 'highways' [KJV], 'where the roads leave the city' [BNTC; GW], 'city exit roads' [NIGTC], 'where a main street leaves the city' [**LN**], 'where highways exit from the city' [WBC], 'country crossroads' [NTC], 'street corners' [NICNT; CEV, NCV, NIV, NLT], 'street crossing' [BAGD]. This noun possibly denotes a street crossing, but more probably the place where a principal thoroughfare crosses a city boundary and extends into the open country [BAGD, LN].

   b. πονηρός (LN 88.110) (BAGD 2.a. p. 691): 'bad' [BNTC, NICNT, NTC, WBC; all versions except GW, NASB], 'evil' [BAGD, BECNT, LN, NIGTC, PNTC; GW, NASB], 'wicked' [BAGD, LN]. This adjective describes someone who is morally corrupt and evil [LN].

   c. ἀγαθός (LN 88.1) (BAGD 1.b.α. p. 3): 'good' [BAGD, LN; all translations]. This adjective describes positive moral qualities of the most general nature [LN].

   d. aorist mid. (deponent = act) infin. of θεάομαι (LN 34.50) (BAGD 1.b. p. 353): 'to see' [BECNT, NIGTC, PNTC; GW, KJV, NCV, NET, NIV, NRSV], 'to go to see' [LN], 'to meet' [CEV, NLT], 'to greet' [BAGD, BNTC], 'to view' [NTC], 'to look at' [ESV, TEV], 'to look over' [NASB], 'to inspect' [NICNT], 'to survey' [WBC], 'to watch' [REB], 'to visit' [LN]. This verb means to go to see a person on the basis of friendship and with helpful intent [LN].

   e. ἔνδυμα (LN 6.162) (BAGD 1. p. 263): 'garment' [BAGD, BNTC, PNTC, WBC; ESV, KJV], 'robe' [BECNT, NTC; NRSV], 'clothes' [NICNT; CEV, GW, NASB, NET, NIV, NLT, TEV], 'clothing' [BAGD, LN], 'apparel' [LN]. The phrase ἐνδεδυμένον ἔνδυμα γάμου 'having been clothed with a wedding garment' is translated 'dressed for a wedding' [NCV, REB]. This noun denotes any kind of clothing [LN].

QUESTION—What does the noun διέξοδος 'intersection' denote?

   It describes the place where main roads cross city boundaries and empty into the open country [BAGD, BNTC, ICC, LN, NIBC, NIGTC, PNTC, WBC], which is where people would congregate [My], especially the poor [PNTC, TRT]. It refers to the forks of roads [EBC, NTC], which would be where the main roads going out from the city divide into smaller streets [NTC]. It is the intersection of country roads [My]. It refers to the main intersections of the town, where people would be most easily found [TH]. It describes where the roads from the country end at the city [Lns].In this context it refers to any place where ordinary people are to be found [NICNT].

QUESTION—Why did the king enter to see the guests?.

He was there to meet and greet the guests [BNTC, TH; CEV, NLT]. He came to see who had come to his feast [NTC, PNTC]. It was an inspection [NIBC, NICNT]. This act of inspecting the guests symbolizes that fact that even those who profess to be Jesus' disciples will come before God for judgment [NIBC].

QUESTION—What does the wedding garment symbolize?

It represents producing the fruit of the Christian life [NICNT, NTC, WBC]. It symbolizes one's righteousness [TRT, WBC], doing the will of God in obedient discipleship [BNTC]. Though entry into the kingdom of heaven is free, there are obligations involved [NICNT]. People who are saved from their sins must exhibit true righteousness [EBC, My]. The wedding garment represents the righteousness that Christ imputes to those who have faith [Lns]. The man without a wedding garment typifies those Jewish leaders who imagine they can participate in the eschatological banquet on their own terms, whereas a person's righteousness would need to exceed that of the scribes and Pharisees if they would enter the kingdom of heaven [NIGTC].

22:12 And he-says to-him, 'Friend,[a] how did-you-come-in here not having a-wedding garment?' And he-was-speechless.[b] **22:13** Then the king said to-the servants, 'Bind him feet and hands and throw- him -out into the outer[c] darkness; there will be weeping[d] and gnashing[e] of teeth there.' **22:14** For many are called[f] but few[g] (are) chosen.[h]'

LEXICON—a. ἑταῖρος (LN 34.16) (BAGD p. 314): friend' [BAGD, BECNT, BNTC, LN, NTC, PNTC, WBC; all versions except REB], 'my friend' [NICNT; REB], 'comrade' [NIGTC]. This noun denotes a person who is associated with someone else, though not necessarily involving personal affection [LN].

  b. aorist pass. indic. of φιμόω (LN 33.123) (BAGD 2. p. 862): 'to be speechless' [BECNT, NICNT, NTC, PNTC; ESV, KJV, NASB, NIV, NRSV], 'to be left speechless' [NIGTC], 'to be silent' [BAGD, BNTC, WBC], 'to say nothing' [NCV, TEV], 'to have no reply' [NLT], 'to have no excuse' [CEV], 'to have nothing to say' [GW, NET, REB], 'to be silenced' [BAGD, LN]. This verb means to cause someone to have nothing to say [LN].

  c. ἐξώτερος (LN 1.23) (BAGD 2. p. 280): 'outer' [BNTC, **LN**, PNTC, WBC; ESV, KJV, NASB, NET, NLT, NRSV], 'outside' [BECNT, LN, NICNT, NIGTC; CEV, GW, NIV, TEV], 'out' [NCV, REB], 'most distant' [NTC], 'farthest, extreme, farthest out' [BAGD]. The idiomatic expression 'the outer darkness' denotes a place or region which is both dark and removed (presumably from the abode of the righteous) and serving as the abode of evil spirits and devils [LN].

  d. κλαυθμός (LN 25.138) (BAGD p. 433): 'weeping' [BAGD, BECNT, BNTC, LN, NICNT, NTC, WBC; ESV, KJV, NASB, NET, NIV, NLT, NRSV], 'wailing' [PNTC; REB], 'crying' [BAGD, LN]. The phrase ἔσται ὁ κλαυθμός 'there will be weeping' is translated 'people will cry' [CEV, GW, NCV], 'he will cry' [TEV]. This noun denotes weeping or wailing, with emphasis upon the noise accompanying the weeping [LN].

e. βρυγμός (LN 23.41) (BAGD p. 148): 'gnashing (of teeth)' [BAGD, BECNT, BNTC, LN, NICNT, NIGTC, PNTC; ESV, KJV, NASB, NET, NIV, NLT, NRSV], 'grinding (of teeth)' [NTC, WBC; REB]. The phrase ἔσται...ὁ βρυγμὸς τῶν ὀδόντων 'there will be...gnashing of teeth' is translated 'people will...grit/grind their teeth in pain' [CEV, NCV], 'he will gnash his teeth' [TEV], 'people will be in extreme pain' [GW]. This noun denotes the grinding or the gnashing of the teeth, whether involuntary as in the case of certain illnesses, or as an expression of an emotion such as anger or of pain and suffering [LN].

f. κλητός (LN **33.318**) (BAGD p. 436): 'called' [BAGD, BECNT, NTC, WBC; CEV, ESV, KJV, NASB, NCV, NET, NLT, NRSV], 'invited' [BAGD, BNTC, **LN**, NICNT, NIGTC, PNTC; CEV, NIV, REB, TEV]. This adjective describes having been invited by someone [LN].

g. ὀλίγος (LN 59.3) (BAGD 1.b. p. 563): 'few' [BAGD, BECNT, BNTC, LN, NICNT, PNTC, PNTC; all versions except CEV, GW, NCV], 'few of those' [GW], 'only a few' [CEV, NCV], 'fewer' [NIGTC], 'not all' [WBC], 'less' [LN]. This adjective describes a relatively small quantity on any dimension [LN].

h. ἐκλεκτός (LN 30.93) (BAGD 1.b. p. 242): 'chosen' [BAGD, LN; all versions except GW], 'chosen to stay' [GW]. This adjective describes that which has been chosen [LN].

QUESTION—Why was that man speechless?

It means that he had no good excuse for not being dressed appropriately [ICC, NICNT, NIGTC, TH; CEV]. His being speechless shows that he knows he is guilty [EBC, NIGTC, NTC, PNTC].

QUESTION—Who is saying 'There will be weeping and gnashing of teeth there'?

1. The king says this [BECNT, BNTC, NIBC, NIGTC, NTC, PNTC, TH, WBC; ESV, GW, NASB, NCV, NET, NIV, NLT, NRSV, REB, TEV]

2. It is part of Jesus' summary comment, along with 'many are called but few are chosen' [My, NICNT; CEV].

QUESTION—Why would some be called but not chosen?

Those who are not chosen either did not respond to the invitation to enter the kingdom, or were not willing to produce its fruit [NICNT, WBC]. Some who are called refuse to come, and others refuse to submit to the norms of the kingdom [EBC]. It is possible that this should be understood in the sense of 'many are invited to apply (i.e., by God) but few are actually selected [LN]. Many are called, but only some respond [ICC]. Not all respond properly [BECNT]. The invitation goes to many, but only those who accept Jesus and follow him are chosen; our decisions and conduct matter [NIBC]. The invitation to come goes out widely, but only those who prepare as the king expects them to will be able to come into the kingdom [BNTC]. The elect are few because so many people eliminate themselves from the gracious invitation [Lns]. Only those who are faithful to the end are finally chosen [TH].

QUESTION—What is meant by 'many' and 'few'?

Since Hebrew and Aramaic do not have comparative forms, comparisons are framed as absolutes, as in this passage. Here it simply means that not all of the called are actually chosen [ICC, PNTC, WBC]. It means that more are called than are chosen [NIGTC]. Many are invited, but some refuse to come and others who do come refuse to submit to the norms of the kingdom and are therefore rejected. Those who remain are called 'chosen' [EBC]. 'Many' probably means 'all' are called [NAC, TRT, WBC], and 'few' means considerably less than all [TRT, NAC].

DISCOURSE UNIT—22:15–23:1–39 [PNTC]. The topic is the Pharisees and Sadducees.

DISCOURSE UNIT—22:15–46 [NICNT]. The topic is three challenges and a counterchallenge.

DISCOURSE UNIT—22:15–22 [CEV, ESV, GW, NASB, NCV, NET, NIV, NLT, NRSV, TEV]. The topic is a question about taxes [GW], the question about paying taxes [NRSV, TEV], is it right to pay taxes or not? [NCV], paying taxes to Caesar [ESV, NET, NIV], taxes for Caesar [NLT], tribute to Caesar [NASB], paying taxes [CEV].

22:15 Then having-departed the Pharisees took counsel-together[a] (about) how they-might-trap[b] him in a-statement. **22:16** And they-send their disciples to-him with (some of the) Herodians saying, "Teacher, we-know that you-are truthful[c] and you-teach the way of-God in truth, and it-does-not -matter[d] to-you about anyone; for you-do- not -regard[e] the face of-men.

LEXICON—a. συμβούλιον (LN 30.74) (BAGD 1. p. 778): 'plans (made against someone), plot' [LN]. The phrase συμβούλιον ἔλαβον 'took counsel' [NIGTC, PNTC, KJV] is also translated 'made plans' [NCV], 'made a plan' [TEV], 'planned together' [BECNT; NET], 'planned' [GW], 'laid plans' [NIV], 'agreed on a plan' [REB], 'plotted' [BNTC, NTC, WBC; ESV, NASB, NRSV], 'met together to plot' [NLT], 'consulted' [NICNT], 'got together and planned' [CEV]. This noun denotes joint planning so as to devise a course of common action, often one with a harmful or evil purpose [LN]. The idiom λαμβάνω συμβούλιον means to consult or to plot [BAGD].

  b. aorist act. subj. of παγιδεύω (LN 27.30) (BAGD p. 602): 'to trap' [BECNT, **LN**, NIGTC, NTC, PNTC, WBC; GW, NASB, NCV, NIV, NLT, REB, TEV], 'to entrap' [BAGD, BNTC, NICNT; NET, NRSV], 'to entangle' [ESV, KJV], 'to trick' [CEV], 'to set a snare' [BAGD], 'to catch off guard, to catch in a mistake' [LN]. This verb means to acquire information about an error or fault, with the purpose of causing harm or trouble [LN].

c. ἀληθής (LN **88.39**) (BAGD 1. p. 36): 'truthful' [BAGD, BNTC, LN, NICNT, NTC; NASB, NET], 'honest' [BAGD, BECNT, **LN**; CEV, NLT], 'true' [NIGTC, PNTC, WBC; ESV, KJV], 'sincere' [NRSV, REB], 'a person/man of integrity' [LN; NIV]. The phrase ἀληθὴς εἶ 'you are truthful' is translated 'you tell the truth' [GW, TEV], 'you are an honest man' [NCV]. This adjective pertains to being truthful and honest [LN].

d. pres. act. indic. of μέλει (LN 30.39) (BAGD 2. p. 500): 'to care for/about' [BAGD, BNTC, NICNT, PNTC; KJV], 'to court favor' [BAGD, NTC; NET, REB], 'to defer to' [BECNT], 'to show deference to' [NRSV], 'to take notice of' [NICNT], 'to be concerned about' [LN], 'to think about' [LN]. The phrase οὐ μέλει σοι περὶ οὐδενός 'it does not matter to you about anyone' is translated 'no one matters specially to you' [WBC], 'you do not care about anyone's opinion' [ESV], 'you are not afraid of what other people think about you' [NCV], 'without worrying about what others think of you' [TEV], 'you are not swayed by men' [NIV], 'you are impartial' [NLT]. The clause 'it does not matter to you about anyone for you do not regard the face of a man' is translated 'you treat everyone with the same respect, no matter who they are' [CEV], 'you don't favor individuals because of who they are' [GW], 'courting no man's favor, whoever he may be' [REB]. This verb means to think about something in such a way as to make an appropriate response [LN].

e. pres. act. indic. of βλέπω (LN **30.120**) (BAGD 5. p. 143): 'to notice, to mark' [BAGD]. The idiom βλέπω εἰς πρόσωπον 'to regard the face' is translated 'to have regard to anyone' [PNTC], 'to regard the status of persons' [WBC], 'to regard with partiality' [NRSV], 'to judge a person on the basis of outward appearance' [**LN**], 'to be partial to' [BECNT, NASB, NTC], 'to show partiality to' [NET], 'to defer to' [NIGTC], 'to pay attention to someone's status' [TEV], 'to regard the person' [KJV], 'to pay attention to who they are' [NCV, NIV], 'to pay attention to outward position' [BNTC], 'to play favorites' [NLT], 'to be impressed by people's status' [NICNT], 'to be swayed by appearances' [ESV]. The idiom is literally 'to see into the face' and it means to judge on the basis of external appearances [LN].

QUESTION—What relationship is indicated by τότε 'then'?

It marks the beginning of a new passage, but does not necessarily mean that these events followed immediately from what went before [TH]. It primarily indicates a sequence of events, but there is also a logical aspect in that the Pharisees were taking counsel together because of what had just occurred [EBC].

QUESTION—Who would make the statement that they thought might trap Jesus?

1. It refers to what Jesus might say that could be a basis for accusation [BECNT, BNTC, ICC, Lns, My, NICNT, NTC, PNTC, TRT, WBC; CEV, ESV, GW, KJV, NASB, NCV, NET, NIV, NLT, NRSV, REB, TEV].

2. It refers to what the Pharisees might be able to say to trap him [NIBC, NIGTC; TEV].

QUESTION—Who were the Herodians?

They were people who supported the rule of the Herods and were favorable toward Roman rule [BECNT, EBC, Lns, NAC, NIBC, NICNT, PNTC, TH, TRT, WBC]. The Pharisees and the Herodians disagreed on whether it was right to pay taxes to Rome [BECNT, Lns, NAC, NTC, TRT]. They were not friends with the Pharisees [BNTC, Lns, NIBC, TRT].

QUESTION—What is implied by the use of the term 'teacher'?

It is a title of respect similar to 'rabbi' [PNTC, WBC], but in the gospel of Matthew is only used by people who are not his disciples [NICNT, NIGTC, WBC]. It is a polite form of address [PNTC].

QUESTION—What is meant by the phrase 'the way of God'?

It refers to Jesus' teaching about righteousness [NIGTC, WBC], about how God wants people to live [ICC, Lns, My, TH, TRT]. It means that he teaches God's law [TH].

22:17 **So tell us what you think. Is-it-lawful[a] to pay poll-tax to Caesar or not?"** **22:18** **But Jesus perceiving[b] their evil-intent[c] said, "Why do-you-test[d] me, (you) hypocrites?** **22:19** **Show me the coin for the poll-tax." And they-brought him a-denarius.**

LEXICON—a. pres. indic. act. of ἔξεστι (LN 71.32) (BAGD 1. p. 275): 'to be lawful' [BECNT, NIGTC, NTC; ESV, KJV, NASB, NRSV], 'to be permitted' [BNTC; REB], 'to be right' [NICNT, WBC; GW, NCV, NET, NIV, NLT], 'to be proper' [PNTC], 'to be against the (Jewish) Law' [TEV], 'must, ought to' [LN]. The verb ἔξεστιν 'is it lawful' is translated 'should we' [CEV]. This verb means to be obligatory [LN].

    b. aorist act. participle of γινώσκω (LN 28.1) (BAGD 4.a. p. 161): 'to perceive' [BAGD, BECNT, PNTC; KJV, NASB], 'to know' [LN, WBC; CEV, NCV, NIV, NLT], 'to discern' [BNTC], 'to recognize' [NICNT; GW], 'to be aware of' [NTC; ESV, NRSV, REB, TEV], 'to know about, to have knowledge of, to be acquainted with' [LN], 'to realize' [BAGD; NET]. This verb means to possess information about something [LN].

    c. πονηρία (LN 88.108) (BAGD p. 690): 'evil intent' [NIGTC, WBC; NIV], 'evil intentions' [NET], 'evil motives' [NLT], 'evil thoughts' [CEV], 'evil plan' [GW, TEV], 'malice' [BECNT, PNTC; ESV, NASB, NRSV], 'malicious intention' [NICNT; REB], 'maliciousness' [BAGD], 'wickedness' [BAGD, BNTC, LN, NTC; KJV]. This noun is translated by a phrase: 'were trying to trick him' [NCV]. This noun denotes an evil, wicked nature [LN].

    d. pres. act. indic. of πειράζω (LN 27.31) (BAGD 2.c. p. 640): 'to test' [BECNT, BNTC, PNTC, WBC; CEV, GW, NASB, NET], 'to put to the test' [BAGD, NIGTC, NTC; ESV, NRSV], 'to try to trap' [LN, NICNT; NCV, NIV, NLT, TEV], 'to tempt' [KJV], 'to catch (someone) out' [REB], 'to attempt to catch in a mistake' [LN]. This verb means to obtain information to be used against a person by trying to cause someone to make a mistake [LN].

QUESTION—Does the question 'is it lawful' ask for an interpretation of some point of Jewish law, or a more basic question of right and wrong?

They are asking if *it is right* to pay taxes to Caesar [EBC, NICNT, PNTC], though for a Jew any such question was ultimately a theological question [EBC]. They are asking if it is lawful, that is, is it in keeping with God's law, the Torah [BECNT, ICC]. The question suggests the possibility that by paying the tax a Jewish person would be disloyal to God and in violation of God's law [Lns, NIGTC].

QUESTION—What would have been the concern about paying taxes to Caesar?

The Jewish people resented the Roman occupation and rule over their nation [ICC, NIBC, NIGTC, PNTC, WBC]. They also considered the denarius used for the tax as idolatrous since it had the image of Caesar on it [BECNT, BNTC, EBC, ICC, NIBC, NICNT, NTC, PNTC, WBC] and because the inscription described Caesar as son of the divine Augustus [BECNT, BNTC, EBC, ICC, NIBC, NICNT, NTC, TRT] and as chief priest [BECNT, EBC, NIBC, NTC, TRT]. They were asking if Jesus thought paying the tax was a violation of Jewish law and duty [BNTC].

22:20 And he-says to-them, "Whose (is) this image[a] and inscription?[b]" **22:21** They-say to him, "Caesar's.[c]" Then he-says to-them, "Then give[d] to-Caesar the-things (that are) Caesar's, and to God the-things (that are) God's." **22:22** And having-heard (this) they-were-amazed,[e] and having left him they-went-away.

LEXICON—a. εἰκών (LN **6.96**) (BAGD 1.a. p. 222): 'image' [BAGD, BNTC, LN, NICNT, NIGTC, WBC; KJV, NCV, NET], 'likeness' [BAGD, BECNT, **LN**, NTC, PNTC; ESV, NASB], 'picture' [CEV, NLT], 'face' [GW, TEV], 'head' [NRSV, REB], 'portrait' [NIV]. This noun denotes an object which has been formed to resemble a person, god, animal, etc. [LN].

b. ἐπιγραφή (LN **33.46**) (BAGD p. 291): 'inscription' [BAGD, BECNT, BNTC **LN**, NICNT, NIGTC, NTC, PNTC, WBC; ESV, NASB, NET, NIV, REB], 'name' [CEV, GW, NCV, TEV], 'superscription' [KJV], 'title' [NLT, NRSV], 'writing' [LN]. This noun denotes a brief notice used primarily for identification [LN].

c. Καῖσαρ (LN **37.74**) (BAGD p. 395): 'Caesar' [BAGD, BECNT, BNTC, NIGTC, NTC, PNTC, WBC; ESV, KJV, NASB, NCV, NET, NIV, NLT, REB], 'the Emperor' [BAGD, LN, NICNT; CEV, GW, NRSV, TEV]. This noun is a title for the Roman Emperor [LN].

d. aorist act. impera. of ἀποδίδωμι (LN **57.153**) (BAGD 1. p. 90): 'to give' [BECNT, NIGTC, WBC; CEV, GW, NCV, NET, NIV, NLT, NRSV], 'to give back' [NICNT], 'to pay' [BAGD, LN; REB, TEV], 'to pay back' [BNTC], 'to render' [**LN**, NTC, PNTC; ESV, KJV, NASB]. This verb means to make a payment, with the implication of such a payment being in response to an incurred obligation [LN].

e. aorist act. indic. of θαυμάζω (LN 25.213) (BAGD 1.a.α. p. 352): 'to be amazed' [BECNT, LN, NICNT, NIGTC; NASB, NCV, NIV, NRSV, TEV], 'to amaze (them)' [NLT], 'to marvel' [BAGD, BNTC, LN, WBC; ESV, KJV], 'to wonder' [BAGD, LN], 'to be astonished' [BAGD, NTC, PNTC], 'to be taken aback' [REB], 'to be stunned' [NET], 'to be surprised' [GW], 'to surprise (them)' [CEV]. This verb means to wonder or marvel at some event or object [LN].

DISCOURSE UNIT—22:23–46 [NASB]. The topic is Jesus answers the Sadducees.

DISCOURSE UNIT—22:23–33 [CEV, ESV, GW, NCV, NET, NIV, NLT, NRSV, TEV]. The topic is some Sadducees try to trick Jesus [NCV], the question about rising from death [TEV], Sadducees ask about the resurrection [ESV], marriage and the resurrection [NET], marriage at the resurrection [NIV], the question about the resurrection [NRSV], discussion about resurrection [NLT], the dead come back to life [GW], life in the future world [CEV].

22:23 On that day there-approached him (some) Sadducees who say/were-saying there-is no resurrection and they-questioned him **22:24** saying, "Teacher, Moses said 'If someone dies not having children, his brother shall-marry[a] his wife and raise-up[b] offspring[c] for- his -brother.'

TEXT—Manuscripts reading λέγοντες 'saying' are given a B rating by GNT to indicate it was regarded to be almost certain. Other manuscripts read οἱ λέγοντες 'those who say'. However, other factors also enter into the decision about whether to translate this participle as 'saying' or as 'those who say'. Consequently it is difficult to determine whether a translation decision has been made on the basis of the textual variant or other considerations.

LEXICON—a. fut. act. indic. or aorist act. impera. of ἐπιγαμβρεύω (LN **34.71**) (BAGD p. 290): 'to marry' [**LN**; all translations], 'to marry as next of kin' [BAGD]. This verb means to marry the childless widow of one's brother [LN].

b. fut. act. indic. or aorist act. impera. of ἀνίστημι (LN **23.59**) (BAGD 1.b. p. 70): 'to raise up' [BECNT, BNTC, NICNT, NIGTC, NTC, PNTC, WBC; ESV, KJV, NASB, NRSV], 'to have (children)' [GW, NCV, NIV, NLT, TEV], 'to father' [NET], 'to provide (an heir)' [REB], not explicit [CEV]. When used with σπέρμα this verb means 'to beget' [**LN**], 'to procreate, to become the father of' [LN], 'to cause to be born' [BAGD]. The idiom ἀνίστημι σπέρμα 'to raise up offspring' describes the male role in begetting children [LN].

c. σπέρμα (LN 10.29) (BAGD 2.b. p. 761): 'offspring' [LN, NICNT, NIGTC], 'children' [BAGD, BNTC, NTC, WBC; ESV, GW, NASB, NCV, NET, NIV, NRSV, TEV], 'a child' [NLT], 'an heir' [REB], 'seed'

[PNTC; KJV], 'descendants [BAGD, BECNT, LN], 'posterity' [BAGD, LN], not explicit [CEV]. This noun denotes posterity, with emphasis upon the ancestor's role in founding the lineage [LN].

QUESTION—Was the comment about the Sadducees not believing in the resurrection intended to describe their views generally, or what they were saying as they approached Jesus?

1. It is a parenthetical comment on their general beliefs [BECNT, EBC, Lns, My, NICNT, NTC, PNTC, TH, TRT; CEV, ESV, GW, KJV, NASB, NCV, NET, NIV, NLT, REB]: Sadducees, who say there is no resurrection.

2. It describes what they were saying to Jesus as they approached him [BNTC, NIGTC, WBC; NRSV, TEV]: Sadducees approached him saying that there is no resurrection.

22:25 Now there-were seven brothers with us; and the first after-marrying died, and not having offspring left[a] his wife to his brother; **22:26** likewise also the second (died) and the third, up-to the seventh. **22:27** And last of-all the woman died. **22:28** So in the resurrection[b] of-which of the seven will-she-be (the) wife? For all had[c] her."

LEXICON—LEXICON—a. aorist act. indic. of ἀφίημι (LN 15:48) (BAGD 3.a. p. 126): 'to leave' [BAGD, BECNT, BNTC, NICNT, NIGTC, NTC, PNTC, WBC; ESV, GW, KJV, NSB, NET, NIV, NRSV, TEV]. The phrase ἀφῆκεν τὴν γυναῖκα αὐτοῦ τῷ ἀδελφῷ αὐτοῦ 'left his wife to his brother' is translated 'his wife was left to his brother' [CEV, REB], 'his brother married the widow' [NCV, NLT]. This verb means to move away from someone [LN].

b. ἀνάστασις (LN 23.93) (BAGD 2.b. p. 60): 'resurrection' [BAGD, BECNT, BNTC, LN, NICNT, NIGTC, NTC, PNTC, WBC; ESV, KJV, NASB, NET, NIV, NLT, NRSV, REB]. The phrase ἐν τῇ ἀναστάσει 'in the resurrection' is translated 'when God raises people from death' [CEV], 'when the dead come back to life' [GW], 'when people rise from the dead' [NCV], 'on the day when the dead rise to life' [TEV]. This noun denotes the event of coming back to life after having once died [LN].

c. aorist act. indic. of ἔχω: (LN 57.1): 'to have' [BNTC, LN. NICNT, NIGTC, NTC, PNTC; ESV, KJV], 'to have as wife' [WBC], 'to marry' [BECNT; NASB, NCV, NET, NRSV, REB, TEV], 'to be married to' [GW, NIV, NLT]. The phrase πάντες ἔσχον αὐτήν 'all had her' is translated 'she had been married to all seven brothers' [CEV]. This verb means to have or possess objects or property in the technical sense of having control over the use of such objects [LN].

QUESTION—Does the statement 'there were seven brothers with us' indicate that this story is being presented as though it had actually happened?

The story is being related as a true story, as having actually occurred [Lns, NIGTC, TH, TRT, WBC]. Although the story is being related as factual, it may have been somewhat embellished [TH]. The story is not necessarily factual [NICNT]. The story was probably fabricated [EBC, ICC, My, NTC], though they presented it as being true [ICC]. It was a hypothetical case [BECNT].

22:29 **And answering Jesus said to-them, "You-err**[a] **(because-of) not knowing the scriptures nor the power of-God.** **22:30** **For in the resurrection neither do-they-marry nor are-given-in-marriage, but they-are as (the) angels in the heaven.** **22:31** **But about the resurrection of-the dead have-you- not -read what was-spoken to you by God, when-saying,** **22:32** **'I am the God of Abraham, and the God of Isaac, and the God of Jacob'? He-is not the God of (the) dead, but of (the) living."** **22:33** **And the crowds having-heard (this) were-amazed**[b] **at his teaching.**

LEXICON—a. pres. pass. indic. of πλανάομαι (LN 31.67) (BAGD 2.c.γ. p. 665): 'to err' [BNTC; KJV], 'to be in error' [NIV], 'to go astray' [BAGD, PNTC], 'to be wide of the mark' [NICNT], 'to be mistaken' [BECNT, NIGTC; GW, NASB], 'to be wrong' [ESV, NRSV, TEV], 'to be completely wrong' [CEV], 'to not understand' [NCV], 'to be deceived' [NET], 'to deceive oneself' [NTC], 'to be misled' [BAGD, WBC], 'to be deluded' [BAGD, 'to be far from the truth' [REB], 'to stray from the truth, to wander from the truth, to go astray from' [LN]. The verb πλανᾶσθε 'you err' is translated 'your mistake is' [NLT]. This verb means to no longer believe what is true, but to start believing what is false [LN].

   b. imperf. pass. indic. of ἐκπλήσσομαι (LN 25.219) (BAGD 2. p. 244): 'to be amazed' [BAGD; NCV, NET, NRSV, REB, TEV], 'to be astonished' [BECNT, BNTC, NICNT, NIGTC, PNTC; ESV, KJV, NASB, NIV, NLT], 'to be surprised' [CEV], 'to be astounded' [NTC], 'to be greatly astounded' [LN]. This passive verb is translated as active: 'he amazed (the crowds)' [GW]. This verb means to be so amazed as to be practically overwhelmed [LN].

QUESTION—What relationship is indicated by γάρ 'for' at the beginning of verse 30?

   It indicates why they were wrong about thinking that if there is life in the future world then marriages would continue as it is here [Lns, PNTC]. This is an explanation about how the power of God will manifest itself in the life inaugurated by the resurrection. There will be a change in sexual relationships and marriage as we know it will be no more [EBC].

QUESTION—Does the phrase 'in the resurrection' refer primarily to the time the dead are raised, or to the continuing state that results afterward?

   It views it as the resurrected state [EBC, ICC, PNTC, TRT, WBC], the life of the resurrection order [WBC]. Others think it refers to the actual day in which the dead will be raised to life [Lns, TH; TEV].

DISCOURSE UNIT—22:34–40 [CEV, ESV, GW, NCV, NET, NIV, NLT, NRSV, TEV]. The topic is the most important command [NCV], the most important commandment [CEV, NLT], the great commandment [ESV, TEV], the greatest commandment [NET, NIV, NRSV], love God and your neighbor [GW].

22:34 **And having-heard that he-had-silenced[a] the Sadducees, the Pharisees gathered-together, 22:35 and one of them, a-lawyer,[b] testing him asked, 22:36 "Teacher, which commandment in the law (is) great?[c]"**

TEXT—Manuscripts reading νομικός 'a lawyer' are given a C rating by GNT to indicate that choosing it over a variant text was difficult. Other manuscripts have νομικὸς τις 'a certain lawyer' and other manuscripts omit the reading altogether. GNT includes νομικός in brackets. Only REB omits it.

LEXICON—a. aorist act. indic. of φιμόω (LN **33.123**) (BAGD 2. p. 861): 'to silence' [BAGD, LN; all translations except CEV, KJV, NCV], 'to put to silence' [BAGD, **LN**; KJV], 'to make (someone) look foolish' [CEV]. The phrase ἐφίμωσεν τοὺς Σαδδουκαίους 'he had silenced the Sadducees' is translated 'the Sadducees could not argue with Jesus' answers to them' [NCV]. This verb means to cause someone to have nothing to say [LN].

b. νομικός (LN 33.338) (BAGD 2. p. 541): 'lawyer' [BAGD, BECNT, BNTC, NICNT, NIGTC, PNTC; ESV, KJV, NASB, NRSV], 'expert in the Law' [LN, WBC; NIV], 'expert in the Jewish law' [CEV], 'law expert' [NTC], 'legal expert' [BAGD], 'an expert in Moses' Teachings' [GW], 'expert on the law of Moses' [NCV], 'expert in religious law' [NET, NLT], 'teacher of the Law' [TEV], 'interpreter of the Law' [LN]. This noun denotes one who is an expert in interpreting Jewish religious law [LN].

c. μέγας (LN **87.22**) (BAGD 2.b.β. p. 498): 'great' [BAGD, BECNT, LN, NICNT, NTC, PNTC, WBC; ESV, KJV, NASB], 'important' [BAGD, LN]. This adjective is also translated as a superlative: 'greatest' [BNTC, NIGTC; GW, NET, NIV, NRSV, REB, TEV], 'most important' [CEV, NCV, NLT]. This adjective describes being great in terms of status [LN].

22:37 **And he-said to-him, "You-shall-love (the) Lord your God with all your heart[a] and with all your soul[b] and with all your mind;[c] 22:38 this is the great/greatest and first[d] commandment. 22:39 And (the) second (is) like it, You-shall-love your neighbor as[e] yourself. 22:40 On these two commands depend[f] the whole law and the prophets."**

LEXICON—a καρδία (LN **26.3**) (BAGD 1.b.ζ. p. 404): 'heart' [BAGD, **LN**; all translations], 'inner self, mind' [LN]. This noun denotes the causative source of a person's psychological life in its various aspects, but with special emphasis upon thoughts [LN].

b. ψυχή (LN 26.4) (BAGD 1.b.γ. p. 893): 'soul' [BAGD, BECNT, BNTC, NICNT, NTC, PNTC; all versions], 'life' [NIGTC, WBC], 'inner self, mind, thoughts, feelings, heart, being' [LN]. This noun denotes the essence of life in terms of thinking, willing, and feeling [LN].

    c. διάνοια (LN 26.14) (BAGD 1. p. 187): 'mind' [BAGD, BECNT, BNTC, LN, NIGTC, NTC, PNTC, WBC; all versions], 'thinking' [NICNT], 'understanding, intelligence' [BAGD]. This noun denotes the psychological faculty of understanding, reasoning, thinking, and deciding [LN].

    d. πρῶτος (LN 65.52) (BAGD 1.c.α. p. 726): 'first' [BAGD, BNTC, NICNT, NIGTC, NTC, PNTC, WBC; all versions except GW, NASB, TEV], 'foremost' [BAGD, BECNT; NASB], 'most important' [BAGD, LN; GW, TEV]. This adjective describes what exceeds everything else in importance [LN].

    e. ὡς (LN 64.12): 'as' [LN; all translations], 'like' [LN]. The phrase ὡς σεαυτόν 'as yourself' is translated 'as you love yourself' [GW, NCV, TEV], 'as much as you love yourself' [CEV]. This conjunction indicates a relatively weak relationship between events or states [LN].

    f. pres. mid. indic. of κρέμαμαι (LN **89.2**) (BAGD 2.b. p. 450): 'to depend' [BAGD, **LN**, NTC; ESV, GW, NASB, NCV, NET, TEV], 'to hang' [BAGD, BECNT, BNTC, NICNT, NIGTC, PNTC, WBC; KJV, NIV, NRSV, REB], 'to be based on' [CEV, NLT]. This verb means to be in a relation of dependency upon something [LN].

QUESTION—What distinction is there between each of these three human faculties?

    Jesus' point is that they must love God with their entire being and with all their faculties [BECNT, BNTC, EBC, ICC, My, NIBC, NIGTC, NTC], with all that one is and has [NICNT]. Love for God must govern our emotions, guide our thoughts, and be the dynamic of all we do [NIBC]. These three categories overlap and are not mutually exclusive [EBC]. The heart refers to the innermost center of one's being, the soul is the life force that energizes a person, and the mind is the faculty of thinking and planning [NIGTC]. The heart is the core of a person's existence and the source of his/her thoughts and actions; the soul is probably to be understood as the seat of emotional activity, and the mind is the source of mental activity, disposition, and attitudes [NTC]. The heart is the whole of the inner sphere and source of conscience, the soul is the capacity to feel and desire, and the mind encompasses the powers of thought and volition [My]. The heart is the center of personality, within which the soul and mind dwell and function; the soul is consciousness and the life that animates the body, and the mind is reason with its functions of thoughts, ideas, and convictions [Lns].

QUESTION—What is meant by 'is like it'?

    It means that it is of equal importance [BNTC, ICC, NAC, NICNT, TH]. Both commands are alike in that the focus of religious duty is outside oneself [NICNT]. They are alike in that they both require love [EBC, Lns, NTC, PNTC]. They are both of the same nature and character [Lns, My]. The command to love one's neighbor is second only to the command to love God [Lns, NIGTC], but the two are alike in the claim they make on human beings [NIGTC].

QUESTION—What is meant by 'as yourself'?

It means to have the same concern for others that we have for ourselves [ICC, NIBC]. It assumes that people naturally love themselves [BECNT, ICC, NAC, NIBC, NICNT, TH]. They love themselves in the sense of being concerned for their own self-interest more than for the interests of others [NICNT]. It means that our treatment of others must be the same as how we would want to be treated [NIGTC].

QUESTION—What does it means that the law and the prophets 'depend' on these two commands?

It means that all other commandments are contained in these two commands [My, NAC, NIGTC]. They are derived from or taken from those two commands [BNTC, TRT]. Fulfilling the law's commands and the teaching of the prophets cannot happen apart from obeying these two commandments about love [WBC]. The law and the prophets summarize these two commands to love, and spell out their practical implications [NICNT]. Nothing in scripture truly holds together nor can scripture be truly obeyed unless these two principles are observed [EBC]. These two fundamental principles are expressed in all other Old Testament teaching [NIBC]. God's love, which demands a response of love, is at the heart of all of the OT commandments [NTC]. Without love none of the other commands in the law can be carried out [PNTC]. The commands to love are the basis for all other commandments and form the basis and essential character of all the rest [My]. These two commands contain ideals on which the rest of scripture elaborates [BECNT]. These two commands give everything else in the Old Testament true meaning and purpose [Lns]. They are the most basic demand made by the law and the prophets and describe their real purpose [ICC].

DISCOURSE UNIT—22:41–46 [CEV, ESV, GW, NCV, NET, NIV, NLT, NRSV, TEV]. The topic is how can David's son be David's Lord? [GW], Jesus questions the Pharisees [NCV], the question about the Messiah [TEV], whose son in the Christ? [ESV, NIV], whose son in the Messiah? [NLT], the Messiah: David's son and lord [NET], the question about David's son [NRSV], about David's son [CEV].

22:41 **And (while) the Pharisees were-assembled Jesus asked them** **22:42** **saying, "What do-you-think about the Christ? Whose son is he?" They-say to-him, "The (son) of David."** **22:43** **He says to-them, "How does- David in**[a] **(the)-Spirit**[b] **-call him Lord saying,** **22:44** **'(The) Lord said to-my Lord, "Sit at my-right (hand) until I-put your enemies beneath your feet."'** **22:45** **If then David calls him Lord, how is-he**[c] **his son?"** **22:46** **And no-one was-able to-answer him a-word nor did- anyone -dare**[d] **from that day to-ask him anything.**

TEXT—Instead of ὑποκάτω τῶν ποδῶν σου 'beneath your feet' some manuscripts have ὑποπόδιον τῶν ποδῶν σου 'a footstool for your feet'. GNT does not mention this variant. It is followed only by CEV and KJV.

LEXICON—a. ἐν (LN 90.6) (BAGD I.5.d. p. 260): 'in' [BAGD, BECNT, BNTC, NIGTC, NTC, PNTC; ESV, KJV, NASB], 'by' [LN, WBC; NET, NIV, NRSV], 'inspired by' [NICNT], 'by inspiration' [REB], 'under the inspiration of' [NLT], 'guided by' [GW], 'speaking by the power of' [NCV], 'from' [LN]. The phrase Πῶς οὖν Δαυὶδ ἐν πνεύματι καλεῖ 'how does David in the Spirit call' is translated 'how could the Spirit have David call' [CEV], 'why did the Spirit inspire David to call' [TEV]. This preposition indicates an agent, often with the implication of an agent being used as an instrument, and in some instances relating to general behavior rather than to some specific event [LN]. It indicates a close connection [BAGD].

    b. πνεῦμα (LN 12.18) (BAGD 5.d.β., 6.c. p. 677): 'Spirit' [BAGD, LN; all translations except KJV, NCV, REB], 'spirit' [KJV], 'Holy Spirit' [LN; NCV], 'Spirit of God' [LN], not explicit [REB]. This noun denotes the title for the third person of the Trinity [LN].

    c. pres. act. indic. of εἰμί (LN 13.4): 'to be' [LN]. The phrase 'how is he' [BECNT, NIGTC, NTC, PNTC, WBC; ESV, KJV, NASB] is also translated 'how can he be' [BNTC, NICNT; NET, NIV, REB], 'how can the Messiah/Christ be' [CEV, NCV, NLT, NRSV, TEV]. This verb means to be identical with [LN].

    d. aorist act. indic. of τολμάω (LN 25.161) (BAGD 1.a. p. 821): 'to dare' [LN, BAGD; all translations except NCV], 'to be brave enough' [BAGD; NCV], 'to have the courage' [BAGD]. This verb means to be so bold as to challenge or defy possible danger or opposition [LN].

QUESTION—What does 'in the Spirit' mean?

    It means he was inspired by the Holy Spirit when he wrote that psalm [BECNT, BNTC, EBC, Lns, My, NAC, NICNT, NTC, PNTC, TH, TRT, WBC].

QUESTION—What does the idiom 'beneath your feet' mean?

    It means they will be under his control or authority [PNTC, TRT]. He will rule them [NAC]. God will defeat them and they will bow down before the Son [TH]. In ancient times conquerors would put their feet on the necks of defeated enemies [Lns, NTC, TRT]. The hostility of Messiah's enemies will be crushed in the end [EBC].

DISCOURSE UNIT—23:1–25:46 [NAC]. The topic is judgment on the temple but also on the nations.

DISCOURSE UNIT—23:1–24:2 [NICNT]. The topic is Jesus' verdict on Jerusalem and its leadership.

DISCOURSE UNIT—23:1–39 [NIGTC, WBC; NIV]. The topic is Jesus criticizes the scribes and Pharisees [NIGTC], castigation of the scribes and Pharisees [WBC], seven woes [NIV].

DISCOURSE UNIT—23:1–36 [CEV, ESV, NCV, NET, NLT, NRSV]. The topic is Jesus accuses some leaders [NCV], seven woes to the scribes and

Pharisees [ESV], seven woes [NET], Jesus denounces scribes and Pharisees [NRSV], Jesus criticizes the religious leaders [NLT], Jesus condemns the Pharisees and the teachers of the Law of Moses [CEV].

DISCOURSE UNIT—23:1–12 [GW, NASB, TEV]. The topic is Jesus disapproves of the example set by scribes and Pharisees [GW], Jesus warns against the teachers of the Law and the Pharisees [TEV], Pharisaism exposed [NASB].

23:1 **Then Jesus spoke to-the crowds and to-his disciples** **23:2** **saying, "The scribes and the Pharisees sit**[a] **in Moses' seat.** **23:3** **Therefore, do**[b] **and observe**[c] **all they-say to-you, but do- not -do according-to their works, for they-say**[d] **and do- not -do.**

LEXICON—a. aorist act. indic. of καθίζω (LN **37.44**) (BAGD 2.a.α. p. 390): 'to sit down' [BAGD]. The phrase Ἐπὶ τῆς Μωϋσέως καθέδρας ἐκάθισαν 'sit in/on Moses' seat' [BNTC, NIGTC; ESV, KJV, NET, NIV, NRSV], is also translated 'sit upon the seat of Moses' [WBC], 'sit in the chair of Moses' [BECNT, NTC], 'have taken their seat on Moses' chair' [NICNT, PNTC], 'have seated themselves in the chair of Moses' [NASB], 'occupy Moses' seat' [REB], 'are experts in the Law of Moses' [CEV], 'teach with Moses' authority' [GW], 'have the authority to tell you what the law of Moses says' [NCV], '(to be an) authority concerning the Law of Moses' [**LN**], 'are the official interpreters of the law of Moses' [NLT], 'are the authorized interpreters of Moses' law' [TEV]. The idiom ἐπὶ τῆς Μωϋσέως καθέδρας καθίζω 'sit in Moses' seat' means to have the capacity to interpret the Law of Moses with authority [LN].

    b. aorist act. impera. of ποιέω (LN 42.7): 'to do' [BECNT, BNTC, LN, NIGTC, NTC, PNTC, WBC; NASB, NRSV], 'to practice' [NICNT; ESV, NLT], 'to observe' [KJV], 'to obey' [NCV, NIV, TEV], 'to pay attention' [NET], 'to carry out, to perform' [LN]. The phrase 'do and observe' is translated 'obey' [CEV], 'do' [GW], 'be careful to do' [REB]. This verb means to do or perform [LN].

    c. pres. act. impera. of τηρέω (LN 36.19) (BAGD 5. p. 815): 'to observe' [BAGD, BECNT, BNTC, NTC, PNTC; ESV, NASB], 'to do' [KJV, NET, NIV], 'to obey' [LN; NLT], 'to follow' [NCV, NRSV, TEV], 'to keep' [BAGD, NICNT, NIGTC, WBC], 'to keep commandments' [LN]. This verb means to continue to obey orders or commandments [LN].

    d. pres. act. indic. of λέγω (LN 33.69): 'to say' [BNTC, LN, NIGTC, NTC, PNTC, WBC; CEV, KJV, NASB, REB], 'to talk' [BECNT, LN, NICNT], 'to preach' [ESV, GW, NIV, TEV], 'to teach' [NET, NLT, NRSV], 'to tell' [LN; NCV], 'to speak' [LN]. This verb means to speak or talk, with apparent focus upon the content of what is said [LN].

QUESTION—How is this discourse connected with chapter 22?

    It is a continuation of Jesus' comments in the temple [EBC, My, Lns, NAC, NICNT, NTC]. It occurred soon after the discourse recorded in chapter 22 [PNTC].

QUESTION—What does Jesus mean when he says that the scribes and the Pharisees sit in Moses' seat?

He is referring to their function as interpreters and teachers of the Law of Moses [BECNT, My, NIGTC, TH, TRT, WBC]. It refers to their teaching office whereby they taught the law Moses handed down [My, NICNT, PNTC]. Each synagogue had a seat of honor which was assigned to the most prominent scribe in that place and who taught the people what God's will was as revealed to Moses; the scribes and Pharisees fulfilled that function in a more general sense as well [NTC]. Synagogues had a prominent seat at the front in which teachers of the law sat, and functioned as successors to Moses by virtue of their authority to teach the law [BNTC, EBC, NAC, NIBC]. After the time of Jesus synagogues did have a chair referred to as 'Moses' seat,' but it's not known if that was the case in Jesus' day [BECNT].

QUESTION—Does Jesus' statement imply that the scribes and Pharisees legitimately occupy the seat of Moses as interpreters of the law, or that they have taken it upon themselves to be the interpreters of the law?

1. He is saying that they actually do have the authority to interpret the law [BECNT, ICC, NAC, NIBC, NICNT, NIGTC, TH, WBC; BNTC, GW, NCV, NLT, TEV].

2. He is saying that they had put themselves in the position of being the interpreters of the law [Lns, My, PNTC; ESV, NASB]. They were usurpers, having appointed themselves to that function [Lns].

QUESTION—Is Jesus affirming the teaching of the scribes and Pharisees when he said 'practice and observe all they say to you'?

He is not saying they must be obeyed in everything, but they should be obeyed to the extent that they faithfully and truly interpret the law [Lns, NAC, NTC, PNTC, WBC], that is, to the degree that they teach what Moses actually taught [My, NIBC, NIGTC, PNTC]. This is biting sarcasm and irony; he is *not* telling them that they should obey what the Pharisees say so much as he is telling them that they should not follow the example of what they do [EBC, NICNT]. He is affirming that people should obey their teachings, but not follow their example [BECNT, BNTC, ICC, TH]. They were a reliable source of information about what the law actually said, though their interpretation of what it meant was questionable [NIGTC].

23:4 And they-tie-up[a] heavy burdens[b] (that are) hard-to-bear[c] and put (them) on the shoulders of-people, but they are- not -willing to-move[d] them with their finger.

TEXT—Manuscripts reading δυσβάστακτα 'hard to bear' are given a C rating by GNT to indicate that choosing it over variant manuscripts that omit it was difficult. It is omitted by BNTC, NIGTC, NTC; CEV, NASB, NIV, REB. It is included in brackets by WBC.

LEXICON—a. pres. act. indic. of δεσμεύω (LN **18.15**) (BAGD 2. p. 175): 'to tie up' [BAGD, BECNT, NICNT, NTC, PNTC, WBC; ESV, NASB, NET, NIV, NRSV], 'to tie' [LN; TEV], 'to bind' [BNTC, **LN**; KJV], 'to

bind up' [NIGTC], 'to pile' [CEV], 'to make (loads)' [GW, REB]. The
clause δεσμεύουσιν δὲ φορτία...ἐπιτιθέασιν ἐπὶ τοὺς ὤμους τῶν
ἀνθρώπων 'they tie up heavy burdens...and put them on the shoulders of
people' is translated 'they make strict rules and try to force people to obey
them' [NCV], 'they crush people with unbearable religious demands'
[NLT]. This verb means to bind or to tie on [LN].

b. φορτίον (LN 15.208) (BAGD 2. p. 865): 'burden' [BAGD, BECNT,
BNTC, LN, NIGTC, NTC, WBC; CEV, ESV, KJV, NASB, NRSV],
'load' [BAGD, LN, NICNT, PNTC; GW, NET, NIV, REB, TEV]. This
noun denotes a relatively heavy object which is carried [LN].

c. δυσβάστακτος (LN 22.34) (BAGD p. 209): 'hard to bear' [BAGD, LN;
ESV, NRSV], 'hard to carry' [BECNT, PNTC; GW, NET, TEV],
'cumbersome' [NICNT], 'difficult to bear' [WBC], 'grievous to be borne'
[KJV], 'difficult' [LN]. This adjective describes that which is difficult to
bear or endure [LN].

d. aorist act. infin. of κινέω (LN 15.3) (BAGD 1. p. 432): 'to move'
[BAGD, BECNT, BNTC, LN, NICNT, NIGTC, NTC, PNTC, WBC;
ESV, GW, KJV, NASB, NET, NIV, NRSV], 'to help' [CEV], 'to help
carry the load' [TEV], 'to ease the burden' [NLT, REB], 'to remove'
[BAGD, LN]. The clause αὐτοὶ δὲ τῷ δακτύλῳ αὐτῶν οὐ θέλουσιν
κινῆσαι αὐτά 'they are not willing to move them with their finger' is
translated 'they are unwilling to help those who struggle under the weight
of their rules' [NCV]. This verb means to cause something to be moved
from a place [LN].

QUESTION—In what sense did these scribes and Pharisees 'tie up' on the
people 'heavy burdens' that they were not willing to lift?

The Pharisees had interpreted the law of Moses in such a way that it was
extremely burdensome for many people to observe [PNTC, NICNT, TH,
TRT, WBC], but they had devised for themselves many ways of mitigating
the difficult requirements [PNTC]. They had disdain for common people and
did not reach out to them in any way [NICNT]. The Pharisaic legislation was
very difficult for people working in various trades to maintain [NIBC]. The
Pharisaic system was a heavy burden compared to Jesus' teachings [BECNT,
BNTC]. They were not willing to help others fulfill the requirements they
taught concerning how the law should be obeyed [BECNT, My, NAC]. They
did more harm than good through the burdensome rules they created [EBC],
and they were not willing to relax rulings and interpretations they issued
concerning the law must be kept [EBC, NIGTC]. They were not willing
themselves to expend the effort required to fulfill all the requirements that
they expected others to follow [NTC]. They failed to recognize the element
of gospel in the Old Testament scriptures, and dealt with it only as laws; they
were unwilling to expend the effort to fulfill the weightier elements of the
teaching of the Old Testament, and focused instead on more trivial things
[Lns].

23:5 They-do all their works to-be-seen[a] by people; for they-broaden their phylacteries[b] and lengthen (their) tassels,[c] **23:6** and they-love the place-of-honor[d] at feasts and the chief-seats[e] in the synagogues **23:7** and greetings in the marketplaces and to be called 'Rabbi'[f] by people.

LEXICON—a. aorist pass. infin. of θεάομαι (LN 24.14) (BAGD 1.c.β. p. 353): 'to be seen' [BNTC, NIGTC, PNTC, WBC; ESV, KJV, NET, NRSV], 'to be noticed' [BAGD, BECNT, NICNT; NASB], 'to attract attention' [BAGD, NTC; GW], 'to show off' [CEV], 'for show' [NLT, REB], 'for (men) to see' [NIV], 'so that (people) will see them' [NCV, TEV], 'to be observed, to be looked at' [LN]. This verb means to observe something with continuity and attention [LN].

   b. φυλακτήριον (LN **6.195**) (BAGD p. 868): 'phylactery' [BAGD, BECNT, BNTC, LN, NICNT, NTC, PNTC, WBC; ESV, KJV, NASB, NET, NIV, NRSV, REB], 'tepillin' [NIGTC], 'headband' [GW], 'prayer box' [NLT], 'box of Scripture' [NCV], 'straps with Scripture verses on them' [TEV]. The phrase πλατύνουσιν τὰ φυλακτήρια αὐτῶν 'they broaden their phylacteries' is translated 'they even make a big show of wearing Scripture verses on their foreheads and arms' [CEV]. This noun denotes a small leather case containing OT scripture verses and it was worn on the arm and forehead by Jews, especially when praying [LN].

   c. κράσπεδον (LN **6.194**) (BAGD 2. p. 448): 'tassel' [BAGD, BECNT, BNTC, **LN**, NIGTC, NTC, PNTC, WBC; CEV, NASB, NET, NIV, NLT, REB, TEV], 'fringe' [NICNT; ESV, NRSV], 'border' [KJV], 'shawl' [GW], 'special prayer clothes' [NCV]. This noun denotes the tassels which Jews were obliged to wear on the four corners of the outer garment [LN].

   d. πρωτοκλισία (LN **87.18**) (BAGD p. 725): 'place of honor' [BAGD, BECNT, BNTC, LN, NTC; ESV, GW, NASB, NET, NIV, NRSV, REB], 'seat of honor' [WBC], 'best seat' [CEV], 'best place' [**LN**; TEV], 'first place' [NIGTC], 'chief couch' [PNTC], 'most prominent couch' [NICNT], 'most important seat' [NCV], 'at the head table' [NLT], 'uppermost room' [KJV]. This noun denotes a position or place of particular importance that indicates the special status of the person occupying it [LN].

   e. πρωτοκαθεδρία (LN **87.18**) (BAGD p. 725): 'chief seat' [BECNT, NTC, PNTC; KJV, NASB, REB], 'seat of honor' [**LN**; NLT], 'place of honor' [BAGD], 'best seat' [BAGD, BNTC, LN; ESV, NET, NRSV], 'front seat' [CEV, GW], 'important seat' [WBC], 'most important seat' [NCV, NIV], 'prime seat' [NIGTC], 'front seat' [NICNT], 'reserved seat' [TEV]. This noun denotes a position or place of particular importance that indicates the special status of the person occupying it [LN].

   f. ῥαββί (LN **33.246**) (BAGD p. 733): 'rabbi' [BAGD, LN; all translations except CEV, NCV, TEV], 'teacher' [**LN**; CEV, NCV, TEV]. This noun denotes a Jewish teacher and scholar recognized for expertise in interpreting the Jewish Scriptures [LN].

QUESTION—What were the phylacteries?

They were small leather boxes or cases which contained slips of paper that had certain passages from the law written on them as a reminder of God's law [BECNT, BNTC, EBC, Lns, NIGTC, NTC, PNTC]. This was normally only worn at the time of daily prayers, but some people apparently wore them at other times as well [Lns, PNTC]. The command to do this is found in Exodus 13:9, 16 and Deuteronomy 6:8; 11:18 [BNTC, EBC, NAC, TRT, WBC], though these passages were probably metaphorical originally [EBC]. The command to do this was taken figuratively until after the exile, when people began to carry it out literally [NIBC]. These boxes were worn on the arms and the forehead [BECNT, NAC, PNTC]. In some cases the phylacteries were superstitiously regarded as charms that could protect the wearer from danger [NTC] or from evil spirits [My, NTC].

23:8 But you(pl), do- not -be-called 'Rabbi'; for one is your(pl) teacher,[a] and you are all brothers. **23:9** And do- not -call anyone on the earth 'Father', for one is your(pl) Father the-one (in) heaven. **23:10** And do- not -be-called teachers,[b] for one[c] is your(pl) teacher, the Christ, and you are all brothers. **23:11** But the-greatest of-you(pl) shall-be your servant.[d] **23:12** And whoever shall-exalt[e] himself shall-be-humbled[f] and whoever humbles himself shall-be-exalted.

LEXICON—a. διδάσκαλος (LN 33.243): 'teacher' [LN; all versions except KJV, NIV, REB], 'Master' [KJV, NIV], 'rabbi' [REB], 'instructor' [LN]. This noun denotes one who provides instruction [LN].

b. καθηγητής (LN **33.245**) (BAGD p. 389): 'teacher' [BAGD, BECNT, BNTC, **LN**; NET, NIV, NLT, REB], 'instructor' [LN, NICNT, PNTC; ESV, NRSV], 'tutor' [WBC], 'personal tutor' [NIGTC], 'leader' [NTC; CEV, GW, NASB, TEV], 'master' [KJV, NCV]. This noun denotes one who provides instruction and guidance [LN].

c. εἷς (LN 60.10) (BAGD 2.b. p. 231): 'one' [LN], 'single, only one' [BAGD]. The phrase 'one is your teacher' [BECNT, NTC, PNTC; NASB], is also translated 'you have one teacher' [BNTC; ESV, NET, NRSV], 'you have one who is your teacher' [NIGTC], 'there is one who is your teacher' [WBC], 'for you there is just one teacher' [NICNT], 'you have only one teacher' [CEV, GW, NCV, NLT, TEV], 'you have one rabbi' [REB], 'you have only one master' [NIV], 'one is your master' [KJV]. This noun denotes one, in contrast to more than one [LN].

d. διάκονος (LN 35.20) (BAGD 1.a. p. 184): 'servant' [BAGD, LN; all translations]. This noun denotes a person who renders service [LN].

e. fut. act. indic. of ὑψόω (LN 87.20) (BAGD 2. p. 851): 'to exalt' [BAGD, BECNT, BNTC, LN, NIGTC, NTC, PNTC, WBC; ESV, KJV, NASB, NET, NIV, NLT, NRSV, REB], 'to be lifted up' [NICNT], 'to put (yourself) above others' [CEV], 'to honor (yourself)' [GW], 'to make (oneself) great' [NCV, TEV], 'to give high status to' [LN]. This verb means to cause someone to have high status [LN].

f. fut. pass. indic. of ταπεινόω (LN 25.198) (BAGD 2.a. p. 804): 'to be humbled' [BAGD, BECNT, BNTC, NIGTC, NTC, PNTC, WBC; all versions except CEV, KJV, NCV], 'to be made humble' [NCV], 'to be brought low' [NICNT], 'to be put down' [CEV], 'to be abased' [KJV], 'to be put to shame' [LN], 'to be humiliated' [BAGD, LN]. This verb means to cause someone to become disgraced and humiliated, with the implication of embarrassment and shame [LN].

QUESTION—What did 'rabbi' originally mean, and what was the use that Jesus is warning them to avoid?

It originally meant 'my great one' [NAC, NIBC, NICNT, PNTC, TH, TRT, WBC], 'my master' [BECNT, WBC], 'my teacher' [BNTC, EBC, Lns], 'my lord' [NTC]. It could be used to designate a slave's master, or a prince or even a king [PNTC]. Here Jesus is telling them to avoid its use to indicate someone of prominence or rank [NTC, PNTC]. He is telling them not to arrogate authority to themselves or to despise others as knowing nothing [Lns]. This title was probably applied to the scribes [NIGTC].

QUESTION—Who might have been addressed as 'Father'?

This could have been used to refer to a prominent teacher or religious leader of the past [EBC, NAC, NTC, PNTC]. It was used to refer to a respected teacher [ICC, Lns, NICNT, TRT, WBC], or to address a member of the Sanhedrin [NTC].

DISCOURSE UNIT—23:13–39 [GW]. The topic is the hypocrisy of the scribes and Pharisees.

DISCOURSE UNIT—23:13–36 [NASB]. The topic is eight woes.

DISCOURSE UNIT—23:13–28 [TEV]. The topic is Jesus condemns their hypocrisy.

23:13 But woe[a] to-you, scribes and Pharisees, hypocrites,[b] for you-shut[c] the kingdom of-the heavens in-front-of[d] people; for you do- not -enter nor do-you-let those-going-in to-enter.

LEXICON—a. οὐαί (LN 22.9) (BAGD 1.a. p. 591): 'woe' [BAGD, BECNT, BNTC, NICNT, NIGTC, NTC, PNTC, WBC; ESV, KJV, NASB, NET, NIV, NRSV], 'alas' [BAGD; REB], 'disaster, horror' [LN]. This particle is translated 'you are in for trouble' [CEV], 'how horrible it will be for you' [GW], 'how terrible for you' [NCV, TEV], 'what sorrow awaits you' [NLT]. It describes a state of intense hardship or distress [LN].

b. ὑποκριτής (LN 88.228) (BAGD p. 845): 'hypocrite' [BAGD, LN; all translations except CEV], 'show off' [CEV], 'pretender' [BAGD, LN], 'dissembler' [BAGD], 'one who acts hypocritically' [LN]. This noun denotes one who pretends to be other than he really is [LN].

c. pres. act. indic. of κλείω (LN 79.112) (BAGD 2. p. 434): 'to shut' [BAGD, BNTC, LN, NICNT, NIGTC, NTC, WBC; ESV, NIV], 'to shut up' [PNTC; KJV], 'to shut off' [BECNT; NASB], 'to shut the door' [NLT, REB], 'to lock the door' [TEV], 'to lock out' [CEV, GW, NET,

NRSV], 'to close' [BAGD, LN], 'to close the door' [NCV], 'to make shut' [LN]. This verb means to cause something to be shut [LN].

d. ἔμπροσθεν (LN 83.33): 'in front of' [LN], 'before' [LN, PNTC], 'from' [BECNT; NASB], 'against' [BNTC; KJV], 'to' [WBC], 'in the face of' [NIGTC]. The phrase ἔμπροσθεν τῶν ἀνθρώπων 'in front of people' is translated 'in men's faces' [NTC; NIV], 'in people's faces' [ESV, NLT, REB, TEV], 'in other people's faces' [NICNT], not explicit [CEV, GW, NCV, NET, NRSV]. This preposition indicates a position in front of an object, whether animate or inanimate, which is regarded as having a spatial orientation of front and back [LN].

QUESTION—Were the scribes and Pharisees present when Jesus said these things?

1. Here he addresses them directly [EBC, Lns, My, NICNT, NIGTC, PNTC, TH], which indicates that some were in the audience [PNTC]. Some were no doubt coming and going in this public place [EBC]. In this chapter the disciples are in the foreground, the crowds are just a little ways back, and the Pharisees, who had withdrawn (see 22:46), are in the background [My].

2. They had already left, and were no longer present when he said this [BECNT, NAC, NTC]. This was spoken to Jesus' disciples as a warning not to imitate the hypocrisy of the scribes and Pharisees [BECNT]. Since no mention is made of their presence, they are being addressed rhetorically [WBC].

QUESTION—What is Jesus expressing with the word οὐαί 'woe' here?

It expresses strong condemnation [BNTC, EBC, Lns, WBC]. It is a condemnation as well as an expression of his sorrow over the judgment that is going to befall them [BECNT, Lns, NTC, PNTC]. It expresses sorrow as well as warning of punishment [NIBC].

QUESTION—What does the term 'hypocrites' mean here?

They were people who sought human approval more than God's approval [BECNT, ICC, PNTC], who were guilty of religious fraud, outwardly appearing to honor God but who were far from him inwardly, having evil intents and thoughts [BECNT]. They wanted to appear to be something other than what they really were [TH, WBC]. They were deceivers [NTC, TH], actors [Lns]. They deceived themselves as well as others with their religious observances [EBC]. They were self-deceived and had a distorted perspective about what really mattered, focusing primarily on external things [NICNT].

QUESTION—How were these people preventing others from entering the kingdom?

They misled others by their teaching [BNTC, ICC, Lns, NAC, NICNT, TH, TRT, WBC]. They were turning others away from faith in Christ [EBC, My, NTC, PNTC] by trying to discredit him [NIGTC, PNTC]. They set a bad example by not following Christ [BNTC]. They hindered people from entering the kingdom by persecuting those who conveyed its message [ICC].

23:14 [[Omitted]]

TEXT—Manuscripts omitting this verse are given a B rating by GNT to indicate the omission was regarded to be almost certain. A variant reading is 'Woe to you, scribes and Pharisees, hypocrites, because you devour widows' houses, and for a pretense you make long prayers; therefore you will receive greater condemnation' [NASB]. This verse is included only by KJV, and NASB, (which puts the verse in parentheses).

23:15 Woe to-you, scribes and Pharisees, hypocrites, for you-travel-about[a] (on) the sea and dry-land to-make a-single proselyte,[b] and whenever he-becomes (one) you-make him twice the son[c] of-hell[d] as-yourselves.

LEXICON—a. pres. act. indic. of περιάγω (LN **15.23**) (BAGD 2. p. 645): 'to travel about' [BNTC, **LN**, NTC], 'to travel about on' [WBC], 'to travel around on' [NASB], 'to travel over' [BECNT, PNTC; CEV, NIV, REB], 'to travel all over' [NICNT], 'to travel across' [ESV, NCV], 'to cross' [GW, NET, NLT, NRSV], 'to cover' [NIGTC], 'to compass' [KJV], 'to go around, to go about' [BAGD]. The phrase περιάγετε τὴν θάλασσαν καὶ τὴν ξηράν 'you travel about on the sea and dry land' is translated 'you sail the seas and cross whole countries' [TEV]. This verb means to move about from place to place, with significant changes in direction [LN].

　　b. προσήλυτος (LN 11.54) (BAGD p. 715): 'proselyte' [BAGD, BECNT, BNTC, **LN**, NICNT, NIGTC, NTC, PNTC, WBC; ESV, KJV, NASB], 'follower' [CEV, GW], 'person who will change to your ways' [NCV], 'convert' [BAGD; NET, NIV, NLT, NRSV, REB, TEV], 'Jewish convert' [LN]. This noun denotes a Gentile who had converted to Judaism [LN].

　　c. υἱός (LN **9.4**) (BAGD 1.c.δ. p. 834): 'son (of)' [BAGD, BNTC, **LN**, NTC, PNTC; NASB, NIV], 'child (of)' [BECNT, NICNT, NIGTC; ESV, KJV, NET, NLT, NRSV], 'offspring (of)' [WBC], 'fit for' [CEV, GW, NCV, REB], 'deserving of going to (hell)' [TEV]. This noun denotes a person of a class or kind, specified by the following genitive construction [LN].

　　d. γέεννα (LN 1.21) (BAGD p. 153): 'hell' [BAGD, BECNT, LN, NICNT, NTC, PNTC; all versions], 'Gehenna' [BAGD, BNTC, LN, NIGTC, WBC]. This noun denotes a place of punishment for the dead [LN].

QUESTION—Who were the proselytes, and what was the nature of their conversion?

　　These were God-fearing Gentiles who were being urged to convert fully to Judaism [BECNT, ICC, NAC, NICNT, NTC] and follow the traditions of the Pharisees [BECNT, Lns, NTC, WBC]. They were being converted to Pharisaism, not just to Judaism [EBC, PNTC]. These were Gentiles who knew little about Judaism, and who were being converted to the Pharisaic form of Judaism [PNTC].

QUESTION—What does 'son of Hell' mean?
They are bound for hell [My, NIBC, NICNT, NTC, PNTC], fit for hell [CEV, GW, NCV, REB], deserving of going to hell [BNTC, ICC, TH, TRT; TEV], destined for God's judgment [WBC]. This is someone whose entire life and character show that he belongs to hell [Lns]. They, like their teachers, are failing to enter the kingdom of heaven because of their rejection of Jesus [EBC].

23:16 Woe to-you, blind guides,[a] (who) say, 'Whoever would-swear[b] by the temple, it-is nothing;[c] but whoever would-swear by the gold in the temple, he-is-obligated.[d] 23:17 Fools[e] and blind-men, for which is greater, the gold or the temple having-sanctified[f] the gold? 23:18 And (you say), 'Whoever would-swear by the altar, it-is nothing; but whoever would-swear by the gift[g] upon it, he-is-obligated.' 23:19 Blind (men), for which (is) greater, the gift or the altar that sanctifies the gift?**

LEXICON—a. ὁδηγός (LN 36.4) (BAGD 2. p. 553): 'guide' [BAGD, BECNT, BNTC, LN, NICNT, NIGTC, NTC, PNTC; all versions except CEV, NCV], 'leader' [BAGD, LN, WBC]. This word is translated as a phrase: 'you guide the people' [NCV], 'you are supposed to lead others' [CEV]. This noun denotes one who guides or leads [LN].

b. aorist act. subj. of ὀμνύω (LN 33.463) (BAGD p. 566): 'to swear' [BAGD, LN; all translations except GW], 'to swear an oath' [GW], 'to take an oath' [BAGD], 'to make an oath' [LN]. This verb means to affirm the truth of a statement by calling on a divine being to execute sanctions against a person if the statement in question is not true [LN].

c. οὐδέν (LN 92.23) (BAGD 2.b.β. p. 592): 'nothing' [BNTC, LN, NICNT, NIGTC, NTC, PNTC, WBC; ESV, KJV, NASB, REB], 'worthless' [BAGD], 'invalid' [BAGD]. The phrase οὐδέν ἐστιν 'it is nothing' is translated 'it means nothing' [NCV, NET, NLT], 'is bound by nothing' [NET, NRSV], 'he isn't bound by his vow' [TEV], 'is not obligated' [BECNT], 'it does not matter' [CEV], 'doesn't mean a thing' [GW]. This adjective is a negative reference to an entity, event, or state [LN].

d. pres. act. indic. of ὀφείλω (LN 71.25) (BAGD 2.b.α. p. 599): 'to be obligated' [BAGD, BECNT, BNTC; NASB], 'to be bound' [BAGD, NIGTC, PNTC; TEV], 'to be bound by the oath' [NICNT, NTC, WBC; ESV, NET, NIV, NRSV, REB], 'to be binding' [NLT], 'ought, to be under obligation' [LN]. The verb ὀφείλει 'he is obligated' is translated 'it does matter' [CEV], 'must keep his oath' [GW], '(they) must keep that promise' [NCV], '(he) is a debtor' [KJV]. This verb means to be obligatory in view of some moral or legal requirement [LN].

e. μωρός (LN 32.55) (BAGD 1. p. 531): 'fool' [BECNT, LN, NICNT, NTC, PNTC; all versions], 'foolish' [BAGD, BNTC, LN, NIGTC, WBC], 'stupid' [BAGD]. This adjective describes being extremely unwise and foolish [LN].

   f. aorist act. participle of ἁγιάζω (LN 53.44) (BAGD 1. p. 8): 'to sanctify' [BAGD, BECNT, NIGTC, NTC, PNTC, WBC; KJV, NASB, REB], 'to make sacred' [BNTC; CEV, ESV, NET, NIV, NLT, NRSV], 'to give sanctity' [NICNT], 'to make holy' [BAGD; GW, NCV, TEV], 'to consecrate' [BAGD, LN], 'to dedicate to God' [LN]. This verb means to dedicate to the service of deity with full loyalty [LN].

   g. δῶρον (LN 57.84) (BAGD 2. p. 211): 'gift' [BNTC, LN, NIGTC, PNTC, WBC; all versions except NASB, REB], 'sacrifice' [NICNT], 'offering' [NTC; NASB, REB], 'present' [LN]. This noun denotes that which is given or granted [LN].

23:20 Therefore the-one swearing by the altar swears by it and by everything on it; and **23:21** and the-one swearing by the temple swears by it and by the-one dwelling-in[a] it, **23:22** and the-one swearing by heaven swears by the throne of-God and by the-one sitting[b] upon it.

LEXICON—a. pres. act. participle of (LN 85.69) (BAGD 2. p. 424): 'to dwell' [BAGD, BECNT, BNTC, LN, NTC, PNTC, WBC; ESV, KJV, NASB, NET, NIV, NRSV, REB], 'to live' [BAGD, NICNT, LN; CEV, GW, NLT, TEV], 'to inhabit' [NIGTC], 'to reside' [BAGD, LN], not explicit [NCV]. This verb means to live or dwell in a place in an established or settled manner [LN].

   b. pres. mid. or pass. (deponent = act.) participle of κάθημαι (LN 17.12) (BAGD 1.a.α. p. 389): 'to sit' [BAGD, LN; all translations except NRSV], 'to be seated' [LN; NRSV], 'to sit down' [LN]. This verb means to be in a seated position or to take such a position [LN].

23:23 Woe to-you, scribes and Pharisees, hypocrites, for you-tithe[a] the mint[b] and the dill[c] and the cumin[d] and you-have-neglected[e] the weightier[f] (things) of-the law, justice[g] and mercy[h] and faithfulness.[i] It-was-necessary to-do these and- not to-neglect -those.

LEXICON—a. pres. act. indic. of ἀποδεκατόω (LN 57.114) (BAGD 1. p. 89): 'to tithe' [BAGD, BECNT, BNTC, LN, NICNT, NIGTC, NTC, PNTC, WBC; ESV, NASB, NLT, NRSV], 'to pay tithe' [KJV, REB], 'to give God a tenth' [CEV, GW, NCV, TEV], 'to give a tenth' [BAGD, LN; NET, NIV]. This verb means to give a tenth of one's income [LN].

   b. ἡδύοσμον (LN 3.23) (BAGD p. 344): 'mint' [BAGD, LN; all translations except KJV, NLT], 'anise' [KJV]. This and the following two nouns are translated 'the tiniest income from your herb gardens' [NLT]. This noun denotes an herb used for seasoning [LN]. It is a garden plant [BAGD].

   c. ἄνηθον (LN 3.24) (BAGD p. 66): 'dill' [BAGD, LN; all translations except NLT]. This noun denotes an herb used for seasoning [BAGD, LN].

   d. κύμινον (LN 3.25) (BAGD p. 457): 'cumin' [BAGD, LN; all translations except NLT]. This noun denotes an herb used for seasoning [LN].

   e. aorist act. indic. of ἀφίημι (LN 31.63) (BAGD 3.b. p. 126): 'to neglect' [BAGD, NICNT, NTC, PNTC, WBC; CEV, ESV, GW, NASB, NET, NIV, NRSV], 'neglect to obey' [TEV], 'to ignore' [NLT], 'to leave undone' [BNTC], 'to abandon' [BAGD, NIGTC], 'to overlook' [REB], 'to omit' [KJV], 'to not obey' [NCV], 'to refuse to listen to, to reject' [LN]. This verb means to no longer pay attention to previous beliefs [LN].

f. βαρύς (LN **65.55**) (BAGD 2.b. p. 134): 'weighty' [BAGD], 'important' [BAGD, **LN**], 'significant' [LN]. This comparative form is translated 'weightier' [BECNT, NICNT, NIGTC, PNTC, WBC; ESV, KJV, NASB, NRSV, REB], 'more important' [BNTC, NTC; CEV, NET, NIV, NLT], 'most important' [GW], 'really important' [NCV, TEV]. This adjective describes being important in view of substantive character [LN].

g. κρίσις (LN 56.25) (BAGD 3. p. 453): 'justice' [BAGD, LN; all translations except KJV], 'judgment' [KJV], 'fairness' [LN]. This noun denotes the administration of justice [LN].

h. ἔλεος (LN 88.76) (BAGD 1. p. 250): 'mercy' [BAGD, LN; all translations]. This noun denotes the act of showing kindness or concern for someone in serious need [LN].

i. πίστις (LN 31.88) (BAGD 1.a. p. 662): 'faithfulness' [BAGD, BECNT, BNTC, LN, NICNT, NTC, PNTC, WBC; CEV, ESV, GW, NASB, NET, NIV], 'faith' [NIGTC; KJV, NLT, NRSV], 'good faith' [REB], 'being loyal' [NCV], 'honesty' [TEV], 'trustworthiness, dependability' [LN]. This noun denotes the state of being someone in whom complete confidence can be placed [LN].

QUESTION—Is Jesus saying that people should tithe mint, dill, and cumin?

Jesus is not focusing on whether they should or should not tithe these herbs, but on the importance of other things that were being missed [BECNT, BNTC, EBC, NAC, NIBC, NICNT, NIGTC, WBC]. Jesus is saying that people should observe God's ordinances about tithing, which covered only the three main products of grain, wine, and oil [NTC, WBC]. Tithing garden herbs was an invalid man-made extension of God's law, not God's law itself [NTC]. Tithing herbs was going beyond what was commanded in scripture [PNTC, WBC], but Jesus was not objecting to it [Lns, PNTC, WBC]. Jesus did not object to tithing herbs, but that may only be by way of concession, since he was obviously concerned about other, more important things that were being neglected [NICNT]. God wanted the Jewish people to obey the Mosaic law while keeping its priorities in mind [NAC].

QUESTION—What is being referred to by 'straining out the gnat'?

People would strain water or wine in order to remove any tiny insects such as gnats, which were ceremonially unclean, that may have gotten into it [ICC, ns, My, NAC, NIBC, NICNT, NIGTC, PNTC, TH].

23:24 Blind guides, straining-out[a] the gnat[b] but swallowing the camel.

LEXICON—a. pres. act. participle of διϋλίζω (LN **46.17**) (BAGD p. 200): 'to strain out' [BAGD, BECNT, BNTC, LN, NICNT, NIGTC, NTC, PNTC, WBC; CEV, ESV, GW, NASB, NET, NIV, NRSV, TEV], 'to strain at' [KJV], 'to strain off' [REB], 'to strain (water)' [NLT], 'to pick out'

[NCV], 'to filter out' [BAGD, **LN**]. This verb means to filter or strain out substances from a liquid [LN].

  b κώνωψ (LN **4.48**) (BAGD p. 462): 'gnat' [BAGD, BECNT, BNTC, **LN**, NICNT, NIGTC, NTC, PNTC, WBC; ESV, GW, KJV, NASB, NET, NIV, NLT, NRSV], 'fly' [NCV, TEV], 'small fly' [CEV], 'midge' [REB], 'mosquito' [BAGD, LN]. The straining of liquids referred to in Matthew 23:24 is based on the regulations in Leviticus 11, in which the gnat is the smallest of the unclean creatures and the camel the largest [LN].

23:25 Woe to-you, scribes and Pharisees, hypocrites, for you-clean[a] the outside of the cup and dish, but inside they-are-full[b] of greed[c] and self-indulgence.[d] **23:26** Blind Pharisee, first cleanse the inside of-the cup, so-that the outside of-it may- also -become clean.

LEXICON—a. pres. act. indic. of καθαρίζω (LN **79.49**) (BAGD 1.a. p. 387): 'to clean' [BECNT, **LN**, NICNT, NIGTC, NTC, PNTC, NTC, WBC; all versions except CEV, NCV], 'to cleanse' [BAGD, BNTC, LN], 'to wash' [CEV, NCV], 'to purify' [BAGD], 'to make clean' [BAGD, LN]. This verb means to cause something to become clean [LN].

  b. pres. act. indic. of γέμω (LN **59.41**) (BAGD 2. p. 153): 'to be full (of)' [BAGD, BECNT, BNTC, **LN**, NICNT, NIGTC, NTC, PNTC; all versions except CEV], 'to be filled with' [WBC], 'to contain' [LN]. The verb γέμουσιν 'they are full of' is translated 'there is nothing but' [CEV]. This verb means to be full of some substance or objects [LN].

  c. ἁρπαγή (LN **57.237**) (BAGD 2. p. 108): 'greed' [BECNT; CEV, ESV, GW, NET, NIV, NLT, NRSV, REB], 'greediness' [WBC], 'plunder' [BAGD, BNTC, LN], 'violence' [NICNT], 'rapacity' [NIGTC], 'extortion' [NTC; KJV], 'robbery' [PNTC; NASB], 'what has been stolen' [BAGD], 'things you got by cheating others' [NCV], 'what you got by violence' [TEV], 'what has been taken by violence' [**LN**], 'booty' [LN]. This noun denotes that which is taken by force or plundered [LN].

  d. ἀκρασία (LN **88.91**) (BAGD p. 33): 'self-indulgence' [BECNT, BNTC, NIGTC, NTC, WBC; ESV, NASB, NET, NIV, NLT, NRSV, REB], 'greed' [NICNT], 'intemperance' [NTC], 'selfishness' [CEV, TEV], 'uncontrolled desires' [GW], 'pleasing only yourselves' [NCV], 'excess' [KJV], 'lack of self-control, failure to control oneself' [LN]. This noun denotes a failure to exercise self-control [LN].

QUESTION—What is Jesus describing as being full of greed and self-indulgence?

  1. His reference to eating utensils is metaphorical, but then he shifts to talking about the inward character of the people using them [BECNT, EBC, ICC, NIBC, NICNT, NIGTC, TRT, WBC].

  2. Jesus is describing the contents of the eating utensils as being food and drink that were taken by dishonest or violent means [BNTC, LN, Lns, My, NAC, NTC, PNTC, TH; NCV, TEV], and consumed in a manner that lacks self-control [Lns, NTC, PNTC].

QUESTION—Why is 'Pharisee' in the singular in v.26?

It helps to sharpen the focus by picturing one person as representative of all the rest [NICNT]. It enhances the effect of what is saying [EBC, NTC]. He speaks as though addressing a typical Pharisee [PNTC], as though addressing a hypothetical opponent in debate style [WBC]. It is a generic singular [ICC, NIGTC], which better fits with the metaphor of the previous verse [ICC].

QUESTION—What does Jesus mean about making the outside of the cup clean by cleaning the inside?

He is telling them that a person's outward actions change when his innermost character has changed [NICNT, PNTC, TRT]. If the inner character is made right the outward appearances will take care of themselves [NAC]. Inward moral renewal will result in appropriate outward religious observances [EBC]. If a person has inward purity of heart he does not need to be concerned about outward ceremonial purity [NTC]. Inward purity must have priority over external purity [WBC]. He is saying that if the contents of the cup were wrongly acquired, then rectifying that problem would make the cup clean by virtue of no longer containing what was wrongly taken, that is, morally unclean [Lns, My].

23:27 Woe to-you, scribes and Pharisees, hypocrites, for you-are-like whitewashed[a] graves, which outwardly appear beautiful,[b] but inside are-full of-bones of-(the)-dead and all-manner[c] of-uncleanness.[d] **23:28** So also outwardly you appear righteous to people, but inside you-are full of hypocrisy and lawlessness.[e]

LEXICON—a. perf. pass participle of κονιάω (LN **45.12**) (BAGD p. 443): 'to be whitewashed' [BAGD, **LN**; CEV], 'to be painted white' [NCV]. This participle is translated as an adjective: 'whitewashed' [BECNT, BNTC, NICNT, NIGTC, NTC, PNTC, WBC; ESV, GW, NASB, NET, NIV, NLT, NRSV, TEV], 'whited' [KJV], 'covered with whitewash' [REB]. This verb means to apply whitewash to a surface [LN].

b. ὡραῖος (LN **79.10**) (BAGD 2. p. 897): 'beautiful' [BAGD, BECNT, BNTC, **LN**, NIGTC, NTC, PNTC, WBC; all versions except NCV, REB, TEV], 'lovely' [BAGD, LN, NICNT], 'fine' [NCV, REB, TEV]. This adjective describes being beautiful, often with the implication of appropriateness [LN].

c. πᾶς (LN 59.23) (BAGD 1.a.β. p. 631): 'every kind of' [BAGD; GW], 'all sorts of' [BAGD, NICNT, WBC; NLT], 'all kinds of' [NIGTC, NTC; NCV, NRSV], 'all' [BECNT, BNTC, LN, PNTC; ESV, KJV, NASB], 'everything' [NET, NIV], 'every' [LN], not explicit [CEV, REB, TEV]. This adjective describes the totality of any object, mass, collective, or extension [LN].

d. ἀκαθαρσία (LN **79.54**) (BAGD 1. p. 28): 'uncleanness' [BECNT, BNTC, NICNT, NIGTC, PNTC; ESV, KJV, NASB], 'impurity' [BAGD, WBC; GW, NLT], 'filth' [**LN**, NTC; CEV, NRSV], 'corruption' [REB], 'unclean things' [NCV], '(everything) unclean' [NET, NIV], 'decaying corpses' [TEV], 'dirt' [BAGD, LN], 'rubbish' [LN], 'refuse' [BAGD]. This noun denotes any substance which is filthy or dirty [LN].

 e. ἀνομία (LN 88.139) (BAGD 1. p. 71): 'lawlessness' [BAGD, BECNT, BNTC, LN, NICNT, NIGTC, NTC, PNTC; ESV, GW, NASB, NET, NLT, NRSV, REB], 'iniquity' [WBC; KJV], 'evil' [CEV, NCV], 'wickedness' [NIV], 'sins' [TEV], 'lawless living' [LN]. This noun denotes behaving with complete disregard for the laws or regulations of a society [LN].

QUESTION—Why were graves whitewashed?

Around Passover time graves were marked with white limestone so that pilgrims from other places would know that they were graves and would not inadvertently make themselves ceremonially unclean by contact with a corpse [BNTC, EBC, My, Lns, NTC, PNTC, TH, TRT, WBC]. Graves were not always together in one place, they were scattered in various places, so a person may have been unaware that he was becoming ritually impure by coming in contact with a grave [PNTC]. This may refer to the practice of putting plaster on tombs for ornamental purposes [ICC, NIBC], and was done to beautify them [NIGTC].

QUESTION—Why did Jesus consider them to be lawless?

He is saying that inwardly they actually despised God's law [NTC], and were opposed to its true content [Lns]. They contravened God's law [NAC], living in a way that is opposite of a life of obedience [BNTC]. By ignoring such things as justice, mercy, and faithfulness, they were refusing to submit to the real demands of God's law [PNTC]. He is saying that they were filled with iniquity, despite wanting to appear righteous [WBC]. They were unrepentant sinners [TRT]. Their basic approach diverged so far from what Jesus taught that they were, in effect, lawless and wicked [EBC]. They were not sensitive to or obedient to the fundamental will of God [NICNT].

DISCOURSE UNIT—23:29–36 [TEV]. The topic is Jesus predicts their punishment.

23:29 Woe to-you, scribes and Pharisees, hypocrites, for you-build[a] the tombs of-the prophets and decorate[b] the monuments[c] of-the righteous,[d] **23:30** and you-say, 'If we-had-been in the days of our fathers, we-would-not -have-been partners[e] in the blood[f] of the prophets.'

LEXICON—a. pres. act. indic. of οἰκοδομέω (LN 45.1) (BAGD 1.a. p. 558): 'to build' [BAGD, LN; all translations except REB, TEV], 'to build up' [REB], 'to make (fine tombs)' [TEV], 'to construct' [LN], 'to erect' [LN]. This verb means to make or erect any kind of construction [LN].

 b. pres. act. indic. of κοσμέω (LN 79.12) (BAGD 2.a.β. p. 445): 'to decorate' [BAGD, NICNT, LN, NTC, PNTC; CEV, ESV, GW, NET, NIV, NLT, NRSV, TEV], 'to adorn' [BAGD, BECNT, BNTC, LN, NIGTC; NASB], 'to beautify' [BAGD, WBC], 'to show honor (to the

graves)' [NCV], 'to embellish' [REB], 'to garnish' [KJV]. This verb
means to cause something to be beautiful by decorating [LN].

c. μνημεῖον (LN **7.75**, 7.76) (BAGD 2. p. 524): 'monument' [BNTC, LN
(7.76), NTC, PNTC, WBC; ESV, GW, NASB, NLT, REB, TEV], 'grave'
[BAGD, BECNT, **LN** (7.75); NCV, NET, NIV, NRSV], 'grave
monument' [NIGTC], 'tomb' [BAGD, LN (7.75), NICNT; CEV],
'sepulcher' [KJV], 'memorial' [LN (7.76)]. This noun may denote a
construction for the burial of the dead [LN (7.75)], or may denote a
monument built as a memorial to someone who has died and which could
also serve as a tomb for the individual in question [LN].

d. δίκαιος (LN 88.12) (BAGD 1.b. p. 195): 'righteous' [BAGD, LN], 'just'
[BAGD, LN], 'upright' [BAGD]. This adjective describes being in
accordance with what God requires [LN].

e. κοινωνός (LN **34.6**) (BAGD 1.c. p. 440): 'partner' [LN], 'associate'
[LN], 'someone who takes part in something with someone' [BAGD],
'one who joins in with' [**LN**]. This noun denotes one who participates
with another in some enterprise or matter of joint concern [LN].

f. αἷμα (LN **20.83**) (BAGD 2.a. p. 22): 'to kill' [BAGD, LN], 'killing'
[LN], 'to commit murder' [**LN**]. The prepositional phrase ἐν τῷ αἵματι
'in the blood' [KJV], is translated 'in shedding the blood' [BECNT,
BNTC, NIGTC, NTC, PNTC; ESV, NASB, NET, NIV, NRSV], 'in
killing' [NICNT, WBC; CEV, NLT], 'to murder' [GW], 'the murder of'
[REB], '(helped them) kill' [NCV], '(what they did and) killed' [TEV].
This noun denotes the act of depriving a person of life by violent means
[LN].

23:31 So[a] you-testify[b] (against)[c] yourselves that you-are sons of those-
having-murdered the prophets. **23:32** Fill-up[d] then the measure[e] of-your
fathers.

LEXICON—a. ὥστε (LN 89.52) (BAGD 1.a. p. 899): 'so' [BAGD, BECNT,
NICNT, NTC; GW, NASB, NIV, REB, TEV], 'and so' [BNTC, LN], 'so
that' [LN, WBC], 'so then' [LN, PNTC], 'thus' [ESV, NRSV],
'wherefore' [KJV], 'therefore' [BAGD, LN], 'in saying that' [NLT], not
explicit [CEV, NCV, NET]. This conjunction indicates result, often in
contexts implying an intended or indirect purpose [LN].

b. pres. act. indic. of μαρτυρέω (LN 33.262) (BAGD 1.a. p. 492): 'to
testify' [BAGD, BECNT, BNTC, NTC, PNTC; GW, NASB, NET, NIV,
NLTR, NRSV], 'to give proof' [NCV], 'to witness' [LN; ESV], 'to bear
witness' [BAGD, WBC], 'to be a witness' [BAGD; KJV]. The phrase
μαρτυρεῖτε ἑαυτοῖς 'you witness against yourselves' is translated 'you
identify yourselves as' [NICNT], 'you prove that you really are' [CEV],
'you acknowledge that you are' [REB], 'you actually admit that you are'
[TEV]. This verb means to provide information about a person or an event
concerning which the speaker has direct knowledge [LN].

  c. There is no lexical entry in the Greek text for this word, but it is supplied
in translation to indicate the dative case relation of the pronoun ἑαυτοῖς.
This relation is translated 'against' [BECNT, BNTC, NTC, PNTC, WBC;
ESV, GW, NASB, NET, NIV, NLT, NRSV], 'unto' [KJV], not explicit
[NICNT; CEV, NCV, REB, TEV].

  d. aorist act. impera. of πληρόω (LN 59.37) (BAGD 1.a. p. 670): 'to fill up'
[BECNT, BNTC, PNTC; ESV, KJV, NASB, NET, NIV, NRSV], 'to
make full' [NTC], 'to fill' [BAGD, LN], 'to bring to the full' [WBC]. The
phrase πληρώσατε τὸ μέτρον τῶν πατέρων ὑμῶν 'fill up then the
measure of your fathers' is translated 'complete your ancestors' task'
[NICNT], 'complete the sin your ancestors started' [NCV], 'go on then,
finish off what your fathers began' [REB], 'go on then and finish up what
your ancestors started' [TEV], 'go ahead, finish what your ancestors
started' [GW, similarly NLT], 'keep on doing everything they did' [CEV].
This verb means to cause something to become full [LN].

  e. μέτρον (LN 81.1) (BAGD 1.a. p. 515): 'measure' [BAGD, BECNT,
BNTC, LN, PNTC, WBC; ESV, KJV, NET, NRSV], 'measure of sin'
[NIV], 'measure of guilt' [NTC; NASB], not explicit [NICNT; CEV, GW,
NCV, NLT, REB, TEV]. This noun denotes unit of measurement, either
of length or volume [LN].

QUESTION—In what sense were they the sons of those who murdered the
prophets?

  Jesus sees the irony in the fact that they are not just descendants of those
who killed the prophets, but that in their character they are so much like
them [BECNT, EBC, My, TH, TRT, WBC]. They have inherited the evil
nature of their ancestors [ICC, NIBC, NIGTC]. Jesus is saying that, since
they are already planning his murder, who is the greatest prophet of all, they
show themselves to be like their ancestors who killed the earlier prophets
[NTC]. They continued in the sins of their ancestors that the prophets had
denounced, and they paid little attention to righteous people of their own day
such as Jesus and his disciples [PNTC]. They share a corporate responsibility
with their ancestors because they have rejected John and Jesus and will soon
participate in the ultimate rebellion of pressing for Jesus' execution
[NICNT].

QUESTION—In what sense should they 'fill up the measure' of their fathers'?

  He is speaking with bitter irony [ICC, Lns, My, NAC, NICNT, NIGTC,
TRT, WBC], telling them to go ahead and finish the evil they intend to do
[Lns, NAC, TRT]. Jesus is using irony to tell them to go on and keep doing
what they are doing, with the inevitable consequences that will follow
[PNTC]. He is defiantly urging them to complete the evil work of their
ancestors [BNTC]. He is telling them to continue the family tradition of
killing the prophets that their fathers began [NIGTC]. The measure of their
fathers is the full scope of their ancestors' sin and guilt [NTC; NASB, NIV].
When the measure gets to a certain point it overflows and judgment ensues

[EBC, NIBC]. He is emphasizing the certainty of the coming judgment [BECNT, Lns].

23:33 Snakes,[a] offspring[b] of-vipers,[c] how (can)-you-escape[d] the judgment[e] of hell?[f]

LEXICON—a. ὄφις (LN **88.123**) (BAGD 2. p. 600): 'snake' [BAGD, BECNT, **LN**, NICNT, NIGTC, NTC, PNTC; all versions except ESV, KJV, NASB], 'viper' [LN], 'serpent' [BAGD, BNTC, WBC; ESV, KJV, NASB], 'evil person' [LN]. This noun denotes a dangerous and despised person [LN].

b. γέννημα (LN 23.53, 58.26) (BAGD p. 156): 'offspring' [BAGD, BECNT, BNTC, LN (23.53, 58.26), NIGTC, NTC, WBC; NET], 'brood' [LN, NICNT, PNTC; ESV, NASB, NIV, NRSV, REB], 'child' [BAGD, LN (23.53), LN (58.26); CEV, TEV], 'generation' [KJV], 'son of' [LN (58.26); NLT], 'kind of, one who has the characteristics of' [LN (58.26)], not explicit [GW]. The phrase γεννήματα ἐχιδνῶν 'offspring of vipers' is translated 'family of poisonous snakes' [NCV]. This noun denotes that which has been produced or born of a living creature [LN (23.53)]. Or, it may denote a kind or class of persons, with the implication of possessing certain derived characteristics [LN (58.26)].

c. ἔχιδνα (LN **88.123**) (BAGD p. 331): 'viper' [BAGD, BECNT, BNTC, **LN**, NICNT, NIGTC, NTC, PNTC, WBC; ESV, KJV, NASB, NET, NIV, NLT, NRSV, REB], 'snake' [LN; CEV, TEV], 'poisonous snake' [GW, NCV], 'evil person' [LN]. This noun denotes a dangerous and despised person [LN].

d. aorist act. subj. of φεύγω (LN **21.14**) (BAGD 2. p. 855): 'to escape' [BAGD, BECNT, BNTC, **LN**, NICNT, NTC, PNTC, WBC; all versions], 'to flee' [NIGTC], 'to avoid' [LN]. This verb means to become safe from danger by avoiding or escaping [LN].

e. κρίσις (LN **38.1**, 56.30) (BAGD 1.a.β. p. 452): 'judgment' [BECNT, BNTC, NIGTC, WBC; NLT], 'God's judgment' [NCV], 'condemnation' [LN (56.30)], 'damnation' [KJV], 'sentence' [NASB], 'punishment' [**LN** (38.1)]. This noun is translated as a verb: 'being condemned' [NICNT; GW, NET, NIV, REB, TEV], 'being sentenced' [NTC, PNTC; ESV, NRSV], 'going to (hell)' [CEV]. It denotes the act of judging a person to be guilty and liable to punishment [LN (56.30)]. This noun denotes punishment, with the implication of having been judged guilty [LN (38.1)].

f. γέεννα (LN 1.21) (BAGD p. 153): 'hell' [BAGD, BECNT, LN, NICNT, NIGTC, PNTC; all versions except NCV], 'Gehenna' [BAGD, BNTC, LN, NIGTC, WBC], not explicit [NCV]. This noun denotes a place of punishment for the dead [LN].

QUESTION—How are the nouns related in the phrase 'judgment of hell'?

The judgment results in being sent to hell [BECNT, BNTC, EBC, ICC, Lns, My, NAC, NICNT, NTC, PNTC, TH, TRT, WBC; CEV, ESV, GW, NET, NIV, NRSV, REB, TEV].

23:34 Therefore[a] behold,[b] I am-sending to you prophets and wise-men[c] and scribes; (some) of-them you-will-kill and you-will crucify and (some) of-them you-will-scourge[d] in your synagogues and you-will-persecute[e] from city to city.

LEXICON—a. διὰ τοῦτο: 'therefore' [BECNT, BNTC, NTC, PNTC; ESV, NASB, NIV, NLT, NRSV, REB], 'wherefore' [KJV], 'so' [NCV], 'and so' [TEV], 'for this reason' [NIGTC; NET], 'in keeping with this' [WBC], not explicit [NICNT; CEV, GW].

   b. ἰδού (LN 91.13) (BAGD 1.b.δ. p. 371): 'behold' [BAGD, BECNT, BNTC; KJV, NASB], 'look' [BAGD, LN, NICNT, NTC, WBC], 'listen' [LN], not explicit [NIGTC, PNTC; all versions except KJV, NASB]. This particle is a prompter of attention, which serves also to emphasize the following statement [LN].

   c. σοφός (LN 32.35) (BAGD 3. p. 760): 'wise man' [BECNT, BNTC, LN, NICNT, NTC, WBC; all versions except CEV, NRSV], 'wise people' [CEV], 'sage' [NIGTC, PNTC; NRSV], 'one who is wise' [LN], 'wise' [BAGD]. This adjective, used here as a noun, denotes a person of professional or semi-professional status who is regarded as particularly capable in understanding the philosophical aspects of knowledge and experience [LN].

   d. fut. act. indic. of μαστιγόω (LN 19.9) (BAGD 1. p. 495): 'to scourge' [BAGD, BNTC, WBC; KJV, NASB], 'to flog' [BAGD, BECNT, NICNT, NTC, PNTC; ESV, NET, NIV, NRSV, REB], 'to have flogged' [NIGTC], 'to flog with whips' [NLT], 'to beat' [CEV, NCV], 'to whip' [BAGD, LN; GW, TEV], 'to beat with a whip' [LN]. This verb means to beat severely with a whip [LN].

   e. fut. act. indic. of διώκω (LN **15.158**) (BAGD 3. p. 201): 'to persecute' [BECNT, BNTC, NICNT, NIGTC, PNTC, WBC; ESV, GW, KJV, NASB], 'to chase' [CEV, NCV, NLT, TEV], 'to pursue' [LN, NTC; NET, NIV, NRSV], 'to hound' [REB], 'to drive away, to drive out' [BAGD], 'to run after, to chase after' [LN]. This verb means to follow with haste, and presumably with intensity of effort, in order to catch up with, for friendly or hostile purpose [LN].

QUESTION—Who are the prophets and wise men and scribes Jesus will send?

He is referring to his disciples whom he would send out as apostles [BECNT, EBC, Lns, My, NAC, NICNT, NIGTC, NTC, WBC], and to Christian teachers [My, NICNT, NIGTC]. His apostles would fill the role of the Old Testament prophets [My]. These are the leaders of the early church [NIBC]. Jesus is speaking in the place of God the Father, and is predicting the persecution of future teachers and bearers of God's message [PNTC]. These terms refer to all messengers whom God or Jesus sends [ICC].

23:35 So-that[a] upon[b] you will-come all (the) righteous[c] blood[d] having-been-shed on the earth from the blood of righteous Abel to the blood of Zechariah son of-Berechiah, whom you-murdered between the sanctuary[e] and the altar.[f] **23:36** Truly I-say to-you, all these-things will-come upon this generation.

LEXICON—a. ὅπως (LN 89.59) (BAGD 2.a.α. p. 577): 'so that' [BECNT, LN, NICNT, NIGTC, NTC, PNTC, WBC; ESV, NASB, NET, NRSV], 'that' [BNTC; KJV], 'so' [NCV, REB], 'and so' [NIV], 'that's why' [CEV], 'in order that' [BAGD], 'in order to, for the purpose of' [LN], 'as a result' [GW, NLT, TEV]. This conjunction indicates purpose for events and states [LN].

b. ἐπί with accusative (LN **90.17**) (BAGD III.1.b.γ. p. 289): 'upon' [BAGD, BNTC, **LN**, NIGTC, NTC, PNTC; KJV, NASB, NIV, NRSV], 'on' [BAGD, LN; ESV, NET, REB]. The phrase 'upon you' is translated 'that you may bear the responsibility for' [NICNT], 'you will be held guilty for' [CEV, NCV], 'you will be held accountable for' [GW], 'you will be held responsible for' [NLT], 'the punishment...will fall on you' [TEV], 'shall be laid to your account' [WBC]. This preposition indicates the one upon whom responsibility falls [LN].

c. δίκαιος (LN 88.12) (BAGD 4. p. 196): 'righteous' [BAGD, BECNT, BNTC, LN, NICNT, NIGTC, NTC, PNTC; ESV, KJV, NASB, NET, NIV, NRSV], 'innocent' [BAGD, WBC; GW, REB, TEV], 'good' [CEV, NCV], 'godly (people)' [NLT], 'just' [LN]. This adjective describes being in accordance with what God requires [LN].

d. αἷμα (LN **20.84**) (BAGD 2.a. p. 23): 'blood' [BAGD, BECNT, BNTC, NICNT, NIGTC, PNTC, WBC; ESV, KJV, NASB, NET, NIV, NRSV], 'the guilt of all the (righteous/innocent) blood' [NTC; REB], 'blood of those murdered' [GW], 'the murder of every (good) person' [CEV], 'the murder of all (innocent) people' [TEV], 'the murder of all (godly) people' [NLT], 'the death of all the (good) people' [NCV], 'responsibility for someone's death' [**LN**]. The noun αἷμα 'blood' when used with the verb ἐκχύννω 'to shed' is an idiom that means to cause the death of someone by violent means [LN].

e. ναός (LN **7.15**) (BAGD 1.a. p. 533): 'sanctuary' [**LN**, NICNT, NIGTC, NTC, PNTC; ESV, NLT, NRSV, REB], 'temple' [BAGD, BECNT, LN, WBC; CEV, GW, KJV, NASB, NCV, NET, NIV, TEV], 'temple building' [BNTC]. This noun denotes a building in which a deity is worshiped, and in the case of the Temple in Jerusalem, a place where God was also regarded as dwelling [LN].

f. θυσιαστήριον (LN 6.114) (BAGD 1.a. p. 366): 'altar' [BAGD, LN; all translations]. This noun denotes any type of altar or object where gifts may be placed and ritual observances carried out in honor of supernatural beings [LN].

QUESTION—What relationship is indicated by the conjunction ὅπως 'so that'?

1. It indicates purpose [ICC, Lns, My, PNTC, TH, WBC]; this will happen so that you will become guilty of all the blood shed from the beginning.
2. It indicates result [CEV, GW, NLT, TEV]; as a result of this occurring, you will become guilty of all the blood shed from the beginning.

QUESTION—Who is the Zechariah that Jesus is referring to here?

1. This is Zechariah the son of Jehoida, whose murder is recorded in 2 Chronicles 24:20–22 [BECNT, EBC, ICC, Lns, My, NIGTC, NTC, PNTC]. Since in the Hebrew Old Testament Genesis was the first book and 2 Chronicles was the last book, Abel and Zechariah represent all martyrs from the beginning to the end of the Old Testament canon [BECNT, EBC, ICC, Lns, My, NICNT, NIGTC, NTC, PNTC, TH, TRT]. As he was being killed in the temple Zechariah called out for vengeance just as Abel's blood did [ICC, NICNT, NIGTC]. It may be that Zechariah's father actually was Berechiah, and that Jehoida was Zechariah's patronymic or family name, taken from his grandfather, just as was the case with another Zechariah who was the Old Testament prophet, and who was called 'son of Berechiah, son of Iddo' in Zech 1:1, but is called Zechariah 'son of Iddo' in Ezra 6:14 [EBC, PNTC]. Zechariah's father probably had two names, Jehoiada and Berechiah [Lns, TRT]. Since the father of the Zechariah of 2 Chronicles 24 is named as Jehoiada, the discrepancy about his name could be accounted for by the possibility that an unknown copyist inserted the name 'Berechiah' from Zech. 1:1 into early manuscripts of Matthew that are now lost to us [NTC].
2. This is the Zechariah who wrote the prophetic book that bears his name [NAC].

DISCOURSE UNIT—23:37–39 [CEV, NASB, NCV, NET, NLT, NRSV, TEV]. The topic is Jesus feels sorry for Jerusalem [NCV], Jesus grieves over Jerusalem [NLT], Jesus loves Jerusalem [CEV], Jesus' love for Jerusalem [TEV], judgment on Israel [NET], the lament over Jerusalem [NRSV], lament over Jerusalem [NASB].

23:37 Jerusalem, Jerusalem, the-one killing the prophets and stoning those having-been-sent to her, how-often[a] I-wanted[b] to-gather-together[c] your(sg) children,[d] the-way a-hen[e] gathers her chicks[f] under the wings, and you(pl) were- not -willing.[g]

LEXICON—a. ποσάκις (LN 67.14) (BAGD p. 694): 'how often' [BAGD, LN; all translations except CEV, NCV, TEV], 'often' [CEV], 'many times' [NCV], 'how many times' [BAGD; TEV]. This adverb describes number of related points of time, occurring in interrogative or exclamatory contexts [LN].

b. aorist act. indic. of θέλω (LN 25.1) (BAGD 2. p. 355): 'to want' [BAGD, BECNT, LN, NICNT, NIGTC, WBC; CEV, GW, NASB, NCV, NLT, TEV], 'to wish' [BAGD, BNTC, LN], 'to long' [NET, NIV, REB], 'to desire' [LN; NRSV]. This verb is translated 'I would have' [NTC, PNTC; ESV, KJV]. This verb means to desire to have or experience something [LN].

c. aorist act. infin. of ἐπισυνάγω (LN **15.126**) (BAGD p. 301): 'to gather together' [BAGD, BECNT, BNTC, **LN**, NICNT, NTC, PNTC; ESV, GW, KJV, NASB, NET, NIV, NLT, NRSV], 'to gather' [BAGD, WBC; CEV, NCV, REB], 'to gather up' [NIGTC], 'to put (my) arms around' [TEV], 'to cause to come together' [LN]. This verb means to cause to come together to, toward, or at a particular location [LN].

d. τέκνον (LN 11.63) (BAGD 2.f.α. p. 808): 'child' [BAGD], 'person of' [LN]. This plural noun is translated 'children' [all translations except CEV, NCV, TEV], 'people' [CEV, NCV, TEV]. It denotes the inhabitants of a particular place [BAGD, LN].

e. ὄρνις (LN **4.38**) (BAGD p. 582): 'hen' [BAGD, BECNT, BNTC, **LN**, NIGTC, NTC, PNTC; all versions], 'bird' [BAGD, LN, NICNT, WBC]. This noun denotes any kind of bird, wild or domestic [LN].

f. νοσσίον (LN **4.39**) (BAGD p. 543): 'chick' [BECNT, BNTC, NICNT; CEV, GW, NASB, NCV, NET, NIV, NLT, TEV], 'chicken' [PNTC; KJV], 'young bird' [**LN**], 'the young of a bird' [BAGD], 'young' [NIGTC, WBC], 'brood' [NTC; ESV, NRSV, REB]. This noun denotes the young of any bird [LN].

g. aorist act. indic. of θέλω (LN 25.1) (BAGD 2. p. 355): 'to want' [BAGD, LN], 'to wish' [BAGD, LN], 'to desire' [LN]. The phrase οὐκ ἠθελήσατε 'you were not willing' [BECNT, NICNT; GW, NIV, NRSV] is also translated 'you were unwilling' [NASB], 'you did not want it' [NIGTC], 'you refused' [BNTC], 'you would not' [NTC, PNTC; ESV, KJV], 'you would not have it' [WBC], 'you would have none of it' [NET], 'you wouldn't let me' [CEV, NLT, REB, TEV], 'you did not let me' [NCV]. This verb means to desire to have or experience something [LN].

QUESTION—Who is being referred to here as 'Jerusalem'?

He is speaking specifically about the inhabitants of Jerusalem [BNTC, ICC, My, NIBC, NICNT, PNTC, TH, WBC], and especially their leadership [My, WBC], concerning what they had done and would later do [PNTC]. Jerusalem symbolizes the entire nation of Israel [BECNT, EBC, Lns, NTC, TRT], of which Jerusalem was the capital and religious citadel [Lns]. It is a metonymy for the leadership of the nation [NAC].

23:38 Behold, your(pl) house[a] is-being-left to-you(pl) desolate.[b] **23:39** For I-say to-you(pl), you(pl)-will- certainly not[c] -see me from now until you(pl)-say, 'Blessed[d] (is) the-one-coming in (the) name of-(the)-Lord.'"

LEXICON—a. οἶκος (LN 7.2) (BAGD 1.a.γ. p. 560): 'house' [LN; all translations except CEV, REB, TEV], 'temple' [LN; CEV, REB, TEV], 'sanctuary' [LN], 'city' [BAGD]. This noun denotes a building consisting of one or more rooms and normally serving as a dwelling place, but also may include certain public buildings, such as a temple [LN].

b. ἔρημος (LN **85.84**) (BAGD 1.a. p. 309): 'desolate' [BAGD, PNTC, WBC; ESV, KJV, NASB, NET, NIV, NRSV], 'a desolation' [NIGTC], 'abandoned' [BAGD, BECNT, BNTC], 'abandoned and desolate' [NLT], 'abandoned and empty' [TEV], 'abandoned, deserted' [GW], 'deserted' [LN, NICNT; CEV], 'a deserted place' [NTC], 'forsaken by God and laid waste' [REB], 'uninhabited' [**LN**], 'empty' [BAGD], 'completely empty' [NCV]. This adjective describes an absence of residents or inhabitants in a place [LN].

c. οὐ μή: 'certainly not' [NIGTC, NTC], 'not' [BNTC, PNTC; all versions except NLT, TEV], 'never' [BECNT, NICNT; NLT, TEV], 'in no wise' [WBC].

d. perf. pass. participle of εὐλογέω (LN 33.470) (BAGD 2.a. p. 322): 'blessed' [BAGD, LN; all translations except NCV, NLT, TEV], 'to be blessed' [LN]. This participle is translated 'God bless' [NCV, TEV], 'blessings on him' [NLT]. This verb means to ask God to bestow divine favor on, with the implication that the verbal act itself constitutes a significant benefit [LN].

QUESTION—What is the 'house' that is being left desolate?

It is the temple [BECNT, BNTC, ICC, NAC, NIBC, NICNT, NIGTC, TH, TRT; CEV, REB, TEV]. It is the city of Jerusalem [BAGD, Lns, My, NTC, PNTC], which includes the temple [NTC]. The temple and the city of Jerusalem were sometimes referred to interchangeably [ICC]. The city represents all Israel [PNTC]. The temple represents the entire nation [NIBC]. The temple and Jerusalem represent all Israel [BECNT]. It includes the temple, Jerusalem and all Israel [EBC, WBC].

QUESTION—What does it mean that it will be left 'desolate'?

It will be deserted [CEV, GW, NCV], abandoned [NICNT, PNTC, TH, TRT, WBC; NLT, TEV], destroyed [My, NAC, PNTC, TRT, WBC]. God will forsake it and destroy it [REB]. It refers to Jesus' departure [BNTC, ICC, NIBC], particularly in view of the fact that they had turned Jesus away, and were now left to themselves [NIBC]. Jesus' leaving is likened to the cloud of the Shekina glory departing from the temple [ICC].

QUESTION—When would the people bless him as the one coming in the name of the Lord?

Jesus is describing an eschatological reality, not something in the immediate future [BECNT, BNTC, EBC, Lns, My, NAC, NTC, PNTC, WBC]. It represents a great turning in faith to Jesus by Jews at the end of the church age [NAC]. It speaks of the time when Christ will return on clouds of glory [NTC]. He is describing the turning to Jesus by a significant number of Jews that happened during the early period of the church's expansion in the first century [NIGTC]. It is a conditional sentence: they will see him only when they bless him in the name of the Lord [ICC, NICNT]. He is saying that such a welcome and blessing is the only condition on which they would ever be restored to a relationship with him, not that there would definitely be a time when it would actually happen [NICNT].

DISCOURSE UNIT—24:1–26:2 [BECNT]. The topic is discourse 5: judgment of Jerusalem and the coming of Christ.

DISCOURSE UNIT—24:1–26:1 [CC]. The topic is the eschatological discourse.

DISCOURSE UNIT—24:1–25:46 [EBC, NIGTC, PNTC, WBC; REB]. The topic is the shape of the future [NIGTC], the Olivet discourse [EBC, PNTC], the fifth discourse: the destruction of the temple [WBC], warnings about the end [REB].

DISCOURSE UNIT—24:1–51 [NLT]. The topic is Jesus foretells the future.

DISCOURSE UNIT—24:1–35 [ICC; GW, NCV, NIV]. The topic is Jesus teaches his disciples on the Mount of Olives [GW], the temple will be destroyed [NCV], signs of the end of the age [NIV], the end of the ages [ICC].

DISCOURSE UNIT—24:1–14 [NASB]. The topic is signs of Christ's return.

DISCOURSE UNIT—24:1–2 [CEV, ESV, NET, NRSV, TEV]. The topic is Jesus speaks of the destruction of the temple [TEV], Jesus foretells destruction of the temple [ESV], the destruction of the temple foretold [NRSV], the destruction of the temple [NET], the temple will be destroyed [CEV].

`24:1` **And having-come out of the temple Jesus was going away, and his disciples approached to-point-out[a] to-him the buildings[b] of the temple. `24:2` And answering he-said to-them, "You-see all these, (do you) not? Truly I-say to-you, not one stone will be left here upon another which will- not -be thrown-down.[c]"**

LEXICON—a. aorist act. infin. of ἐπιδείκνυμι (LN 24.25) (BAGD 1. p. 291): 'to point out' [BAGD, BECNT, NIGTC; ESV, NASB, NLT, NRSV], 'to proudly point out' [GW], 'to point to' [REB], 'to show' [BAGD, BNTC, LN, PNTC, WBC; KJV, NCV, NET], 'to draw attention to' [NICNT], 'to call attention to' [NTC; NIV, TEV]. The phrase 'to point out to him the buildings' is translated 'look at all these buildings!' [CEV]. This verb means to cause to be seen [LN].

 b. οἰκοδομή (LN 7.1) (BAGD 2.a. p. 559): 'building' [BAGD, LN; all translations], 'structure' [LN]. This noun denotes any type of building or structure which encloses an area, but the area may be open to the sky, as in the case of amphitheaters [LN].

 c. fut. pass. indic. of καταλύω (LN 20.54) (BAGD 1.a. p. 414): 'to be thrown down' [BAGD, BNTC, NTC, PNTC; ESV, KJV, NIV, NRSV, REB, TEV], 'to be thrown down to the ground' [NCV], 'to be torn down' [BECNT, LN; CEV, GW, NASB, NET], 'to be pulled down' [NIGTC], 'to be broken down' [WBC], 'to be demolished' [NICNT], 'to be

completely demolished' [NLT], 'to be destroyed' [LN]. This verb means
to destroy completely by tearing down and dismantling [LN].

QUESTION—What is the significance of Jesus' going away from the temple?
His leaving symbolizes his abandoning the temple [BECNT, NICNT,
PNTC].

QUESTION—What were the disciples pointing out to Jesus?
The noun ἱερός 'temple' refers in this case to the entire area of the temple
complex [BNTC, My, NIBC, NICNT, TH], which includes the porticos,
gates, walls, and buildings [BNTC, My].

DISCOURSE UNIT—24:3–25:46 [NICNT]. The topic is Jesus answers the
question about the parousia and the end of the age.

DISCOURSE UNIT—24:3–14 [CEV, ESV, TEV]. The topic is troubles and
persecutions [TEV], signs of the close of the age [ESV], warning about trouble
[CEV].

DISCOURSE UNIT—24:3–8 [NET, NRSV]. The topic is signs of the end of
the age.

24:3 And he having-sat-down on the Mount of Olives, the disciples came
to-him privately, saying, "Tell us when these-things will-be, and what (will-
be) the sign[a] of-your coming[b] and of-(the)-end[c] of-the age[d]?"

LEXICON—a. σημεῖον (LN **33.477**) (BAGD 1. p. 747): 'sign' [BAGD, **LN**; all
translations except NLT, TEV], 'distinguishing mark, token, indication'
[BAGD]. The phrase 'the sign of your coming' is translated 'what sign
will signal your return' [NLT], 'what will happen to show that it is the
time for your coming?' [TEV]. This noun denotes an event which is
regarded as having some special meaning [LN].

  b. παρουσία (LN **15.86**) (BAGD 2.b.α. p. 630): 'coming' [BAGD, BECNT,
BNTC, **LN**, NIGTC, NTC, PNTC, WBC; all translations except GW,
NCV, NLT], 'visitation' [NICNT], 'advent' [BAGD], 'return' [NLT]. The
phrase τῆς σῆς παρουσίας 'of your coming' is translated 'that you are
coming again' [GW], 'that it is time for you to come again' [NCV]. This
noun denotes the act of coming to be present at a particular place [LN].

  c. τέλος (LN 67.66) (BAGD 1.b. p. 811): 'end' [BAGD, BECNT, BNTC,
LN, NICNT, NTC; all versions except ESV, NCV], 'completion'
[NIGTC], 'consummation' [PNTC, WBC], 'close' [ESV], 'conclusion,
last part' [BAGD]. This noun is translated as a verb infinitive: 'to end'
[NCV]. This noun denotes a point of time marking the end of a duration
[LN].

  d. αἰών (LN 67.143) (BAGD 2.a. p. 27): 'age' [BAGD, BECNT, BNTC,
LN, NICNT, NIGTC, NTC, PNTC, WBC; ESV, NASB, NCV, NET,
NIV, NRSV, REB, TEV], 'world' [CEV, GW, KJV, NLT], 'era' [LN].
This noun denotes a unit of time as a particular stage or period of history
[LN].

QUESTION—How many questions are being asked here by the disciples?

There are only two questions: when will the destruction happen and what will be the sign connected with his coming and the end of the age [BECNT, Lns, My, NAC, NICNT, NIGTC, PNTC, TH, WBC]. The fact that there is one definite article for the two nouns 'coming' and 'end' indicates that those two events were seen as occurring at the same time [BECNT, Lns, My, NIBC, NICNT, PNTC]. The disciples evidently understood the end of the temple to mean the end of the age as well [BECNT, EBC, ICC, My, NICNT, NIGTC, NTC, WBC].

QUESTION—How is the material in this chapter about the destruction of Jerusalem and the end times to be understood?

Although much of this material focuses on the destruction of Jerusalem, it also anticipates the terrible tribulation of the last days [BECNT, EBC, Lns, My, NIBC, NTC, WBC]. Verses 29–31 describe the second coming of Christ [EBC, BECNT, my, NAC, NIBC, NTC, PNTC, WBC].

1. In this discourse Jesus describes tribulation such as will characterize the entire period before the second coming of Christ [BECNT, EBC, ICC, NAC, NIBC, NTC, PNTC, TRT]. This period is described primarily in vv.4–14 [BECNT, PNTC, NIBC, NTC, TH, TRT], or, alternately, in all of vv.4–28 [EBC]. The tribulation of vv.4–14 is especially severe for the first generation of believers, including Jesus' own disciples [PNTC]. (Note that this view allows for a considerable period of time between the immediate distress and the final tribulation of the last days.)

1.a Verses 15–28 describe a great tribulation prior to the second coming, with the destruction of Jerusalem being a foreshadowing of the great tribulation that will come later [NTC].

1.b Verses 15–20 describe the coming destruction of Jerusalem, and vv.21–28 describe a tribulation such as will characterize the entire period before Jesus returns, just as in vv.4–14 [NAC, TRT].

1.c Verses 15–22 describe the coming destruction of Jerusalem, and vv.23–28 describe a tribulation that will characterize the entire period before Jesus returns, just as in vv.4–14 [NIBC].

1.d Verses 4–28 describe tribulation for Jesus' followers such as will characterize the entire period before Jesus returns, with a violent display of judgment early on in the fall of Jerusalem in vv.15–21 [EBC].

1.e Verses 4–28 describe tribulation such as will characterize the entire period before Jesus returns. After the distress connected with the destruction of Jerusalem has come, then the end will come, although that date cannot be known [ICC].

1.f Verses 4–14 are Jesus' stern warning and exhortation for the disciples to remain faithful to their role as disciples; vv.15–28 and 32–35 describe the destruction of Jerusalem, and vv.29–31, 36 describe the second coming, the timing of which only God knows [TH].

2. Verses 4–35 describe the destruction of Jerusalem and the temple within that present generation, and that answers the disciples' first question in v.3. Then the disciples' second question in v.3 about the sign of his coming is answered in vv.36ff, but no one can predict when that sign will appear [NICNT].

3. Christ's coming will immediately follow the destruction of Jerusalem and the temple, and all will occur within the lifespan of the generation then living. Verses 4–14 describe signs of the close of the age; vv.15–28 describe the destruction of Jerusalem and warnings about false Messiahs; and vv.29ff describe Christ's second coming, which will immediately follow the destruction of Jerusalem [My, NIGTC, WBC]. Despite the fact that Jesus did not teach that his second coming was imminent, Matthew and the other disciples understood the destruction of Jerusalem and the temple to be closely tied together. Matthew mistakenly reports that Jesus was describing something that would occur within the time of the generation then living [WBC]. (Note that My and NIGTC assume that Jesus wrongly believed that he would return immediately after the fall of Jerusalem, while WBC assumes that Matthew incorrectly understood what Jesus meant.)

QUESTION—What did the disciples mean when they spoke of the coming of Jesus?

In that day the term 'coming' was used to refer to visits by royalty or important officials and concerned either their 'presence' or 'appearance' [ICC, NIBC, NICNT, NIGTC, NTC, PNTC, TH, WBC]. The term can refer to ones 'presence', 'arrival', or 'coming' [EBC, Lns ,without implying an eschatological or end-time event [EBC]. It can also connote a manifestation or visitation by a divine figure [NICNT, NIGTC].

1. They understood it to mean that he would depart and then return [BECNT, My, NAC, NIBC, NTC], although their understanding of all that meant was incomplete [BECNT].

2. It would be inaccurate to translate παρουσία as 'return' within the context of the disciples' question [ICC, NIGTC, TH], but they did understand it to be an end-time event of some kind [ICC]. In the disciples' thinking it would not be a 'coming' in the same clear sense that ἐρχόμενος 'coming' has in Jesus' reply in v.30 [NIGTC].

24:4 **Answering Jesus said to-them, "Watch-out[a] (that) no-one lead-you(pl) -astray.[b] 24:5 For many will-come in my name, saying, 'I am the Christ!' and they-will-lead-astray many. 24:6 And you-are-about to-hear of wars and rumors[c] of wars. See (that) you-are- not -alarmed.[d] It-is-necessary for (this) to-take-place, but the end is not-yet.**

LEXICON—a. present act. impera. of βλέπω (LN 27.58) (BAGD 6. p. 143): 'to watch out' [NET, NIV, TEV], 'to watch out for' [LN], 'to watch' [BAGD], 'to see to it' [BECNT; NASB], 'to see (that)' [NIGTC; ESV], 'to beware' [BAGD, LN; NRSV], 'to take care (lest/that)' [BNTC, NTC,

PNTC; REB], 'to be careful' [NICNT, WBC; GW, NCV], 'to take heed' [KJV], 'to pay attention to' [LN], not explicit [CEV, NLT]. This verb means to be ready to learn about future dangers or needs, with the implication of preparedness to respond appropriately [LN].

b. aorist act. subj. of πλανάω (LN **31.8**) (BAGD 1.b. p. 665): 'to lead astray' [NIGTC; ESV, NRSV], 'to be led astray' [PNTC], 'to deceive' [BAGD, BECNT, **LN**, NICNT, WBC; GW, KJV, NIV], 'to mislead' [BAGD, BNTC, LN, NTC; NASB, NET, NLT, REB], 'to fool' [CEV, NCV, TEV]. This verb means to cause someone to hold a wrong view and thus be mistaken [LN].

c. ἀκοή (LN 33.213) (BAGD 2.a. p. 31): 'rumor' [BAGD, BECNT, BNTC, NIGTC, NTC, PNTC, WBC; ESV, GW, KJV, NASB, NET, NIV, NRSV, REB], 'a talk about' [NICNT], 'threat' [CEV, NLT], 'story' [NCV], 'report' [BAGD, LN], 'news, information' [LN]. The phrase ἀκούειν πολέμους καὶ ἀκοὰς πολέμων 'hear of wars and rumors of wars' is translated 'hear the noise of battles close by and the news of battles far away' [TEV]. This noun denotes the content of the news which is heard [LN].

d. pres. pass. impera. of θροέομαι (LN 25.262) (BAGD p. 364): 'to be alarmed' [BECNT, NICNT, NIGTC; ESV, GW, NET, NIV, NRSV, REB], 'to be disturbed' [BAGD, NTC], 'to be frightened' [BAGD, BNTC, WBC; NASB], 'to be troubled' [PNTC; KJV, TEV], 'to be afraid' [CEV, NCV], 'to panic' [NLT], 'to be startled' [LN]. This verb means to be in a state of fear associated with surprise [LN].

QUESTION—What is meant by people coming in Jesus' name?

They claim to be the Messiah [BECNT, BNTC, ICC, Lns, NIBC, NIGTC, PNTC, TH, WBC], or possibly even to be Christ himself [EBC, WBC]. They claim to succeed and replace Jesus as the Christ [BNTC], to speak with his authority [NIBC]. This describes would-be liberators who, though not claiming to be Jesus himself, claim the role and title which belong to Jesus [NICNT].

QUESTION—What does 'the end is not yet' mean?

The events Jesus describes do not necessarily indicate that the coming of Christ is imminent or near [BECNT, EBC, NIGTC, PNTC, WBC] or that the end of the world is at hand [TH, TRT]. Such things will occur throughout history, from the first century all the way to the second coming [EBC]. He is referring to the end of Jerusalem and the temple, which would not necessarily be near just because there was news of wars [NICNT].

24:7 For nation will-rise-up[a] against nation, and kingdom against kingdom, and there-will-be famines[b] and earthquakes in-various-places;[c] **24:8** but all these (are) (just)[d] (the) beginning of birth-pains.[e]

TEXT—Manuscripts reading λιμοὶ καὶ σεισμοί 'famines and earthquakes' are given a B rating by GNT to indicate it was regarded to be almost certain.

Manuscripts reading λιμοὶ καὶ λοιμοὶ καὶ σεισμοί 'famines and pestilences and earthquakes' are followed by KJV.

LEXICON—a. fut. pass. indic. of ἐγείρομαι (LN 55.2) (BAGD 2.d. p. 215): 'to rise up' [BECNT, NIGTC, WBC], 'to rise up in arms' [BAGD, LN, NTC; NET], 'to rise' [BNTC; ESV, KJV, NASB, NIV, NRSV], 'to be raised up' [PNTC], 'to fight' [NICNT; GW, NCV, TEV], 'to go to war' [CEV, NLT, REB], 'to make war against [LN]. This verb means to go to war against [LN].

    b. λιμός (LN 23.33) (BAGD 2. p. 475): 'famine' [BAGD, LN; all translations except CEV, NCV], 'hunger' [LN]. The phrase ἔσονται λιμοί 'there will be famines' is translated 'there will be times when there is no food for people to eat' [NCV], 'people will starve to death' [CEV]. This noun denotes a widespread lack of food over a considerable period of time and resulting in hunger for many people [LN].

    c. τόπος (LN 80.1) (BAGD 1.d. p. 822): 'place' [LN], 'region, district' [BAGD]. The phrase κατὰ τόπους 'in various places' [BECNT, NICNT, NTC; GW, ESV, GW, NASB, NET, NIV, NRSV] is also translated 'in some places' [CEV], 'in many places' [PNTC; REB], 'in different places' [NCV], 'in divers places' [KJV], 'from place to place' [NIGTC], 'in place after place' [WBC], 'in many parts of the world' [NLT], 'everywhere' [TEV]. This noun denotes an area of any size, regarded in certain contexts as a point in space [LN].

    d. There is no lexical entry for 'just' in the Greek text, but it is supplied to convey something that is implied. This implied sense is represented in translation as 'just' [BECNT, NICNT; CEV], 'only' [BNTC, NTC; GW, NLT], 'but' [NIGTC; ESV, NRSV], 'merely' [NASB], not explicit [PNTC; KJV, NCV, NET, NIV, REB, TEV].

    e. ὠδίν (LN **24.87**) (BAGD 2.b. p. 895): 'birth pains' [BAGD, BECNT, BNTC, LN (23.54), NTC; ESV, NET, NIV, NLT], 'birth pangs' [PNTC, WBC; NASB, NRSV], 'birth pangs of the new age' [REB], 'labor pains' [NICNT, NIGTC], 'pains of childbirth' [TEV], 'pains' [GW], 'pains when something new is about to be born' [NCV], 'trouble' [CEV], 'sorrows' [KJV], 'great suffering' [**LN** (24.87)], 'great pain' [LN (24.87)]. This noun denotes intense suffering [LN (24.87)], or the pain associated with giving birth [LN (23.54)].

DISCOURSE UNIT—24:9–14 [NET, NRSV]. The topic is the persecution of disciples [NET], persecutions foretold [NRSV].

24:9 "Then they-will-hand- you -over[a] for persecution[b] and they-will-kill you, and you-will-be hated by all the nations[c] because-of my name. **24:10** And then many will-fall-away[d] and they-will-betray[e] one-another and they-will-hate one-another.

LEXICON—a. fut. act. indic. of παραδίδωμι (LN 37.111) (BAGD 1.b. p. 615): 'to hand over' [BAGD, BECNT, BNTC, LN, NICNT, NIGTC, PNTC, WBC; GW, NET, NRSV], 'to arrest (and) hand over' [NCV, TEV], 'to be handed over' [NTC; NIV, REB], 'to turn over to' [BAGD, LN], 'to deliver (someone) up' [ESV, KJV], 'to deliver' [NASB], 'to give (someone) up to' [BAGD], 'to betray' [LN]. The phrase παραδώσουσιν ὑμᾶς 'they will hand you over' is translated 'you will be arrested' [CEV, NLT]. This verb means to deliver a person into the control of someone else, involving either the handing over of a presumably guilty person for punishment by authorities or the handing over of an individual to an enemy who will presumably take undue advantage of the victim [LN].

b. θλῖψις (LN 22.2) (BAGD 1. p. 362): 'persecution' [LN], 'oppression' [BNTC, NIGTC], 'affliction' [BAGD], 'tribulation' [BAGD, BECNT, NTC, WBC; ESV, NASB], 'trouble' [PNTC], 'punishment' [REB], 'trouble and suffering, suffering' [LN]. The phrase εἰς θλῖψιν 'for persecution' is translated 'to be persecuted' [NET, NIV], 'to be ill-treated' [NICNT], 'to be afflicted' [KJV], 'to be hurt' [NCV], 'to be tortured' [NRSV], 'to be punished' [TEV], 'to those who will torture you' [GW], 'you will be persecuted' [NLT], '(you will be...) punished' [CEV]. This noun denotes trouble involving direct suffering [LN].

c. τὰ ἔθνη (plural only) (LN 11.37): 'nations, people' [LN (11.55)], 'heathen, pagans' [LN (11.37)]. The phrase πάντων τῶν ἐθνῶν 'all nations' [BECNT; ESV, GW, KJV, NASB, NIV, NRSV, REB] is also translated 'all the nations' [BNTC, NICNT, NIGTC, NTC, PNTC, WBC; NET], 'people of all nations' [CEV], 'people' [NCV], 'all over the world' [NLT], 'everyone' [TEV]. This noun denotes the largest unit into which the people of the world are divided on the basis of their constituting a socio-political community [LN (11.55)]. It may also denote those who do not belong to the Jewish or Christian faith [LN (11.37)].

d. fut. pass. indic. of σκανδαλίζομαι (LN 31.77) (BAGD 1.a. p. 752): 'to fall away' [BAGD, BECNT, NTC, WBC; ESV, NASB, NRSV], 'to fall from faith' [REB], 'to be caused to fall' [BAGD], 'to be caused to stumble' [NICNT, NIGTC], 'to be tempted to sin' [BNTC], 'to be led into sin' [NET], 'to be entrapped' [PNTC], 'to give up' [CEV], 'to give up (one's) faith' [TEV], 'to lose faith' [GW, NCV], 'to be offended' [KJV], 'to turn away from the faith' [NIV], 'to turn away from Christ' [NLT], 'to cease believing, to give up believing' [LN]. This verb means to give up believing what is right and let oneself believe what is false [LN].

e. fut. act. indic. of παραδίδωμι (LN 37.111) (BAGD 1.b. p. 614): 'to betray' [BAGD, BECNT, BNTC, LN, NICNT, NTC, WBC; all versions except NCV], 'to hand (someone) over' [BAGD, LN, NIGTC, PNTC], 'to turn over to' [BAGD, LN], 'to turn against (someone)' [NCV]. This verb means to deliver a person into the control of someone else, involving either the handing over of a presumably guilty person for punishment by the authorities, or the handing over of an individual to an enemy who will take undue advantage of the victim [LN].

QUESTION—What relationship is indicated by 'then' in v.9 and 'and then' in v.10?

It refers to the time throughout history in which Christ's followers will be persecuted; there is no suggestion of a sequence between what is described in the previous two verses and what is describe in v.9 [EBC]. It refers to a time near the end of the age when these troubles, called 'birth pangs' begin to become especially intense [Lns]. In v.9 it indicates something additional that begins during the time of what is described as occurring in vv.7–8. Then in v.10 it indicates a chronological sequence, but also a logical connection, in that what is described follows naturally as a result of what has just been described [NIGTC]. It refers to Jewish persecution of Christians prior to the time of the destruction of Jerusalem [NICNT]. It points generally to the time of messianic 'birth pangs' prior to the end, which is described in v.8 [WBC].

QUESTION—What does 'because of my name' mean?

They will be hated because they are his disciples and are governed by their loyalty to him [BNTC, TH], because they bear the name 'Christian' [PNTC], because of their vital connection with Christ [NTC]. The name represents him as a person and all he stands for, particularly as is made known in the gospel [Lns].

24:11 **And many false-prophets will-arise**[a] **and will-lead- many -astray.**
24:12 **And because lawlessness**[b] **will-be-increased, the love of-many will-grow-cold.**[c]

LEXICON—a. fut. pass. indic. of ἐγείρω (LN 13.83) (BAGD 2.e. p. 215): 'to rise up' [BECNT], 'to arise' [BNTC, NICNT, NIGTC, NTC, PNTC, WBC; ESV, KJV, NASB, NRSV, REB], 'to be raised up' [LN], 'to come' [CEV, NCV], 'to appear' [BAGD; GW, NET, NIV, NLT, TEV]. This verb means to cause to come into existence [LN].

b. ἀνομία (LN 88.139) (BAGD 1. p. 72): 'lawlessness' [BAGD, BECNT, BNTC, LN, NICNT, NIGTC, NTC, PNTC; ESV, GW, NASB, NET, NRSV, REB], 'iniquity' [WBC; KJV], 'wickedness' [NIV], 'evil' [TEV], 'lawless living' [LN]. The phrase πληθυνθῆναι τὴν ἀνομίαν 'lawlessness will be increased' is translated 'evil will spread' [CEV], 'there will be more and more evil in the world' [NCV], 'sin will be rampant everywhere' [NLT]. This verb means to behave with complete disregard for the laws or regulations of a society [LN].

c. fut. pass. indic. of ψύχομαι (LN 78.39) (BAGD p. 894): 'to grow cold' [BAGD, BECNT, BNTC, NTC, PNTC, WBC; all versions except CEV, KJV, NCV], 'to become cold' [BAGD, LN, NICNT], 'to wax cold' [KJV], 'to diminish greatly' [**LN**], 'to be snuffed out' [NIGTC], 'to be extinguished' [BAGD]. The phrase ψυγήσεται ἡ ἀγάπη τῶν πολλῶν 'the love of many will grow cold' is translated '(cause) many people to stop loving others' [CEV], 'people will stop showing their love for each other' [NCV]. This verb means to diminish significantly in intensity [LN].

QUESTION—What does it mean for love to grow cold?

This describes professing Christians falling away from the faith [BECNT, ICC, Lns, NAC, NICNT, NIGTC], and as they become more and more lawless their love and concern for others, especially believers, will wane [BECNT, ICC]. It means that some will desert the Christian fellowship [BNTC]. Lawlessness is a lifestyle outside of the law of God, which can characterize even scrupulous people whose love for God and others has grown cold [NICNT]. It means that there will be general lawlessness, in which lawless people will be concerned only for themselves and have no regard for others [BECNT, PNTC]. Because of the spread of evil many people will no longer love other people [TH; CEV, NCV].

24:13 "But the one-having-endured[a] to (the) end will-be-saved. **24:14** And this good-news[b] of-the kingdom will-be-proclaimed[c] in all the world as a-testimony[d] to-all the nations; and then the end[e] will-come.

LEXICON—a. aorist act. participle of ὑπομένω (LN 25.175) (BAGD 2. p. 845): 'to endure' [BECNT, BNTC, LN, NIGTC, NTC, PNTC, WBC; ESV, GW, KJV, NASB, NET, NLT, NRSV, REB], 'to remain faithful' [NICNT], 'to continue to be faithful' [CEV], 'to keep one's faith' [NCV], 'to stand firm' [NIV], 'to hold out' [TEV], 'to bear up, to demonstrate endurance, to put up with' [LN]. This verb means to continue to bear up despite difficulty and suffering [LN].

b. εὐαγγέλιον (LN 33.217) (BAGD 1.c, 2.b.α. p. 316): 'the good news' [BAGD, LN, NICNT, WBC; CEV, GW, NCV, NLT, NRSV, TEV], 'the gospel' [BAGD, BECNT, BNTC, LN, NIGTC, NTC, PNTC; ESV, KJV, NASB, NET, NIV, REB]. This noun denotes the content of good news (in the NT a reference to the gospel about Jesus) [LN].

c. fut. pass. indic. of κηρύσσω (LN 33.256) (BAGD 2.b.β. p. 431): 'to be preached' [BECNT, BNTC, LN, NTC, WBC; CEV, KJV, NASB, NCV, NET, NIV, NLT, TEV], 'to be proclaimed' [NICNT, NIGTC, PNTC; ESV, NRSV, REB], 'to be spread' [GW], 'to be proclaimed aloud' [BAGD]. This verb means to publicly announce religious truths and principles while urging acceptance and compliance [LN].

d. μαρτυρία (LN 33.262) (BAGD 1.a. p. 494): 'testimony' [BAGD, BECNT, BNTC, NIGTC, NTC, PNTC; ESV, GW, NASB, NET, NIV, NRSV, REB], 'witness' [LN, NICNT, WBC; KJV, TEV], not explicit [NCV]. The phrase εἰς μαρτύριον 'as a witness' is translated '(has been) told' [CEV], 'will hear it' [NLT]. This noun denotes the act of providing information about a person or an event concerning which the speaker has direct knowledge [LN].

e. τέλος (LN **67.66**) (BAGD 1.b. p. 811): 'end' [BAGD, LN; all translations], 'close, conclusion' [BAGD]. This noun denotes a point of time marking the end of a duration [LN].

QUESTION—To what does 'the end' refer in v.13?

For the individual believer it refers to the end of one's life [EBC, Lns], and for the church it refers to the end of the age [EBC]. Here it means that believers must endure for as long as is necessary [NICNT, NIGTC]. Tribulation will have to be endured until the end of the age [NIGTC, WBC].

QUESTION—Does the noun 'testimony' have a positive or a negative connotation?

It has a positive connotation in that all nations shall hear the truth of the gospel [NIBC, NICNT, NIGTC, PNTC, TRT, WBC]. It is a testimony or witness intended to be accepted as truth, but when rejected is a testimony against the person who rejects it [Lns]. It has both positive and negative connotations [EBC, ICC, Lns].

DISCOURSE UNIT—24:15–28 [CEV, ESV, NASB, NET, NRSV, TEV]. The topic is the awful horror [TEV], the horrible thing [CEV], the abomination of desolation [ESV, NET], the desolating sacrilege [NRSV], perilous times [NASB].

24:15 "So when you-see the abomination[a] of-desolation[b] which was-spoken-of by the prophet Daniel standing in (the) holy place (let- the reader -understand), **24:16** then those in Judea let-them-flee to the mountains,

LEXICON—a. βδέλυγμα (LN 25.187, **53.38**) (BAGD 3. p. 138): 'abomination' [BAGD, BNTC, **LN** (53.38), PNTC, WBC; ESV, KJV, NASB, NET, NIV, REB], 'sacrilege' [BECNT, NIGTC, NTC; NRSV], 'sacrilegious object' [NLT], 'pollution' [NICNT], 'terror' [NCV], 'horror' [TEV], 'horrible thing' [CEV], 'disgusting thing' [GW], 'detestable thing' [BAGD], 'what is detestable, what is abhorrent' [LN (25.187)]. This noun denotes that which is utterly detestable and abhorrent [LN (25.187)], or in a specifically religious context, an abomination (either an object or an event) which defiles a holy place and thus causes it to be abandoned and left desolate [**LN** (53.38)].

b. ἐρήμωσις (LN **53.38**) (BAGD p. 309): 'desolation' [PNTC, WBC; ESV, KJV, NASB, NET, REB], 'devastation, destruction, depopulation' [BAGD], 'that which desolates or defiles' [**LN**], 'that causes desolation' [NIV], 'that causes desecration' [NLT], 'desolating' [BECNT, BNTC, NIGTC, NTC; NRSV], 'devastating' [NICNT], 'destroying' [NCV], 'awful' [TEV], not explicit [CEV, GW].

QUESTION—Does the section beginning in v.15 and going through v.21 (or v.22) describe the great tribulation before the coming of the anti-Christ, or only the fall of Jerusalem in the first century?

It focuses on the period around the time of the fall of Jerusalem [EBC, Lns, NICNT, NIGTC, PNTC, TRT, WBC]. It describes both periods; the destruction of Jerusalem was a foretaste of the horrors of the future end times [BECNT, NTC]. The destruction of Jerusalem is a type or foreshadowing of the end of the world [Lns].

QUESTION—What relationship is indicated by οὖν 'so'?

It indicates instructions by Jesus about the coming destruction of Jerusalem, but which are drawn as an inference from his description of the tribulations that will come at the end of the world [Lns]. It indicates an inference to be drawn from the statement 'then the end will come' in the previous verse [NICNT]. It indicates a further instruction to them concerning what he has told them in v.2 about the destruction of the temple, and answers the question raised by the disciples about that in v.3 [NIGTC]. It simply indicates a transition and has little or no inferential force [EBC].

QUESTION—How are the nouns related in the genitive phrase 'abomination of desolation'?

The sacrilege makes desolate or causes desolation [BECNT, BNTC, EBC, ICC, **LN**, Lns, NIGTC, NTC, PNTC, TRT, WBC; NIV, NRSV], it devastates or destroys [NICNT; GW, NCV]. It is a sacrilege that causes desecration [Lns, TH; NLT]. It also causes a sense of horror [ICC].

QUESTION—What is the abomination of desolation?

It refers to a blasphemous invader who would come and destroy the temple [BNTC], or who would defile the temple [NICNT, PNTC, WBC]. It was the desecration of the temple, prior to the siege by the Roman general Titus, in which Jewish Zealots and Idumeans slaughtered 8,500 victims there [Lns]. The act of sacrilege would be a warning sign to people that disaster will soon occur [NICNT].

QUESTION—What is the 'holy place'?

It is the temple [BNTC, Lns, NICNT, NIGTC, PNTC, TH, WBC].

QUESTION—What does the parenthetical comment 'let the reader understand' mean?

1. It is spoken by Jesus, and is telling anyone who reads Daniel 9:27 and 12:11 to recognize that what Daniel spoke of would appear soon [EBC, ICC, Lns, PNTC].

2. It is a parenthetical comment inserted by the author of the gospel [NIBC, NICNT, NIGTC, WBC; NCV, NLT, TEV]. It refers to anyone reading the Daniel passage [NIGTC, WBC]. It could refer to the reader of the Daniel passage [NICNT], or to the reader of the gospel account [NICNT, WBC].

24:17 the-one on the housetop[a] must- not -go-down to-carry-away[b] the-things from his house; **24:18** and the-one in-the field must- not -turn-back to-carry-away his cloak. **24:19** Woe to-those (who are) pregnant and to-those nursing (infants) in those days! **24:20** And pray that your flight may-not -be in-winter or on-a-sabbath. **24:21** For then there-will-be great tribulation,[c] such-as has- not -been from (the) beginning (of-the) world until now, no, and-never will-be.

LEXICON—a. δῶμα (LN **7.51**) (BAGD p. 210): 'housetop' [BAGD, BECNT, BNTC, LN, NTC, PNTC; ESV, KJV, NASB, NRSV], 'roof' [BAGD, NICNT; GW, NET, REB], 'rooftop' [NIGTC, WBC], 'roof of a house'

[CEV, NCV, NIV, TEV], 'deck of a roof' [NLT], 'the top of the house'
[**LN**]. This noun denotes the area on the top of a flat-roof house [LN].

b. aorist act. infin. of αἴρω (LN 15.203) (BAGD 3. p. 24): 'to carry (away)'
[BAGD, LN], 'to get' [BECNT, NTC; CEV, GW, NASB, NCV, TEV],
'to take' [NICNT, WBC; ESV, KJV, NET, NIV, NRSV], 'to pick up'
[BNTC], 'to fetch' [PNTC; REB], 'to remove' [BAGD, LN], 'to carry off,
to take (away)' [LN]. The phrase ἆραι τὰ ἐκ τῆς οἰκίας αὐτοῦ 'to carry
away the things from his house' is translated 'to pack' [NLT]. This verb
means to lift up and carry (away) [LN].

c. θλῖψις (LN **22.2**) (BAGD 1. p. 362): 'tribulation' [BAGD, BECNT,
BNTC, NTC, WBC; ESV, KJV, NASB], 'distress' [NICNT, PNTC; NIV,
REB], 'oppression' [NIGTC], 'suffering' [**LN**; CEV, NET, NRSV],
'misery' [GW], 'anguish' [NLT], 'trouble' [NCV, TEV], 'trouble and
suffering, persecution' [LN], 'oppression, affliction' [BAGD]. This noun
denotes trouble involving direct suffering [LN].

QUESTION—What is the meaning of οὐαὶ 'woe' in this passage?

Jesus is expressing his compassion and sorrow for what will happen to them
[BNTC, EBC, Lns, NICNT, NIGTC, NTC, WBC].

QUESTION—What would be problematic about traveling on the Sabbath?

Such travel would require breaking the Sabbath [BNTC, ICC, NIBC,
NIGTC, PNTC, TH, TRT, WBC]. Few people would be willing to help, and
some may try to prevent others from traveling further than the distance
allowed for a Sabbath [EBC, Lns, PNTC]. On the Sabbath it would be
difficult to buy needed supplies or to leave a walled city [BECNT].

QUESTION—What relationship is indicated by γάρ 'for' in v.21?

It indicates the reason for the fleeing urged in vv.17–20, which is that there
will be terrible suffering [BECNT, EBC, Lns, WBC].

QUESTION—What period of tribulation is he describing here?

It refers to the destruction of Jerusalem, and all the horrendous suffering and
carnage that happened then [EBC, Lns, NIBC, NICNT, NIGTC, PNTC]. It
describes the destruction of Jerusalem, but will also reflect the horrors of the
last days [BECNT, WBC]. Beginning in v.21 he has shifted to describing a
period of terrible suffering that will occur just before his return [NTC].

24:22 "And if those days had- not -been-shortened,[a] no flesh[b] would-be-
saved; but for-the-sake-of the elect[c] those days will-be-cut-short. **24:23**
Then if anyone says to-you, 'Look! Here (is) the Christ[d]!' or 'There (he is)!'
do- not -believe (it).

LEXICON—a. aorist pass. indic. of κολοβόω (LN **59.71**) (BAGD 2. p. 442):
'to be shortened' [BAGD, BNTC, **LN**, NIGTC, PNTC; KJV, NLT], 'to be
cut short' [BECNT, NICNT, NTC, WBC; ESV, NASB, NET, NIV,
NRSV, REB], 'to make short' [NCV], 'to reduce the number' [GW], 'to
reduce the number of days' [TEV], 'to be decreased, to be reduced in
number' [LN]. This passive verb is translated as active: 'to make shorter'

[CEV]. This verb means to cause something to be reduced in number or extent [LN].

b. σάρξ (LN 9.11) (BAGD 3. p. 743): 'people, human being' [LN]. This noun denotes humans as physical beings [LN]. The phrase οὐκ...πᾶσα σάρξ 'no flesh' [KJV] is also translated 'no one of all flesh' [NIGTC], 'no one' [BECNT, BNTC, NTC, PNTC; CEV, GW, NCV, NET, NIV, NRSV], 'nobody' [BAGD; TEV], 'nobody at all' [NICNT], 'no person' [BAGD], 'not a single person' [NLT], 'no human being' [WBC; ESV], 'no living thing' [REB], 'no life' [NASB].

c. ἐκλεκτός (LN 30.93): 'elect' [BECNT, BNTC, NIGTC, NTC, PNTC, WBC; ESV, KJV, NASB, NET, NIV, NRSV], 'chosen people' [NICNT], 'God's chosen ones' [CEV, NLT], 'God's chosen' [REB], 'the people he has chosen' [NCV], 'his chosen people' [TEV], 'those whom God has chosen' [GW], 'chosen' [LN]. This adjective (used pronominally here) describes that which has been chosen [LN].

d. Χριστός (LN 53.82) (BAGD 1. p. 887): 'the Christ' [BAGD, BNTC, LN, NIGTC, NTC, WBC; ESV, KJV, NASB, NCV, NET, NIV], 'the Messiah' [BAGD, BECNT, LN, NICNT, PNTC; CEV, GW, NLT, NRSV, REB, TEV]. In the NT this noun is used as a title for Jesus as the Messiah [LN].

QUESTION—To whom does οὐκ πᾶσα σάρξ 'no flesh' refer?

It refers to all believers [NAC]. It refers to the whole Jewish nation [Lns]. It refers primarily to believers, but includes others in the city who by God's mercy would be spared along with believers [NIGTC]. It refers to all people [TRT].

QUESTION—What period of time is described by 'those days'?

1. 'Those days' refers to the period from 66 AD to 70 AD, which resulted in the destruction of Jerusalem [Lns, NICNT, NIGTC, WBC].

2. 'Those days' refers to the destruction of Jerusalem, but ultimately also applies to the period of intense distress before Christ's return [BECNT].

3. 'Those days' refers to all Jesus says in vv.4–28 describing a general period of distress that stretches throughout the church age, of which vv.15–21 (describing the destruction of Jerusalem) are but one part. 'No flesh' describes all of humanity and 'the elect' describes all true believers [EBC, PNTC].

QUESTION—Does 'saved' refer to physical survival or spiritual salvation?

It refers to physical survival [Lns, NAC, NICNT, NIGTC, PNTC, TH, TRT, WBC], particularly of believers [NAC, NICNT], but also to spiritual survival [NICNT]. It refers to the survival of the Jews, who remain as a symbol of what it means to be sovereignly chosen by God [Lns].

QUESTION—What relationship is indicated by τότε 'then' in v.23?

1. It is temporal [ICC, Lns, NICNT, NIGTC, PNTC, TRT]. It indicates a period of time during the period of tribulation when Jerusalem was to be besieged [ICC, Lns, NICNT, NIGTC]. It refers to a time after that period

of intense tribulation, though not necessarily immediately after; it may be that a considerable period of time follows [PNTC].

2. It indicates a logical conclusion to be drawn from previous warnings; because these things are so, don't let anyone deceive you [NAC].

24:24 **For false-Christs and false-prophets will-arise and will-perform great signs[a] and wonders[b] so-as-to[c] lead-astray, if possible, even the elect. 24:25 Behold, I-have-told- you -beforehand.[d]**

LEXICON—a. σημεῖον (LN 33.477) (BAGD 2.b. p. 748): 'sign' [BAGD, BECNT, BNTC, LN, NICNT, NIGTC, NTC, PNTC, WBC; ESV, KJV, NASB, NET, NIV, NLT, NRSV, REB], 'spectacular, miraculous sign' [GW], 'wonder' [BAGD; NCV], 'miracle' [BAGD; CEV, TEV]. This noun denotes an event which is regarded as having some special meaning [LN].

b. τέρας (LN 33.480): 'wonder' [BECNT, BNTC, NICNT, NIGTC, PNTC, WBC; ESV, KJV, NASB, NET, NLT, REB, TEV], 'wonderful thing' [GW], 'miracle' [NTC; NCV, NIV], 'sign' [LN; CEV], 'omen' [NRSV], 'portent' [LN]. This adjective describes an unusual sign, especially one in the heavens, serving to foretell impending events [LN].

c. ὥστε (LN 89.61) (BAGD 2.a.β. p. 900): 'so as to' [BNTC, NICNT, NIGTC, NTC, PNTC; ESV, NASB, NLT], 'so that' [BAGD, LN, WBC], 'insomuch that' [KJV], 'in order to' [LN; TEV]. Purpose is indicated by translating this conjunction as a finite verb: 'They will try' [CEV, NCV]. This conjunction is also translated as a simple infinitive: 'to (deceive, lead astray, etc.)' [BECNT; GW, NET, NIV, NRSV, REB]. This conjunction indicates purpose, with the implication that what has preceded serves as a means [LN].

d. perf. act. indic. of προλέγω (LN 33.281, 33.423) (BAGD 1. p. 704): 'to tell beforehand' [BAGD, BNTC; ESV, NRSV], 'to tell before' [KJV], 'to tell ahead of time' [BECNT, LN (33.281), NIGTC, NTC; NET, NIV], 'to tell in advance' [WBC; NASB], 'to foretell' [BAGD, PNTC], 'to tell something before it happens' [GW], 'to predict' [LN (33.281)], 'to forewarn' [NICNT; REB], 'to warn ahead of time' [CEV], 'to warn before it happens' [NCV], 'to warn' [LN (33.423)]. This verb means to say in advance what is going to happen [LN (33.281)], or it can mean to tell someone that some future happening is dangerous and may lead to serious consequences [LN (33.423)].

QUESTION—Does 'so as to lead astray' indicate purpose or result?

It indicates the intended purpose of the would-be deceivers [EBC, Lns, NTC, PNTC, TH, WBC; CEV, NCV], though not the result [EBC, Lns, NTC, PNTC, WBC].

QUESTION—Is he saying that it is not possible to lead the elect astray?

God will protect them from being deceived [Lns, PNTC, WBC]. Though it is unlikely that they would be led astray, they are not immune to deception [NAC, NICNT]; however, God will ultimately keep them from outright apostasy [NAC] because they will have the spiritual resources to resist being deceived [NICNT].

24:26 "So if they-say to-you, 'Look! He-is in the wilderness,[a]' do- not -go-out. (Or) 'Look! (He is) in the inner-rooms,[b]' do- not -believe (it). **24:27** For as the lightning comes from (the) east and flashes as-far-as (the) west, so will-be the coming of-the Son of-Man. **24:28** Wherever the corpse is, there the vultures[c] will-gather.

LEXICON—a. ἔρημος (LN 1.86) (BAGD 2. p. 309): 'wilderness' [BAGD, BECNT, BNTC, LN, NICNT, NIGTC, NTC, PNTC, WBC; ESV, NASB, NET, NRSV, REB], 'desert' [BAGD, LN; CEV, GW, KJV, NCV, NIV, NLT, TEV], 'lonely place' [LN]. This noun denotes a largely uninhabited region, normally with sparse vegetation [LN].

  b. ταμεῖον (LN 7.28) (BAGD 2. p. 803): 'inner room' [BAGD, BECNT, BNTC, LN, NTC, PNTC, WBC; ESV, NASB, NCV, NET, NIV, NRSV, REB], 'storeroom' [NICNT, NIGTC], 'secret place' [CEV, GW], 'secret chamber' [KJV], 'innermost, secret, or hidden room' [BAGD]. The phrase ἐν τοῖς ταμείοις 'He is in the inner rooms' is translated 'he is hiding here' [NLT, TEV]. This noun denotes a room in the interior of a house, normally without windows opening to the outside [LN].

  c. ἀετός (LN 4.42) (BAGD p. 19): 'vulture' [BAGD, **LN**; all translations except CEV, KJV], 'buzzard' [CEV], 'eagle' [LN; KJV].

QUESTION—What is the connotation of the 'inner rooms'?

It indicates secrecy, which is the opposite of what will happen when he actually returns [Lns, NICNT, TH, WBC]. It describes a hidden setting restricted to a few initiates [EBC], out of the reach of ordinary people [PNTC].

QUESTION—What bird is referred to in this proverb?

It is the vulture [BAGD, BECNT, EBC, LN, NAC, NIBC, NICNT, NIGTC, PNTC, TH, TRT]. It is not the eagle [EBC, NIBC, NICNT], as eagles do not normally feed on carrion [EBC, NICNT, PNTC], nor do they flock together around a carcass [NIBC, NICNT, PNTC]. The basic distinction between eagles and vultures is that eagles either capture their prey or feed upon dead carcasses, while vultures only feed upon dead carcasses. In the Western Hemisphere these are seen as two distinct families of birds [LN].

QUESTION—What is the point of the parable of the vultures and the corpse?

Although it is difficult to determine what the vultures and the corpse refer to, the basic meaning of the proverb is that certain things always occur together, so where one is evident, the other will be present [ICC]. This proverb illustrates the unmistakable nature of Christ's parousia, which is something that cannot possibly be missed, and just as vultures gather at a dead body, so also all people will see Christ when he returns [ICC, NAC, NICNT, TH, WBC]. Just as surely as a gathering of vultures indicates the presence of a corpse, so also these signs will indicate that the end is at hand [NLT]. It may

mean that it will be as difficult for people not to see the coming of the Son of
Man as for vultures not to see a decaying corpse [EBC]. He was saying that
they won't have to search at all for him, because he will appear wherever his
disciples are, just as vultures appear where a body is [BNTC]. He was saying
that false prophets and Messiahs would flock like vultures on a dead body
[NIBC]. He is likening the false Christs and false prophets to the birds, and
the decadent Jewish nation, who are prone to believe the false Christs, to the
decaying body [Lns]. The spiritually dead will attract judgment just like a
dead body attracts vultures [PNTC]. He is graphically describing the final
eschatological battle with a common symbol of death [BECNT]. The
disciples of Jesus do not need prompting by anyone to be drawn to him,
because they will be drawn to him just as surely as vultures are to a corpse
[NIGTC].

24:29 "And immediately after the suffering[a] of-those days the sun will-be-
darkened,[b] and the moon will- not -give its light;[c] and the stars will-fall[d]
from the heaven, and the powers[e] of-the heavens[f] will-be-shaken.[g]

LEXICON—a. θλῖψις (LN 22.2) (BAGD 1. p. 362): 'tribulation' [BAGD,
    BECNT, BNTC, NTC, WBC; ESV, KJV, NASB], 'distress' [NICNT,
    PNTC; NIV, REB], 'oppression' [BAGD, NIGTC], 'suffering' [LN;
    CEV, NET, NRSV], 'anguish' [NLT], 'misery' [GW], 'trouble' [NCV,
    TEV], 'trouble and suffering, persecution' [LN], 'affliction' [BAGD].
    This noun denotes trouble involving direct suffering [LN].

  b. fut. pass. Indic. of σκοτίζομαι (LN **14.55**) (BAGD 1. p. 757): 'to be
    darkened' [BAGD, BECNT, BNTC, NICNT, NIGTC, NTC, PNTC; ESV,
    KJV, NASB, NET, NIV, NLT, NRSV, REB], 'to be made dark' [WBC],
    'to become dark' [BAGD, **LN**; CEV], 'to turn dark' [GW], 'to grow dark'
    [NCV, TEV]. This verb means to change from a condition of being light
    to one of being dark [LN].

  c. φέγγος (LN **14.36**) (BAGD p. 854): 'light' [BAGD, **LN**; all translations
    except CEV, TEV]. The phrase 'the moon will not give its light' is
    translated 'the moon will no longer shine' [CEV, TEV]. This noun
    denotes light, in contrast with darkness [LN].

  d. fut. mid. (deponent = act.) indic. of πίπτω (LN 15.118) (BAGD 1.a.
    p. 659): 'to fall' [BAGD, LN; all translations]. This verb means to fall
    from one level to another [LN].

  e. δύναμις (LN 12.44) (BAGD 5. p. 208): 'power' [BAGD, LN; all
    translations except NIV], 'authority, lordship, ruler, wicked force' [LN].
    The phrase δυνάμεις τῶν οὐρανῶν 'powers of the heavens' is translated
    'heavenly bodies' [NIV]. This noun denotes a supernatural power having
    some particular role in controlling the destiny and activities of human
    beings [LN].

  f. οὐρανός (LN 1.5) (BAGD 1.c. p. 594): 'heaven' [BAGD; BECNT,
    BNTC, NICNT, NIGTC, NTC, PNTC, WBC; ESV, KJV, NASB, NCV,
    NET, NLT, NRSV], 'sky' [LN; CEV], 'universe' [GW], 'space' [TEV].

This noun is translated as an adjective: 'heavenly' [NIV], 'celestial' [REB]. This noun denotes the space above the earth that includes the vault arching high over the earth from one horizon to another, as well as the sun, moon, and stars [LN].

g. fut. pass. indic. of σαλεύω (LN 16.7) (BAGD 1. p. 740): 'to be shaken' [LN, BAGD; all translations except TEV]. The phrase αἱ δυνάμεις τῶν οὐρανῶν σαλευθήσοντα 'the powers of the heavens will be shaken' is translated 'the powers in space will be driven from their courses' [TEV]. This verb means to cause something to move back and forth rapidly, often violently [LN].

QUESTION—To what specific time period does 'those days' refer?

In interpreting Jesus' predictions in this chapter it is important to recognize that the destruction of Jerusalem in 70 AD can be understood as a foreshadowing of similar events that would occur at the end of the age [BECNT, EBC, Lns, NIBC, NTC].

1. 'Those days' refers to the desecration of the temple spoken of in v.15ff [ICC, NIGTC, NICNT, WBC].

2. It refers to the entire period of affliction that extends throughout the church age up to the parousia of Christ [EBC, NAC, NIBC, TRT]. He is speaking of all that is predicted in vv.4–28, but especially in vv.9–11, which speaks of persecution that will occur generally, though particularly in the end times, but also in vv.15–22, which describes the suffering involved in the destruction of Jerusalem [NIBC].

3. It is the distress occurring in the last days [BECNT, Lns, NTC, PNTC], particularly as described in v.9 and v.21 [PNTC]. It is a time of intense suffering just before the return of Christ [NTC]. It refers to a future time of terrible anguish described in vv.15–28, which also describes the terrible suffering involved in the destruction of Jerusalem [BECNT].

QUESTION—Is the description given here to be taken literally or metaphorically?

1. These signs of the last days are described metaphorically in language drawn from apocalyptic imagery [ICC, NAC, NIBC, NICNT, NIGTC], though some of this may actually happen physically [NAC, NIGTC].

2. These signs are probably intended to be understood literally, as things that will actually happen [EBC, Lns, PNTC, WBC]. At least some of this, though not necessarily all of it, will literally happen [NTC]. Apocalyptic imagery is used to describe unusual phenomena in the sky [WBC].

QUESTION—What are the 'powers of the heaven'?

1. He is referring to literal objects in the sky such as the sun, moon, and stars [BNTC, Lns, NIBC, WBC].

2. He is referring to angelic or demonic spirits [ICC, NAC, PNTC].

3. In the ancient world it was believed that there was a correspondence between stars and certain celestial or supernatural powers represented by

those stars, so here it could refer both to the stars themselves as well as spiritual powers that supposedly controlled the stars [TH].

QUESTION—In what sense will the powers of the heavens be shaken?

1. This verb may be being used figuratively in this passage in the sense of deposing the hosts of the spiritual realm from their positions of power [LN]. The powers that are opposed to God are still subject to his will, and will be disturbed and curtailed when it is time for the Son of Man to return, because he will inaugurate the reign of God in the earth [PNTC]. The lights in the sky are metaphorically applied to the Jewish governing power structures of the first century, which will be brought to an end [NICNT].

2. There will be actual cosmic upheaval [BECNT, LN, My, NIBC, NIGTC]. All of the luminaries of the sky will be disturbed in a way that is unimaginable [Lns].

24:30 **Then the sign[a] of-the Son of Man will-appear in heaven,[b] and then all the tribes[c] of-the earth will-mourn,[d] and they-will-see the Son of-Man coming on the clouds of heaven with power[e] and great glory.**

LEXICON—a. σημεῖον (LN 33.477) (BAGD 1. p. 747): 'sign' [BAGD, LN; all translations], 'distinguishing mark, token, indication' [BAGD]. This noun denotes an event which is regarded as having some special meaning [LN].

b. οὐρανός (LN 1.11) (BAGD 2.b. p. 595): 'heaven' [BAGD, BNTC, LN, NICNT, NIGTC, PNTC; ESV, KJV, NET, NLT, NRSV, REB], 'sky' [BECNT, NTC, WBC; CEV, GW, NASB, NCV, NIV, TEV]. This noun denotes the supernatural dwelling place of God and other heavenly beings [LN].

c. φυλή (LN **11.56**) (BAGD 2. p. 869): 'tribe' [BECNT, BNTC, NICNT, NIGTC, NTC, PNTC, WBC; ESV, KJV, NASB, NET, NRSV], 'nation' [BAGD, **LN**; CEV, NIV], 'people' [BAGD, LN; GW], 'peoples' [NCV, NLT, REB, TEV]. This noun denotes a relatively large unit of people who constitute a sociopolitical group, sharing a presumed biological descent [LN].

d. fut. mid. indic. of κόπτομαι (LN 52.1) (BAGD 2. p. 444): 'to mourn' [BAGD, BECNT, BNTC, LN, NICNT, NIGTC, NTC, WBC; ESV, KJV, NASB, NET, NIV, NRSV], 'to lament' [LN, PNTC], 'to make lamentation' [REB], 'to weep' [CEV, TEV], 'to cry in agony' [GW], 'to cry' [NCV], 'to beat the breast' [BAGD, LN]. This verb is translated as a noun phrase: 'there will be deep mourning' [NLT]. This verb means to beat the breast and lament as an expression of sorrow [LN].

e. δύναμις (LN 76.1): 'power' [BECNT, LN; all translations]. This noun denotes the potentiality to exert force in performing some function [LN].

QUESTION—What is the sign of the Son of Man?

It is a standard or ensign that will be unfurled in the heavens [EBC, ICC], and it will be a signal to those who will fight in the great eschatological battle to come for battle [ICC]. The sign is the cross appearing in the sky

[ICC]. Whatever the sign, it will be unmistakable to everyone everywhere [ICC, NIBC, PNTC]. It refers to all the glorious ways the Son of Man will manifest himself at his coming on the clouds [Lns]. The sign is the visible manifestation of Christ's heavenly rule, as shown through the destruction of the old order (which the temple represents) and the gathering to him of his chosen people who are being incorporated into the church [NICNT]. It will be a sign that the Son of Man is coming [NLT, REB].

QUESTION—Does 'in heaven' indicate where the sign will appear, or where the Son of Man is, and will appear?

1. The sign will appear in heaven [BECNT, BNTC, EBC, ICC, Lns, NIGTC, PNTC; ESV, NET, NLT, NRSV, REB], that is, in the sky [BECNT, NIBC, NTC, TH, WBC; CEV, GW, NASB, NCV, NIV, TEV].

2. The Son of Man is in heaven [BAGD, NICNT]. This refers to his enthronement in heaven, which is manifested by the physical destruction of the temple and his reign being expressed in his chosen people who are being gathered to him through both Gentile and Jewish people coming to faith [NICNT]. He will appear visibly in his heavenly glory [BAGD].

QUESTION—Why will the peoples of the earth mourn?

They will mourn over their impending judgment [BNTC, Lns, NICNT, NIGTC, PNTC, TH, WBC]. They will mourn in contrition over their past sins, especially for having persecuted believers in Christ [EBC]. They will mourn over how they have been wrong about who Jesus is and about his messianic claims [NIBC]. Since 'earth' can mean 'the land', probably referring to the land of Israel, the mourning will be that of all Israel grieving over Christ's crucifixion, possibly to the point of repentance [NAC].

QUESTION—To what people or group of people does πᾶσαι αἱ φυλαὶ τῆς γῆς 'all the tribes of the earth' refer?

It refers to all the nations of the earth [BECNT, EBC, Lns, NIGTC, PNTC, TH, WBC]. It refers to the tribes of Israel, taking τῆς γῆς as meaning all the land, that is, the land of Israel [NAC, NICNT].

QUESTION—What do the clouds symbolize?

They symbolize God's presence [BECNT, EBC, Lns, ICC, PNTC], his heavenly majesty [Lns].

QUESTION—What is meant by the Son of Man coming μετὰ δυνάμεως 'with power'?

He has divine power to judge and to save [BNTC]. His appearance will be majestic [PNTC]. People will recognize that he has great power [TH]. His omnipotent power is shown in what happens to the heavenly bodies [Lns]. When he comes to judge the earth, he will have been endowed with power to exercise the dominion granted him in the scene from Daniel 7:13–14 where the Son of Man is enthroned in God's presence [NIGTC]. His coming with power refers not to his coming to earth again, but to his coming in heaven for enthronement in the presence of God as in Daniel 7 [NICNT]. His power will overshadow all the power of deceivers and false messiahs [ICC].

QUESTION—What noun or nouns does the adjective 'great' modify?
1. It modifies 'glory' [BECNT, BNTC, EBC, Lns, NIGTC, NTC, PNTC, TH, WBC; CEV, ESV, GW, KJV, NASB, NET, NIV, NLT, NRSV, REB, TEV].
2. It modifies both 'power' and 'glory' [NICNT; NCV].

24:31 And he-will-send-out his angels with a-great[a] trumpet-sound, and they-will-gather[b] his elect from the four winds,[c] from (one) end[d] of heaven to (the other) end.

TEXT—Manuscripts reading σάλπιγγος μεγάλης 'great trumpet-sound' are given a B rating by GNT to indicate it was regarded to be almost certain. Other manuscripts read σάλπιγγος φονῆς μεγάλης 'great trumpet sound' and this is followed by KJV.

LEXICON—a. μέγας (LN 78.2) (BAGD 2.a.γ. p. 497): 'great' [LN], 'loud' [BAGD], 'intense, terrible' [LN]. The phrase σάλπιγγος μεγάλης 'great trumpet sound' [LN (6.93)] is also translated 'great trumpet blast' [LN (6.93), NICNT, NIGTC], 'trumpet blast' [REB], 'great trumpet call' [WBC], 'loud trumpet' [PNTC; NCV], 'loud trumpet blast' [NTC; NET], 'loud trumpet call' [BNTC; ESV, GW, NIV, NRSV], 'sound of a loud trumpet' [CEV], 'great sound of a trumpet' [KJV], 'mighty blast of a trumpet' [NLT], 'great trumpet' [BECNT; NASB]. It is also translated as a verb phrase: 'the great trumpet will sound' [TEV]. This adjective describes the upper range of a scale of extent, with the possible implication of importance in relevant contexts [LN].

b. fut. act. indic. of ἐπισυνάγω (LN 15.126) (BAGD p. 301): 'to gather' [BAGD, NIGTC, NTC, PNTC; all versions except CEV, KJV, NASB], 'to gather together' [BAGD, BECNT, LN, NICNT, WBC; KJV, NASB], 'to bring together' [CEV], 'to assemble' [BNTC], 'to cause to come together' [LN]. This verb means to cause to come together to, toward, or at a particular location [LN].

c. ἄνεμος (LN 14.4) (BAGD 1.b. p. 64): 'wind' [BECNT, BNTC, LN, NICNT, NIGTC, NTC, PNTC, WBC; ESV, KJV, NASB, NET, NIV, NRSV, REB], 'direction(s), cardinal point(s)' [BAGD]. The phrase ἐκ τῶν τεσσάρων ἀνέμων ἀπ᾽ ἄκρων οὐρανῶν ἕως [τῶν] ἄκρων αὐτῶν 'from the four winds, from one end of heaven to the other end' is translated 'from all over the world—from the farthest ends of the earth and heaven' [NLT], 'from one end of the world to the other' [TEV], 'from all over the earth' [CEV], 'from every direction under the sky' [GW], 'all around the earth...every part of the world' [NCV]. This noun denotes air in relatively rapid movement, but without specification as to the force of the movement [LN].

d. ἄκρον (LN **80.7**) (BAGD p. 34): 'end' [BAGD, BECNT, BNTC, **LN**, NICNT, NTC, PNTC, WBC; ESV, KJV, NASB, NET, NIV, NLT, NRSV, TEV], 'bounds' [REB], 'boundary' [NIGTC], 'extreme boundary, final limit' [LN], 'extreme limit' [BAGD], not explicit [CEV, GW, NCV].

This noun denotes the extreme limit of a space [LN]. The phrase 'the four winds, from one end of heaven to the other' is translated 'from all over the earth' [CEV].

DISCOURSE UNIT—24:32–41 [NASB]. The topic is the parable of the fig tree.

DISCOURSE UNIT—24:32–35 [CEV, ESV, NET, NRSV, TEV]. The topic is the parable of the fig tree [NET], the lesson of the fig tree [ESV, NRSV, TEV], a lesson from a fig tree [CEV].

24:32 "Learn the parable[a] from the fig-tree. As-soon-as its branch becomes tender[b] and puts-forth its leaves, you know that the summer is near.[c] **24:33** So you also, when you-see all these-things, you-know that he/it- is -near, (right) at (the) gates.[d] **24:34** Truly I-say to-you, this generation[e] will-certainly-not -pass-away[f] until all these-things take-place. **24:35** The heaven and the earth will-pass-away, but my words will- certainly-not - pass-away.

LEXICON—a. παραβολή (LN 33.15) (BAGD 2. p. 612): 'parable' [BAGD, BECNT, BNTC, LN, NIGTC, PNTC; KJV, NASB, NET], 'meaning of the parable' [WBC], 'lesson' [NICNT, NTC; CEV, ESV, NCV, NIV, NLT, NRSV, REB, TEV], 'story' [GW], 'illustration' [BAGD], 'figure, allegory, figure of speech' [LN]. This noun denotes a relatively short narrative with symbolic meaning [LN].

b. ἁπαλός (LN **79.101**) (BAGD p. 80): 'tender' [BAGD, BECNT, BNTC, LN, NICNT, NIGTC, NTC, WBC; ESV, GW, KJV, NASB, NET, NIV, NRSV, REB], 'green and tender' [TEV], 'green and soft' [NCV]. The phrase ὁ κλάδος αὐτῆς γένηται ἁπαλός 'its branch becomes tender' is translated 'its branches sprout/bud' [CEV, NLT]. This adjective pertains to being tender, that is, yielding readily to pressure [LN].

c. ἐγγύς (LN 67.61) (BAGD 2.a. p. 214): 'near' [BAGD, LN; all translations except KJV], 'nigh' [KJV]. This noun denotes a point of time subsequent to another point of time, but relatively close [LN].

d. θύρα (LN **67.58**) (BAGD 2.a. p. 365): 'gates' [NIGTC, NTC; ESV, NRSV]. This plural noun is translated as a singular noun: 'door' [BAGD, BECNT, BNTC, PNTC, WBC; GW, KJV, NASB, NET, NIV, NLT, REB], 'threshold' [NICNT]. The idiomatic phrase πρὸ θυρῶν 'at the gates' is translated 'ready to come' [NCV], 'ready to begin' [TEV], 'soon' [LN]. The phrase ἐγγύς ἐστιν ἐπὶ θύραις 'he/it is near, right at the gates' is translated 'the time has almost come' [CEV]. The idiom πρὸ θυρῶν 'right at the gates' denotes a point of time subsequent to another point of time and it indicates imminence, that is to say, the subsequent event is regarded as almost begun [LN].

e. γενεά (LN 11.4 or 10.4) (BAGD 2. p. 154): 'generation' [BAGD, all translations except CEV, NCV, TEV], 'people of this time' [NCV], 'people now living' [TEV], 'those of the same time, those of the same generation' [LN (11.4)], 'some of the people of this generation' [CEV], 'people of the same kind' [LN (10.4)]. This noun denotes people living at the same time and belonging to the same reproductive age-class [LN (11.4)], or it denotes an ethnic group exhibiting cultural similarities [LN (10.4)].

   f. aor. act. subj. of παρέρχομαι (LN **67.85**) (BAGD 1.b.α. p. 626): 'to pass away' [BAGD, BECNT, BNTC, NICNT, NIGTC, NTC, PNTC, WBC; ESV, NASB, NET, NIV, NRSV], 'to pass' [**LN**; KJV], 'to pass from the scene' [NLT], 'to disappear' [GW], 'to come to an end' [BAGD]. The phrase οὐ μὴ παρέλθῃ 'will certainly not pass away' is translated 'are still living' [NCV], '(some) will still be alive' [CEV], 'will live to see (it all)' [REB], 'before…(the people now living) have all died' [TEV]. This verb means to mark the passage of time, with focus upon completion [LN].

QUESTION—How is the word 'parable' used here?

It describes a lesson to be learned from the example of the fig tree [EBC, ICC, NIBC, NICNT, NIGTC, TH, WBC]. This 'parable' is an instructive comparison of one thing to another [NTC, PNTC].

QUESTION—To what does πάντα ταῦτα 'all these things' in v.34 refer?

It refers to all that is described in vv.4–28 [BECNT, EBC, Lns, PNTC, WBC], or in vv.4–31 [ICC]. Verses 4–28 describe the tribulation that Christ's followers experience throughout the period of time from his ascension until his return [EBC]. It refers to the approach of the Roman armies and the defiling of the temple in the Jewish war that occurred from 66 AD to 70 AD [NICNT, WBC].

QUESTION—Is the implied subject of ἐγγύς ἐστιν 'he/it is near' Christ ('he'), or the time of his return ('it')?

   1. It refers to Christ ('he') being near [BECNT, BNTC, ICC, NIGTC, WBC; ESV, GW, NASB, NET, NRSV].

   2. It refers to the time of his return ('it') being near [Lns, NICNT, NTC, PNTC; CEV, KJV, NCV, NIV, NLT, TEV], of the end being near [NIBC; REB]. It refers to the end of Jerusalem being near [NICNT].

QUESTION—How might Christ's coming have been 'near' to those who heard these words?

It is the next major step in God's program of redemption for humanity [EBC]. After these things all transpired in the first century, all was in readiness such that the Son of Man could come at any time [WBC]. The most decisive event of history has already occurred in Christ's ministry, death, resurrection, and ascension, so his coming can now occur at any moment. Whatever happens after the decisive event of Christ's ministry, etc.) is an interlude granted by God's mercy to allow people to repent, and however long it maybe, it is only an epilogue and is short in the sense that Christ could come at any time [NAC]. Jesus' generation saw those things happen, but similar things will also happen again in the last days, when his coming is truly near [BECNT]. All these signs have occurred repeatedly since the time Jesus said this [Lns]. Jesus was referring to the destruction of Jerusalem in the first century, which occurred within about forty years or less of when he said this [NICNT].

QUESTION—In what sense does Jesus use the phrase 'this generation'?

1. It refers to the generation of people living at that time [BECNT, BNTC, EBC, ICC, NAC, NICNT, NIGTC, PNTC, TH, WBC; NCV, TEV].
2. It refers to the unbelieving Jewish people throughout history up to the very end [Lns].

QUESTION—In what sense would all those things take place in that generation?

1. Jesus is referring to the distress that was described in vv.4–28, including the fall of Jerusalem [BECNT, EBC, PNTC]. Prophecy can have multiple fulfillments. The events leading up to the destruction of Jerusalem typify a greater and more total catastrophe that will happen again just before the final judgment [BECNT, NIBC, PNTC]. He is referring to the events described in vv.1–26 concerning the destruction of Jerusalem, all of which had transpired by the time Jerusalem finally fell [NAC, NICNT, WBC].
2. Unbelieving Jewish people will see these things occur throughout the centuries but they will still persist in their unbelief [Lns].

QUESTION—What is the significance of Jesus' statement about his words not passing away?

Jesus is claiming an authority and eternal validity of his words that are equal to the authority and validity of God's words [BECNT, EBC, ICC, NICNT, TRT, WBC]. This is a far-reaching claim [PNTC].

DISCOURSE UNIT—24:36–25:30 [ICC]. The topic is eschatological vigilance.

DISCOURSE UNIT—24:36–51 [ESV, GW, NCV, NIV]. The topic is that no one knows when the Son of Man will return [GW], when will Jesus come again? [NCV], no one knows that day and hour [ESV], the day and the hour unknown [NIV].

DISCOURSE UNIT—24:36–44 [NET, NRSV, TEV]. The topic is that no one knows the day and hour [TEV], be ready! [NET], the necessity of watchfulness [NRSV].

24:36 "But about[a] that day and hour no-one knows, neither the angels of heaven, nor the Son, but only the Father. **24:37** For as the days of Noah (were), so will-be the coming of the Son of Man. **24:38** For as in those days before the flood they-were eating and drinking, marrying and giving-in-marriage, until the day Noah went-into the ark, **24:39** and they did- not -understand[b] until the flood came and took- them-all -away,[c] so too will-be the coming of the Son of Man.

TEXT—In verse 36, manuscripts reading οὐδὲ ὁ υἱός 'nor the Son' are given a B rating by GNT to indicate it was regarded to be almost certain. Manuscripts that omit this phrase are followed by KJV, NET.

TEXT—In verse 38, manuscripts reading ἡμέραις ἐκείναις 'those days' are given a C rating by GNT to indicate that choosing it over a variant text was difficult. This reading is followed by NIGTC, NTC, PNTC; ESV, NASB, NCV, NET, NLT, NRSV. It is included in brackets by BECNT, GNT, WBC. Others manuscripts omit ἐκείναις 'those'. It is omitted by BNTC, NICNT; CEV, GW, KJV, NIV, REB, TEV, though with some translations the omission of this variant may be more for the sake of English style than for textual considerations.

LEXICON—a. περί with the genitive (LN 89.6) (BAGD 1.h. p. 645): 'about' [NICNT, NIGTC, NTC; NRSV, REB], 'concerning' [BAGD, BNTC, LN, WBC; ESV], 'of' [BECNT; KJV, NASB], 'as for' [PNTC; NET], 'in relation to, with regard to' [LN], 'with reference to' [BAGD], not explicit [CEV, GW, NCV, NIV, NLT, TEV]. This preposition indicates a relation, usually involving content or topic [LN].

b. aorist act. indic. of γινώσκω (LN 32.16) (BAGD 3.b. p. 161): 'to understand' [BAGD], 'to come to understand, to perceive' [LN], 'to comprehend' [BAGD, LN]. The phrase οὐκ ἔγνωσαν 'did not understand' [BECNT, BNTC; NASB] is also translated 'knew nothing' [NICNT, PNTC; NET, NRSV, REB], 'knew not' [KJV], 'did not know' [NIGTC, WBC], 'were unaware' [ESV], 'knew nothing about what was happening/would happen' [NCV, NIV], 'didn't know anything was happening' [CEV], 'didn't realize what was going to happen/was happening' [NLT, TEV], 'were not aware of what was happening' [GW], 'not recovering their senses' [NTC]. This verb means to come to an understanding as the result of ability to experience and learn [LN].

c. aorist act. indic. of αἴρω (LN **15.203**) (BAGD 4. p. 24): 'to take away' [BAGD, BECNT, LN, NIGTC, PNTC; KJV, NASB, NET, NIV], 'to sweep away' [BNTC, NICNT, NTC; CEV, ESV, GW, NLT, NRSV, REB, TEV], 'to destroy' [WBC; NCV], 'to carry (away)' [**LN**], 'to carry off' [LN], 'to remove' [BAGD, LN].

24:40 "Then two (men)[a] will-be in the field; one is-taken[b] and one will-be-left. **24:41** Two (women) are-grinding[c] at[d] the mill;[e] one will be taken and one will be left.

LEXICON—a. There is no lexical entry for this word in the Greek text, but the gender of the two people working in the field is suggested by the masculine form of the adjective εἷς 'one', though that could also be used generically for a person of unstated gender. The plural of this implied noun is translated 'men' [BNTC, NICNT, NIGTC, NTC, PNTC, WBC; all versions except KJV, NRSV], 'people' [BECNT], not explicit [KJV, NRSV]. Likewise, in v.41 the word 'women' does not appear in the Greek text, but the gender of those milling is specified by the feminine form of the adjective μία 'one' and by the feminine form of the participle ἀλήθουσα 'are grinding'. The implied subject of this participle is translated 'women' [all translations].

b. pres. pass. indic. of παραλαμβάνω (BAGD 1. p. 619): 'to be taken' [BAGD, all translations except TEV], 'to be taken away' [TEV].

c. pres. act. participle of ἀλήθω (LN **46.16**) (BAGD p. 37): 'to grind' [BAGD, BECNT, BNTC, NIGTC, NTC, PNTC, WBC; ESV, KJV, NASB, NIV, REB], 'to grind grain' [**LN**, NICNT; CEV, NCV, NET], 'to grind flour' [NLT], 'to grind meal' [NRSV, TEV], 'to work' [GW]. This verb means to grind grain in a mill [LN]. Such mills were usually operated by two women [BAGD].

d. ἐν (LN 83.23): 'at' [BNTC, LN, NIGTC, PNTC, WBC; ESV, GW, KJV, NASB, NLT, REB, TEV], 'with' [BECNT, NICNT, NTC; NCV, NET, NIV], not explicit [CEV, NRSV]. This preposition describes a position in proximity to or in the immediate vicinity of an object [LN].

e. μύλος (LN 7.68) (BAGD 1. p. 529): 'mill' [BAGD, BNTC, LN, NIGTC, PNTC, WBC; all versions except CEV, NIV, NRSV], 'hand mill' [BAGD, BECNT, NICNT, NTC; NIV], not explicit [CEV, NRSV]. This noun denotes a construction of two flat stones between which grain was ground into flour by rotating the top stone [LN].

QUESTION—Where are they to be taken and who is being taken?

1. Christ's elect are taken to be with him, and those who are left will face judgment [BNTC, ICC, Lns, PNTC, TH, WBC]. They are taken to share in the blessings of being with Christ [PNTC]. They are taken for salvation [NIGTC].

2. Unbelievers are taken away for judgment [NAC, NIBC, NICNT], and only Christ's people remain behind to be with him [NAC]. This does not refer to a 'rapture' [NAC].

3. The passage does not discuss which ones are taken and which are left; the main point is that there is a separation between believers and unbelievers [BECNT, EBC]. It is neither clear nor important whether 'taken' means taken in judgment' as in verse 39 or 'taken to be gathered with the elect' as in verse 31 [EBC].

DISCOURSE UNIT—24:42–51 [NASB]. The topic is be ready for his coming.

24:42 "Therefore be-alert,[a] for you-do- not -know what day your Lord is-coming. **24:43** But understand this, that if the owner-of-the-house[b] had-known in which watch-of-the-night[c] the thief was-coming, he-would-have-stayed-awake and would- not -have-let his house be-broken-into. **24:44** Therefore you also be ready,[d] for the Son of Man is-coming at-an-hour you-do- not -expect.

TEXT—Manuscripts reading ἡμέρα 'day' are given a B rating by GNT to indicate it was regarded to be almost certain. Other manuscripts that read ὥρα 'hour' are followed by BNTC; KJV.

LEXICON—a. pres. act. impera. of γρηγορέω (LN 27.56) (BAGD 2. p. 167): 'to be ready' [NCV], 'to be alert' [BECNT, LN; GW], 'to be on the alert' [BAGD, NTC; NASB], 'to stay alert' [NET], 'to watch' [BNTC, PNTC, WBC; KJV], 'to watch out' [TEV], 'to keep watch' [NIV, NLT], 'to be on your guard' [CEV], 'to keep awake' [NICNT; NRSV, REB], 'to stay awake' [NIGTC; ESV], 'to be watchful' [BAGD, LN], 'to be vigilant' [BAGD, LN]. This verb is a figurative extension of meaning of ἀγρυπνέω 'to keep oneself awake' and it means to be in continuous readiness and alertness to learn of what might be a potential future threat [LN].

b. οἰκοδεσπότης (LN 57.14) (BAGD p. 558): 'owner of the house' [BECNT, NTC; NCV, NET, NIV, NRSV, TEV], 'master of the house' [BAGD, NICNT, NIGTC, WBC; ESV], 'master of the household' [LN], 'head of the house' [NASB], 'householder' [BNTC, PNTC; REB], 'homeowner' [CEV, GW, NLT], 'goodman of the house' [KJV]. This noun denotes one who owns and manages a household, including the family, servants, and slaves [LN].

c. φυλακή (LN 67.196) (BAGD 4. p. 868): 'watch of the night' [BAGD, NTC], 'watch' [LN, NIGTC, PNTC; KJV], 'time of night' [NICNT; GW, NASB, NCV, NET, NIV, REB], 'part of the night' [BECNT; ESV, NRSV], 'night-watch' [WBC], 'time' [TEV], 'hour' [BNTC], 'a fourth of the night' [LN], not explicit [CEV]. The phrase ποίᾳ φυλακῇ 'in which watch of the night' is translated 'exactly when' [NLT]. This noun denotes one of four periods of time into which the night was divided, during which time certain assigned persons would be on the lookout. In Matthew 24:43, however, it is possible that the reference is to three night watches, as was typical among Hebrews and Greeks [LN].

d. ἕτοιμος (LN 77.2) (BAGD 2. p. 316): 'ready' [BAGD, LN; all translations], 'prepared' [BAGD, LN]. This adjective describes a state of readiness [LN].

QUESTION—Is 'understand' an imperative or indicative?

1. It is imperative [BECNT, BNTC, NICNT, NIGTC, PNTC, TH, WBC; ESV, KJV, NASB, NCV, NET, NIV, NLT, NRSV, REB].
2. It is indicative [EBC, ICC, NTC; GW].

QUESTION—How is the coming of the Son of Man to be compared with the coming of a thief?

They must be ready for the coming of the Son of Man like the householder must be ready for the coming of a thief in just one respect, which is the unexpectedness of the coming [EBC]. The hour of the coming is one that they do not expect [PNTC, WBC].

24:45 **"Who then is the faithful[a] and wise[b] slave,[c] whom the master has-put-in-charge[d] over his household[e] to-give to-them their food at (the) proper-time[f]? 24:46 Blessed (is) that slave whom his master having-arrived will-find working thus. 24:47 Truly I-tell you that he-will-put- him -in-charge over all his possessions.[g]**

LEXICON—a. πιστός (LN 31.87) (BAGD 1.a.α. p. 664): 'faithful' [BAGD, BECNT, BNTC, LN, NIGTC, NTC, PNTC, WBC; all versions except NCV], 'trustworthy' [BAGD, LN, NICNT], 'loyal' [NCV], 'dependable' [BAGD, LN], 'reliable' [LN]. This adjective pertains to being trusted [LN].

b. φρόνιμος (LN 32.31) (BAGD p. 866): 'wise' [BAGD, LN, NIGTC, WBC; all versions except NASB, NLT], 'prudent' [BAGD, BNTC], 'sensible' [BAGD, NICNT, NTC, PNTC; NASB, NLT], 'thoughtful' [BAGD, BECNT]. This adjective describes an understanding resulting from insight and wisdom [LN].

c. δοῦλος (LN 87.76) (BAGD 1.a. p. 205): 'slave' [BAGD, BNTC, LN, PNTC; NASB, NET, NRSV], 'servant' [BNTC, NTC, WBC; all versions except NASB, NET, NRSV], 'bondservant' [LN]. This noun denotes one who is a slave in the sense of becoming the property of an owner (though in ancient times it was frequently possible for a slave to earn his freedom) [LN].

d. aorist act. indic. of καθίστημι (LN **37.104**) (BAGD 2.a. p. 390): 'to put in charge of' [BAGD, BECNT, BNTC, LN, NTC; CEV, GW, NASB, NET, NIV, NRSV], 'to place in charge' [TEV], 'appointed to take charge of' [NICNT], 'to appoint' [BAGD, LN], 'to appoint over' [PNTC, WBC], 'to set over' [NIGTC; ESV], 'to make ruler over' [KJV], 'to trust (to)' [NCV], 'to give the responsibility of managing' [NLT], 'to be charged with responsibility to manage' [REB], 'to designate' [LN]. This verb means to assign to someone a position of authority over others [LN].

e. οἰκετεία (LN **46.6**) (BAGD p. 557): 'household servants' [LN]. The phrase τῆς οἰκετείας αὐτοῦ 'his household servants' [LN, WBC] is also translated 'his household' [BNTC, NICNT, PNTC; ESV, KJV, NASB, NET, NRSV, REB], 'his other household servants' [NLT], 'the servants in his household' [NIV], 'the other servants' [CEV, GW, NCV, TEV], 'the household slaves' [BECNT], 'the slaves in his household' [BAGD], 'the other slaves in the household' [NIGTC], 'his household employees'

[NTC]. This noun denotes the group of servants working in a particular household [LN]. It denotes the slaves in a household [BAGD].

  f. καιρός (LN 67.1) (BAGD 2. p. 395): 'proper time' [BAGD, BECNT, BNTC, NICNT, NIGTC, NTC, PNTC; CEV, ESV, NASB, NET, NIV, NRSV, REB, TEV], 'right time' [BAGD, WBC; GW, NCV], 'due season' [KJV], 'time, occasion' [LN], not explicit [NLT]. This noun denotes points of time consisting of occasions for particular events [LN].

  g. pres. act. participle of ὑπάρχω (LN **57.16**) (BAGD 1. p. 838): 'possessions' [BAGD, BECNT, BNTC, LN, NTC, WBC; ESV, NASB, NET, NIV, NRSV], 'goods' [NIGTC, PNTC; KJV], 'property' [BAGD, **LN**; GW, REB, TEV], 'means' [BAGD]. This noun is translated as a verb phrase: 'that he possesses' [NICNT],] 'everything/all the master/he owns' [CEV, NCV, NLT]. This participle denotes that which constitutes someone's possession [LN].

QUESTION—What relationship is indicated by ἄρα 'then'?

  It indicates a conclusion to be drawn from the immediately preceding context about readiness [ICC, Lns, NTC] and about the unexpectedness of his coming [Lns]. The conclusion to be drawn is that readiness implies faithfulness [NTC], or that the slave who is carrying out his responsibility will be blessed as described in v.46 [ICC].

24:48 "But if that wicked[a] slave says in his heart,[b] 'My master is-delaying,[c]' **24:49** and he-begins to-beat[d] his fellow-slaves and eats and drinks with the drunkards, **24:50** the master of that slave will-come on a day in-which he-does- not -expect and at an-hour that he-does- not -know.

LEXICON—a. κακός (LN 88.106) (BAGD 1.a. p. 397): 'wicked' [NICNT, NIGTC, NTC, PNTC; ESV, GW, NIV, NRSV], 'evil' [BECNT, BNTC, WBC; CEV, KJV, NASB, NCV, NET, NLT], 'bad' [BAGD, LN; REB, TEV]. This adjective pertains to being bad in the sense of being harmful and damaging [LN].

  b. καρδία (LN 26.3) (BAGD 1.b.β. p. 403): 'heart' [BECNT, BNTC, LN, NIGTC, NTC, PNTC, WBC; KJV, NASB], 'mind' [BAGD, LN], 'inner self' [LN]. The phrase εἴπῃ...ἐν τῇ καρδίᾳ αὐτοῦ 'says in his heart' is translated 'says to himself' [BAGD, NICNT; ESV, NET, NIV, NRSV, REB], '(will) tell himself' [TEV], 'thinks to himself' [NCV], 'thinks' [CEV, GW, NLT]. This noun denotes the causative source of a person's psychological life in its various aspects, but with special emphasis upon thoughts [LN].

  c. pres. act. indic. of χρονίζω (LN 67.122) (BAGD 1, 2. p. 887): 'to delay' [BAGD 2, BECNT], 'to delay (one's) return/coming' [BNTC, WBC; KJV], 'to be delayed' [PNTC; ESV, NRSV], 'to be away a long time' [NICNT], 'to stay away a long time' [NET, NIV], 'to not come/come back for a long time' [NASB, TEV], 'to not be back for a while' [NLT], 'to not come back soon' [NCV], 'to take (one's) time' [BAGD, NIGTC], 'to not return until late' [CEV], 'to be a long time coming' [REB], 'to linger, fail to come' [BAGD 1], 'to be late' [LN]. The phrase Χρονίζει μου ὁ κύριος 'my master is delaying' is translated 'it will be a long time before (his) master comes' [GW]. This verb means to extend a state or an event beyond an expected time [LN].

d. pres. act. infin. of τύπτω (LN 19.1) (BAGD 1. P. 830): 'to beat' [BAGD, BECNT, BNTC, LN, NIGTC, PNTC, WBC; all versions except KJV, REB], 'to beat up' [NTC], 'to hit' [LN, NICNT], 'to smite' [KJV], 'to bully' [REB], 'to strike' [BAGD, LN]. This verb means to strike or hit an object one or more times [LN].

24:51 He-will-cut- him -in-two[a] and put[b] him in a place with the hypocrites.[c] In-that-place there-will-be weeping[d] and gnashing[e] of-teeth."

LEXICON—a. fut. act. indic. of διχοτομέω (LN 19.19, **38.12**) (BAGD p. 200): 'to cut in two' [BAGD, BNTC, LN (19.19), NICNT, NIGTC, PNTC; NET], 'to cut in/to pieces' [BECNT, NTC, WBC; ESV, NASB, NCV, NIV, NLT, NRSV, REB, TEV], 'to cut asunder' [KJV], 'to punish severely' [**LN** (38.12); GW], 'to punish with utmost severity' [BAGD], 'to punish' [LN (38.12)]. This active verb is translated as passive: 'to be punished' [CEV]. This verb means to cut an object into two parts [LN (19.19)]. It may also mean to punish with great severity [LN (38.12)].

b. fut. act. indic. of τίθημι (LN 85.32) (BAGD I.1.b.ε. p. 816): 'to put, to place' [BAGD, LN]. The phrase τὸ μέρος αὐτοῦ μετὰ τῶν ὑποκριτῶν θήσει 'put him in a place with' is translated 'assign him a/his place with/among' [BECNT, BNTC, NTC; GW, NASB, NET, NIV, NLT, REB], 'allocate him his place with' [NIGTC], 'give him a place with' [PNTC], 'appoint him his portion with' [KJV], 'put him with' [ESV, NRSV], 'consign him to the fate of' [NICNT], 'make him share the fate of' [TEV], 'put their inheritance among' [WBC], 'they will be thrown out (with the ones)' [CEV], 'send him away to be with' [NCV]. This verb means to put or place someone in a particular location [LN].

c. ὑποκριτής (LN 88.228) (BAGD p. 845): 'hypocrite' [BAGD, LN; all translations except CEV], 'pretender' [BAGD, LN], 'one who pretends to serve their master' [CEV], 'one who acts hypocritically' [LN], 'dissembler' [BAGD]. This noun denotes one who pretends to be other than he really is [LN].

d. κλαυθμός (LN 25.138) (BAGD p. 433): 'weeping' [BAGD, BECNT, BNTC, LN, NICNT, NIGTC, NTC, WBC; ESV, KJV, NASB, NET, NIV, NLT, NRSV], 'wailing' [PNTC; REB], 'crying' [BAGD, LN]. This noun is translated as a verb phrase: 'they/people/he will cry' [CEV, GW, NCV, TEV]. This noun denotes the act of weeping or wailing, with emphasis upon the noise accompanying the weeping [LN].

e. βρυγμός (τῶν ὀδόντων) (LN 23.41) BAGD p. 148): 'gnashing (of teeth)' [BAGD, BECNT, BNTC, LN, NICNT, NIGTC; ESV, KJV, NASB, NET, NIV, NLT, NRSV], 'grinding (of teeth)' [LN, NTC, PNTC,

WBC; REB]. This noun phrase is translated 'he will gnash his teeth' [TEV], 'they will grit their teeth in pain' [CEV], 'people will grind their teeth with pain' [NCV], 'people will be in extreme pain' [GW]. This noun denotes the grinding or the gnashing of the teeth, whether involuntary as in the case of certain illnesses, or as an expression of an emotion such as anger or of pain and suffering LN.

QUESTION—Would a slave master ever go so far as to cut a slave in two, or is this only a figurative statement?

1. This is a figurative way of describing severe and final punishment [BNTC, PNTC, TH, TRT]. It probably means to be cut off in the OT sense of being banned from the Israelite community [NAC, WBC].

2. This was meant to be understood as a literal punishment that a slave might actually receive [EBC, ICC, NIBC, NICNT]. Slaves who disappointed their masters could be subjected to very cruel treatment [NIGTC, NTC].

DISCOURSE UNIT—25:1–13 [CEV, ESV, GW, NASB, NCV, NET, NIV, NLT, NRSV, TEV]. The topic is the story about ten bridesmaids [GW, NCV], a story about ten girls [CEV], the parable of the ten girls [TEV], the parable of the ten bridesmaids [NLT, NRSV], the parable of the ten virgins [ESV, NET, NIV], parable of ten virgins [NASB].

25:1 "Then[a] the kingdom of heaven will-be-compared to-ten girls[b] who having-taken their lamps/torches[c] went to meet the bridegroom.[d] 25:2 Five of them were foolish,[e] and five (were) wise.[f] 25:3 For the foolish-ones having-taken their lamps/torches, took no oil with them. 25:4 But the wise-ones took oil in-flasks[g] with their lamps/torches.**

LEXICON—a. τότε (LN 67.47): 'then' [BECNT, BNTC, LN, NICNT, NIGTC, NTC, PNTC, WBC; ESV, KJV, NASB, NLT, NRSV], 'at that time' [NCV, NET, NIV, TEV], 'when the end comes' [GW], 'when the day comes' [REB], not explicit [CEV]. This adverb describes a point of time subsequent to another point of time [LN].

b. παρθένος (LN 9.39) (BAGD 1. p. 627): 'girl' [NICNT, NTC, PNTC; CEV, REB], 'virgin' [BAGD, BECNT, LN, WBC; ESV, KJV, NASB, NET, NIV], 'maiden' [BNTC, NIGTC], 'bridesmaid' [GW, NCV, NLT, NRSV], 'young woman' [LN; TEV]. This noun denotes a female person beyond puberty but not yet married and a virgin (though in some contexts virginity is not a focal component of meaning) [LN].

c. λαμπάς (LN 6.104) (BAGD 2. p. 465): 'lamp' [BAGD, BECNT, BNTC, LN, NTC; all translations except CEV, GW, TEV], 'oil lamp' [CEV, GW, TEV], 'torch' [NICNT, NIGTC, PNTC, WBC]. This noun denotes a light made by burning a wick saturated with oil contained in a relatively small vessel [LN].

d. νυμφίος (LN 10.56) (BAGD p. 545): 'bridegroom' [BAGD, BECNT, BNTC, LN, NICNT, NIGTC, NTC, PNTC, WBC; all translations except CEV, GW], 'groom' [CEV, GW]. This noun denotes a man who is about to be married or has just been married [LN].

e. μωρός (LN 32.55) (BAGD 1. p. 531): 'foolish' [BAGD, BECNT, BNTC, LN, NIGTC, NTC, PNTC, WBC; all versions], 'silly' [NICNT], 'unwise' [LN]. This adjective describes someone who is extremely unwise and foolish [LN].

f. φρόνιμος (LN 32.31) (BAGD p. 866): 'wise' [BECNT, LN, NIGTC, WBC; all translations except NASB, REB, TEV], 'prudent' [BNTC; NASB, REB, TEV], 'sensible' [NICNT, NTC, PNTC], 'with understanding, with insight' [LN]. This adjective describes someone who has the insight and wisdom to understand what should be done [LN].

g. ἀγγεῖον (LN **6.120**) (BAGD p. 6): 'flask' [BAGD, BECNT, PNTC, WBC; NASB, NET, NRSV, REB], 'vessel' [BAGD, **LN**, NTC; KJV], 'container' [BAGD, BNTC, LN, NIGTC; TEV], 'jar' [NICNT; NCV, NIV]. The phrase ἔλαιον ἐν τοῖς ἀγγείοις 'oil in flasks' is translated 'flasks of oil' [ESV], 'extra oil' [CEV, GW, NLT]. This noun denotes a container that is primarily used for liquids or wet objects. In this context it would have been relatively small, containing probably not more than a liter (about a quart) [LN].

QUESTION—What relationship is indicated by τότε 'then'?

It refers to the time of judgment at the coming of the Son of Man spoken of in the immediately preceding passage [EBC, Lns, My, NIGTC, PNTC, TH; GW, NCV, NET, NIV, REB, TEV]. It refers to the time near the end, but before the Lord has returned [BNTC].

QUESTION—Why is the verb ὁμοιωθήσεται 'will be compared' in the future tense?

It is in the future tense because the event it describes had not yet happened [NICNT, WBC].

QUESTION—What were the λαμπάδας 'lamps/torches' carried by the girls?

1. They were lamps [BAGD (2), BNTC, NTC, WBC; CEV, ESV, GW, KJV, NASB, NCV, NET, NIV, NLT, NRSV, REB, TEV]. It was an oil lamp [ICC, My, TH], or some form of lantern [ICC]. Perhaps they carried oil lamps tied to the top of poles like torches [WBC]. It was a lamp with a wick and space for oil [BAGD, NTC]. The burning of the lamps while the girls slept is the reason the oil ran low [BNTC]. They should have had an extra supply of oil in separate jars, but the foolish girls brought no extra oil [ESVSB].

2. They carried torches [BECNT, EBC, ESVSB, Lns, NAC, NIBC, NICNT, NIGTC, PNTC, TRT]. These were large dome-shaped torches that were fueled by rags soaked in oil. They were used while walking outdoors, and such torches would last for several hours if there were extra containers of oil [ESVSB]. The torches would have been able to burn for only about 15 minutes before needing to be re-soaked with oil [NICNT, TRT]. The torches would not be burning while inside the house [Lns, NIGTC, NTC, PNTC, TRT]. The torches had not yet been lit since they were only going to be used when the bridegroom actually approached [Lns, NIGTC]. After

the torches were lit, they would soon run out of oil [NICNT] and it was foolish to think that the amount of oil that a torch could hold would be sufficient [PNTC].

QUESTION—Do the various elements in the story symbolize anything?

The bridegroom is Christ [BECNT, EBC, Lns, WBC], the wise and foolish girls are faithful and unfaithful followers of Christ [WBC], or alert disciples and careless disciples [BECNT], and the rejection by the bridegroom at the door stands for the final judgment [BECNT, WBC]. The oil has no symbolic meaning [EBC, NICNT, WBC], and it serves only to support the focus of the parable about preparedness [WBC]. The overriding theme is being prepared for the coming of the Son of Man [EBC]. The story shifts from a parable that corresponds more or less realistically to everyday life to application at the end when he says "I do not know you" [ICC, NAC, NICNT, NTC].

25:5 **The bridegroom being-delayed,[a] they-all became-drowsy[b] and began-sleeping. 25:6 But at-midnight there-was a-cry, 'Behold, the bridegroom! Come-out to-meet him.' 25:7 Then all the girls rose and trimmed[c] their lamps.**

LEXICON—a. pres. act. participle of χρονίζω (LN **67.122**) (BAGD 1. p. 887): 'to be delayed' [PNTC; ESV, NLT, NRSV], 'to be late' [**LN**; GW, NCV], 'to delay' [BECNT, BNTC; NASB], 'to delay a long time' [NET], 'to delay one's coming' [WBC], 'to be late arriving' [CEV], 'to be a long time coming' [NICNT; NIV, REB], 'to be late in coming' [TEV], 'to take one's time' [NIGTC, NTC], 'to tarry' [KJV], 'to linger, to fail to come for a long time' [BAGD]. This verb means to extend a state or an event beyond an expected time [LN].

  b. aorist act. indic. of νυστάζω (LN **23.67**) (BAGD 1. p. 547): 'to become drowsy' [BAGD, BECNT, BNTC, NICNT, WBC; CEV, ESV, GW, NET, NIV, NLT, NRSV], 'to grow drowsy' [**LN**, NTC], 'to get drowsy' [NASB], 'to nod off' [NICNT, PNTC], 'to nod' [BAGD; TEV], 'to become sleepy' [NCV], 'to slumber' [KJV], 'to doze off' [REB], 'to doze' [BAGD]. This noun denotes the process of becoming sleepy. In some languages 'to grow drowsy' may have to be rendered 'to begin to nod' or 'their heads fell' or 'their eyes gradually closed' [LN].

  c. aorist act. indic. of κοσμέω (BAGD 1. p. 445): 'to trim' [BAGD, BECNT, BNTC, NTC, PNTC; ESV, KJV, NASB, NET, NIV, NRSV, REB, TEV], 'to trim a wick' [WBC], 'to get (something) ready' [NICNT, NIGTC; CEV, GW, NCV], 'to prepare' [NLT], 'to put in order' [BAGD].

QUESTION—Is there any significance in the use of the aorist of 'became drowsy' and the imperfect of 'began sleeping'?

The aorist verb 'became drowsy' introduces the following ongoing activity of the imperfect verb 'began sleeping' [BECNT, PNTC].

25:8 **And the foolish-ones said to-the wise-ones, 'Give us some-of your oil, for our lamps are-going-out.[a]' 25:9 But the wise-ones answered saying, 'There-will- not[b] -be-enough for-us and for-you; instead go to those-who-**

sell[c] and buy (some) for-yourselves.' **25:10** And while- they -were-going-
away to-buy, the bridegroom came, and those- (who were) -ready[d] went-in
with him into the wedding-banquet,[e] and the door was-shut.[f]

TEXT—In verse 9 manuscripts reading μήποτε οὐ μὴ ἀρκέσῃ 'there will not be
enough' are followed by GNT, which does not mention any variant reading.
This text is followed by BECNT, NICNT, NIGTC, PNTC, WBC; CEV,
ESV, GW, NASB, NET, NLT, NRSV, REB, TEV. A variant reading is
μήποτε οὐκ ἀρκέσῃ 'there might not be enough.' This reading is followed
by BNTC, NTC; KJV, NCV, NIV.

LEXICON—a. pres. pass. indic. of σβέννυμι (LN 14.70) (BAGD 1. p. 745): 'to
go out' [BAGD; all translations], 'to be extinguished' [BAGD, LN], 'to
be put out' [BAGD, LN]. This verb means to cause a fire to be
extinguished [LN].

   b. μήποτε (LN 71.18) (BAGD 4. p. 519): 'probably' [BAGD], 'perhaps'
[BAGD], 'can be, might be, whether perhaps' [LN]. This conjunction
describes a situation of not being certain [LN]. If the manuscript reading
μήποτε οὐ μή is followed, it would indicate an emphatic negation (LN
69.5): 'by no means, certainly not' [LN]. It is translated 'there would
never be' [NICNT, REB], 'there will certainly not be' [NIGTC], 'there
would by no means be' [WBC]. This manuscript reading may also be
translated as indicating a simple negation: 'there will not be' [BECNT,
PNTC; ESV, GW, NASB, NET, NRSV], 'there is not' [CEV, TEV], 'we
don't have' [NLT]. However, where the manuscript reading μήποτε οὐκ
is followed, it is translated as indicating uncertainty or possibility:
'perhaps there will not be' [BNTC], 'there may/might not be' [NTC;
NCV, NIV], 'lest there not be' [KJV].

   c. pres. act. participle of πωλέω (LN **57.186**) (BAGD 1. p. 731): 'to sell'
[BAGD, LN]. This plural participle 'those who sell' [**LN**, NTC] is also
translated 'those who sell oil' [NET, NIV], 'them that sell' [KJV], 'people
who sell' [NCV], 'dealers' [BAGD, BNTC; ESV, NASB, NRSV, REB],
'sellers' [BAGD, BECNT, NICNT, NIGTC, PNTC], 'someone to sell'
[GW], 'the-shops/a-shop' [WBC; NLT], 'store' [TEV], not explicit
[CEV]. This verb means to dispose of property or provide services in
exchange for money or other valuable considerations [LN].

   d. ἕτοιμος (LN 77.2) (BAGD 2. p. 316): 'ready' [BAGD, LN; all
translations], 'prepared' [LN]. This adjective describes a state of readiness
[LN].

   e. γάμος (LN 34.68) (BAGD 1.b. p. 151): 'wedding banquet' [BAGD,
BNTC, NIGTC, WBC; NET, NIV, NRSV, REB], 'wedding feast'
[BECNT, NICNT; NASB, NCV, TEV], 'wedding' [LN, NTC, PNTC;
CEV], 'marriage feast' [ESV, NLT], 'marriage' [KJV], 'wedding hall'
[GW]. This noun denotes the ceremony associated with becoming married
[LN].

f. aorist pass. indic. of κλείω (LN **79.112**) (BAGD 1. p. 434): 'to be shut'
[BAGD, BECNT, LN, NIGTC, NTC, PNTC, WBC; ESV, GW, KJV,
NASB, NET, NIV, NRSV, REB], 'to be closed' [BAGD, BNTC, **LN**,
NICNT; CEV, TEV], 'to be closed and locked' [NCV], 'to be locked'
[BAGD; NLT]. This verb means to cause something to be shut [LN].

QUESTION—Does the reply of the five wise girls about not having enough oil
express uncertainty or certainty?

No matter which text is followed, the effect is the same: the foresight and
preparedness of the wise virgins cannot benefit the foolish virgins [EBC].
1. It is emphatic and expresses certainty [ICC, Lns, My, NICNT, NIGTC,
TH, WBC; REB]. Although not emphatic, it expresses no uncertainty
[BECNT, PNTC; CEV, ESV, GW, NASB, NET, NLT, NRSV, TEV].
2. It expresses uncertainty or possibility [BNTC, NTC; KJV, NCV, NIV].

QUESTION—What is the likelihood that they would have found a vendor for
oil at that hour?

Since there was a wedding celebration going on in the town, they probably
could have found someone to sell them oil late at night [ICC, NAC, NIBC,
TH, WBC]. It appears from verse 11 that they were able to buy oil [WBC].
They may have had difficulty finding someone to sell oil at that hour
[NIGTC].

25:11 And later the other girls came also, saying, 'Lord/Sir[a], lord/sir, open
to-us. **25:12** But answering he-said, 'Truly, I-say to-you, I-do- not -know[b]
you.' **25:13** Watch[c] therefore, for you-do- not -know the day nor the hour.

TEXT—Some manuscripts include ἐν ᾗ ὁ υἱὸς τοῦ ἀνθρώπου ἔρχεται 'in
which the Son of Man comes' after τὴν ὥραν 'the hour'. It is omitted by
GNT with an A rating, indicating that the text is certain. It is included by
KJV and NCV only. NLT adds 'of my return' though this may be for clarity
in the English rendering only.

LEXICON—a. κύριος (LN 87.53) (BAGD 1.b. p. 459): 'lord' [BAGD,
BECNT, BNTC, NICNT, WBC; ESV, NASB, NCV, NET, NLT, NRSV],
'Lord' [KJV], 'master' [NIGTC], 'sir' [BAGD, LN, NTC, PNTC; CEV,
GW, NIV, REB, TEV]. This noun is a title of respect used in addressing a
man [BAGD, LN].

b. perf. act. indic. (with present tense meaning) of οἶδα (LN 28.1) (BAGD 2.
p. 556): 'to know' [LN; all translations except GW, NCV], 'to know
about, to have knowledge of' [LN], 'to be acquainted with' [BAGD, LN],
'to stand in a close relation to' [BAGD]. The phrase οὐκ οἶδα ὑμᾶς 'I do
not know you' is translated 'I don't know who you are' [GW], 'I don't
want to know you' [NCV], 'I have nothing to do with you' [BAGD]. The
verb means to possess information about someone [LN].

c. pres. act. impera. of γρηγορέω (LN 27.56) (BAGD 2. p. 167): 'to watch'
[BNTC, PNTC, WBC; ESV, KJV], 'to keep watch' [NIV, NLT], 'to
watch out' [TEV], 'to be alert' [BECNT, LN; NET], 'to be on the alert'
[BAGD, NTC; NASB], 'to be ready' [CEV, NCV], 'to be awake'

[NICNT, NIGTC], 'to be watchful, 'to be vigilant' [BAGD, LN]. The force of the present tense imperative is expressed with a helping verb: 'to keep (awake, etc.)' [NICNT, NTC; NRSV, REB], 'to stay (awake, etc.)' [NIGTC; GW, NET]; by a temporal adverb 'to always be (ready)' [CEV, NCV].

QUESTION—What is meant by the statement 'I do not know you'?

It indicates repudiation [BAGD, ICC, Lns, NIBC, NICNT, NIGTC, PNTC, TH, TRT; NCV]. He does not recognize them as his own [My, NAC, NTC].

QUESTION—How should the exhortation to 'keep watch' be understood?

It is a warning to be prepared [BECNT, BNTC, EBC, ICC, Lns, My, NAC, NIBC, NICNT, NIGTC, NTC, PNTC, WBC]. This parable means that people must be prepared for the return of the Son of Man and the coming of the kingdom [EBC].

DISCOURSE UNIT—25:14–30 [CEV, ESV, GW, NASB, NCV, NET, NIV, NLT, NRSV, TEV]. The topic is a story about three servants [CEV, GW, NCV], the parable of the three servants [NLT, TEV], the parable of the talents [ESV, NET, NIV, NRSV], parable of the talents [NASB].

25:14 "For (it will be) like[a] a man going-away-on-a-journey,[b] (who) called his-own servants[c] and handed-over[d] to-them his possessions.[e] **25:15** To-one he-gave five talents,[f] to-one (he gave) two, to-one (he gave) one, to-each according-to his-own ability,[g] and he-went-away.

LEXICON—a. ὥσπερ (LN **64.13**) (BAGD 1. p. 899): 'like' [BECNT, NTC, PNTC, WBC; ESV, GW, NCV, NET, NIV, REB, TEV], 'like when' [NICNT], 'like what happened' [CEV], 'just like' [BNTC; NASB], 'as if' [NIGTC; NRSV], 'just as' [BAGD, LN], 'as in the case of' [**LN**], 'as' [BAGD, LN; KJV], 'can be illustrated by the story of' [NLT]. This conjunction is a somewhat emphatic marker of similarity between events and states [LN].

b. pres. act. participle of ἀποδημέω (LN 15.47) (BAGD 1. p. 90): 'to go on a journey' [BAGD, BECNT, WBC; ESV, NASB, NET, NIV, NRSV], 'to leave on a journey' [BNTC], 'to leave home on a trip' [TEV], 'to go on a trip/long-trip' [GW, NLT], 'to go away from home' [NICNT, NIGTC], 'to go away' [CEV], 'to go abroad' [NTC, PNTC; REB], 'to travel into a far country' [KJV], 'to go to another place for a visit' [NCV], 'to leave home on a journey, to be away from home on a journey' [LN]. This verb means to journey away from one's home or home country, and it implies being away for a considerable period of time and at quite a distance [LN].

c. δοῦλος (LN 87.76) (BAGD 1.a. p. 205): 'servant' [BECNT, BNTC, NTC, PNTC, WBC; all versions except NASB, NET, NRSV], 'slave' [BAGD, BECNT, LN, NICNT, NIGTC; NASB, NET, NRSV], 'bondservant' [LN]. This noun denotes one who is a slave in the sense of becoming the property of an owner (though in ancient times it was frequently possible for a slave to earn his freedom) [LN].

d. aorist act. indic. of παραδίδωμι (LN 57.77) (BAGD 1.a. p. 614): 'to hand over' [BAGD, BNTC, LN, NIGTC, PNTC], 'to give over' [BAGD, LN, WBC], 'to entrust' [BAGD, BECNT, NICNT; ESV, GW, NASB, NET, NIV, NLT, NRSV, REB], 'to place in someone's hand' [NTC], 'to deliver' [BAGD; KJV], 'to put in charge of' [CEV, TEV], 'to tell to take care of (something)' [NCV]. This verb means to hand over to or to convey something to someone, particularly a right or an authority [LN].

e. pres. act. participle of ὑπάρχω (used as a noun) (LN 57.16) (BAGD 1. p. 838): 'possessions' [BAGD, BECNT, BNTC, LN, NICNT; NASB], 'property' [BAGD, LN, NTC, PNTC; ESV, NET, NIV, NRSV, TEV], 'capital' [NIGTC; REB], 'money' [WBC; GW, NLT], 'all (he) owned' [CEV], 'goods' [KJV], 'things' [NCV]. This noun denotes that which constitutes someone's possession [LN].

f. τάλαντον (LN **6.82**) (BAGD p. 803): 'talent' [BAGD, BECNT, BNTC, **LN**, NICNT, NIGTC, NTC, PNTC, WBC; ESV, KJV, NASB, NET, NIV, NRSV]. The phrase πέντε τάλαντα 'five talents' is translated 'five thousand coins' [CEV], 'five thousand gold coins' [TEV], 'five bags of gold' [NCV, REB], 'five bags of silver' [NLT], 'ten thousand dollars' [GW]. This noun denotes a Greek monetary unit (also a unit of weight) with a value which fluctuated, depending upon the particular monetary system which prevailed at a given period of time (a silver talent was worth approximately six thousand denarii with gold talents worth at least thirty times that much) [LN].

g. δύναμις (LN 74.1) (BAGD 2. p. 208): 'ability' [BAGD, LN; all translations except CEV, NCV], 'capability' [BAGD, LN]. The phrase ἑκάστῳ κατὰ τὴν ἰδίαν δύναμιν 'to each according to his ability' is translated 'to each one as much as he could handle' [NCV], 'he knew what each servant could do' [CEV]. This noun denotes the ability to perform a particular activity or to undergo some experience [LN].

QUESTION—What is being described here as indicated by the word ὥσπερ 'like'?

He is still describing the kingdom of heaven, as in the previous passage [Lns, NAC, TH, PNTC]. He is describing what will happen when the kingdom of heaven is manifested at last [NTC]. This parable is associated so closely with verses 1–13 that they share the same introduction (in verse 1) [EBC].

QUESTION—What was the value of a talent?

It is not possible to know exactly what the value was since 'talent' was a weight [NICNT, NTC, PNTC, WBC], and it could have referred to the weight of gold, silver, or copper [EBC, NICNT, NTC, PNTC]. This may have been a talent of silver since the word for 'money' in verse 18 is actually the word for 'silver' [EBC, PNTC], though this is not conclusive [EBC]. A talent of silver was equivalent to 6,000 denarii (a denarius being a day's wage for a laborer) [BECNT, EBC, ICC, NICNT, NTC, TH, WBC]. Even one talent was quite a large sum of money [BECNT, ICC, NICNT, NIGTC,

NTC, PNTC]. A talent could have hired one hundred day laborers for a year [NIGTC].

QUESTION—What do the talents represent in this parable?

The talents represent opportunities and responsibilities for serving the Lord [BECNT, ICC, Lns, NICNT, NTC, PNTC], as well as abilities he has given for doing so [BECNT, Lns]. They represent resources God puts at our disposal, and which must be used and developed [EBC]. They represent the time, abilities, and resources that God gives people to enable them to serve him [NAC]. Faithful serving will be rewarded with more opportunity for faithful serving [PNTC].

At-once^a 25:16 the-one having-received the five talents went and traded^b with them, and he-gained^c five more. 25:17 Likewise the-one (having-received) the two (talents) made two more. 5:18 But the-one having-received the one having-gone dug (in) (the) ground and hid^d his master's money.

TEXT—Manuscripts that punctuate verses 15–16 in such a way that the adverb εὐθέως 'At once' goes with 16 to describe the actions of the first servant are given a B rating by GNT to indicate that this reading was regarded to be almost certain. Other manuscripts punctuate verses 15–16 in such a way that εὐθέως 'immediately' goes with verse 15 to describe the action of the master. Only KJV follows that reading.

LEXICON—a. εὐθέως (LN 67.53): 'at once' [BNTC, NTC, PNTC; ESV, GW, NIV, NRSV, REB, TEV], 'immediately' [BECNT, LN, NIGTC, WBC; NASB], 'straight off' [NICNT], 'as soon as (the man had gone)' [CEV], 'straightway' [KJV], 'quickly' [NCV], 'right away' [LN; NET], 'then' [LN], not explicit [NLT]. This adverb describes a point of time immediately subsequent to a previous point of time (the actual interval of time differs appreciably, depending upon the nature of the events and the manner in which the sequence is interpreted by the writer) [LN].

b. aorist mid. (deponent = act.) indic. of ἐργάζομαι (LN **57.198**) (BAGD 1. p. 307): 'to trade' [**LN**, NICNT; ESV, KJV, NASB, NRSV], 'to do business' [BECNT, LN], 'to engage in business' [BNTC], 'to employ in business' [REB], 'to use (them)' [CEV], 'to work with' [BAGD, NIGTC, PNTC, WBC], 'to put (them/the money) to work' [NTC; NET, NIV], 'to invest' [GW, NCV, NIV, TEV]. This verb means to be involved in business, with focus upon the work that is involved [LN].

c. aorist act. indic. of κερδαίνω (LN **57.189**) (BAGD 1.a. p. 429): 'to gain' [BAGD, BNTC, LN, NIGTC, NTC, PNTC, WBC; NASB, NET, NIV], 'to earn' [**LN**; CEV, NCV, NIV, TEV], 'to make' [BECNT; ESV, KJV, NRSV], 'to make a profit' [BAGD, LN; REB]. The phrase ἐκέρδησεν ἄλλα πέντε 'he made five more' is translated 'he doubled his money' [GW]. This verb means to gain something by means of one's activity or investment [LN].

d. aorist act. indic. of κρύπτω (LN **21.12**) (BAGD 1.a. p. 454): 'to hide'
[BAGD, BECNT, BNTC, **LN**, NIGTC, NTC, PNTC, WBC; all versions],
'to bury' [NICNT], 'to keep safe, to cause to be protected, to protect'
[LN]. This verb means to cause something to be safe or protected by
hiding it so that it cannot be found [LN].

25:19 Now after a-long time the master of-those servants comes and settles[a]
accounts with them. **25:20** And having-come-forward the-one having-
received the five talents brought five talents more, saying, 'Master, you-
entrusted[b] to-me five talents; see[c] I-have-made five talents more.'
LEXICON—a. pres. act. indic. of συναίρω (LN 57.229) (BAGD p. 783): 'to
settle accounts' [BAGD, BECNT, BNTC, LN, NICNT, NIGTC, NTC,
PNTC, WBC; ESV, GW, NASB, NET, NIV, NRSV, REB, TEV], 'to
reckon' [KJV], 'to check on accounts' [LN]. The phrase συναίρει λόγον
'settles accounts' is also translated 'asked what they had done with his
money' [CEV, similarly NCV], 'called them to give an account of how
they had used his money' [NLT]. This verb means to settle or check on
accounts with someone [LN].
  b. aorist act. indic. of παραδίδωμι (LN 57.77) (BAGD 1.a. p. 614): 'to
entrust' [BAGD, BECNT, WBC; NASB, NET, NIV], 'to hand over to'
[BAGD, BNTC, LN, NIGTC, PNTC; NRSV], 'to leave (something) with'
[NICNT; REB], 'to place in (someone's) hands' [NTC], 'to give' [CEV,
GW, NLT, TEV], 'to give over' [BAGD, LN], 'to deliver' [BAGD; ESV,
KJV], 'to trust to care for' [NCV]. This verb means to hand over to or to
convey something to someone, particularly a right or an authority [LN].
  c. ἴδε (LN 91.13) (BAGD 3. p. 369): 'look' [BECNT, LN, NICNT, NIGTC,
PNTC, WBC; REB, TEV], 'behold' [BNTC; KJV], 'see' [NASB, NET,
NIV, NRSV], 'here' [ESV], 'here is' [BAGD], 'pay attention, listen'
[LN], not explicit [CEV, GW, NCV, NLT]. This particle calls for
attention and serves to emphasize the statement that follows [LN].

25:21 His master said to-him, 'Well-done,[a] good[b] and faithful[c] servant.
You have been faithful over[d] a-little; I-will-set- you -over much. Enter-into
the joy[e] of your master.' **25:22** And having-come-forward the-one (having-
received) the two talents said, 'Master, you-entrusted to-me two talents; see,
I-have-made two talents more.' **25:23** His master said to-him, 'Well-done,
good and faithful servant. You have been faithful over a-little; I-will-set-
you -over much. Enter-into the joy of your master.'
LEXICON—a. εὖ (LN **65.23**) (BAGD p. 317): 'well done' [BAGD, **LN**; all
translations except CEV, GW, NCV], 'you did well' [NCV], 'good job!'
[GW], 'wonderful' [CEV], 'well, excellent' [BAGD, LN], 'fine, good'
[LN]. This adverb describes events which measure up to their intended
purpose [LN].
  b. ἀγαθός (LN **65.20**) (BAGD 1.a.α. p. 2): 'good' [BAGD, LN; all
translations], 'fit, capable, useful' [BAGD]. This adjective pertains to

having the proper characteristics or performing the expected function in a fully satisfactory way [LN].

c. πιστός (LN **31.87**) (BAGD 1.a.α. p. 664): 'faithful' [BAGD, BECNT, BNTC, **LN**, NIGTC, NTC, PNTC, WBC; all versions except NCV, NRSV], 'trustworthy' [BAGD, LN, NICNT; NRSV], 'loyal' [NCV], 'dependable, reliable' [BAGD, LN]. This adjective pertains to being trusted and here it has the idea of being one whom he can trust [LN].

d. ἐπί with accusative (LN 37.9) (BAGD III.1.b.α. p. 289): 'over' [BECNT, BNTC, LN, NICNT, NIGTC, NTC, PNTC, WBC; ESV, KJV], 'in charge of' [CEV], 'in handling' [NLT], 'in managing' [TEV], 'in' [NET, NRSV, REB], 'with' [GW, NASB, NCV, NIV], 'with responsibility for' [LN]. This preposition indicates the object over which someone exercises control or authority [LN].

e. χαρά (LN 25.123) (BAGD 2.b., c. p. 875): 'joy' [BAGD, BECNT, BNTC, LN, NIGTC, PNTC, WBC; ESV, KJV, NASB, NCV, NET, NRSV, REB], 'happiness' [NICNT, NTC; CEV, GW, NIV, TEV], 'gladness, great happiness' [LN], 'a state of joyfulness' [BAGD 2.b.], 'festive dinner, banquet' [BAGD 2.c.]. The phrase εἴσελθε εἰς τὴν χαρὰν τοῦ κυρίου σου 'enter into the joy of your master' is translated 'let's celebrate together' [NLT]. This noun denotes a state of joy and gladness [LN].

QUESTION—What is meant by entering into the joy of his master?

They share each other's joy at the successful outcome of the investments [NTC]. Since the master is happy with the outcome, the servant can also participate in that happiness [My]. When a servant has the warm approval of his master his future will be characterized by joy [PNTC]. At this point Jesus leaves the parable and describes actual eternal realities [Lns]. In the application of the parable this joy represents a joy that will be experienced at the time of the messianic banquet [ICC], the blessings of the eschatological era [WBC], the delight of the consummated kingdom [EBC, BNTC]. It indicates participation in the eschatological feast that will happen when Jesus' reign on earth begins [BECNT]. To those who have done well as stewards of what God has put at their disposal he will grant happiness, along with commendation and eternal life [NAC].

25:24 And **having-come-forward the-one having-received the one talent said, 'Master, I-know that you-are a-hard**[a] **man, reaping where you did- not -sow, and gathering where you-did- not -scatter,**[b] **25:25 and having-been-afraid,**[c] **and having-gone I-hid your talent in the ground. See, you-have what (is) yours.'**

LEXICON—a. σκληρός (LN **88.136**) (BAGD 2. p. 756): 'hard' [BAGD, LN, NICNT, NIGTC, NTC, PNTC, WBC; ESV, KJV, NASB, NCV, NET, NIV, REB, TEV], 'hard to get along with' [CEV], 'hard to please' [GW], 'cruel' [BAGD, BECNT], 'harsh' [BAGD, BNTC; NLT, NRSV], 'severe'

[LN], 'demanding' [**LN**], 'strict, merciless' [BAGD]. This adjective
pertains to being hard and demanding in one's behavior [LN].
  b. aorist act. indic. of διασκορπίζω (LN **15.136**) (BAGD p. 188): 'to
     scatter' [BAGD, BNTC, **LN**, NICNT, NTC, PNTC, WBC; REB], 'to
     scatter seed' [BECNT, NIGTC; CEV, ESV, GW, NASB, NET, NIV,
     NRSV, TEV], 'to sow seed' [NCV], 'to cultivate' [NLT], 'to strow'
     [KJV], 'to disperse, to winnow' [BAGD], 'to cause to disperse' [LN].
  c. aorist pass. participle of φοβέομαι (LN 25.252) (BAGD 1.a. p. 862): 'to
     be afraid' [BAGD, LN; all translations except CEV], 'to be frightened'
     [CEV], 'to fear' [LN]. This verb means to be in a state of fearing [LN].
QUESTION—What does the 'scattering' refer to here?
  1. It refers to winnowing or threshing [LN, Lns, My, PNTC]. The sowing
     and the scattering refer to the processes that began and completed the
     getting in of the crop. At the end of the harvest they plied the winnowing
     shovel to scatter the mingled chaff and grain in order to separate the two
     [PNTC]. In this verse it may be important to indicate clearly what was
     scattered. This could not be a reference to sowing since sowing has
     already been mentioned in the previous statement. What is scattered in
     this clause may be chaff or manure [LN (**88.132**)].
  2. It again refers to the sowing of seed [BECNT, ICC, NICNT, NIGTC, TH,
     WBC; CEV, ESV, GW, NASB, NCV, NET, NIV, NRSV, TEV]. The two
     clauses seem to be equivalents, an example of synonymous parallelism
     [WBC]. The final verb 'scatter' could mean 'scatter seed' or 'winnow
     chaff'. Probably 'scatter seed' is best in this context. In either case the
     idea of taking profits where someone else has done the work is clear [TH].
QUESTION—What relationship is indicated by the participial form φοβηθείς
'having been afraid'?
  It indicates a conclusion being drawn from the statement of the previous
  sentence: 'You are a hard man so I was afraid' [BECNT, NICNT, NIGTC;
  ESV, NCV, NET, NIV, NRSV, REB]. It indicates the reason he went and
  hid the money: 'Because I was afraid I went and hid' [BNTC, NTC, PNTC,
  WBC; GW, NLT, TEV].
QUESTION—What was the servant supposedly afraid of?
  He was afraid of failure [WBC], that he would lose some or all of the
  master's money [EBC, Lns, My, NICNT, NTC, PNTC, WBC; NLT], or of
  not being able to satisfy the master [My]. However, the master attributes the
  servant's actions to laziness, not to fear [ICC].

25:26 "But answering his master said to-him, '(You) wicked[a] and lazy[b]
servant! You-knew that I-reap where I-did- not -sow and I-gather where I
did not scatter? 25:27 Then you ought to have invested[c] my money with-
the bankers,[d] and having-come I would have-received-back what (was) my-
own with interest.[e]
LEXICON—a. πονηρός (LN 88.110) (BAGD 1.b.α. p. 690): 'wicked' [BAGD,
     BECNT, BNTC, LN, NICNT, NIGTC, NTC, PNTC; ESV, KJV, NASB,

NCV, NIV, NLT, NRSV], 'evil' [BAGD, LN, WBC; GW, NET], 'good for nothing' [CEV], 'worthless' [BAGD; REB], 'bad' [BAGD; TEV]. This adjective pertains to being morally corrupt and evil [LN].

b. ὀκνηρός (LN 88.250) (BAGD 1. p. 563): 'lazy' [BAGD, BECNT, BNTC, LN, NTC, PNTC, WBC; all versions except ESV, KJV], 'indolent' [BAGD, NIGTC], 'slothful' [ESV, KJV], 'cowardly' [NICNT], 'idle' [BAGD], 'lacking in ambition' [LN]. This adjective describes the trait of shrinking from or hesitating to engage in something worthwhile, possibly implying lack of ambition [LN].

c. aorist act. infin. of βάλλω (LN **57.217**) (BAGD 2.b. p. 131): 'to deposit' [BAGD, BECNT, BNTC, **LN,** NICNT; NET, NLT, TEV], 'to put (with bankers/exchangers)' [NIGTC, PNTC; KJV], 'to put in a bank' [LN, WBC; CEV, NASB, NCV], 'to put on deposit' [NIV, REB], 'to invest' [NTC; ESV, GW, NRSV]. This verb means to deposit money with a banker with the intent of earning interest [LN].

d. τραπεζίτης (LN **57.216**) (BAGD p. 824): 'banker' [BAGD, BECNT, BNTC, **LN,** NICNT, NIGTC, NTC, PNTC; ESV, GW, NET, NIV, NRSV], 'bank' [WBC; CEV, NASB, NCV, NLT, TEV], 'exchanger' [KJV], not explicit [REB]. This noun denotes a person who manages or works in a bank [LN].

e. τόκος (LN 57.212) (BAGD p. 821): 'interest' [BAGD, LN; all translations except KJV], 'usury' [KJV]. This noun denotes the interest on money that has been loaned [LN].

QUESTION—What is the relation between 'wicked' and 'lazy'?

Laziness is what is wicked about this servant [ICC]. Not all wicked people are lazy, but those who are lazy are wicked for being so [NTC]. The servant's wickedness consisted of his misrepresentation of his master's character as a cover for his own faults [NTC]. His wickedness was his bad stewardship, as shown in his laziness [WBC]. He was wicked for failing to use the money entrusted to him to the best advantage, and his motive was laziness [BECNT, PNTC]. He was wicked for not wanting the master to gain a profit, and lazy in that he did not want to work to provide a profit [Lns].

QUESTION—What is the nature of the question in verse 26?

The master is using the servant's own words against him without necessarily admitting that the charge was true, which it was not [Lns, My, NAC, NIGTC, NTC, TRT]. It might be a statement of fact, indicating that what the servant thought was actually correct [TH].

25:28 So take the talent from him and give (it) to-the-one-having the ten talents. **25:29** For to-everyone having more-will-be-given, and he-will-be-caused-to-have-(an)-abundance,[a] but from-the-one not having, even what he has will-be-taken-away from him. **25:30** And throw the useless[b] servant into the outer[c] darkness; there-will-be weeping and gnashing of teeth there.'

LEXICON—a. fut. pass. indic. of περισσεύω (LN 59.54) (BAGD 2.a. p. 651): 'to have an abundance' [BECNT, BNTC, PNTC; ESV, KJV, NASB, NIV, NLT, NRSV], 'to have in abundance' [NIGTC], 'to have more than enough' [NICNT; CEV, GW, NET, TEV], 'to have more than one needs' [NCV], 'to have enough and to spare' [REB], 'to have plenty' [NTC], 'to be caused to be abundant, to be provided in abundance, to be provided a great deal of' [LN], 'to be caused to abound' [BAGD]. The verb περισσευθήσεται 'he will be caused to have an abundance' is translated 'it will be multiplied' [WBC]. This verb means to cause something to exist in an abundance [LN].

   b. ἀχρεῖος (LN **65.33**) (BAGD p. 128): 'useless' [BAGD, LN, NICNT, NTC, WBC; GW, NCV, NLT, REB, TEV], 'worthless' [BAGD, BECNT, BNTC, **LN**, NIGTC; CEV, ESV, NASB, NET, NIV, NRSV], 'unprofitable' [PNTC; KJV], 'unworthy' [BAGD], 'not useful' [LN]. This adjective describes not being useful [LN].

   c. ἐξώτερος (LN 1.23) (BAGD 2. p. 280): 'outer' [BNTC, LN, PNTC, WBC; ESV, KJV, NASB, NET, NLT, NRSV], 'outside' [LN, NICNT, NIGTC; GW, NCV, NIV, TEV], 'most distant' [NTC], 'out in (the darkness/dark)' [CEV, REB], 'farthest out' [BAGD]. The idiomatic expression τὸ σκότος τὸ ἐξώτερον 'the outer darkness' denotes a place or region which is both dark and removed (presumably from the abode of the righteous) and serving as the abode of evil spirits and devils [LN].

QUESTION—What is it that people will have or not have?

In the parable, the one who 'has' is the person who has more capital than before because he has increased what he was given [ICC]. This verse is laying down a principle of the spiritual life. Anyone who has a talent of any kind and uses it to the full will find that his talent develops and grows. But he will forfeit it should he fail to use it [Lns, PNTC]. 'Having' refers to what they have accomplished with what has been given them [NAC]. 'The one having' refers to faithfulness, and the faithful person will be given more in which to be faithful [NIBC, TRT, WBC]. Those who give themselves to God in faithful service will find themselves spiritually enriched [NTC]. 'Success' as defined by effective discipleship will bring further similar success [NICNT]. Those who prove to be trustworthy with what they have been entrusted will experience even greater blessings [BECNT, My]. The one who has and uses resources faithfully will be granted more [BNTC].

DISCOURSE UNIT—25:31–46 [CEV, ESV, GW, NASB, NCV, NET, NIV, NLT, NRSV, TEV]. The topic is the judgment [NASB, NET], Jesus will judge the world [GW], the king will judge all people [NCV], the final judgment [CEV, ESV, NLT, TEV], the judgment of the nations [NRSV], the sheep and the goats [NIV].

25:31 **"When the Son of Man comes in his glory, and all the angels with him, then he-will-sit on (the) throne of-his glory.**[a] **25:32** **Before him will-be-gathered all the nations, and he-will-separate**[b] **people one from another as the shepherd separates the sheep from the goats.** **25:33** **And he-will-place the sheep on his right, but the goats on (the) left.**

LEXICON—a. δόξα (LN 14.49) (BAGD 1.a. p. 203): 'brightness, radiance' [BAGD, LN], 'splendor' [BAGD], 'shining' [LN]. The phrase θρόνου δόξης αὐτοῦ 'the throne of his glory' [NIGTC, NTC; KJV, NRSV] is also translated 'his throne in heavenly glory' [NIV], 'his glorious throne' [BECNT, BNTC, NICNT, PNTC, WBC; ESV, GW, NASB, NET, NLT, REB], 'his royal throne' [CEV, TEV], 'his great throne' [NCV]. This noun denotes the state of brightness or shining [LN].

   b. fut. act. indic. of ἀφορίζω (LN **63.28**) (BAGD 1. p. 127): 'to separate' [BAGD, LN; all translations except TEV], 'to set one apart from another' [**LN**], 'to divide' [TEV]. The phrase ἀφορίσει αὐτοὺς ἀπ᾽ ἀλλήλων 'he will separate people one from another' is translated 'he will separate them/people into two groups' [NCV, REB]. This verb means to separate into two or more parts or groups, often by some intervening space [LN].

QUESTION—Who are 'all the nations' in this scene?

   1. It refers to all the people of the world and not to the nations as such [BECNT, BNTC, EBC, ICC, LN, Lns, NAC, NIBC, NICNT, NIGTC, NTC, PNTC, TH, WBC].

   2. It refers to all Christians [My].

QUESTION—What is the reason for the practice of separating sheep from goats, and how does that illustration apply in this passage?

   Goats are less able to keep themselves warm, so shepherds put them in a warmer place at night than the sheep would need [EBC, ICC, NIBC, PNTC, TH, TRT]. Sheep respond to the shepherd when called, whereas goats do not [NTC]. Goats were not viewed negatively, so the distinction made here is not based on any intrinsic superiority in value of sheep, but rather as a convenient way of referring to making a distinction between one group and another [NICNT].

QUESTION—Why are those favored put on the king's right, and those disfavored put on his left?

   A king's right side was a place of honor [BECNT, BNTC, EBC, NAC, NICNT, NIGTC, PNTC, TH, TRT, WBC], and also of power [EBC]. The right side was considered superior [ICC].

25:34 Then the king will-say to-those on his right, 'Come, the-ones-blessed[a] of my Father, inherit[b] the kingdom prepared for-you from (the) foundation[c] of-(the)-world.

LEXICON—a. perf. pass. participle of εὐλογέω (LN 88.69) (BAGD 3. p. 322): 'to be blessed' [BAGD, BECNT, BNTC, LN, NICNT, NIGTC, NTC, PNTC, WBC; ESV, KJV, NASB, NET, NIV, NLT, NRSV, TEV], 'to be treated kindly' [LN], 'to be provided with benefits' [BAGD]. This passive participle is translated as an active verb phrase: 'my Father has blessed you' [CEV, GW], 'my Father has given you his blessing' [NCV], 'you have my Father's blessing' [REB]. This verb means to provide benefits, often with the implication of certain supernatural factors involved [LN].

    b. aorist act. indic. of κληρονομέω (LN 57.131) (BAGD 2. p. 434): 'to inherit' [BECNT, BNTC, NICNT, NIGTC, NTC, PNTC, WBC; ESV, GW, KJV, NASB, NET, NLT, NRSV], 'to take an inheritance' [NIV], 'to receive' [LN; CEV, NCV], 'to take possession of' [REB], 'to come and possess' [TEV], 'to be given, to gain possession of' [LN], 'to come into possession of, to acquire' [BAGD]. This verb means to receive something of considerable value which has not been earned [LN].

    c. καταβολή (LN **42.37**) (BAGD 1. p. 409): 'foundation' [BAGD, BECNT, BNTC, NICNT, NIGTC, PNTC, WBC; ESV, KJV, NASB, NET, NRSV], 'founding' [NTC], 'creation' [**LN**; GW, NIV, NLT, TEV], 'beginning' [BAGD]. The phrase ἀπὸ καταβολῆς κόσμου 'from the foundation of the world' is translated 'before the world was created' [CEV], 'since the world was made' [NCV, REB]. This noun denotes creation, particularly of the world, with focus upon the beginning phase [LN].

QUESTION—What relationship is indicated by the genitive construction τοῦ πατρός μου 'of my Father'?

    1. It indicates that the Father is the agent of blessing [BECNT, BNTC, EBC, Lns, NICNT, NIGTC, NTC, TH, TRT; CEV, ESV, GW, NCV, NET, NIV, NLT, NRSV, REB, TEV].

    2. It indicates that those who are blessed belong to the Father [PNTC, WBC; probably KJV, NASB].

QUESTION—What does it mean to 'inherit' the kingdom?

To inherit means to receive a benefit one has not earned [NTC, PNTC], which is especially significant in that this blessing has come about as a result of Jesus' death [PNTC]. It means to receive something freely from God [TH].

QUESTION—In what sense do they inherit the kingdom?

They are receiving a secure place in it [PNTC]. They experience the blessing of the eschatological kingdom in the fullest way possible [WBC]. They fully and freely experience all the blessings of salvation [NTC]. They actually are given the status of kings, co-reigning with Jesus [Lns, NICNT], or something very similar [NIGTC].

25:35 For I-was-hungry and you gave me (food) to-eat, I-was-thirsty and you-gave- me -drink, I-was a-stranger[a] and you-welcomed[b] me, **25:36** (I was) naked[c] and you-clothed[d] me, I-was-sick and you-visited me, I-was in prison and you-came to me.'

LEXICON—a. ξένος (LN **11.73**) (BAGD 2.a p. 548): 'stranger' [BAGD, BECNT, BNTC, **LN**, NIGTC, NTC, PNTC, WBC; all versions except NCV], 'foreigner' [LN, NICNT], 'alone and away from home' [NCV], 'alien' [BAGD]. This noun denotes a person belonging to a socio-political group other than the reference group [LN].

   b. aorist act. indic. of συνάγω (BAGD 5. p. 782): 'to welcome' [BECNT, NTC, PNTC; CEV, ESV, NRSV], 'to welcome in' [NIGTC], 'to take in' [KJV], 'to invite in' [NASB, NET, NIV], 'to invite into one's house/home' [NCV, NLT], 'to take into one's home' [GW, REB], 'to receive into one's home' [TEV], 'to receive as a guest' [BAGD, BNTC, WBC], 'to make (someone) a guest' [NICNT], 'to invite as a guest' [BAGD].

   c. γυμνός (LN 49.22) (BAGD 3. p. 168): 'naked' [BECNT, LN, NICNT, NIGTC, PNTC, WBC; all versions except GW, NCV, NIV], 'scantily clad' [BNTC], 'without clothes' [NCV], 'in need of clothes' [NTC], 'needed clothes' [GW, NIV], 'poorly dressed' [BAGD]. This adjective describes wearing no clothing or being very scantily clothed [LN].

   d. aorist act. indic. of περιβάλλω (LN 49.3) (BAGD 1.b.ε. p. 646): 'to clothe' [BAGD, BECNT, BNTC, LN, NIGTC, NTC, PNTC, WBC; ESV, KJV, NASB, NIV, REB, TEV], 'to give clothing' [NET, NLT, NRSV], 'to give clothes' [NICNT], 'to give clothes to wear' [CEV], 'to give something to wear' [GW, NCV]. This verb means to put on clothes, implying the clothing being completely around [LN].

QUESTION—What is the tie between their good works and the fact that they are inheriting the kingdom?

   Their good deeds are evidence of their right relationship with God, not the cause [Lns, EBC, NIBC]. Salvation is by grace, and results in righteous deeds [PNTC, WBC]. They were brought into the kingdom by grace, and their good deeds are the result and the evidence of what that grace has done in them [NTC, PNTC]. A transformed heart produces ethical fruit [ICC]. Their faith is shown by their works [BECNT]. They are judged to be righteous on the basis of their good works, and thus worthy of inheriting the kingship that they share with Jesus in ruling over the world [NICNT].

QUESTION—Does 'naked' mean that they had no clothes at all?

   They were poorly clad, having very little to wear [BNTC, Lns, NAC, NTC, PNTC, TRT; GW, NIV].

25:37 Then the righteous[a] will-answer him, saying, 'Lord, when did-we-see you-hungering and we-fed-(you), or thirsting and we-gave- (you) -drink? **25:38** And when did-we-see you a-stranger and we-welcomed (you), or naked and we-clothed (you)? **25:39** And when did-we-see you being-sick or in prison and we-came to you?' **25:40** And answering the king will-say to-them, 'Truly, I-say to-you, in as-much-as[b] you-did (it) for[c]-one of-the least[d] of-these my brothers,[e] you-did-it for-me.'

LEXICON—a. δίκαιος (LN 88.12) (BAGD 1.b. p. 195): 'righteous' [BAGD, LN; all translations except CEV, GW, NCV], 'just' [BAGD, LN]. This plural noun is translated 'the ones who pleased the Lord' [CEV], 'the people who have God's approval' [GW], 'the good people' [NCV]. This adjective describes being in accordance with what God requires [LN].

   b. ὅσος (LN 59.19): 'as much as' [LN, NIGTC; KJV], 'so far as' [BNTC, NICNT, PNTC, WBC], 'just as' [NET, NRSV], 'to the extent that' [NASB], 'as long as' [LN]. The phrase ἐφ' ὅσον ἐποιήσατε 'in as much as you did it' is translated 'whatever you did' [BECNT, NTC; GW, NIV], 'anything you did' [NCV, REB], 'whenever/when you did it' [CEV, NLT, TEV], 'as you did it' [ESV]. This adjective describes a comparison of a quantity [LN].

   c. There is no lexical entry for the preposition 'for' in the Greek text, but it is used in English translation to express the dative case relationship of the adjective εἷς 'one'. The meaning of this dative case relationship is translated as 'for' [BECNT, NICNT, NIGTC, NTC; CEV, GW, NCV, NET, NIV, REB, TEV], 'to' [BNTC, PNTC, WBC; ESV, NASB, NLT, NRSV], 'unto' [KJV].

   d. ἐλάχιστος (LN 87.66) (BAGD 2.a. p. 248): 'least' [BECNT, BNTC, NIGTC, NTC, PNTC, WBC; ESV, KJV, NASB, NCV, NET, NIV, NLT, NRSV], 'smallest' [NICNT], 'however insignificant' [REB], 'no matter how unimportant they seemed' [GW], 'most unimportant, insignificant' [BAGD], 'lowest, least important, last' [LN]. The phrase 'the least of these my brothers' is translated 'my people, no matter how unimportant they seemed' [CEV], 'one of the least important of these followers of mine' [TEV]. This adjective refers to being of the lowest status [LN].

   e. ἀδελφός (LN 11.23) (BAGD 2. p. 16): 'brother' [BAGD, BNTC, NTC, PNTC; ESV, KJV, NASB, NIV, REB], 'fellow believer, (Christian) brother' [LN]. This plural noun ἀδελφῶν 'brothers' is also translated 'brothers and sisters' [BECNT, NICNT; NLT], 'brothers or sisters' [NIGTC, WBC; GW, NET], 'members of my family' [NRSV], 'followers of mine' [TEV], 'my people' [CEV, NCV]. This noun denotes a close associate of a group of persons having a well-defined membership (in the NT ἀδελφός refers specifically to fellow believers in Christ) [LN].

QUESTION—Who are the 'brothers' Jesus is referring to?

   1. They are all Christians, that is, all of Jesus' disciples or followers [BECNT, EBC, Lns, My, NICNT, NIGTC, NTC, PNTC, WBC], although the same kind of benevolence should also be shown for all people generally, whether or not they are Christians [NAC, PNTC]. They are the messengers of Christ, and those who respond positively to the messengers also respond rightly to the message itself [NAC].

2. They are all people, whether Christian or not [BNTC, ICC].

3. Jesus' brothers (or sisters) are anyone who does the will of Jesus' Father, or anyone who suffers and is needy [TH].

25:41 Then **he-will-say to-those on (his) left, 'Depart[a] from me, (you) accursed-ones,[b] into the eternal fire (that) has-been-prepared for the devil and his angels. 25:42 For I-was-hungry and you-gave me no (food) to-eat, I-was-thirsty and you-gave- me no -drink, 25:43 (I was) a-stranger and you-did- not -welcome me, naked and you-did- not -clothe me, sick and in prison and you-did- not -visit me.**

LEXICON—a. pres. mid. or pass. (deponent = act.) impera. of πορεύομαι (LN 15.34) (BAGD 1. p. 692): 'to depart' [BAGD, BECNT, BNTC, NIGTC, NIGTC, NTC, WBC; ESV, KJV, NASB, NET, NIV, NRSV], 'to go away' [LN, NICNT, PNTC; NCV], 'to get away' [CEV, GW], 'to leave' [LN]. The command πορεύεσθε ἀπ' ἐμοῦ 'depart from me' is translated 'away with you' [NLT], 'away from me' [TEV], 'go from my sight' [REB]. This verb means to move away from a reference point [LN].

b. perf. pass. participle of καταράομαι (LN 33.471) (BAGD p. 417): 'to be cursed' [BAGD, LN]. This passive participle is translated 'accursed' [BECNT, BNTC, NTC; NASB, NET, NRSV], 'cursed' [PNTC, WBC; ESV, KJV, NIV, NLT], 'you who have been cursed' [NICNT], 'you who are cursed' [NIGTC], 'you are under God's curse' [CEV, TEV], 'a curse is on you' [REB], 'God has cursed you' [GW], 'you will be punished' [NCV]. This verb means to cause injury or harm by means of a statement regarded as having some supernatural power, often because a deity or supernatural force has been evoked [LN].

25:44 Then **they- also will-answer, saying, 'Lord, when did-we-see you hungering or thirsting or a-stranger or naked or sick or in prison, and did-not -minister[a] to-you?' 25:45 Then he-will-answer them, saying, 'Truly, I-say to-you, inasmuch-as you-did- not -do (it) to-one of-the least of-these, you-did- not -do (it) to-me.' 25:46 And these-will-go-away into eternal punishment,[b] but the righteous into eternal life."**

LEXICON—a. aorist act. indic. of διακονέω (LN 35.37) (BAGD 4. p. 184): 'to minister to' [BNTC, WBC; ESV, KJV], 'to help' [BAGD, BECNT; CEV, GW, NCV, NIV, NLT, TEV], 'to look after' [NICNT], 'to wait on' [NTC], 'to do service to' [PNTC], 'to take care of' [LN, NIGTC, NIGTC; NASB, NRSV], 'to give whatever is needed' [NET]. The phrase οὐ διηκονήσαμέν σοι 'did not minister to you' is translated 'did nothing for you' [REB]. This verb means to take care of someone by rendering humble service to that person [LN].

b. κόλασις (LN 38.2) (BAGD 2. p. 441): 'punishment' [BAGD, **LN**; all translations except CEV, NCV]. The phrase κόλασιν αἰώνιον 'everlasting punishment' is translated 'will/to be punished forever' [CEV,

NCV]. This noun denotes punishment, with the implication of severe suffering resulting [LN].

QUESTION—Does this statement indicate ongoing conscious punishment for the unsaved?

1. It indicates punishment that is everlasting [BECNT, BNTC, EBC, ICC, Lns, My, NAC, NIBC, NTC, PNTC, WBC]. The adjective αἰώνιος 'eternal' has the same meaning with reference to punishment as well as to life [BECNT, BNTC, EBC, Lns, NAC, NIBC, NTC, WBC], which is that they go on and on [NTC] and shows the seriousness of the issue at stake [WBC].

2. It indicates a punishment with eternal consequences, which is the loss of the life of the age to come, but does not necessarily mean that the punishment goes on forever [NICNT].

DISCOURSE UNIT—26:1–28:20 [CC, NAC, WBC]. The topic is Jesus' ultimate destiny [NAC], the story of Jesus' death and resurrection [WBC], passion, resurrection, and great commission from Galilee [CC].

DISCOURSE UNIT—26:1–28:15 [NICNT]. The topic is Jerusalem: the Messiah rejected, killed, and vindicated.

DISCOURSE UNIT—26:1–27:66 [NAC, NIGTC, PNTC; REB]. The topic is the passion and crucifixion [NAC], the passion account [NIGTC], the passion story [PNTC], the trial and crucifixion of Jesus [REB].

DISCOURSE UNIT—26:1–16 [NICNT]. The topic is setting the scene.

DISCOURSE UNIT—26:1–5 [CEV, ESV, GW, NASB, NCV, NET, NIV, NLT, NRSV, TEV]. The topic is the plot to kill Jesus [CEV, ESV, GW, NASB, NLT, NRSV], the plan to kill Jesus [NCV], the plot against Jesus [NET, NIV, TEV].

26:1 **And it-happened when Jesus had-finished saying all these sayings, he-said to-his disciples, 26:2 "You-know that after two days the Passover[a] will-occur, and the Son of-Man is-to-be-handed-over[b] to be-crucified."**

LEXICON—a. πάσχα (LN 51.6) (BAGD 1. p. 633): 'Passover' [BAGD, LN; all translations except KJV, NCV, TEV], 'Passover festival' [BAGD, LN; TEV], 'Passover feast' [NCV], 'feast of the Passover' [KJV]. This noun denotes the Jewish festival commemorating the deliverance of Jews from Egypt [LN].

b. pres. pass. indic. of παραδίδωμι (LN 37.111) (BAGD 1.b. p. 615): 'to be handed over' [BAGD, BNTC, LN, NICNT, NIGTC, NTC, PNTC, WBC; all translations except ESV, KJV, NCV], 'to be betrayed' [LN; KJV], 'to be delivered up' [BECNT; ESV], 'to be given to one's enemies' [NCV], 'to be turned over to' [LN]. This present tense verb is translated as future: 'will be (handed over, etc.)' [NICNT, PNTC, WBC; all versions except KJV, NASB], 'is to be (delivered, etc.) [BECNT; NASB]. It is translated as present: 'is (handed over, etc.)' [BNTC, NIGTC, NTC; KJV]. This verb means to deliver a person into the control of someone else, involving either the handing over of a presumably guilty person for punishment by authorities or the handing over of an individual to an enemy who will presumably take undue advantage of the victim [LN].

QUESTION—To what does 'all these things' refer?

It refers to the previous discourse from chapter 23 to chapter 25 [NIBC, PNTC]. It refers to what Jesus has said in chapters 24–25 [My, NICNT, WBC]. It also marks the end of Jesus' entire teaching ministry [BECNT, NICNT, PNTC, TH, WBC]. It marks the end of all the discourses in Matthew's gospel [BNTC, ICC, Lns]. It is the completion of his teaching about God's rule [BECNT].

QUESTION—On what day of the week did Jesus say this, and what day was Jesus referring to when he said 'after two days'?

He means 'the day after tomorrow' [NICNT]. It is difficult to say on which day this was spoken because in Jewish reckoning the day started in the evening, so 'the Passover' could refer either to the afternoon of Thursday 14 Nisan, in which the Passover lamb would have been sacrificed, or to Thursday evening, which in Jewish reckoning would have been counted as the beginning of Friday 15 Nisan, when the Passover meal would have been eaten [NICNT, NIGTC, TH]. He said this on Tuesday [BNTC, Lns, My, NAC], though possibly it was late Tuesday afternoon or Tuesday evening [BECNT, EBC, NAC, NTC, PNTC, WBC], which by Jewish reckoning was the beginning of what we call Wednesday, and the Passover began on Thursday afternoon when the Passover lamb was slaughtered [EBC, NTC]. This comment would have been made on Tuesday or Wednesday of that week as we count it [PNTC]. It was on Wednesday [ICC, NIBC]. The Passover that year would have been on Thursday, 14 Nisan [BECNT, Lns, My, NAC, NIBC]. The Passover would have been on Friday 15 Nisan [ICC, WBC]. In English 'after two days' is better expressed as 'two days from now' or 'in two days' [TH].

DISCOURSE UNIT—26:3–28:20 [BECNT]. The topic is epilogue/conclusion: passion, resurrection, and commission.

DISCOURSE UNIT—26:3–46 [BECNT]. The topic is preliminary events and preparation of the disciples.

26:3 Then the chief priests and the elders of the people gathered-together in the palace[a] of-the high-priest, the one-called Caiaphas, **26:4** and they took-counsel-together[b] that-they-would-arrest[c] Jesus by-stealth[d] and kill (him). **26:5** But they-said, "Not during the festival,[e] lest there-be a-riot[f] among the people."

LEXICON—a. αὐλή (LN **7.6**) (BAGD 4. p. 121): 'palace' [BAGD, BNTC, **LN**, NTC, PNTC, WBC; ESV, GW, KJV, NCV, NET, NIV, NRSV], 'court' [BECNT; NASB], 'courtyard' [NICNT], 'courtyard of the palace'

[NIGTC], 'home' [CEV], 'house' [REB], 'residence' [NLT], 'dwelling, mansion' [LN]. This noun denotes any dwelling having an interior courtyard and it was often a relatively elaborate structure [LN].

b. aorist mid. indic. of συμβουλεύω (LN 33.294) (BAGD 2.a. p. 778): 'to take counsel together' [WBC], 'to plot' [BAGD, NTC; NIV, NLT], 'to plot together' [ESV, NASB], 'to make a plot' [BNTC], 'to plan' [CEV, NCV, NET], 'to make plans' [GW], 'to conspire' [BECNT; NRSV], 'to confer together' [NIGTC], 'to discuss' [NICNT; REB], 'to counsel' [LN], 'to consult' [BAGD, PNTC; KJV]. This verb means to tell someone what he or she should plan to do [LN].

c. aorist act. subj. of κρατέω (LN 37.110) (BAGD 1.a. p. 448): 'to arrest' [BAGD, BECNT, LN, NICNT, PNTC, WBC; ESV, GW, NCV, NET, NIV, NRSV], 'to have someone arrested' [CEV], 'to take into custody' [BAGD, NTC], 'to take' [KJV], 'to apprehend' [BAGD], 'to seize' [BNTC, LN, NIGTC; NASB, REB], 'to capture' [NLT]. This verb means to take a person into custody for alleged illegal activity [LN].

d. δόλος (LN **88.154**) (BAGD p. 203): 'stealth' [BECNT, NICNT; ESV, NASB, NET, NRSV], 'treachery' [BAGD, LN, NIGTC], 'deceit' [BAGD, WBC], 'cunning' [BAGD, BNTC], 'trick' [NTC], 'scheme' [REB], 'subtlety' [KJV]. This noun in the dative case is translated 'sneak around' [CEV], 'craftily' [PNTC], 'secretly' [NLT], 'in an underhanded way' [GW], 'in some sly way' [NIV], 'to set a trap' [NCV]. This noun denotes deception through trickery and falsehood [LN].

e. ἑορτή (LN 51.2) (BAGD p. 280): 'festival' [BAGD, BECNT, LN, NICNT, NIGTC, NTC; GW, NASB, NRSV, REB], 'feast' [BAGD, BNTC, LN, PNTC, WBC; ESV, NCV, NET, NIV], 'feast day' [KJV], 'the Passover' [CEV], 'the Passover celebration' [NLT], 'celebration' [LN]. This noun denotes the events associated with the celebration of a festival or feast [LN].

f. θόρυβος (LN **39.42**) (BAGD 3.b. p. 363): 'riot' [BECNT, NICNT, NIGTC, NTC, WBC; GW, NASB, NET, NIV, NRSV], 'rioting' [REB], 'uproar' [BNTC; ESV, KJV], 'tumult' [PNTC]. This noun is translated as a verb: 'to riot' [**LN**; CEV, NLT], 'to cause a riot' [NCV]. This noun denotes disorderly behavior of people in violent opposition to authority [LN].

QUESTION—What relationship is indicated by τότε 'then' that begins the paragraph?

It could indicate either time or a logical connection of one event to the other [NAC]. It is a loose connective [EBC, PNTC], and does not indicate a particularly close sequence in time [PNTC]. By placing this passage immediately after verses 1–2 it gives a hint of God's sovereign control over the events that are transpiring [EBC]. It shows the plot of the Jewish authorities to be the fulfillment of what Jesus has just predicted [BNTC, Lns, WBC]. Jesus accurately foretold the time of his death, and then the authorities made their own plan for it at a different time, which ultimately was not the timing that actually came about [NTC]. Ironically, the plotting of the chief priests and elders happened at the same time that Jesus was telling his disciples about his impending death [My].

QUESTION—Was the αὐλή a courtyard or a palace?

The noun can refer either to a palace or to a courtyard [EBC, ICC]. It can refer either to the palace, or to a hall in the palace [Lns]. It was a residence [BNTC, **LN**, NTC, PNTC, TH, WBC; ESV, GW, KJV, NCV, NET, NIV, NRSV; CEV, NLT, REB]. It was a court or courtyard [BECNT, My, NAC, NICNT, NIGTC; NASB].

QUESTION—What is the makeup of the group that plotted Jesus' death?

This is the Sanhedrin [BNTC, EBC, Lns], including both clerical and lay members [EBC]. The scribes do not figure into this account because there is no discussion of scripture, of which they were considered the experts, and the Pharisees are missing from this meeting because the plot was primarily motivated by concern on the part of the priestly hierarchy for political considerations and their eagerness to conform to the expectations of the Romans [PNTC]. These priests and elders represented the more politically minded of the groups that comprised the Sanhedrin [NICNT]. It was the priestly aristocracy that opposed him at the end [ICC]. The scribes were not mentioned, but probably would have been represented there [NTC].

QUESTION—Why did they say 'not during the festival'?

They wanted to wait until after the festival when the crowds that might support Jesus would be gone [BECNT, BNTC, EBC, ICC, Lns, My, NAC, NTC, TH, TRT, WBC], but when Judas offered to hand Jesus over at a time that avoided public notice they decided to go ahead and do it during the time of the festival [BECNT, EBC, ICC, NAC, NTC]. They were probably trying to avoid the crowd of the festival, not the time of the festival itself [NIBC, NICNT].

DISCOURSE UNIT—26:6–28:20 [EBC]. The topic is the passion and resurrection of Jesus.

DISCOURSE UNIT—26:6–27:66 [EBC]. The topic is the passion.

DISCOURSE UNIT—26:6–30 [PNTC]. The topic is Jesus and his followers.

DISCOURSE UNIT—26:6–13 [CEV, ESV, GW, NASB, NCV, NET, NIV, NLT, NRSV, TEV]. The topic is a woman prepares Jesus' body for the tomb [GW], perfume for Jesus' burial [NCV], Jesus is anointed at Bethany [TEV], Jesus anointed at Bethany [ESV, NIV, NLT], the anointing at Bethany [NRSV], at Bethany [CEV], Jesus' anointing [NET], the precious ointment [NASB].

26:6 Now (when) Jesus was in Bethany in (the) house of Simon the leper,[a]
26:7 a-woman came to-him having an-alabaster-jar[b] of-very-costly[c]
perfumed-oil,[d] and she-poured (it) on his head (as) he-reclined (at the
table).

LEXICON—a. λεπρός (LN 23.162) (BAGD p. 472): 'leper' [BECNT, BNTC,
LN, NICNT, NIGTC, NTC, PNTC, WBC; ESV, KJV, NASB, NET, NIV,
NRSV, REB], 'leprous' [BAGD]. The phrase 'the leper' is translated
'who had leprosy' [CEV], 'who had previously had leprosy' [NLT], 'who
had a skin disease' [NCV], 'who had suffered from a skin disease/a
dreaded skin disease' [GW, TEV]. This noun denotes a person suffering
from a dread skin disease [LN].

   b. ἀλάβαστρος (LN 6.131) (BAGD p. 34): 'alabaster jar' [LN, NTC, WBC;
NCV, NET, NIV, NRSV, TEV], 'a beautiful alabaster jar' [NLT],
'alabaster vial' [BECNT, NASB], 'alabaster flask' [BAGD, BNTC,
NIGTC, PNTC; ESV], 'alabaster box' [KJV], 'bottle' [CEV, GW, REB],
'vase' [NICNT]. This noun denotes a jar made of alabaster stone, which
normally had a rather long neck that would be broken off for the contents
to be used. It served primarily as a container for precious substances such
as perfumes [LN].

   c. βαρύτιμος (LN **65.3**) (BAGD p. 134): 'very costly' [BECNT, BNTC,
PNTC; NASB, NRSV, REB], 'very expensive' [BAGD, NICNT, WBC;
ESV, GW, NIV], 'expensive' [**LN**; CEV, NCV, NET, NLT, TEV], 'of
great worth' [NIGTC], 'very precious' [BAGD, NTC; KJV], 'valuable'
[LN]. This adjective describes something of great value or worth,
implying in some contexts a monetary scale [LN].

   d. μύρον (LN 6.205) (BAGD p. 530): 'perfumed oil' [LN; NET], 'perfume'
[BAGD, LN, NIGTC, NTC, PNTC; CEV, GW, NASB, NCV, NIV, NLT,
REB, TEV], 'ointment' [BAGD, BECNT, BNTC, WBC; ESV, KJV,
NRSV], 'anointing oil' [NICNT]. This noun denotes a strongly aromatic
and expensive ointment [LN].

QUESTION—When did this event occur?

   This happened shortly before Palm Sunday [EBC, NAC, NTC], probably on
Saturday evening [Lns, NAC, NTC]. Matthew places the story here, out of
chronological sequence, because of thematic connections with Jesus' death
[EBC, NAC]. This might have been on Tuesday or Wednesday evening
[BNTC, My].

QUESTION—What is the relationship between this story and the account of
Jesus being anointed in Luke 7, Mark 14, and John 12?

   The account in Luke is of a different incident, but the accounts in Mark and
John are of the same event that Matthew relates here, one in which John
identifies the woman as being Mary the sister of Martha and Lazarus [EBC,
My, NIBC, NTC, PNTC, WBC]. Luke's story occurs in Galilee in the home
of a Pharisee, and in that account Jesus is anointed by a sinful woman,
whereas this account occurs in Bethany in Judea and the woman is Mary of
Bethany [EBC]. In John's account this occurs six days before the Passover,

so Matthew's account evidently does not follow the events of verses 1–5 sequentially; Matthew has gone back in time several days for this story, which occurred on Saturday evening [NTC].

26:8 But having-seen (this), the disciples were-indignant[a] saying, "Why[b] this waste[c]? **26:9** For it-could-have-been-possible (for) this ointment to-be-sold for much (money), and (the money) be-given to-(the) poor."

LEXICON—a. aorist act. indic. of ἀγανακτέω (LN 88.187) (BAGD p. 4): 'to be indignant' [BAGD, BNTC, LN, NICNT, NTC, PNTC, WBC; NASB, NIV, NLT, REB, ESV], 'to become indignant' [BECNT; NET], 'to become angry' [NIGTC; CEV, TEV], 'to be angry' [BAGD, LN; NRSV], 'to be irritated' [GW], 'to have indignation' [KJV], 'to be upset' [NCV], 'to be aroused' [BAGD]. This verb means to be indignant against what is judged to be wrong [LN].

   b. εἰς τι: 'why' [BECNT, BNTC, NICNT, NIGTC, NTC, PNTC; all versions except GW, KJV, NLT], 'what is the point of' [WBC], 'to what purpose' [KJV], 'why did she' [GW]. The question 'why this waste?' is translated as an emphatic statement: 'What a waste!' [NLT].

   c. ἀπώλεια (LN 65.14) (BAGD 1. p. 103): 'waste' [BAGD, BECNT, BNTC, LN, NICNT, NTC, PNTC, WBC; all versions except GW, NCV], 'loss' [NIGTC], 'ruin' [LN], 'destruction' [BAGD]. The noun 'waste' is translated as a verb: 'to waste' [GW, NCV]. This noun denotes an action demonstrating complete disregard for the value of something [LN].

26:10 But Jesus, knowing (this), said to-them, "Why do-you-make trouble[a] for-the woman? For she has done a-good[b] deed[c] to-me. **26:11** For you-always -have the poor with you, but you-do- not always -have me. **26:12** For by-pouring this ointment on my body she-did (it) to-prepare- me -for-burial.[d] **26:13** Truly I-say to-you, wherever this good-news is-proclaimed in (the) whole world, what she-has-done will-be-told in remembrance of-her.

LEXICON—a. κόπος (LN 22.7) (BAGD 1. p. 443): 'trouble' [BAGD, BECNT, BNTC, LN, WBC; KJV, REB], 'difficulty' [BAGD], 'distress' [LN]. The phrase κόπους παρέχετε 'to make trouble' is translated 'to trouble' [**LN**; ESV, NCV, NRSV], 'to bother' [NIGTC, NTC, PNTC; CEV, GW, NASB, NET, NIV, TEV], 'to give a hard time to' [NICNT], 'to criticize' [NLT]. This noun denotes a state characterized by troubling circumstances [LN].

   b. καλός (LN 88.4) (BAGD 2.b. p. 400): 'good' [BAGD, BECNT, BNTC, LN, NIGTC, WBC; KJV, NASB, NET, NLT, NRSV], 'beautiful' [NTC, PNTC; CEV, ESV, GW, NIV], 'fine' [LN; REB], 'fine and beautiful' [TEV], 'lovely' [NICNT], 'excellent' [NCV], 'praiseworthy' [BAGD, LN]. This adjective describes a positive moral quality, with the implication of being favorably valued [LN].

    c. ἔργον (LN 42.11) (BAGD 1.c.β. p. 308): 'deed' [BAGD, BNTC, LN, NIGTC; NASB], 'work' [BECNT, WBC; KJV], 'thing' [NICNT, NTC, PNTC; CEV, ESV, GW, NCV, NIV, NLT, REB, TEV], 'service' [NET, NRSV], 'act' [LN]. This noun denotes that which is done, with possible focus on the energy or effort involved [LN].

    d. aorist act. infin. of ἐνταφιάζω (LN 52.6) (BAGD p. 268): 'to prepare for burial' [BAGD, LN; all translations except GW, KJV, TEV], 'to get ready for burial' [TEV], 'preparation for burial' [LN]. This verb is translated 'she did it for my burial' [KJV]. This clause is translated 'she poured this perfume on my body before it is placed in a tomb' [GW]. This verb means to prepare a body for burial [LN].

QUESTION—How did Jesus become aware of what they were saying?

    1. Jesus' knowledge may not have been supernatural [EBC, PNTC]. Their comments were not made openly, and possibly were whispered or muttered [EBC, My, NICNT, PNTC], but Jesus may have sensed what was happening because it troubled the woman [EBC]. Their sentiments would have been apparent to all present, though Jesus is certainly depicted in Matthew as being able to read people's hearts [NIGTC]. He probably heard what they said [BNTC, Lns].

    2. He had supernatural knowledge of what they were thinking [WBC].

QUESTION—In what sense was the woman's action καλός 'good' or 'beautiful'?

    Jesus considered it to be a beautiful expression of devotion [PNTC], a unique expression of sacrificial love, which makes it a 'good work' [NAC]. It was a good work, a special work of righteousness [WBC]. The term καλός has an aesthetic tone that contrasts sharply with the disciples' pragmatic concerns; her action was an extravagant expression of loyalty that, for believers, accents the value of Jesus' death [NICNT]. It was beautiful in that it was prompted by heartfelt gratitude and love that was willing to be extravagant [NTC]. It was a spontaneous expression of loyal devotion and love [BNTC, TH]. It was a good work such as is mentioned in 5:16, which draws other people to glorify God [NIGTC]. It was excellent in every way [Lns]. It was morally beautiful, as opposed to the stinginess shown in the attitudes of the disciples [My].

QUESTION—Was the woman consciously aware that she was preparing Jesus' body for burial?

    The body of an executed criminal normally would not be anointed for burial, so this anointing had to occur prior to Jesus' execution [EBC, NAC, NICNT, PNTC].

    1. She knew that she was preparing his body for burial by anointing him [BNTC, Lns]. She was aware of his approaching death [My].

    2. It is possible that she knew this [BECNT, NTC, PNTC]. She perceived that Jesus' remaining time on earth was short [BECNT]. It is also possible that she didn't know, and Jesus was interpreting her action based on his

own knowledge of what was to occur [BECNT, NAC, NICNT, NIGTC, TH, TRT, PNTC].

3. She did not know that she was preparing his body for burial [ICC, WBC].

DISCOURSE UNIT—26:14–19 [NASB]. The topic is Judas' bargain.

DISCOURSE UNIT—26:14–16 [CEV, ESV, GW, NCV, NET, NLT, NRSV, TEV]. The topic is Judas plans to betray Jesus [GW], Judas becomes an enemy of Jesus [NCV], Judas agrees to betray Jesus [NLT, NRSV, TEV], Judas to betray Jesus [ESV], the plan to betray Jesus [NET], Judas and the chief priests [CEV].

26:14 Then one of-the twelve, the-one called Judas Iscariot, having-gone to the chief-priests **26:15** said, "What are-you-willing to-give me, and[a] I-will-hand- him -over[b] to-you?" And they weighed-out[c] for-him thirty (pieces of) silver. **26:16** And from that-moment he-was-seeking an-opportunity[d] that-he-might-hand- him -over.[e]

LEXICON—a. καί (LN 89.87): 'and' [BNTC, LN, NICNT, NIGTC, PNTC; KJV], 'and then' [LN]. This conjunction indicates a relation that is translated as indicating a conditional clause: 'if I (hand him over, etc)' [NTC; CEV, ESV, GW, NIV, NRSV, TEV]. It is translated as indicating purpose: 'so I will (betray, etc)' [WBC], 'to (betray, etc)' [BECNT; NASB, NET, NLT, REB], 'for (giving)' [NCV]. This conjunction links a sequence of closely related events [LN].

　b. fut. act. indic. of παραδίδωμι (LN 37.111) (BAGD 1.b. p. 614): 'to hand over' [BAGD, BECNT, LN, NICNT, NIGTC, NTC; GW, NIV], 'to betray' [BNTC, LN, PNTC, WBC; NASB, NET, NLT, NRSV, REB, TEV], 'to deliver over/unto' [ESV, KJV], 'to turn over (to)' [BAGD, LN], 'to give to' [NCV], 'to give up' [BAGD]. The phrase κἀγώ ὑμῖν παραδώσω αὐτόν 'and I will hand him over to you' is translated 'if I help you arrest Jesus' [CEV]. This verb means to deliver a person into the control of someone else, involving either the handing over of a presumably guilty person for punishment by authorities or the handing over of an individual to an enemy who will presumably take undue advantage of the victim [LN].

　c. aorist act. indic. of ἵστημι (LN **57.158**) (BAGD II.2.c. p. 382): 'to weigh out' [BECNT, BNTC, NIGTC, NTC; NASB, REB], 'to pay' [**LN**; CEV, ESV, NRSV], 'to count out' [NIV, TEV], 'to give' [NCV, NLT], 'to agree on' [NICNT], 'to set for (him)' [PNTC], 'to set out (for him)' [NET], 'to set with (him)' [WBC], 'to offer' [BAGD; GW], 'to covenant with (him)' [KJV], 'to set or fix (a price), to allow' [BAGD]. This verb means to pay, possibly in the sense of to weigh out or to count out a sum of money [LN].

　d. εὐκαιρία (LN 67.5) (BAGD p. 321): 'opportunity' [BECNT, LN, NTC, PNTC; ESV, KJV, NET, NIV, NLT, NRSV, REB], 'good opportunity'

[NICNT; NASB], 'favorable opportunity' [BAGD, **LN**], 'suitable opportunity' [BNTC], 'opportune time' [WBC], 'opportune moment' [NIGTC], 'the right moment' [BAGD], 'chance' [GW], 'good chance' [CEV, TEV], 'best time' [NCV], 'good occasion, favorable time' [LN]. This noun denotes a favorable occasion for some event [LN].

e. aorist act. subj. of παραδίδωμι (LN **37.111**) (BAGD 1.b. p. 614): 'to hand over' [BAGD, LN, NICNT, NIGTC, NTC; NIV, TEV], 'to betray' [BNTC, **LN**, PNTC, WBC; all versions except NCV, NIV, TEV], 'to give (someone) up' [BAGD, BECNT], 'to turn (someone) in' [NCV], 'to turn over to' [BAGD, LN].

QUESTION—What relationship is indicated by the beginning adjective τότε 'then'?

It indicates sequence of action, but it also shows a logical connection with what was just narrated [EBC, Lns]; Judas concluded that Jesus was not acting very much like a king, and in fact was conceding defeat by talking of death, and he also resented Jesus' rebuke [EBC]. This occurred several days after the anointing and very soon after the meeting of the chief priests to plot Jesus' death [NTC]. It connects Jesus' statement showing his lack of interest in money with Judas' going to the priests to ask for money [ICC]. It is a loose temporal connection [TH].

QUESTION—What is the specific meaning of ἵστημι 'to weigh out'?

Even though coins had a standard value, older coins that were more worn with age would have less actual silver, and must be weighed to assure that they actually contained the value of silver that they represented [Lns]. Weighing was still practiced for large sums paid from the temple treasury [My]. They weighed the silver on scales [Lns, NIBC]. Since coins were standardized by that time, here it simply means to strike a bargain [NICNT]. The wording is taken from Zech 11:13 [EBC, ICC, NICNT, NIGTC, NTC, WBC].

QUESTION—What is significant about the sum of money paid to Judas?

It recalls Zech 11:12–13 which indicates that same sum as being a rather insignificant amount, and what would be paid for a slave that was gored by an ox [BECNT, BNTC, EBC, ICC, Lns, NIBC, NICNT, NTC, PNTC, TH, WBC]. The sum reflects the low estimation of him by Judas [EBC, TRT], and by the priests as well [EBC].

QUESTION—What was the value of the amount Judas received for his betrayal?

It was probably worth about four months' wages for a laborer [BECNT, EBC, ICC, NAC, TRT]. It was probably worth about two to three months' wages [NIGTC]. It was worth about a month's wages [BNTC].

QUESTION—What is implied by the term εὐκαιρία 'opportunity'?

Judas was seeking a time that would be convenient or suitable in the sense that the chief priests wanted to arrest Jesus when there were no supportive crowds around, in order to avoid provoking a riot [ICC, My, NICNT, PNTC, WBC].

DISCOURSE UNIT—26:17–46 [NICNT]. The topic is Jesus' last hours with the disciples.

DISCOURSE UNIT—26:17–30 [NIV, NLT]. The topic is the Lord's supper [NIV], the last supper [NLT].

DISCOURSE UNIT—26:17–25 [CEV, ESV, NCV, NET, NRSV, TEV]. The topic is Jesus eats the Passover meal [NCV], Jesus eats the Passover meal with his disciples [CEV, TEV], the Passover with the disciples [ESV, NRSV], the Passover [NET].

DISCOURSE UNIT—26:17–20 [GW]. The topic is preparations for the Passover.

26:17 **On the first-day of-the Unleavened-Bread**[a] **the disciples came to Jesus, saying, "Where do-you-want us-to-prepare for-you to-eat the Passover-meal**[b]**?" 26:18 And he said, "Go into the city to a-certain-man,**[c] **and say to-him, 'The Teacher says, "My time**[d] **is near; I-will-keep**[e] **the Passover**[f] **at your-(place) with my disciples."'" 26:19 And the disciples did as Jesus directed them, and they-prepared the Passover-meal.**

LEXICON—a. ἄζυμος (LN 5.13) (BAGD 1.b. p. 20): 'Unleavened Bread' [BECNT, BNTC, NICNT, NIGTC, PNTC; ESV, NASB, NRSV, REB], 'the Feast Of Unleavened Bread' [NTC; KJV, NCV, NET, NIV], 'the Festival Of Unleavened Bread' [BAGD, WBC; GW, NLT, TEV], 'the Festival Of Thin Bread' [CEV], 'unleavened, without yeast, not having yeast' [LN]. This adjective describes the absence of yeast [LN].

b. πάσχα (LN 51.7) (BAGD 2. p. 633): 'Passover meal' [LN, NICNT, WBC; CEV, GW, NCV, NLT, TEV], 'Passover supper' [NTC], 'Passover' [BAGD, BECNT, BNTC, NIGTC, PNTC; ESV, KJV, NASB, NET, NIV, NRSV, REB], 'paschal lamb' [BAGD]. This noun denotes the Passover meal eaten in connection with the Passover festival [LN]. (Regarding the Passover festival see 51.6 in verse 2 above and item d. in verse 18 below).

c. δεῖνα (LN **92.19**) (BAGD p. 173): 'a certain man' [BAGD, BECNT, BNTC, **LN**; all versions except KJV], 'certain' [LN], 'so-and-so' [BAGD, NICNT, NTC, PNTC], 'such-and-such' [NIGTC], 'such a man' [KJV], 'the man' [WBC], 'a man' [LN], 'somebody' [BAGD, LN]. This noun denotes an entity which one cannot or does not wish to make explicit and in the NT it only refers to a man. Although in many translations δεῖνα is translated as 'certain', this can give a wrong impression since it would imply that the individual is known to the parties involved or has been identified by the context. [LN].

d. καιρός (LN 67.1) (BAGD 2.b. p. 395): 'time' [BAGD, BECNT, BNTC, LN, NICNT, NIGTC, NTC, PNTC, WBC; CEV, ESV, GW, NASB, NET, NLT, NRSV, REB], 'appointed time' [NIV, REB], 'hour' [TEV], 'occasion' [LN]. The phrase καιρός μου 'my time' is translated 'the chosen time' [NCV]. This noun denotes points of time consisting of occasions for particular events [LN].

e. pres. act. indic. of ποιέω (LN 90.45) (BAGD I.1.b.ζ. p. 681): 'to keep' [BAGD, BECNT, BNTC, PNTC; ESV, KJV, NASB, NRSV, REB], 'to observe' [NET], 'to celebrate (a festival)' [BAGD, NTC, WBC; GW, NIV, TEV], 'to hold' [NICNT], 'to do' [BAGD, LN, NIGTC], 'to eat (the Passover meal)' [CEV, NLT], 'to have' [NCV]. This verb describes an agent relation with a numerable event [LN].

f. πάσχα (LN 51.6, 51.7) (BAGD 3. p. 633): 'Passover' [BECNT, BNTC, LN (51.6), NIGTC, NTC, PNTC, WBC; all versions except CEV NLT], 'Passover festival' [LN (51.6)], 'Passover meal' [BAGD, LN (51.7), NICNT; CEV, NLT]. This noun denotes the Jewish festival commemorating the deliverance of Jews from Egypt [LN (51.6)]. It may also denote the Passover meal itself, which was eaten in connection with the Passover festival [LN (51.7)].

QUESTION—What is the first day of Unleavened Bread?

The Passover was followed by the seven day Feast of Unleavened Bread, so the day of Passover was often considered the first day of that eight-day observance [BECNT, BNTC, ICC, Lns, My, NAC, NIBC, NICNT, NIGTC, NTC, PNTC, TRT, WBC].

QUESTION—Why do Matthew, Mark, and Luke indicate that the last supper occurred on the day of Passover, but John records it as being the day before Passover?

Two different calendars were observed in Judea at that time, and Jesus and the disciples may have used the calendar observed in Galilee, which observed the Passover a day earlier than the priests would have observed it based on the calendar they used [PNTC, WBC]. The preparations were being made on Thursday afternoon, but by the time the meal came it was evening, which in Jewish reckoning was considered the beginning of the next day, which was Passover [BECNT, EBC, NTC]. Jesus observed Passover a day early (Thursday evening), though without the lamb, which would have to have been sacrificed at the temple on Friday because he was going to be executed on Passover, which was Friday [NICNT].

QUESTION—What did Jesus mean by 'my time is near'?

Jesus recognizes that the time of his death is approaching [BECNT, BNTC, EBC, Lns, NAC, NIBC, NIGTC, NTC, PNTC, TH, WBC], although neither the man being addressed nor the disciples would his understood Jesus' ambiguous statement to imply that [EBC, PNTC, WBC]. He knew that it was time for his suffering, which was foreordained by God [NICNT]. It refers to a time that God had set for him, which was the time of Jesus' death [TH, TRT]. The man would have understood that Jesus was referring to his impending death [Lns]. The disciples and the man they were to meet may have understood that Jesus was referring to his own death [TRT].

DISCOURSE UNIT—26:20–25 [NASB]. The topic is the last Passover.

26:20 **And evening having-come, he-reclined[a] (at table) with the twelve.**

TEXT—Manuscripts reading μετὰ τῶν δώδεκα 'with the twelve' are given a C
rating by GNT to indicate that choosing it over a variant text was difficult.
Translations that follow this reading are BECNT, BNTC, NIGTC, NTC,
PNTC, WBC; ESV, KJV, NET, NIV, and NRSV. Manuscripts reading μετὰ
τῶν δώδεκα μαθητῶν 'with the twelve disciples' are followed by NICNT;
CEV, NASB, REB, NLT, TEV. GW reads 'the twelve apostles', and NCV
has 'his twelve followers', though this choice may be due to textual
considerations or to concern for clarity of English style.

LEXICON—a. imperf. mid. or pass. (deponent = act.) indic. of ἀνάκειμαι (LN
17.23) (BAGD 2. p. 55): 'to recline at table' [BECNT, BNTC, NIGTC,
NTC, WBC; ESV, NASB, NIV], 'to recline' [BAGD, LN, PNTC], 'to sit
at table' [NICNT; NCV], 'to sit down at table' [NLT], 'to be at table'
[BAGD, LN; GW], 'to take one's place at the table' [NET], 'to eat' [LN;
CEV], 'to sit down' [KJV, REB], 'to sit down to eat' [LN; TEV], 'to dine'
[LN]. The verb ἀνέκειτο 'he reclined at table' is translated 'he took his
place' [NRSV]. This verb means to be in a reclining position as one eats
(with the focus either upon the position or the act of eating) [LN].

DISCOURSE UNIT—26:21–25 [GW]. The topic is Jesus knows who will
betray him.

26:21 **And (while) they-were-eating, he said, "Truly I-say to-you, that one
of you will-betray[a] me." 26:22 And being- greatly -distressed[b] each one
began to-say to him, "Surely- I am –not[c] (the one), Lord?"**

LEXICON—a. fut. act. indic. of παραδίδωμι (LN 37.111) (BAGD 1.b. p. 614):
'to betray' [BECNT, BNTC, LN, NICNT, NTC, PNTC, WBC; ESV, GW,
KJV, NASB, NET, NIV, NLT, NRSV, REB, TEV], 'to hand (someone)
over' [BAGD, LN, NIGTC], 'to hand (someone) over to enemies' [CEV],
'to turn against' [NCV], 'to turn over to' [BAGD, LN], 'to give someone
up' [BAGD]. This verb means to deliver a person into the control of
someone else and it may involve either the handing over of a presumably
guilty person for punishment by authorities or the handing over of an
individual to an enemy who will presumably take undue advantage of the
victim [LN].

   b. pres. pass. participle of λυπέομαι (LN 25.274) (BAGD 2.b. p. 481): 'to
be/become distressed' [BAGD, LN, NIGTC, WBC; NET, NLT, NRSV,
REB], 'to be filled with distress' [NTC], 'to be sad' [BAGD, LN, PNTC;
CEV, NIV], 'to be made sad' [NCV], 'to be grieved' [BAGD, BECNT,
BNTC; NASB], 'to be sorrowful' [ESV, KJV], 'to be horrified' [NICNT],
'to feel deeply hurt' [GW], 'to be upset' [TEV]. This verb means to be sad
as the result of what has happened or what one has done [LN].

c. μήτι (LN 69.16) (BAGD p. 520): 'surely not?' [BAGD]. The question μήτι ἐγώ εἰμι 'surely I am not the one?' is translated 'surely not I?' [BECNT, NTC; NASB, NET, NIV, NRSV], 'surely it is not I?' [BNTC], 'could it be I?' [NIGTC], 'is it I?' [PNTC; ESV, KJV], 'am I the one?' [NLT], 'I'm not the one, am I?' [WBC], 'you don't mean me, do you?' [NICNT; GW], 'you can't mean me?' [CEV], 'surely you do not mean me?' [REB, TEV], 'surely I am not the one who will turn against you?' [NCV]. This interrogative particle indicates a somewhat emphatic negative response [LN].

26:23 And he-answered, "The-one having-dipped his hand into the bowl with me (is) the one who-will-betray me. **26:24** The Son of-Man goes[a] just-as it-is-written of him, but woe[b] to that man by whom the Son of-Man is-betrayed! It-would-have-been better for-him if that man had- not -been-born." **26:25** And Judas, the-one betraying him, said, "Surely- I am -not (the one), Rabbi?" He-says to-him, "You said[c] (it)."

LEXICON—a. pres. act. indic. of ὑπάγω (LN 15.35) (BAGD 3. p. 837): 'to go' [BAGD, BECNT, BNTC, LN, NIGTC, NTC, PNTC, WBC; ESV, KJV, NASB, NET, NIV, NRSV, REB], 'to go away' [NICNT], 'to die' [CEV, GW, NCV, NLT, TEV], 'to go away from, to depart, to leave' [LN]. This verb means to move away from a reference point [LN].

b. οὐαί (LN 22.9) (BAGD 1.a. p. 591): 'woe!' [BAGD, BECNT, BNTC, NICNT, NIGTC, NTC, PNTC, WBC; ESV, KJV, NASB, NET, NIV, NRSV], 'alas!' [BAGD; REB], 'disaster, horror' [LN]. The phrase οὐαὶ τῷ ἀνθρώπῳ ἐκείνῳ 'woe to that man' is translated 'it's going to be terrible for the one' [CEV], 'how horrible/terrible it will be for that person/one' [GW, NCV, NLT], 'how terrible for that man' [TEV]. This particle describes a state of intense hardship or distress [LN].

c. aorist act. indic. of εἶπον (LN 33.69) (BAGD II.1.e. p. 469): 'to say' [LN; all translations except GW, NCV, NIV], 'to declare, to maintain' [BAGD]. The statement σὺ εἶπας 'you said it' [BECNT, NTC, PNTC], is translated 'you have said it' [NICNT, NIGTC; NLT, REB], 'you have said it yourself' [NASB, NET], 'you have said so' [ESV, NRSV], 'you have said' [BNTC], 'thou hast said' [KJV], 'you have said the truth' [WBC], 'yes, it is you' [NCV, NIV], 'yes, I do' [GW], 'so you say' [TEV], 'That's what you say! Jesus replied. But later, Judas did betray him' [CEV]. This verb means to speak or talk, with apparent focus upon the content of what is said [LN].

QUESTION—What is the significance of Jesus saying that the traitor is one who has dipped his hand in the bowl?

Jesus is not identifying who the traitor is, but emphasizing the fact that it is someone who was eating from the one common bowl with him, sharing table fellowship with him [BNTC, EBC, ICC, Lns, NICNT, NTC, PNTC, TH, TRT]. Eating together was a sign of fellowship, intimacy, and solidarity, which makes the betrayal that much worse [NIBC, TH, WBC]. All of them would have dipped their hand in the dish at the same time as Jesus at some point or other during the meal [EBC, NAC, NTC].

QUESTION—What significance is there in the fact that Judas calls Jesus 'Rabbi' but not 'Lord' as the others did?

He addresses him not as his lord, as the other disciples do, but as a teacher [Lns, NAC, NIBC, NTC, PNTC, WBC]. This difference in address is significant [NIBC]. In this gospel only disciples or potential disciples call him 'lord', whereas those who oppose or resist him or who are outside the group of disciples use other titles such as this one [NICNT, WBC].

QUESTION—What did Jesus mean with his cryptic answer 'You have said it'?

It is an indirect way of saying 'yes' [BECNT, BNTC, NAC, NIGTC, TRT, WBC]. Jesus affirms what Judas has said, though in a way that shows that he knows that Judas is insincere in the question he is asking [BECNT, Lns, NICNT, NTC]. In saying it this way Jesus is telling Judas that he has indicted himself with his own words [NAC]. Jesus did not take the initiative to tell Judas that he knew of his treachery, but when asked, he had to acknowledge that he knew [PNTC]. It was somewhat ambiguous to the other disciples, but Judas would have immediately realized that Jesus knew what he was intending to do [BECNT, EBC, NAC, NIGTC]. Jesus' answer to Judas was probably spoken privately [NAC, NICNT].

QUESTION—At what point did Judas leave the meal?

He left immediately at this point [Lns, My, NTC, WBC]. He left when he realized that Jesus knew what he intended to do [My, NTC]. He probably left after they had partaken of the bread and the wine [NICNT]. He left after the Passover meal, when Jesus and the other disciples were going to the Mount of Olives [BECNT, BNTC].

QUESTION—Were the other disciples aware that Jesus had identified Judas as the betrayer?

1. They were not aware that Jesus had identified Judas as the traitor [BECNT, EBC, NAC, NIGTC].

2. They were aware of what Jesus said and meant [Lns].

DISCOURSE UNIT—26:26–35 [NASB]. The topic is the Lord's Supper instituted.

DISCOURSE UNIT—26:26–30 [CEV, GW, NCV, NET, NRSV, TEV]. The topic is the Lord's supper [CEV, GW, NCV, NET, TEV], the institution of the Lord's supper [NRSV].

DISCOURSE UNIT—26:26–29 [ESV]. The topic is the institution of the Lord's Supper.

26:26 (While) they were-eating, Jesus taking a-loaf-of-bread, and having-blessed[a] (it/God) he broke (it), and giving it to-the disciples he-said, "Take, eat; this is my body." **26:27** And having-taken (the) cup, and having-giving-thanks[b] he gave (it) to-them saying, "Drink from it, all (of you), **26:28** for this is my blood of-the covenant,[c] (which is) poured-out[d] for many for (the) forgiveness[e] of-sins. **26:29** And I-tell-you, from now-on I-will- not -drink from this fruit of-the vine until that day when I drink it with you new[f] in my Father's kingdom."

TEXT—Manuscripts reading τῆς διαθήκης 'of the covenant' are given a B rating by GNT to indicate it was regarded to be almost certain. Other manuscripts reading τῆς διαθήκης καινῆς 'of the new covenant' are followed by KJV, NCV.

LEXICON—a. aorist act. participle of εὐλογέω (LN 33.470, 33.356) (BAGD 1. or 2.b., p. 322): 'to bless (God)' [WBC], 'to bless the bread/it' [CEV, ESV, GW, KJV, NLT, NRSV], 'to say a/the blessing' [NICNT, NIGTC; REB], 'to pronounce the blessing' [BNTC], 'to give thanks' [NTC, PNTC; NET, NIV], 'to give a prayer of thanks' [TEV], 'to thank (God)' [BECNT; NCV], 'to bless' [BAGD 2.b, LN (33.470)], 'to praise' [BAGD 1, LN (33.356)], 'to consecrate' [BAGD 2.b]. This participle is translated as a noun: '(after) a blessing' [NASB]. This verb means to ask God to bestow divine favor on, with the implication that the verbal act itself constitutes a significant benefit [LN (33.470)], or it may mean to speak of something in favorable terms, that is to praise God [LN (33.356)].

b. aorist act. participle of εὐχαριστέω (LN 33.349) (BAGD 2. p. 328): 'to give thanks' [BNTC, NICNT, NIGTC, NTC, PNTC, WBC; ESV, KJV, NASB, NET, NIV, NRSV], 'to give thanks to God' [CEV, NLT, TEV], 'to offer thanks to God' [REB], 'to thank God' [BECNT; NCV], 'to speak a prayer of thanksgiving' [GW], 'to thank' [LN]. This verb means to express gratitude for benefits or blessings [LN].

c. διαθήκη (LN 34.44) (BAGD 2. p. 183): 'covenant' [BAGD, BECNT, BNTC, LN, NICNT, NIGTC, NTC, PNTC, WBC; ESV, NASB, NET, NIV, NLT, NRSV, REB, TEV], 'agreement' [CEV, NCV], 'promise' [GW], 'testament' [KJV], 'pact' [LN]. This noun denotes the verbal content of an agreement between two persons specifying reciprocal benefits and responsibilities [LN].

d. perf. pass. participle of ἐκχύννομαι (LN **23.112**) (BAGD 1. p. 247): 'to be poured out' [BAGD; all versions except KJV, REB], 'to be shed' [BAGD, BNTC; KJV, REB]. The idiom ἐκχύννεται τὸ αἷμα means to die, with the implication of a sacrificial purpose [LN].

e. ἄφεσις (LN **40.8**) (BAGD 2. p. 125): 'forgiveness' [BAGD, BECNT, BNTC, **LN**, NICNT, NIGTC, NTC, PNTC, WBC; ESV, NASB, NET, NIV, NRSV, REB, TEV], 'remission' [KJV], 'pardon' [BAGD]. This noun is translated as a verb phrase: 'will have their sins forgiven' [CEV], 'so that sins are forgiven' [GW], 'to forgive their/the sins' [NCV, NLT]. This noun denotes the removal of the guilt resulting from wrongdoing [LN].

f. καινός (LN 58.71) (BAGD 3.b. p. 394): 'new' [BAGD, BECNT, BNTC, LN, NICNT, NTC, PNTC, WBC; all versions except NIV], 'anew'

[NIGTC; NIV]. This adjective describes that which is new or recent and hence superior to that which is old [LN].

QUESTION—Was this leavened or unleavened bread?

1. It was unleavened [BECNT, BNTC, EBC, Lns, My, NAC, NICNT, NIGTC, NTC, TRT].

2. It could have been either leavened or unleavened [PNTC].

QUESTION—What is the object of the aorist active participle εὐλογήσας 'having blessed'?

The blessing said over the meal consists of a blessing of God himself in the action of giving thanks by means of a prayer that begins 'Blessed are you, O Lord' [EBC, ICC, NICNT, PNTC], and it is not a blessing of any physical object [PNTC, TRT]. Jesus is thanking God for the bread [BECNT, BNTC, ICC, Lns, My, NIBC, NICNT, NIGTC, NTC, PNTC, TH, TRT, WBC; NCV, NET, NIV, TEV]. This is translated as though Jesus is blessing the bread itself or saying a blessing over the bread that they are about to eat [CEV, ESV, GW, KJV, NASB, NLT, NRSV, REB].

QUESTION—How is the verb ἐστιν 'is' to be understood in the statements 'this is my body...this is my blood'?

In the Aramaic language that Jesus was probably speaking this verb normally would be left out as unnecessary and implied [ICC, Lns, NAC, NIBC, PNTC]. The verb itself has a very wide range of potential meanings and can prove very little [EBC, ICC, NICNT]; what must be kept in focus is how it links with the redemption history of the Passover meal [EBC]. The action of breaking the bread is essential to understanding what Jesus meant [BNTC].

1. Since Jesus is physically present with them it should not be taken literally [My, NAC, NICNT, NTC, WBC], yet it must be taken seriously as involving deep and significant symbolism [NTC, WBC]. The bread and the cup *represent* Jesus' broken body and shed blood [BECNT, My]. It does not indicate a relationship of identity, meaning that the bread actually *is* his body, though it probably means more than that it just *represents* his body [NIBC].

2. He means that the bread actually *is* his body [Lns].

QUESTION—What does the 'blood of the covenant' mean?

It is a reference to Exodus 24:8 [BECNT, BNTC, EBC, ICC, Lns, My, NAC, NIBC, NICNT, NIGTC, NTC, PNTC, TRT, WBC]. It is the blood of Jesus that inaugurates the new covenant prophesied in Jeremiah 31:31–34 [EBC, NAC, NICNT, NIGTC, PNTC, TRT, WBC], as is evidenced by the addition of the phrase 'for the forgiveness of sins' [EBC, PNTC, WBC]. To speak of God freshly establishing his covenant with his people is very similar to saying that his kingdom is coming [NIGTC].

QUESTION—What relationship is indicated by περί 'for' in the phrase 'for many'?

It has the same meaning here as ὑπέρ 'for' in Mark's account [EBC, My, PNTC], of something given vicariously for or in the place of someone else [EBC, PNTC], on behalf of someone else [BNTC, WBC], or for someone else's benefit [BNTC, Lns, My, NICNT]. It has the sense of substitution [EBC, NICNT, NIGTC, PNTC].

DISCOURSE UNIT—26:30-35 [ESV]. The topic is Jesus foretells Peter's denial.

26:30 **And having-sung-a-hymn,**[a] **they-went out to the Mount of Olives.**

LEXICON—a. aorist act. participle of ὑμνέω (LN **33.113**) (BAGD 2. p. 836): 'to sing a hymn' [BAGD, **LN**; BECNT, BNTC, NIGTC, NTC, PNTC, WBC; all versions], 'to sing the psalms' [NICNT], 'to sing a song of praise' [LN]. It was 'the Passover hymn' [REB]. This verb means to sing a song associated with religion and worship [LN].

QUESTION—What did they sing?

The Hallel, consisting of Psalms 113–118, was usually sung at the Passover, with Psalms 115–118 being sung at the end [BNTC, Lns, My, PNTC, TRT, WBC]. They would have sung the last part of the Hallel [NIGTC, TH], probably Psalms 115–118 [BECNT, EBC, Lns, NAC, NIBC, NICNT, NTC, PNTC, TRT, WBC]. It was a hymn specifically used at Passover [REB]. These psalms would have been chanted [NICNT].

DISCOURSE UNIT—26:31–27:26 [PNTC]. The topic is Jesus brought to trial.

DISCOURSE UNIT—26:31-35 [CEV, GW, NCV, NET, NIV, NLT, NRSV, TEV]. The topic is Jesus predicts Peter's denial [GW, NIV, NLT, TEV], Jesus' followers will leave him [NCV], the prediction of Peter's denial [NET], Peter's denial foretold [NRSV], Peter's promise [CEV].

26:31 **Then Jesus says to-them, "All of-you will-fall-away**[a] **because-of**[b] **me this night; for it-is-written, 'I-will-strike**[c] **the shepherd, and the sheep of-the flock will-be-scattered.'** **26:32** **But after my being-raised**[d] **I-will-go-ahead-of you to Galilee."**

LEXICON—a. fut. pass. indic. of σκανδαλίζομαι (LN 31.77) (BAGD 1.b. p. 752): 'to fall away' [BECNT, WBC; ESV, NASB, NET, NIV], 'to take offense' [BAGD, BNTC, NIGTC], 'to be offended' [KJV], 'to be brought down' [PNTC], 'to be caused to stumble' [NICNT], 'to stumble in one's faith' [NCV], 'to lose faith' [REB], 'to be led into sin' [BAGD], 'to cease believing, to give up believing' [LN]. The phrase 'fall away because of me' is translated 'become untrue to me' [NTC], 'reject me' [CEV], 'abandon me' [GW], 'run away and leave me' [TEV], 'desert me' [NLT], 'become deserters' [NRSV]. This verb means to give up believing what is right and let oneself believe what is false [LN].

b. ἐν (LN 89.26): 'because of' [BECNT, LN, NICNT, PNTC, WBC; ESV, KJV, NASB, NET, NRSV, REB], 'at' [BNTC, NIGTC], 'on account of' [LN; NCV, NIV], 'by reason of' [LN], not explicit [NTC; CEV, GW, NLT, TEV]. This preposition indicates cause or reason, with focus upon instrumentality, either of objects or events [LN].

c. fut. act. indic. of πατάσσω (LN 20.73) (BAGD 1.c. p. 634): 'to strike' [BECNT, NICNT, NIGTC, PNTC, WBC; ESV, GW, NET, NIV, NLT, NRSV, REB], 'to strike down' [BAGD, BNTC, LN, NTC; CEV, NASB], 'to smite' [KJV], 'to kill' [NCV, TEV], 'to slay' [BAGD, LN]. This verb means to slay by means of a mortal blow or disease [LN].

d. aorist pass. infin. of ἐγείρω (LN 23.94) (BAGD 2.c. p. 215): 'to be raised' [BAGD, BECNT, NICNT, NTC, PNTC, WBC; NASB, NET, REB], 'to be raised to life' [LN; CEV, TEV], 'to be raised up' [NIGTC; ESV, NRSV], 'to be raised from the dead' [NLT], 'to be brought back to life' [GW], 'to rise' [BAGD, BNTC; NIV], 'to rise from the dead' [NCV], 'to rise again' [KJV], 'to be made to live again' [LN]. This verb means to cause someone to live again after having once died [LN].

QUESTION—What relationship is indicated by the initial adverb Τότε 'Then'?

It indicates that what is reported here took place as they were going to Gethsemane [Lns, My, NIBC, NTC]. It is used for transition but does not indicate a temporal relation [EBC].

QUESTION—What is the connotation of 'fall away'?

They would fall away in the sense of abandoning or forsaking him [EBC, ICC, My, NAC, NIBC, TRT, WBC; CEV, GW, NLT, NRSV, TEV]. It means they would fall into serious spiritual failure [NICNT]. It means they would stumble in their faith and almost abandon it [BECNT]. They would be trapped into becoming untrue to him [NTC]. They would have a grievous lapse and fail him, but they would not abandon faith altogether [PNTC]. They will be trapped in some kind of sin by being caught and overwhelmed by what would happen to him [Lns, PNTC].

QUESTION—In what sense would Jesus 'go ahead' of them?

It means that he will go to Galilee before they do and will meet them there [BECNT, BNTC, EBC, Lns, NTC, TRT, TH, WBC]. It continues the shepherding metaphor, implying that he will be at the head of the flock of disciples [BECNT, ICC, NIBC, NIGTC, WBC]. They will follow him in Galilee once again, as they did before [ICC, Lns, My, NAC, NIGTC, PNTC].

26:33 But answering Peter said to-him, "(Even) if[a] all fall-away because of you, I will- never fall-away." **26:34** Jesus said to-him, "Truly I-say to-you that in this (very) night, before (the) cock crows, you-will-deny[b] me three-times." **26:35** Peter says to-him, "Even-if it-is-necessary for-me to-die with you, I-will- certainly-not -deny you." And all the disciples said likewise.

LEXICON—a. εἰ (LN 89.65) (BAGD I.1.a. p. 219): 'even if' [BECNT; CEV, GW, NIV, NLT], 'if' [BAGD, BNTC, LN, NICNT, NIGTC, WBC; NET], 'even though' [NTC; NASB, TEV], 'though' [PNTC; ESV, KJV, NRSV], '(everyone else) may' [NCV, REB]. This conjunction indicates a condition, real or hypothetical, actual or contrary to fact [LN].

   b. fut. mid. (deponent=act.) indic. of ἀπαρνέομαι (LN **33.277**) (BAGD p. 81): 'to deny' [BECNT, BNTC, **LN**, NICNT, NIGTC, NTC, PNTC, WBC; ESV, KJV, NASB, NET, NRSV], 'to disown' [NIV, REB], 'to deny knowing someone' [BAGD; NLT]. The phrase ἀπαρνήσῃ με 'you will deny me' is translated 'you will say that you don't know me' [CEV, GW, NCV, TEV]. This verb means to say that one does not know about or is in any way related to a person or event [LN].

QUESTION—At about what time would the rooster have crowed?
   It would have crowed about 12:30 AM [EBC] or 1:30 AM [NAC]. It would have crowed during the third of the four watches of the night as Romans counted them [EBC, My, NTC, PNTC, TH] (which would have been between about midnight and about 3:00 AM). It simply means that it will be sometime before dawn [Lns, NIGTC, WBC].

DISCOURSE UNIT—26:36–46 [CEV, ESV, GW, NASB, NCV, NET, NIV, NLT, NRSV, TEV]. The topic is Jesus prays [CEV], Jesus prays alone [NCV], Jesus prays in the garden of Gethsemane [GW], Jesus prays in Gethsemane [ESV, NLT, NRSV, TEV], the garden of Gethsemane [NASB], Gethsemane [NET, NIV].

26:36 Then Jesus goes with them to a-place[a] called Gethsemane; and he says to-the disciples, "Sit here while I-go-away over-there to-pray." **26:37** And taking Peter and the two sons of Zebedee, he-began to-be-grieved[b] and to-be-distressed.[c] **26:38** Then he-says to-them, "My-soul is deeply-grieved[d] to-the-point-of[e] death; remain here and watch[f] with me."

LEXICON—a. χωρίον (LN 1.95) (BAGD 1. p. 890): 'place' [BAGD, BECNT, BNTC, NTC, PNTC; all versions except NLT], 'estate' [NICNT], 'area' [WBC], 'field' [BAGD, LN], 'plot of land' [NIGTC], 'olive grove' [NLT], 'piece of land' [BAGD], 'land' [LN]. This noun denotes land under cultivation or used for pasture [LN].

   b. pres. pass. infin. of λυπέομαι (LN 25.274) (BAGD 2.b. p. 481): 'to be grieved' [BAGD, BECNT, BNTC, NIGTC; NASB, NRSV], 'to be sorrowful' [PNTC, WBC; ESV, KJV, NIV], 'to be filled with sorrow' [NTC], 'to become anguished' [NET, NLT], 'to be very sad' [CEV, NCV], 'to be sad, to be distressed' [BAGD, LN]. The phrase λυπεῖσθαι καὶ ἀδημονεῖν 'to be grieved and to be distressed' is translated 'to be overcome with distress' [NICNT], 'to feel deep anguish' [GW], 'distress and anguish overwhelmed him' [REB], 'grief and anguish came over him' [TEV]. This verb means to be sad as the result of what has happened or what one has done [LN].

c. pres. act. infin. of ἀδημονέω (LN 25.247) (BAGD p. 16): 'to be distressed' [BAGD, BNTC, LN, NIGTC, PNTC; NASB, NET, NLT], 'to be filled with anguish' [NTC], 'to be troubled' [BAGD, BECNT, LN; CEV, ESV, NCV, NIV], 'to be anxious' [WBC], 'to be agitated' [NRSV], 'to be very heavy' [KJV], 'to be in anxiety' [BAGD], 'to be upset' [LN]. This verb means to be distressed and troubled, with the probable implication of anguish [LN].

d. περίλυπος (LN **25.277**) (BAGD p. 648): 'deeply grieved' [BAGD, BECNT, NIGTC; NASB, NET, NRSV], 'grieved' [BNTC], 'deeply distressed' [NICNT], 'overwhelmed with sorrow' [NTC; NIV], 'very sorrowful' [PNTC; ESV], 'exceeding sorrowful' [KJV], 'sorrowful' [**LN**], 'full of sorrow' [NCV], 'crushed with grief' [NLT], 'very sad' [BAGD, LN, WBC], 'sad' [CEV]. The phrase περίλυπός ἐστιν ἡ ψυχή μου 'my soul is deeply grieved' is translated 'my anguish is so great' [GW], 'the sorrow in my heart is so great' [TEV], 'my heart is ready to break with grief' [REB]. This adjective describes being very sad or deeply distressed [LN].

e. ἕως (LN **78.51**) (BAGD II.4. p. 335): 'to the point of' [BECNT, **LN**, NICNT, NTC, PNTC; NASB, NCV, NIV, NLT], 'even to the point of' [NET], 'unto' [BAGD, BNTC], 'even unto' [KJV], 'to' [NIGTC], 'even to' [WBC; ESV, NRSV], 'to the extent of, to the degree that, up to' [LN], not explicit [REB]. The phrase ἕως θανάτου 'to the point of death' is translated 'that I feel as if I am dying' [CEV, GW], 'that it almost crushes me' [TEV]. This preposition indicates a degree extending to a particular point as marked by the context [LN].

f. pres. act. impera. of γρηγορέω (LN 23.72) (BAGD 1. p. 167): 'to watch' [BNTC, NIGTC, PNTC, WBC; ESV, KJV, NCV], 'to keep watch' [BECNT; NASB, NIV, NLT, TEV], 'to be watchful' [LN], 'to keep awake' [BAGD, NICNT, NTC; CEV], 'to stay awake' [LN; GW, NET, NRSV, REB]. This verb means to remain awake because of the need to continue alert [LN].

QUESTION—Where was Gethsemane?

It was on the western slope of the Mount of Olives [BNTC, EBC, NAC, NIBC, NICNT, NIGTC, NTC, WBC], fairly low on that slope [BNTC, NIGTC, WBC], just across the Kidron brook [BNTC, WBC].

QUESTION—What was the cause of Jesus being so deeply grieved?

He was anguished not so much by the knowledge of his impending death as by the fact of his having to die the death due to sinners [EBC, Lns, NIBC, PNTC, WBC]. He knew he would be forsaken by his Father [NTC, PNTC], and he was already beginning to sense his aloneness and isolation [NTC].

His death was unique, and for that reason his anguish was also unique [EBC].

QUESTION—What does 'to the point of death' mean?

His sorrow was so deep it almost killed him [BECNT, EBC, ICC, My, NIBC, PNTC, TRT, TH]. It is a hyperbole expressing intense emotion [NICNT, NIGTC]. He was hardly able to bear it [WBC]. He knew that he was on the verge of death [Lns].

QUESTION—What does 'watch' mean here?

He wanted them to be awake nearby for company and emotional support so he would not be completely alone [Lns, My, NTC, PNTC, WBC]. He wanted their support and human sympathy [NIBC], their human companionship [NICNT]. He wanted them stay awake so they could uphold him in prayer [EBC, NAC]. He wanted them to keep watch for any approaching danger [BNTC]. He wanted them to be spiritually alert and ready for what was to come [ICC, NIGTC], but also to be physically alert [ICC]. He wanted them to be alert in order to avoid falling into sin [TRT].

26:39 And **having-gone-forward a-little (farther), he-fell**[a] **on his face praying and saying, "My Father, if it-is possible, let- this cup**[b] **-pass**[c] **from-me; yet not as I want but as you (want)."** **26:40** **And he-comes to the disciples and he-finds them sleeping; and he-says to Peter, "So,**[d] **were-you-not -able to-watch with me one hour?**

LEXICON—a. aorist act. indic. of πίπτω (LN 17.22) (BAGD 1.b.α. p. 659): 'to fall' [BECNT, BNTC, NICNT, NIGTC, WBC; ESV, KJV, NASB], 'to fall down' [BAGD], 'to fall down before' [LN], 'to fall to the ground' [BAGD; NCV], 'to prostrate oneself before' [LN]. The phrase 'he fell on his face' is translated 'he threw himself down' [REB], 'he threw himself on the ground' [NRSV], 'he threw himself face down/downward to the ground' [NTC; TEV], 'he threw himself down with his face to the ground' [NET], 'he fell face downward' [PNTC], 'he fell with his face to the ground' [NIV], 'he knelt/bowed with his face to the ground' [CEV, GW, NLT]. This verb means to prostrate oneself before someone, implying supplication [LN].

b. ποτήριον (LN 90.97) (BAGD 2. p. 695): 'cup' [BAGD, BECNT, BNTC, NICNT, NIGTC, NTC, PNTC, WBC; ESV, KJV, NASB, NET, NIV, NRSV, REB], 'cup of suffering' [BAGD; GW, NCV, NLT, TEV]. The idiom παραφέρω τὸ ποτήριον ἀπό 'take the cup from' means to cause someone to not undergo some trying experience [LN].

c. aorist act. third person impera. of παρέρχομαι (LN 15.28) (BAGD 1.b.γ. p. 626): 'to pass' [BAGD, BECNT, BNTC, WBC; ESV, KJV, NASB, NET, NRSV], 'to pass (me) by' [LN, NIGTC; REB], 'to be spared (me)' [NTC], 'to be taken' [NIV], 'to be taken away' [GW, NLT], 'to go by' [LN]. The phrase παρελθάτω ἀπ᾽ ἐμοῦ τὸ ποτήριον τοῦτο 'let this cup pass from me' is translated 'do not give me this cup of suffering' [NCV], 'take this cup of suffering from me' [TEV], 'don't make me suffer by having me drink from this cup' [CEV]. This verb means to move past a reference point [LN].

d. οὕτως (LN 61.9) (BAGD 1.b. p. 597): 'so' [BECNT, BNTC, LN, NICNT, NIGTC, NTC, PNTC; ESV, NASB, NET, NRSV], 'thus' [LN, WBC], 'what!' [KJV, REB], 'how is it that' [TEV], 'in this way' [LN], not explicit [CEV, GW, NCV, NIV, NLT]. This adverb refers to that which precedes [LN], or it may be used to introduce a question [BAGD].

QUESTION—What relationship is indicated by οὕτως 'so'?

It introduces Jesus' question, which is really a statement of dismay [KJV, REB, TEV].

QUESTION—What does the cup symbolize?

It symbolizes suffering [BECNT, BNTC, NICNT, TH, WBC], death and wrath [Lns]. In the Old Testament it symbolizes suffering and God's wrath [EBC, ICC, NIBC, PNTC, TRT, WBC]. It symbolizes the suffering he will endure as he suffers the wrath of God for human sin [NAC, PNTC]. Here it represents his coming death, and has symbolic ties to the cup of the Passover meal [NIGTC].

QUESTION—What relationship is indicated by οὕτως 'so'?

It introduces Jesus' question, which is really a statement of dismay [My, NICNT; KJV, REB, TEV]. It emphasizes what he found on his return to the disciples [NIGTC].

QUESTION—Who is Jesus addressing in verse 40?

Even though he addresses Peter, he is speaking to all three of them as evidenced by the second person plural form of the verb 'watch' [EBC, ICC, NAC, NIBC, NICNT, NIGTC, PNTC, TH, WBC]. Even though he is addressing all three of them, he is singling Peter out because of his having taken the lead in pledging his loyalty and even boasting about it [My, NTC]. He addresses Peter as representing the others [ICC].

26:41 **Watch and pray, so-that you-may- not –come-into temptation;[a] the spirit[b] indeed (is) willing,[c] but (the) flesh[d] (is) weak.[e]"**

LEXICON—a. πειρασμός (LN 88.308) (BAGD 2.b. p. 641): 'temptation' [BAGD, BECNT, BNTC, LN, NICNT, NIGTC, NTC, PNTC; ESV, KJV, NASB, NCV, NET, NIV, NLT, TEV], 'testing' [WBC], 'time of trial' [NRSV], 'the test' [REB]. This noun is translated as a verb: 'to be put to the test' [NICNT], 'to be tested' [CEV], 'to be tempted' [GW]. This noun describes the endeavor or attempt to cause someone to sin [LN].

b. πνεῦμα (LN 26.9) (BAGD 3.b. p. 675): 'spirit' [BAGD, LN; all translations except CEV, GW], 'spiritual nature, inner being' [LN], not explicit [CEV]. This noun denotes the non-material, psychological faculty which is potentially sensitive and responsive to God [LN].

c. πρόθυμος (LN 25.69) (BAGD p. 706): 'willing' [BAGD, BECNT, BNTC, LN, NIGTC, PNTC, WBC; all versions except CEV, GW, NCV], 'eager' [BAGD, LN, NICNT, NTC], 'ready' [BAGD]. The phrase τὸ...πνεῦμα πρόθυμον 'the spirit is willing' is translated as a verb phrase: 'you want to do what is right' [CEV, GW], 'the spirit wants to do what is right' [NCV]. This adjective describes being eager to do something [LN].

d. σάρξ (LN 26.7) (BAGD 7. p. 744): 'flesh' [BAGD, BECNT, BNTC, NICNT, NIGTC, NTC, PNTC, WBC; ESV, KJV, NASB, NET, NRSV, REB, TEV], 'human nature' [LN (26.7)], 'body' [LN (8.4); NCV, NIV, NLT], 'physical body' [LN (8.4)]. The phrase ἡ...σάρξ ἀσθενής 'the flesh is weak' is translated 'you are weak' [CEV, GW]. This noun denotes the psychological aspect of human nature which contrasts with the spiritual nature; in other words, that aspect of human nature which is characterized by or reflects typical human reasoning and desires in contrast with those aspects of human thought and behavior which relate to God and the spiritual life [LN (26.7)]. It may also denote a living body [LN (8.4)].

e. ἀσθενής (LN 74.25) (BAGD 1.b. p. 115): 'weak' [BAGD, LN; all translations], 'unable' [LN]. This adjective describes a state of limited capacity to do or be something [LN].

QUESTION—What temptation was he referring to?

It was the temptation to be untrue to him, which he knew would soon come upon them [EBC, BNTC, My, NIB, NICNT, NIGTC, NTC, WBC]. He is aware of their spiritual defection that will soon occur [EBC]. He knew they were experiencing a severe testing concerning staying awake to watch with him [PNTC].

QUESTION—What does πνεῦμα 'spirit' refer to?

It refers to the human spirit, in which intentions may be good [EBC, Lns, My, NAC, NIB, NICNT, NIGTC, TH, TRT, WBC]. Jesus is talking about the fact that the disciples wanted to do what he was asking [BECNT, PNTC]. The spirit is the inward aspect of the person which is able to be in touch with God and worship God [ICC, NTC]. When translating 'spirit' all translations use a lower case 's' or some similar device to indicate that the human spirit is meant, and not the Spirit of God. Jesus knew Peter and the others wanted to stay awake, even though they failed to do so [all translations]. This word as it is used here refers to part of the inner life, namely, that which concerns the will [BAGD].

QUESTION—What aspect of human life or capacity does σάρξ 'flesh' refer to?

It refers to their physical weakness and failure, here expressed by their succumbing to sleep [BECNT, EBC, NTC, PNTC, TH, WBC]. It is human weakness and lack of moral stamina, by which people fail to do the good they want to do [NICNT]. It is the human nature [NIB], the sinful human nature [Lns, NAC], the human weakness that can be corrupted by sin and darkness [ICC]. The flesh is human weakness and vulnerability to temptation [NIGTC]. It is the physical self, along with its wants and emotions, which is likely to avoid suffering and thus compromise spiritual loyalty [BNTC]. It is that aspect of human beings that gives up too easily [BAGD]. Where the influence of the physical senses is strong, it is hard to resist the temptation to be unfaithful [My].

26:42 Again going-away a second time he prayed saying, "My Father, if this cannot pass unless I-drink it, your will be done." **26:43** And again coming he found them sleeping, for their eyes were weighed-down.[a] **26:44** And leaving them again, having-gone-away he-prayed for (the) third-time, saying the same thing again. **26:45** Then he comes to-the disciples and says to-them, "Are-you-sleeping still[b] and taking- (your) -rest[c]? See, the hour is-at-hand,[d] and the Son of-Man is-being-betrayed into (the) hands of-sinners. **26:46** Get-up, let-us-be-going. See, the-one betraying me is-at-hand.[e]"

LEXICON—a. perf. pass. participle of βαρέω (LN **23.69**) (BAGD p. 133): 'to be weighed down' [BAGD, BNTC, NICNT, NIGTC], 'to be heavy' [BECNT, PNTC; ESV, KJV, NASB, NCV, NIV, NRSV, REB], 'to become heavy' [WBC], 'to be heavy with sleep' [NTC]. The idiom ἦσαν οἱ ὀφθαλμοὶ βεβαρημένοι 'their eyes were weighed down' is translated 'they were very sleepy' [**LN**], 'they could not keep their eyes open' [CEV, GW, NET, NLT, TEV]. It means to become excessively or exceedingly sleepy [LN].

b. λοιπός (LN 63.21) (BAGD 3.a.α. p. 480): 'still' [BAGD], 'meanwhile' [BAGD]. It is difficult to decide how to translate this adjective, and the decision of how to render it is dependent on whether the two verbs 'sleeping' and 'taking your rest' are understood to be imperative or indicative. It is translated adverbially as modifying the continuation of the action of indicative verbs: 'still' [BECNT; CEV, NASB, NCV, NET, NIV, NRSV, REB, TEV], 'for the time that was left' [NIGTC]. It is translated as indicating the continuation of the action of imperative verbs: '(sleep) on now' [BNTC, NICNT, NTC, PNTC; KJV], 'now' [GW], 'for the time that remains' [WBC], 'go ahead' [NLT]; or as describing postponement of the action: 'later on' [ESV].

c. pres. mid. indic. of ἀναπαύομαι (LN 23.80) (BAGD 2. p. 59): 'to take one's rest' [BAGD, BNTC, NIGTC, NTC, PNTC; ESV, KJV, NRSV], 'to rest' [BAGD, BECNT, LN, NICNT, WBC; CEV, NASB, NCV, NET, NIV, REB, TEV], 'to have one's rest' [NLT], not explicit [GW]. This verb means to become physically refreshed after ceasing activity or work [LN].

d. perf. act. indic. of ἐγγίζω (LN 67.21) (BAGD 5.b. p. 213): 'to be at hand' [BECNT, NTC; ESV, KJV, NASB, NRSV], 'to be near' [BNTC; GW, NIV], 'to draw near' [NIGTC], 'to come' [NICNT, PNTC; CEV, NCV, NLT, REB, TEV], 'to come near' [BAGD, LN, WBC], 'to approach' [BAGD, LN; NET]. This verb describes the occurrence of a point of time close to a subsequent point of time [LN].

e. perf. act. indic. of ἐγγίζω (LN 15.75) (BAGD 5.a. p. 213): 'to be near'
[BAGD, BECNT, BNTC, NTC; GW], 'to come near' [LN, WBC], 'to
draw near' [LN, NIGTC], 'to be close' [PNTC], 'to arrive' [NICNT], 'to
be here' [CEV, NCV, TEV], 'to come here' [NCV, NIV], 'to be at hand'
[ESV, KJV, NASB, NRSV], 'to approach' [BAGD, LN; NET], 'to be
upon (us)' [REB].

QUESTION—Does the εἰ 'if' in verse 42 express uncertainty about this cup
passing from him?

The εἰ 'if' is followed by the indicative verb, indicating that there is no
question about the condition; he now knew that it was the Father's will that
he go through this suffering [NAC, PNTC]. Jesus now acknowledges the fact
that this suffering is in fact the Father's will [BECNT, ICC, My, NICNT].
He now expresses the likelihood that it will not be possible to avoid the cup
[NIGTC, WBC].

QUESTION—To what does 'saying the same thing' refer?

The one constant aspect in each of his prayers was his yielding to God's will
[BECNT, EBC, NIBC, NICNT, NTC, PNTC, TH]. They were the same in
substance, even if not expressed in exactly the same words [Lns]. He was
praying the same thing as in verse 42 [My].

QUESTION—Are the two verbs βαρέω 'to sleep' and ἀναπαύομα 'to rest' to
be taken as indicative verbs in a question or imperative verbs in a command?

1. This is a question [BECNT, NAC, NIBC, NIGTC, TH; CEV, NASB,
   NCV, NET, NIV, NRSV, REB, TEV]: 'are you still sleeping and taking
   your rest?' If this is the case, it is a rebuke that means 'How can you still
   be sleeping and taking your rest?' [TH].
2. This is an imperative command [BNTC, EBC, ICC, Lns, My, NICNT,
   NTC, PNTC, WBC; ESV, GW, KJV, NLT], 'sleep and rest'. If this is a
   command, it means that the disciples may as well continue to sleep,
   because they have missed their opportunity to stay awake and keep watch
   with Jesus [PNTC, TH]. This exhortation may simply point to Jesus' final
   resignation to, and acceptance of, what lay ahead of him. The final
   sequence of events is about to begin, and now there is nothing the
   disciples can do [WBC]. It was a gently ironic command now that it was
   too late to pray and gain strength for the temptations ahead [EBC]. A
   different explanation is that having been strengthened through prayer,
   Jesus no longer needs them to stay awake to support him, so he graciously
   forgives them for sleeping when he needed them [NTC].

DISCOURSE UNIT—26:47–27:26 [BECNT, NICNT]. The topic is the arrest
and trial [BECNT], the arrest and trials of Jesus [NICNT].

DISCOURSE UNIT—26:47–56 [CEV, ESV, GW, NASB, NCV, NET, NIV,
NLT, NRSV, TEV]. The topic is Jesus is betrayed and arrested [NLT], Jesus is
arrested [CEV, GW, NCV], Jesus arrested [NIV], the arrest of Jesus [TEV],
betrayal and arrest of Jesus [ESV, NRSV], Jesus' betrayal and arrest [NASB],
betrayal and arrest [NET].

26:47 And while he (was) still speaking, behold, Judas, one of-the twelve, arrived and with him (was) a-large crowd with swords and clubs[a] from the chief-priests and elders of-the people. 26:48 Now the-one betraying him had-given them a-sign,[b] saying, "The-one I-will-kiss[c] is the-one; arrest[d] him." 26:49 And at-once coming-up to-Jesus he-said, "Greetings, Rabbi!" and kissed-him. 26:50 But Jesus said to-him, "Friend,[e] (do that) for which you-are-here." Then coming-forward they-laid[f] hands on Jesus and arrested him.

LEXICON—a. ξύλον (LN 6.31) (BAGD 2.b. p. 549): 'club' [BECNT, BNTC, LN, NIGTC, NTC, PNTC, WBC; all versions except KJV, REB], 'stick' [NICNT], 'stave' [KJV], 'cudgel' [BAGD; REB]. This noun denotes a heavy stick used in fighting [LN].

b. σημεῖον (LN 33.477) (BAGD 1. p. 747): 'sign' [BAGD, BECNT, BNTC, LN, NIGTC, NTC, PNTC, WBC; ESV, KJV, NASB, NET, NRSV, REB], 'signal' [BAGD, LN, NICNT; GW, NCV, NIV, TEV], 'pre-arranged signal' [NLT], not explicit [CEV]. This noun denotes an event which is regarded as having some special meaning [LN].

c. aorist act. subj. of φιλέω (LN **34.62**) (BAGD 2. p. 859): 'to kiss' [BAGD, LN; all translations except CEV, NLT], 'to greet with a kiss' [CEV, NLT]. This verb means to kiss, either as an expression of greeting or as a sign of special affection and appreciation [LN]. To greet someone with a kiss, whether on the hand or foot, was a show of respect, the equivalent of using an honorific. The text does not say where Judas kissed Jesus, and neither should the translation [TH].

d. aorist act. impera. of κρατέω (LN 37.110) (BAGD 1.a. p. 448): 'to arrest' [BAGD, BECNT, BNTC, LN, NICNT; CEV, GW, NCV, NET, NIV, NLT, NRSV, TEV], 'to seize' [LN, WBC; ESV, NASB, REB], 'to take hold of' [NIGTC], 'to lay hold on' [PNTC], 'to grab' [NTC], 'to hold fast' [KJV], 'to take into custody' [BAGD]. This verb means to take a person into custody for alleged illegal activity [LN].

e. ἑταῖρος (LN 34.16) (BAGD p. 314): 'friend' [BAGD, BECNT, BNTC, LN, NIGTC, NTC, PNTC; all versions except CEV, NLT], 'companion' [BAGD, LN]. This vocative form is translated 'my friend' [NICNT; CEV, NLT]. This noun denotes a person who is associated with someone else, though not necessarily involving personal affection [LN].

f. aorist act. indic. of ἐπιβάλλω (LN 37.110) (BAGD 1.b. p. 289): 'to lay (hands) on' [BAGD, BNTC, NICNT, NIGTC, NTC, PNTC; ESV, KJV, NASB, NRSV], 'to grab' [CEV, NCV, NLT], 'to take hold of' [GW, NET], 'to seize' [BECNT, LN; NIV, REB], 'to arrest' [LN; TEV]. The idiom ἐπιβάλλω τὰς χεῖρας 'to lay (hands) upon means to take a person into custody for alleged illegal activity [LN].

QUESTION—What was the makeup of the crowd?

There were temple police [BECNT, BNTC, EBC, ICC, Lns, NIB, NICNT, NTC, PNTC, WBC], a detachment of Roman soldiers [EBC, Lns, NAC,

NIBC, NTC, WBC], Jewish leaders [EBC, NAC, NTC], and possibly a few hired men [WBC]. There were probably also various disreputable or undesirable persons [NAC, PNTC]. The temple police were representatives of the Sanhedrin [PNTC]. The chief priests and elders would not have been in the crowd [NIGTC].

QUESTION—What is the connotation of Ἑταῖρε 'friend' by which Jesus addresses Judas?

It is a distancing form of address [BECNT, EBC, Lns, My, NAC]. Here it is used with irony [BECNT, PNTC, TRT]. It recognizes the close association they previously had shared [BNTC, NIGTC, WBC], though here the tone may be ironic [NIGTC]. It also attempts to strike Judas' conscience one last time [Lns]. It shows only friendliness to the betrayer [ICC].

QUESTION—Is the first sentence in verse 50 a command or a question?

1. It is a command with an implied imperative: (Do) what you came for [My, NICNT, NIGTC, PNTC, TH; ESV, NASB, NCV, NET, NIV, NLT, NRSV, REB, TEV].
2. It is a question: What did you come for? [BECNT, BNTC, ICC, NTC; CEV, GW, KJV], or a rhetorical question: Are you here for this? [NTC]. It expresses disappointment in Judas, that he would have come for such a thing as this [WBC].

26:51 And behold,[a] one of-those with Jesus having-stretched-out[b] (his) hand withdrew (his) sword and having-struck the servant[c] of-the high priest, cut-off his ear. **26:52** Then Jesus says to-him, "Return your sword to its place; for all-those having-taken[d] (the) sword will-die[e] by (the) sword.

LEXICON—a. ἰδού (LN 91.13): 'behold' [BNTC; ESV, KJV, NASB], 'look' [LN, NTC, PNTC, WBC], not explicit [NIGTC; CEV, TEV]. The phrase καὶ ἰδού 'and behold' is translated 'suddenly' [BECNT; GW, NRSV], 'just then' [NICNT], 'at that moment' [REB], 'when that happened' [NCV], 'with that' [NIV], 'but' [NET, NLT], 'listen, pay attention' [LN]. This particle is a prompter of attention, which serves to emphasize the following statement [LN].

b. aorist act. participle of ἐκτείνω (LN 16.19) (BAGD 1. p. 245): 'to stretch out' [BAGD, BNTC, LN, NICNT, NIGTC, NTC, PNTC; ESV, KJV], 'to reach out' [BECNT, LN], 'to reach with' [WBC], 'to reach' [NASB], 'to reach for' [NCV, NIV, REB], 'to grab (his sword)' [NET], 'to put (his hand on his sword)' [NRSV], 'to extend' [BAGD, LN]. The words 'having stretched out his hand withdrew his sword' may be translated more naturally as a single action 'drew his sword' [TH; TEV], 'pulled out his sword' [GW, NLT] 'pulled out a sword' [CEV]. This verb means to cause an object to extend in space by becoming straight, unfolded, or uncoiled [LN].

c. δοῦλος (LN 87.76) (BAGD 1.a. p.205): 'servant' [BNTC, NTC, WBC; CEV, ESV, GW, KJV, NCV, NIV, REB], 'slave' [BAGD, BECNT, LN, NICNT, NIGTC, PNTC; NASB, NET, NLT, NRSV, TEV], 'bondservant'

[LN]. This noun denotes one who is a slave in the sense of becoming the property of an owner (though in ancient times it was frequently possible for a slave to earn his freedom) [LN].

d. aorist act. participle of λαμβάνω (LN 18.1): 'to take' [BNTC, NTC, PNTC, WBC; ESV, KJV, NRSV, REB, TEV], 'to take up' [NICNT, NIGTC; NASB], 'to take hold of' [LN; NET], 'to draw' [BECNT, LN; NIV], 'to use' [GW, NCV, NLT], 'to grasp, to grab' [LN]. The phrase πάντες γὰρ οἱ λαβόντες μάχαιραν 'for all those having taken the sword' is translated 'for anyone who lives by fighting' [CEV]. This verb means to take hold of something or someone, with or without force [LN].

e. fut. mid. indic. of ἀπόλλυμαι (LN **23.106**): 'to die' [BECNT, BNTC, **LN**, NICNT; CEV, NET, NIV, NLT, REB, TEV], 'to perish' [LN, NIGTC, NTC, PNTC, WBC; ESV, KJV, NASB, NRSV], 'to be killed' [GW, NCV]. This verb means to die [LN].

QUESTION—Was the servant of the high priest whose ear was cut off a person of importance to the high priest, or merely a slave?

He represented the high priest himself [Lns, NIGTC, PNTC], and an attack on the slave could be viewed as an attack on the high priest [PNTC]. He might have led the band that was arresting Jesus [BNTC, ICC, Lns, NICNT].

QUESTION—Was Jesus' comment about the use of weapons a call to pacifism?

He is not calling for pacifism as a general rule [BECNT, Lns, NAC, NIBC, NTC], but he is using a proverb to describe how violence tends to spawn violence in a fallen world [BECNT]. This passage specifically addresses the issue of the use of weapons in the context of defending Jesus [EBC, NICNT, NIGTC, NTC], but it is not a general principle [EBC, NICNT, NTC]. Jesus does disdain the use of weapons to impose one's will on others [NIGTC]. The use of weapons is legitimate for properly established authorities, but not for individuals who resort to violence out of purely personal motives [Lns, My]. Jesus is saying that those who are aggressive and warlike tend to die at the hands of others who are aggressive and warlike [NAC, PNTC]. It is not a call to pacifism, though peacemaking is preferable to hostility and conflict. Neither is it a justification for militarism because sometimes war is necessary to combat worse evils [NAC]. The use of the sword violates the principle Jesus set forth in Matthew 5:39 [ICC, WBC]. It is better to suffer injustice than to resort to violence [TH]. Jesus is warning against fighting persecutors [ICC].

26:53 Or do-you-think that I-cannot call-upon[a] my Father, and he-will- at-once -send me more-than twelve legions[b] of-angels? **26:54** (But) how then would- the scriptures -be-fulfilled, that it-is-necessary to-happen in-this-way?" **26:55** At that hour Jesus said to-the crowds, "Have-you-come-out with swords and clubs to arrest me as-though (I were) a-bandit[c]? Day after day I-sat in the temple teaching, and you-did- not -arrest me. **26:56** But all

this has-taken-place so-that the scriptures of-the prophets would-be-9fulfilled." Then all the disciples having-deserted^d him, fled.^e

LEXICON—a. aorist act. infin. of παρακαλέω (LN 33.168) (BAGD 1.c.
p. 617): 'to call upon/on' [BECNT, NICNT, NTC, WBC; GW, NET,
NIV, TEV], 'to call upon for help' [BAGD], 'to appeal to' [LN, NIGTC;
ESV, NASB, NRSV], 'to appeal for help' [REB], 'to petition' [PNTC],
'to ask' [CEV, NCV], 'to ask for' [NLT], 'to ask for (earnestly)' [LN], 'to
pray' [KJV], 'to request' [BNTC, LN]. This verb means to ask for
something earnestly and with propriety [LN].

    b. λεγιών (LN **55.8**) (BAGD p. 468): 'legion' [BAGD, BECNT, BNTC,
LN, NICNT, NIGTC, NTC, PNTC, WBC; ESV, GW, KJV, NASB, NET,
NIV, NRSV, REB], 'army' [LN; CEV, NCV, TEV]. The phrase 'twelve
legions of angels' is translated 'thousands of angels' [NLT]. This noun
denotes a Roman army unit of about six thousand soldiers. The expression
'twelve legions of angels' indicates a very large group of angels, and the
meaning may be rendered as 'many, many angels' or 'thousands of
angels. [LN].

    c. λῃστής (LN 39.37) (BAGD 2. p. 473): 'bandit' [BNTC, NICNT, NIGTC;
NRSV, REB], 'insurrectionist' [BAGD, LN, WBC], 'robber' [NTC,
PNTC; ESV, NASB], 'rebel' [BECNT, LN], 'criminal' [CEV, GW,
NCV], 'outlaw' [NET, TEV], 'dangerous revolutionary' [NLT],
'revolutionary' [BAGD], 'leading a rebellion' [NIV], 'thief' [KJV]. This
noun denotes a person who engages in insurrection [LN].

    d. aorist act. participle of ἀφίημι (LN 15.48) (BAGD 3.a. p. 126): 'to desert'
[BECNT; NIV, NLT, NRSV, REB], 'to leave' [BAGD, BNTC, LN,
NICNT, NIGTC, NTC, PNTC; CEV, ESV, NASB, NCV, NET, TEV], 'to
abandon' [BAGD, WBC; GW], 'to forsake' [KJV]. This verb means to
move away from, with the implication of resulting separation [LN].

    e. aorist act. indic. of φεύγω (LN 15.61) (BAGD 1. p. 855): 'to flee'
[BAGD, BECNT, BNTC, LN, NIGTC, NTC, WBC; ESV, KJV, NASB,
NET, NIV, NLT, NRSV], 'to run away' [LN, NICNT, PNTC; CEV, GW,
NCV, REB, TEV]. This verb means to move quickly from a point or area
in order to avoid presumed danger or difficulty [LN].

QUESTION—How many soldiers would be in twelve legions?

There are up to six thousand soldiers in a legion, so twelve legions could
potentially represent as many as seventy two thousand angels [BECNT,
EBC, ICC, Lns, NAC, NIBC, NICNT, NIGTC, NTC, TH, WBC]. However,
the specific number is not important here [NIGTC, TRT]. The expression
represents a vast army [TH].

QUESTION—Does λῃστής 'robber' denote a criminal or an insurrectionist?

It denotes a criminal [BNTC, Lns, NICNT, NIGTC, NTC, PNTC, TH; CEV,
ESV, GW, KJV, NASB, NCV, NET, NRSV, REB, TEV]. It can be used to
refer to a brigand [ICC, NTC, PNTC]. It denotes a revolutionary [BECNT,
EBC, LN, NAC, NIBC, WBC; NIV, NLT].

DISCOURSE UNIT—26:57–68 [CEV, ESV, GW, NASB, NCV, NET, NIV, NLT, NRSV, TEV]. The topic is the trial in front of the Jewish council [GW], Jesus before the leaders [NCV], Jesus before the council [NLT, TEV], Jesus is questioned by the council [CEV], Jesus before the high priest [NRSV], Jesus before Caiaphas and the council [ESV], Jesus before Caiaphas [NASB], condemned by the Sanhedrin [NET], before the Sanhedrin [NIV].

26:57 And those having-arrested Jesus took-him to Caiaphas the high priest, where the scribes and the elders had-gathered. **26:58** But Peter was-following him from a-distance, up-to the courtyard[a] of-the high priest, and having-gone inside, he-was-sitting-down with the guards to-see the outcome.[b]

LEXICON—a. αὐλή (LN 7.56) (BAGD 1. p. 121): 'courtyard' [BAGD, BECNT, BNTC, LN, LN, NICNT, NIGTC, NTC, PNTC, WBC; ESV, GW, NASB, NET, NIV, NLT, NRSV, REB], 'palace' [KJV], 'courtyard of the...palace' [CEV], 'courtyard of the...house' [NCV, TEV]. This noun denotes a walled enclosure either to enclose human activity or to protect livestock [LN].

   b. τέλος (LN **89.40**) (BAGD 1.c. p. 811): 'outcome' [BAGD, LN, NTC, WBC; NASB, NET, NIV], 'result' [**LN**], 'end' [BAGD, BNTC, LN, NICNT, NIGTC, PNTC; ESV, KJV]. This noun is translated as a phrase: 'how it/this would end' [BECNT; NRSV], 'how it would all end' [NLT, REB], 'what was going to happen' [CEV], 'what would happen' [NCV], 'how this would turn out' [GW], 'how it would all come out' [TEV].

26:59 Now the chief-priests and the whole Sanhedrin were-seeking false-testimony against Jesus so-that they-might-put- him –to-death, **26:60** but they-found none, (though) many false-witnesses having-come-forward. But finally two having-come-forward **26:61** said, "This-fellow[a] said, 'I-am-able to-destroy the temple of God and to-build (it) in three days.'" **26:62** And having-stood-up the high priest said to-him, "Do-you-answer nothing? What do- these -testify-against you?" **26:63** But Jesus was-silent. And the high priest said to-him, "I-put- you -under-oath[b] before the living God that you-tell us if you-are the Messiah, the Son of God." **26:64** Jesus says to-him, "You said[c] (it). But I-say to-you, from now-on[d] you-will-see the Son of-Man seated at (the) right-hand of-Power[e] and coming on the clouds of heaven."

LEXICON—a. οὗτος (LN 92.29): 'this fellow' [BNTC, NIGTC, NTC, PNTC; KJV, NIV, NRSV], 'this man' [BECNT, NICNT, WBC; CEV, ESV, GW, NASB, NCV, NET, NLT, TEV], 'this, this one' [LN], not explicit [REB]. This pronominal adjective describes an entity that is regarded as a part of the discourse setting, with pejorative meaning in certain contexts [LN].

   b. pres. act. indic. of ἐξορκίζω ((LN **33.467**) (BAGD p. 277): 'to put under oath' [BAGD, LN, NICNT; NRSV, TEV], 'to put under solemn oath' [NIGTC], 'to charge under/on oath' [BAGD, PNTC; NET, NIV], 'to adjure' [BAGD, BNTC, NTC, WBC; ESV, KJV, NASB], 'to charge' [REB], 'to command (to tell)' [NCV], 'to insist that one take an oath, to require that one swear' [LN], 'to charge one to swear' [**LN**]. The phrase ἐξορκίζω σε κατὰ τοῦ θεοῦ τοῦ ζῶντος 'I put you under oath before the living God' is translated 'with the living God looking on, you must tell the truth' [CEV], 'swear an oath in front of the living God' [GW], 'I demand in the name of the living God' [NLT]. This verb means to demand that a person take an oath as to the truth of what is said or as to the certainty that one will carry out the request or command [LN].

c. aorist act. indic. of εἶπον (LN 33.69) (BAGD 1. p. 226): 'to say' [BAGD, LN]. The phrase σὺ εἶπας 'you said it' [BECNT, NTC, PNTC] is translated 'you have said' [BNTC], 'thou hast said' [KJV], 'you have said it' [NICNT, NIGTC; NLT], 'you have said it yourself' [NASB, NET], 'so you say' [TEV], 'you have said so' [ESV, NRSV], 'you have said the truth' [WBC], 'that's what you say' [CEV], 'those are your words' [NCV], 'the words are yours' [REB], 'yes, it is as you say' [NIV], 'yes, I am' [GW]. This verb means to speak or talk, with apparent focus upon the content of what is said [LN].

d. ἄρτι (LN 67.38) (BAGD 3. p. 110): 'now' [BAGD, LN]. The phrase ἀπ' ἄρτι 'from now on' [BECNT, BNTC, NICNT, NIGTC, NTC; ESV, GW, NET, NRSV, REB] is also translated 'from this time on' [TEV], 'hereafter' [PNTC; KJV, NASB], 'in the future' [WBC; NCV, NIV, NLT], 'soon' [CEV]. This adverb describes a point of time simultaneous with the event of the discourse itself [LN].

e. δύναμις (LN 12.44) (BAGD 1. p. 207): 'power' [BAGD, LN, NICNT; KJV], 'Power' [BECNT, BNTC; ESV, NASB, NRSV], 'the Power' [NIGTC, NTC, PNTC, WBC; NET], 'God All-Powerful' [CEV], 'God, the Powerful One' [NCV], 'the Mighty One' [NIV], 'the Almighty' [REB, TEV]. The phrase καθήμενον ἐκ δεξιῶν τῆς δυνάμεως 'seated at the right hand of Power' is translated 'in the highest position in heaven' [GW], 'seated in the place of power at God's right hand' [NLT]. This noun denotes a supernatural power having some particular role in controlling the destiny and activities of human beings [LN].

QUESTION—What is meant by 'the whole Sanhedrin'?

It refers to the entire group of those who had hastily assembled during the night [EBC, NAC, WBC], of which the required quorum was only twenty three of the seventy members of that larger body [EBC, NAC]. It means that all the constituent elements of the Sanhedrin were represented, not that all members were present [NICNT, PNTC]. One third of the seventy one members of the Sanhedrin constituted a quorum for conducting official business [NICNT]. It means the Sanhedrin generally, though not necessarily every member of it [My].

QUESTION—What is the connotation of the phrase 'this fellow'?

It is contemptuous here [ICC, Lns, PNTC, TH, TRT].

QUESTION—Does verse 62 express one question or two?

1. There are two questions: Do you answer nothing? What are these people testifying against you? [BNTC, EBC, Lns, My, NIGTC, NTC, PNTC; CEV, ESV, KJV, NASB, NCV, NET, NIV, NLT, NRSV].
2. There is one question: Do you answer nothing to what these people testify against you? [BECNT, GNT, ICC, NICNT, WBC; GW, REB, TEV].

QUESTION—What does the high priest mean by 'the Messiah, the Son of God'?

1. The high priest probably equates the two titles as synonymous [BNTC, My, NAC, WBC]. In first century Judaism the two would often have been considered equivalent [EBC]. At that time 'Son of God' was interpreted messianically [BECNT].
2. The high priest would have seen 'Son of God' as implying more than just being the Messiah, as it would have involved a claim to deity that is not conveyed by 'Messiah' alone [Lns].

QUESTION—What is communicated by Jesus' answer 'you said it'?

He is acknowledging that he is what the high priest said, though not necessarily as the high priest may have meant it [BNTC, EBC, Lns, NICNT, NIGTC, PNTC, TH, WBC], or would have intended to use that information [NIGTC]. It affirms what the high priest said, though in a veiled way [BECNT, NAC, TRT]. He is saying 'Yes indeed!' [NTC]. He is acknowledging that the high priest already knows that the answer is 'yes' [ICC, NIBC].

QUESTION—Does ἀπ' ἄρτι 'from now on' indicate a time beginning when Jesus spoke these words, or does it refer to some point in the future?

1. It means 'from now on' [BECNT, BNTC, EBC, Lns, My, NICNT, NIGTC, NTC, TH; ESV, GW, NET, NRSV, REB, TEV]. It meant that they would no longer see him as he was standing before them, but only as the sovereign judge and undisputed king and Messiah [WBC]. Caiaphas himself will be confronted with the reality of Jesus' resurrection and thereby see the exaltation of Jesus [BECNT]. In the near future Jesus would proclaim that he has all power in heaven and earth (Matthew 28:18) [NICNT]. As in two previous uses, this phrase anticipates a future reality as though it were already present, beginning with the confession of the guards that he is the Son of God, continuing with the report of his resurrection by the guards at the tomb, and by the spread of the gospel by the apostles, and eventually culminating in his parousia [NIGTC]. They will see it in the miracles surrounding his death and resurrection [Lns]. They will 'see' it, albeit in a non-physical sense, in the way his mighty influences in affairs manifest his sovereign sway as he rules from his position at God's right hand [My]. From now on the Son of Man would only be seen in his triumphant state, as he who has all power and who will return to judge the earth [TH].

2. It refers to some point in the future [NIGTC, PNTC, WBC; CEV, KJV, NASB, NCV, NIV, NLT]. It speaks of a future reality, though one that would begin at the resurrection and continue in the form of his ruling from heaven's throne [WBC].

QUESTION—What would it mean for Jesus to claim to be the Son of Man seated at God's right hand and coming on the clouds of heaven?

He will return as universal judge, and occupy the most honored position anywhere, at God's right hand and second only to his Father [NAC]. He is saying that he will return and judge those who are unjustly judging him [BECNT, ICC, Lns, NICNT]. He was equating himself with God [NAC], claiming divine privileges [BECNT]. He will rise from death, exalted, he will be the ultimate judge, and he will rule everything everywhere [PNTC]. He exalts himself above David, and also associates himself with the glory of the parousia [EBC]. He is claiming that it is he who will judge all the nations and exert dominion forever [NTC]. He is saying that he will have the authority of God himself [NICNT], exercising divine power, rule and majesty [Lns]. This explains what Jesus meant by the titles 'Messiah' and 'Son of God' [BNTC, Lns]. It is a clear reference to his future return, his parousia, and is also a claim to be deity [NIBC].

26:65 Then the high-priest tore his robes[a] and said, "He-has-blasphemed![b] Why do-we- still -have-need of-witnesses? See you-have- now -heard the blasphemy. **26:66** What do- you -think?" And answering they-said, "He-is deserving-of[c] death." **26:67** Then they-spat in his face and they-struck[d] him and they-slapped[e] him **26:68** saying, "Prophesy to-us, Messiah! Who is-it that hit[f] you?"

LEXICON—a. ἱμάτιον (LN 6.172) (BAGD 3. p. 376): 'robe' [BAGD, LN, NICNT, NTC, PNTC; CEV, ESV, GW, REB], 'clothes' [BECNT, NIGTC; KJV, NCV, NET, NIV, NRSV, TEV], 'clothing' [NLT], 'cloak' [BAGD, LN], 'garment' [BAGD, BNTC, WBC], 'coat' [LN]. This noun denotes any type of outer garment [LN].

    b. aorist act. indic. of βλασφημέω (LN 33.400) (BAGD 2.b.α. p. 142): 'to blaspheme' [BAGD, BECNT, BNTC, LN, NICNT, NIGTC, NTC, PNTC, WBC; NET, NRSV], 'to utter blasphemy' [ESV], 'to speak blasphemy' [KJV, NIV], 'to dishonor God' [GW], 'to say things against God' [NCV], 'to revile' [BAGD, LN]. The verb ἐβλασφήμησεν 'he has blasphemed' is translated 'This man claims to be God' [CEV], 'Blasphemy!' [NLT, TEV], 'This is blasphemy!' [REB]. This verb means to speak against someone in such a way as to harm or injure his or her reputation (occurring in relation to persons as well as to divine beings) [LN].

    c. ἔνοχος (LN **88.313**) (BAGD 2.b.α. p. 267): 'deserving of' [BAGD, NIGTC], 'worthy of' [NIGTC, PNTC; NIV], 'guilty of' [KJV], 'guilty and deserving' [**LN**]. The phrase ἔνοχος θανάτου ἐστίν 'he is deserving of death' is translated 'he deserves to die' [BECNT, NICNT], 'he deserves death' [BNTC; ESV, NRSV], 'he is guilty' [NCV], 'he is guilty and deserves death' [NET], 'he is guilty and should die' [WBC; similarly REB, TEV], 'he is guilty and deserves to die' [CEV, similarly NLT], 'he deserves the death penalty' [GW]. This adjective describes being guilty and thus deserving some particular penalty [LN].

d. aorist act. indic. of κολαφίζω (LN **19.7**) (BAGD 1. p. 441): 'to strike with the fist' [BAGD, BECNT, LN, NTC; NET, NIV, REB], 'to strike' [BNTC, NIGTC, PNTC, WBC; ESV, NRSV], 'to hit with the fist' [CEV, GW], 'to buffet' [KJV], 'to beat' [BAGD, NICNT; TEV], 'to beat with the fist' [**LN**; NASB, NCV, NLT]. This verb means to strike or beat with the fist, either once or repeatedly [LN].

e. aorist act. indic. of ῥαπίζω (LN 19.4) (BAGD p. 734): 'to slap' [BAGD, LN; all translations except KJV, REB], 'to smite with the palm of the hand' [KJV], 'to hit' [LN], 'to beat' [LN; REB]. This verb means to hit or strike with the open hand, the fist, or an instrument (for example, club, rod, or whip) [LN].

f. aorist act. participle of παίω (LN 19.1) (BAGD 1. p. 605): 'to hit' [BAGD, LN; all translations except ESV, KJV, NRSV], 'to strike' [BAGD, LN; ESV, NRSV], 'to beat' [LN], not explicit [KJV]. This verb means to strike or hit an object, one or more times [LN].

QUESTION—What is conveyed by the tearing of the robes?

It shows outrage or grief [EBC, NAC, NTC], and was the expected action in response to blasphemy [EBC, NIBC]. It expresses disgust and extreme anger [BECNT]. It expresses horror [BNTC, PNTC, WBC] and a repudiation of Jesus' claims [BNTC, PNTC].

QUESTION—What action or statement of Jesus provoked the charge of blasphemy?

It was not blasphemous to claim to be the Messiah [NIBC, PNTC], but in their view Jesus was claiming too close a kinship with God [NAC, PNTC], equating himself with God [Lns, NAC, TH, WBC], claiming a role and power that are appropriate only to God [BNTC], claiming divine honor and authority [My]. He was seen as insulting the majesty of God by claiming to be the Son of God, to have a heavenly throne, and to be the Son of Man described in Daniel 7 [ICC]. The primary issue was his claiming that he would occupy a place at the right hand of God [NIBC, NICNT] and come again on the clouds of heaven [NIBC]. They saw Jesus as having claimed divine prerogatives for himself [BECNT, ICC, Lns, NIGTC, NTC, WBC], such as the role of judging the nations and having everlasting dominion that the Son of Man passage in Daniel 7 described [NIGTC, NTC]. As the figure from Daniel 7 who will be given glory and dominion and an eternal kingship, and whom everyone would serve, he was claiming a rank equal with God [WBC]. He was also viewed as speaking and acting against God's temple and God's appointed leaders [NICNT].

DISCOURSE UNIT—26:69–75 [CEV, ESV, GW, NASB, NCV, NET, NIV, NLT, NRSV, TEV]. The topic is Peter denies Jesus [ESV, GW, NLT, TEV], Peter disowns Jesus [NIV], Peter says he doesn't know Jesus [CEV, NCV], Peter's denials [NASB, NET], Peter's denial of Jesus [NRSV].

`26:69` Now Peter was-sitting outside in the courtyard; and one servant-girl[a] came to-him saying, "You also were-with Jesus the Galilean." `26:70` But he-denied[b] (it) before all (of them), saying, "I-do- not -know what you-are-talking-about." `26:71` And having-gone-out to the gateway,[c] another (servant-girl) saw him and she-says to-those there, "This-man was with Jesus of Nazareth." `26:72` And again he-denied (it) with an-oath,[d] "I-do-not -know the man."

TEXT—Manuscripts reading οὗτος 'this man' are given a B rating by GNT to indicate it was regarded to be almost certain. Other manuscripts reading καί οὗτος 'this man (was) also' are followed by KJV only.

LEXICON—a. παιδίσκη (LN 87.83) (BAGD p. 604): 'servant girl' [BAGD, BECNT, BNTC, NICNT, NIGTC, NTC, WBC; CEV, ESV, NASB, NCV, NIV, NLT, NRSV, REB], 'slave girl' [LN, PNTC; NET], 'female servant' [GW], 'female slave' [BAGD], 'damsel' [KJV], 'servant woman' [TEV], 'slave woman' [LN], 'maid' [BAGD]. This noun denotes a female slave [LN].

b. aorist mid. (deponent = act.) indic. of ἀρνέομαια (LN 33.277) (BAGD 3.a. p. 108): 'to deny' [BAGD, LN; all translations except CEV, NCV], 'to repudiate, to disown' [BAGD]. The phrase ἠρνήσατο 'he denied it' is translated 'Peter said, "That isn't so!"' [CEV], 'Peter said he was never with him' [NCV]. This verb means to say that one does not know about or is in any way related to a person or event [LN].

c. πυλών (LN **7.38**) (BAGD 3. p. 729): 'gateway' [BAGD, BNTC, LN, NICNT, NTC, PNTC; NASB, NET, NIV, REB], 'gate' [CEV, NCV, NLT], 'entrance' [BAGD, BECNT, LN, WBC; ESV, GW], 'entrance of the courtyard' [TEV], 'entranceway' [NIGTC], 'porch' [KJV, NRSV], 'vestibule' [**LN**]. This noun denotes the area associated with the entrance into a house or building [LN].

d. ὅρκος (LN 33.463) (BAGD p. 581): 'oath' [BAGD, LN; all translations except NCV, TEV]. The phrase ἠρνήσατο μετὰ ὅρκου 'he denied with an oath' is translated 'Peter said/answered…I swear (I don't know this man)' [NCV, TEV]. This noun denotes the act of affirming the truth of a statement by calling on a divine being to execute sanctions against a person if the statement in question is not true [LN].

QUESTION—What is conveyed by the use of μία 'one' with 'servant girl'?
It is used here as the equivalent of an indefinite article (which Greek lacks). [BECNT, EBC]. It distinguishes her from another servant girl mentioned in verse 71 [My, NIGTC], but also communicates that she is *only* one servant girl [NICNT, WBC], which emphasizes her insignificance [NICNT]. It means 'a certain' servant girl [Lns, NIGTC].

26:73 After a-little-while[a] those standing (there) coming-up say to-Peter, "Surely[b] you- also -are one-of them, for your speech[c] makes (it) clear[d] about-you." **26:74** Then he-began to-call-down-curses[e] and to-swear-an-oath[f] that "I-do- not -know the man!" And immediately (the) cock crowed. **26:75** Then Peter remembered the word of-Jesus that "Before (the) cock crows, you-will-deny me three-times." And having-gone outside he-wept bitterly.[g]

LEXICON—a. μικρός (LN 67.106) (BAGD 3.e. p. 521): 'a little while' [BAGD, BECNT, BNTC, LN, NIGTC, NTC, WBC; CEV, ESV, GW, NET, NIV, NRSV, TEV], 'a while' [KJV], 'a little (later)' [NASB, NLT], 'a bit (later)' [NICNT], 'a little time' [PNTC], 'shortly (afterwards)' [REB], 'a short time' [BAGD, LN; NCV]. This adjective describes a relatively brief extent of time [LN].

b. ἀληθῶς (LN 70.3) (BAGD 1. p. 37): 'surely' [BECNT; KJV, NASB, NCV, NIV], 'truly' [BAGD, LN, NIGTC, WBC], 'certainly' [NTC, PNTC; ESV, NRSV], 'in truth' [BAGD], 'really' [BAGD, BNTC, LN, NICNT; NET], 'it's obvious' [GW], 'you must be' [NLT, REB], 'of course' [TEV], not explicit [CEV]. This adverb describes being real and not imaginary [LN].

c. λαλιά (LN 33.102) (BAGD 2.a. p. 464): 'speech' [BNTC, NIGTC, PNTC, WBC; KJV], 'accent' [**LN**, NICNT, NTC; ESV, GW, NET, NIV, NRSV, REB], 'Galilean accent' [NLT], 'the way (you) talk' [NASB, NCV], 'form of speech' [BAGD], 'way of speaking' [BAGD, BECNT], 'the way one speaks' [**LN**; TEV], 'you talk like someone (from Galilee)' [CEV]. This noun denotes particular manner of speech [LN].

d. δῆλος (LN 28.58) (BAGD p. 178): 'clear' [BAGD, BECNT, LN, NIGTC, PNTC], 'evident, plain' [BAGD, LN], 'clearly known, easily known' [LN]. The phrase δῆλόν σε ποιεῖ 'makes it clear about you' is translated 'gives you away' [BNTC, NICNT, NTC; GW, NASB, NET, NIV, REB, TEV], 'betrays you' [WBC; ESV, KJV, NRSV], 'shows it' [NCV], 'we can tell' [CEV, NLT]. This adjective describes being clearly and easily able to be known [LN].

e. pres. act. infin. of καταθεματίζω (LN **33.472**) (BAGD p. 410): 'to call down a curse/curses' [NTC; NIV], 'to curse' [BAGD, BECNT, BNTC, **LN**, NICNT, PNTC, WBC; CEV, GW, KJV, NASB, NET, NRSV, REB], 'to invoke a curse' [NIGTC], 'to invoke a curse on oneself' [ESV], to place a curse on oneself' [NCV]. The phrase ἤρξατο καταθεματίζειν καὶ ὀμνύειν 'he began to call down curses and swear with an oath' is translated 'Peter swore, "A curse on me if I'm lying"' [NLT], 'I swear that I am telling the truth! May God punish me if I am not!' [TEV]. This verb means to invoke divine harm if what is said is not true or if one does not carry out what has been promised [LN].

f. pres. act. infin. of ὀμνύω (LN **33.463**) (BAGD p. 566): 'to swear' [BAGD, BECNT, BNTC, **LN**, NICNT, NIGTC, NTC, PNTC, WBC;

CEV, ESV, KJV, NASB, NCV, NIV, TEV], 'to swear with an oath' [GW, NET, NRSV], 'to declare with an oath' [REB], 'to take an oath' [BAGD], 'to make an oath' [LN], not explicit [NLT]. This verb means to affirm the truth of a statement by calling on a divine being to execute sanctions against a person if the statement in question is not true [LN].

  g. πικρῶς (LN **25.284**) (BAGD p. 657): 'bitterly' [BAGD, **LN**; all translations except CEV, NCV], 'hard' [CEV], 'painfully' [NCV], 'with agony' [LN]. This adverb describes feeling mental agony [LN].

QUESTION—What was the object or content of the swearing?

  1. The swearing was the invoking of a solemn curse on himself if he were to be lying [BECNT, EBC, Lns, My, NIGTC, NTC, TH, TRT; NLT, TEV]. He swore on oath that he did not know Jesus [EBC, Lns, NAC, NTC, PNTC]. It was not profanity [EBC]. He falsely invoked God by these oaths [BECNT].

  2. He called down curses on Jesus [ICC, NICNT]. He may have cursed Jesus [WBC].

DISCOURSE UNIT—27:1–10 [GW, NASB, NIV, NLT]. The topic is the death of Judas [GW], Judas hangs himself [NIV, NLT], Judas' remorse [NASB].

DISCOURSE UNIT—27:1–2 [CEV, ESV, NCV, NET, NRSV, TEV]. The topic is Jesus is taken to Pilate [CEV, NCV, TEV], Jesus delivered to Pilate [ESV], Jesus brought before Pilate [NET, NRSV].

27:1 Early-morning having-come, all the chief priests and the elders of-the people took counsel-together against Jesus in-order-to put- him -to-death.[a] **27:2** And having-bound[b] him, they-led- him -away and handed- him -over[c] to-Pilate the governor.[d]

TEXT—Manuscripts reading Πιλάτῳ 'Pilate' are given a B rating by GNT to indicate it was regarded to be almost certain. Manuscripts reading Ποντίῳ Πιλάτῳ 'Pontius Pilate' are followed by NICNT; KJV.

LEXICON—a. aorist act. infin. of θανατόω (LN 20.65) (BAGD 1. p. 351): 'to put to death' [BECNT, BNTC, NIGTC, NTC, PNTC, WBC; ESV, KJV, NASB, NIV, NLT, TEV], 'to have (someone) executed' [NICNT], 'to execute' [LN; GW, NET], 'to bring about (someone's) death' [NRSV], 'to plan the death of' [REB], 'to kill' [LN]. This active transitive verb is translated as a passive verb: 'decided that Jesus should be put to death' [CEV]; as an intransitive verb: 'decided that Jesus should die' [NCV]. This verb means to deprive a person of life, with the implication of this being the result of condemnation by legal or quasi-legal procedures [LN].

  b. aorist act. participle of δέω (LN 18.13) (BAGD 1.b. p. 177): 'to bind' [BAGD, BECNT, BNTC, NIGTC, NTC, PNTC, WBC; ESV, KJV, NASB, NIV, NLT, NRSV, REB], 'to tie up' [LN, NICNT; CEV, GW, NET], 'to tie' [BAGD, LN; NCV], 'to put in chains' [TEV]. This verb means to tie objects together [LN].

c. aorist act. indic. of παραδίδωμι (LN 37.111) (BAGD 1.b. p. 614): 'to hand over to' [BAGD, BECNT, LN, NICNT, NIGTC, NTC, PNTC, WBC; GW, NET, NIV, NRSV, REB, TEV], 'to deliver to' [BNTC, KJV, NASB], 'to deliver over to' [ESV], 'to turn over to' [BAGD, LN; NCV], 'to take to' [NLT], not explicit [CEV]. This verb means to deliver a person into the control of someone else, involving either the handing over of a presumably guilty person for punishment by authorities or the handing over of an individual to an enemy who will presumably take undue advantage of the victim [LN].

d. ἡγεμών (LN 37.83) (BAGD 2. p. 343): 'governor' [BAGD, LN; all translations except NLT, REB, TEV], 'Roman governor' [NLT, REB, TEV], 'prefect' [LN], 'procurator' [BAGD]. This noun denotes a person who ruled over a minor Roman province [LN].

QUESTION—About what time of day is 'early morning' in this verse?

It refers to the first light of day [NICNT, TRT, WBC], at daybreak [BNTC, ICC, NIBC, NIGTC, NTC]. Roman officials tended to conduct their business in the early morning [PNTC].

DISCOURSE UNIT—27:3–10 [CEV, ESV, NCV, NRSV, TEV]. The topic is Judas kills himself [NCV], the death of Judas [CEV, TEV], Judas hangs himself [ESV], the suicide of Judas [NRSV].

DISCOURSE UNIT—27:3–9 [NET]. The topic is Judas' suicide.

27:3 Then Judas, the one-betraying him, having-seen that (Jesus) was-condemned,[a] having-regretted[b] (it) he-returned the thirty (pieces of) silver to the chief-priests and elders **27:4** saying, "I-have-sinned in-having-betrayed innocent blood.[c]" But they-said, "What[d] (is that) to us? See-to[e] (that) yourself."

LEXICON—a. aorist pass. indic. of κατακρίνω (LN 56.31) (BAGD p. 412): to be condemned' [BAGD, BECNT, BNTC, LN, NICNT, NIGTC, NTC, PNTC; all versions except CEV, NCV, NLT], 'to be condemned to die' [NLT], 'to be condemned to death' [BAGD, WBC], 'to be sentenced to death' [CEV], 'to be rendered a verdict of guilt' [LN]. The phrase ὅτι κατεκρίθη 'that he had been condemned' is translated 'that they had decided to kill him' [NCV]. This verb means to judge someone as definitely guilty and thus subject to punishment [LN].

b. aorist passive (deponent = act.) participle of μεταμέλομαι(LN 25.270) (BAGD p. 511): 'to regret (one's action/what one has done)' [BAGD, BECNT, LN, NICNT, WBC; NET], 'to regret what has happened' [GW], 'to feel regret' [BAGD], 'to be sorry (for what one has done)' [CEV], 'to be very sorry (for what one has done)' [NCV], 'to repent' [BNTC; NRSV, TEV], 'to repent oneself' [KJV], 'to change one's mind' [NIGTC; ESV], 'to feel remorse' [NASB], 'to be filled with remorse' [PNTC; NLT], 'to be seized with remorse' [NTC; NIV, REB], 'to feel sad about, to feel sorry because of' [LN]. This verb means to feel regret as the result of what one has done [LN].

c. αἷμα (LN 23.107) (BAGD 2.b. p. 22): 'blood, death, violent death' [LN]. The phrase παραδοὺς αἷμα ἀθῷον 'in having betrayed innocent blood' [WBC] is also translated 'by betraying innocent blood' [ESV, NASB. NET, NRSV], 'in-that/for I have betrayed innocent blood' [KJV, NIV], 'I betrayed innocent blood' [PNTC], 'in having handed over innocent blood' [NIGTC], 'by betraying an innocent man' [GW], 'by betraying an innocent man to death' [TEV], 'for I have betrayed an innocent man' [NLT], 'by betraying a man who has never done anything wrong' [CEV], 'I handed over to you an innocent man' [NCV],'I have brought an innocent man to his death' [REB]. This noun is a figurative extension of meaning of the word 'blood' that refers to the death of a person, generally as the result of execution [LN]. 'Blood' is used figuratively as the seat of life, and to shed blood means to kill [BAGD].

e. τίς (LN 92.14): 'what?' [LN]. The phrase τί πρὸς ἡμᾶς; 'what is that to us?' [BECNT, BNTC, NIGTC, NTC, PNTC; ESV, KJV, NASB, NCV, NET, NIV, NRSV, REB] is also translated 'what difference is that to us?' [WBC], 'what has that to do with us?' [NICNT], 'what do we care?' [GW, NLT], 'what do we care about that?' [TEV]. This adjective is an interrogative reference to someone or something [LN].

f. aorist act. impera. or future mid. (deponent = act.) of ὁράω (LN **13.134**) (BAGD 2.b. p. 578): 'to see to something' [BAGD, **LN**], 'to see to it that something happens' [LN], 'to take care' [BAGD], 'to arrange for something to happen' [LN]. The phrase σὺ ὄψῃ 'see to that/it yourself' [NIGTC, PNTC; ESV, NASB, NRSV] is translated as an aorist imperative: 'you take care of it yourself' [NET], 'see thou to that' [KJV], 'you deal with that' [BECNT]; as a future tense verb: 'you will answer for that' [BNTC]; as a simple statement: 'that's your problem' [NICNT, NTC, WBC; CEV, GW, NLT], 'that's your problem, not ours' [NCV], 'that's your responsibility' [NIV], 'that is your business' [TEV], 'it is your concern' [REB]. This verb means to take responsibility for causing something to happen [LN].

QUESTION—Did Judas only regret what he had done, or did he truly repent of what he had done?

The verb μεταμέλομαι indicates regret and remorse [BNTC, My, NAC, NIBC, NICNT, TRT, WBC], but not necessarily repentance [NAC, NICNT, WBC]. A different verb, μετανοέω, is more commonly used to indicate repentance [BECNT, NAC, NIBC, WBC]. It was not a godly repentance, but the kind of 'repentance' that leads to despair [My]. The two verbs have some overlap in usage, but here Judas' remorse does not seem to be the same as repentance [EBC]. Judas showed no evidence of genuine repentance [BECNT, Lns, NTC], only regret for the consequences of what he had done [Lns, NTC]. It indicates repentance, sorrow, and regret [NIGTC]. It may have been true repentance [ICC].

27:5 And having-thrown-down[a] the (pieces of) silver in the temple,[b] he-left and having-gone-away he-hanged-himself.[c]

LEXICON—a. aorist act. participle of ῥίπτω (LN 15.217) (BAGD 1. p. 736): 'to throw down' [ESV, NLT, NRSV, REB, TEV], 'to throw' [BECNT, BNTC, LN, NICNT, NIGTC, NTC, WBC; CEV, GW, NASB, NCV, NET, NIV], 'to cast down' [KJV], 'to throw away' [BAGD], 'to hurl' [LN, PNTC]. This verb means to throw with considerable force [LN].

   b. ναός (LN 7.15) (BAGD 1.a. p. 533): 'temple' [BAGD, BECNT, LN, NTC, PNTC, WBC; all versions except NASB], 'temple building' [BNTC], 'temple sanctuary' [NASB], 'sanctuary' [LN, NICNT, NIGTC]. This noun denotes a building in which a deity is worshiped (in the case of the Temple in Jerusalem, a place where God was also regarded as dwelling) [LN].

   c. aorist mid. indic. of ἀπάγχομαι (LN **20.81**) (BAGD p. 79): 'to hang oneself' [BAGD, LN; all translations], 'to commit suicide' [LN]. This verb means to cause one's own death by hanging [LN]. Some languages will require an instrument, such as 'he hanged himself with a rope'. Others may need to make it explicit that it brought about his death, such as 'he hanged himself and died' [TH].

QUESTION—Where exactly did Judas throw the coins?

He probably threw them into a holy area where only priests are allowed to go [Lns, My, NIGTC, WBC], possibly through a gate or over a wall [WBC]. He seems to have thrown it into a holy place nearby [Lns, PNTC]. He may have actually run into the forbidden area of temple where he was not allowed to go in order to throw the money away [EBC, My], since he felt he was already guilty and condemned anyway [EBC]. It was probably in the temple treasury room [NAC, NTC], which was part of the larger Court of Women [NTC]. He went into the inner court where the altar of burnt offering was and threw it toward the door of the main temple building [BNTC]. He may have stood in the Court of Israel and thrown it across the Court of the Priests toward the entrance to the sanctuary [NICNT].

27:6 But the chief-priests having-taken the (pieces of) silver, said, "It-is-not -lawful to-put them into the treasury,[a] since it-is (the) price[b] of-blood." **27:7** After taking counsel-together, they-bought with them the potter's[c] field for a-burial-place for-strangers.[d] **27:8** For-this-reason that field has-been-called (the) Field of-Blood to this day.

LEXICON—a. κορβανᾶς (LN **7.33**) (BAGD p. 444): 'treasury' [BECNT, LN, NICNT, NIGTC, WBC; ESV, KJV, NIV, NRSV], 'Temple treasury' [BAGD, BNTC, **LN**, NTC, PNTC; CEV, GW, NASB, NET, NLT, TEV], 'temple fund' [REB], 'temple money' [NCV]. This noun denotes a room in the Temple used as a treasury [LN].

   b. τιμή (LN 57.161) (BAGD 1. p. 817): 'price' [BAGD, LN], 'amount, cost' [LN], 'value' [BAGD]. The phrase τιμὴ αἵματός 'price of blood'

[NICNT, NIGTC, KJV, NASB] is translated 'blood money' [BECNT, BNTC, NTC, PNTC, WBC; ESV, GW, NET, NIV, NRSV, REB, TEV], 'money paid to have a man killed' [CEV], 'payment for murder' [NLT], '(it has) paid for a man's death' [NCV]. This noun denotes the amount of money or property regarded as representing the value or price of something [LN].

   c. κεραμεύς (LN 6.129) (BAGD p. 428): 'potter' [BAGD, LN; all translations except CEV], 'someone who made clay pots' [CEV]. This noun denotes one who makes earthenware vessels [LN].

   d. ξένος (LN 11.73, 28.34) (BAGD 2.a. p. 548): 'stranger' [BAGD, BECNT, BNTC, LN (11.73), NICNT, NIGTC; ESV, GW, KJV, NASB, NCV], 'foreigner' [LN (11.73), NTC, PNTC; CEV, NET, NIV, NLT, NRSV, REB, TEV], 'alien' [BAGD, WBC], 'unknown' [LN (28.34)]. As a noun this word denotes a person belonging to a socio-political group other than the reference group [LN (11.73)]. As an adjective it may describe something or someone unknown or unfamiliar [LN (28.34)].

QUESTION—Where would this money have come from to begin with?

   It probably came from the temple treasury [PNTC, TRT, WBC].

QUESTION—Who are the 'strangers' referred to here?

   They would have been Jews from outside Jerusalem who were attending religious festivals there [BECNT, BNTC, Lns, My, NTC] or were there for business [BNTC]. They would have been foreigners [EBC], resident aliens [NAC]. These would have been non-Jews, who would not have been allowed to be buried in the same cemetery as Jews [WBC]. It probably refers to Jews from other countries [PNTC].

27:9 Then was-fulfilled[a] what had-been spoken by the prophet Jeremiah: "And they-took the thirty (pieces of) silver, the price of-the one whose price had-been-set[b] by the sons of-Israel; **27:10** and they-gave them for the potter's field, as (the) Lord commanded me."

LEXICON—a. aorist pass. indic. of πληρόω (LN 13.106) (BAGD 4.a. p. 671): 'to be fulfilled' [BAGD, BECNT, BNTC, LN, NICNT, NIGTC, NTC, PNTC, WBC; ESV, KJV, NASB, NET, NIV, NRSV], 'to come true' [CEV, GW, NCV, TEV], 'to cause to happen, to make happen' [LN]. This passive verb is translated '(this) fulfilled' [NLT], 'fulfillment was given' [REB]. This verb means to cause to happen, with the implication of fulfilling some purpose [LN].

   b. perf. pass. participle of τιμάω (LN 57.165) (BAGD 1. p. 817): 'to have a price set on (someone)' [BAGD, BNTC, **LN**; NRSV], 'to be priced' [NIGTC, PNTC], 'to be valued' [BAGD; KJV]. The participle τοῦ τετιμημένου 'the one having been priced' is translated 'the one/man whose price was set' [NICNT, NTC], 'upon whom a price had been set' [WBC]. The clause 'the price of the one whose price had been set by the sons/people of Israel' [BECNT; NASB, NET] is also translated 'the price of him on whom a price had been set by some of the sons of Israel'

[ESV], 'the price the people of Israel had placed on him' [GW], 'the price at which he was valued by the people of Israel' [NLT], 'the price set on a man's head (for that was his price among the Israelites)' [REB], 'that's how little the Israelites thought he was worth' [NCV], 'the price set on him by the people of Israel' [NIV], 'the amount the people of Israel had agreed to pay for him' [TEV], 'the price of a person among the people of Israel' [CEV]. This verb means to determine the amount to be used in paying for something [LN].

QUESTION—What was shown by the price being set at thirty pieces of silver?

It means that Jesus was esteemed as being of little worth [BNTC, ICC, Lns, NTC, PNTC; CEV, NCV, REB, TEV]. Thirty pieces of silver was the price of a slave [EBC, ICC].

QUESTION—Why is this prophecy attributed to Jeremiah?

It is a composite from Jeremiah and Zechariah [BNTC, BECNT, EBC, ICC, NAC, NIBC, NICNT]. It was not unusual for a quotation from the prophets to be put together from more than one source and then credit it to just the more well-known of those prophets [NAC, NIBC, NTC]. Here the mention of a potter reminds one of Jeremiah 18, buying a field recalls Jeremiah 32 [NIBC, NICNT, NIGTC, TH], and Zechariah 11:12–13 mentions the thirty pieces of silver thrown to the potter in the house of the Lord [NIBC, NICNT]. Matthew picks up on Jeremiah's theme of Israel's rejection of divinely appointed leaders [NAC, WBC], as well as innocent blood, the potter, and the renaming of a place in the valley of Hinnom [NAC]. Although Matthew borrows the wording from Zechariah, this passage probably recalls the incident in Jeremiah 19:1–13 when Jeremiah rebukes and warns the Jewish leaders and refers to 'innocent blood' (Jeremiah 19:4) [BECNT, EBC, NICNT, NTC]; there are also thematic similarities in that in Jeremiah 19 a place name associated with a potter is changed to a name denoting violence, and which will be used in the future as a burial ground. [EBC, ICC, NAC, NTC]. Matthew sees the prophetic texts as being fulfilled typologically in the events that transpired, but not as a direct prediction of the events themselves [BECNT, EBC, NAC]. Zechariah 11 and Jeremiah 19 both show patterns of rejection of and apostasy from God that will be repeated in the rejection of Jesus [BECNT, EBC]. Although Matthew quotes from various prophetic sources in his gospel, he only mentions the major prophets Isaiah, Jeremiah, and Daniel by name [NICNT]. The third part of the Jewish Bible, known as the prophets, began with Jeremiah, and consequently the whole collection was sometimes referred to by the name 'Jeremiah' [Lns, TRT].

QUESTION—In what sense does this event fulfill prophecy?

Matthew sees the prophetic passages not as directly predicting specific events but as foreshadowing what transpires in Jesus' passion [BECNT, NAC, NIBC, WBC]. Here Matthew is drawing on scriptural motifs [NICNT]. The prophecy in Zechariah is symbolic [Lns].

DISCOURSE UNIT—27:11–26 [NASB, NIV, NLT]. The topic is Jesus before Pilate [NASB, NIV], Jesus' trial before Pilate [NLT].

DISCOURSE UNIT—27:11–23 [NET]. The topic is Jesus and Pilate.

DISCOURSE UNIT—27:11–14 [CEV, ESV, GW, NCV, NRSV, TEV]. The topic is Pilate questions Jesus [CEV, GW, NCV, NRSV, TEV], Jesus before Pilate [ESV].

27:11 **And Jesus stood before the governor, and the governor asked him saying, "Are you the King of-the Jews?" And Jesus said, "You say^a (so)." 27:12 And when being-accused^b by the chief-priests and elders, he-did-not answer. 27:13 Then Pilate says to-him, "Do-you- not -hear how-many (things) they testify-against you?" 27:14 And he-did- not –answer him, not-with-one-word/not-about-one-charge,^{c} so-as to amaze^d the governor greatly.**

LEXICON—a. pres. act. indic. of λέγω (LN 33.69) (BAGD II.1.e. p. 469): 'to say' [LN], 'to maintain, to declare' [BAGD]. The phrase σὺ λέγεις 'you say so' [BECNT, BNTC; NET, NRSV], is translated 'you say it' [NICNT], 'you are saying it' [NIGTC, PNTC], 'thou sayest' [KJV], 'you said/have said it' [NTC; NLT], 'you have said so' [ESV], 'that is what you maintain' [BAGD], 'so you say' [TEV], 'those are your words' [CEV, NCV], 'the words are yours' [REB], 'it is as you say' [NASB], 'yes, it is as you say' [NIV], 'you speak the truth' [WBC], 'yes I am' [GW]. This verb means to speak or talk, with apparent focus upon the content of what is said [LN].

   b. pres. pass. infin. of κατηγορέω (LN 33.427) (BAGD 1.a. p. 423): 'to be accused' [BAGD, BECNT, BNTC, LN, NICNT, NIGTC, NTC, PNTC, WBC; ESV, KJV, NASB, NET, NIV, NRSV], 'to have charges brought (against one)' [BAGD, LN]. This passive verb is translated as active: 'to accuse' [GW, NCV], 'to make accusations' [NLT], 'to bring charges' [CEV, REB]. It is translated as a noun: 'accusations' [TEV]. This verb means to bring serious charges or accusations against someone, with the possible connotation of a legal or court context [LN].

   c. ῥῆμα(LN **33.9**) (BAGD 1. p. 735): 'charge' [BECNT, NICNT, NTC, WBC; ESV, NASB, NIV, NLT, NRSV], 'accusation' [NET]. Others take it to mean 'word' [BAGD, BNTC, **LN**, NIGTC, PNTC; KJV, REB, TEV]. In place of a rendering such as 'refused to answer a single word,' it may be more idiomatic to just say 'said nothing' or 'refused to speak.' [LN], The interpretation 'he did not answer him, not with one word' is simplified by some translations: 'Jesus did not say anything' [CEV], 'Jesus said absolutely nothing in reply' [GW], 'Jesus said nothing in answer to Pilate' [NCV]. This noun denotes a minimal unit of discourse, often a single word [LN]. It refers to that which is said; [BAGD].

   d. pres. act. infin. of 25.213 θαυμάζω (LN 25.213) (BAGD 1.a.α. p. 352): 'to be amazed' [BECNT, LN, NIGTC, WBC; CEV, ESV, NASB, NET,

NRSV], 'to marvel' [BAGD, BNTC, LN; KJV], 'to be surprised' [NICNT; GW, NCV, REB, TEV], 'to be astonished' [NTC, PNTC], 'to wonder' [BAGD, LN], 'to be astonished' [BAGD]. This verb is translated as a noun phrase: 'to the amazement of' [NIV], 'to the surprise of' [NLT], 'to the (governor's) astonishment' [REB]. This verb means to wonder or marvel at some event or object [LN].

QUESTION—Where does this interrogation by Pilate occur?

It is probably at Herod's old palace in the western part of Jerusalem [EBC, NICNT, NIGTC, WBC].

QUESTION—Why does Jesus reply 'you say so'?

Jesus affirms the truth of what Pilate has said but in a qualified way, in that he does not mean the same thing by it that Pilate would mean [BNTC, EBC, NAC, NIBC, NICNT, NIGTC, PNTC, TH, TRT, WBC]. It was a qualified affirmation that Pilate had spoken the truth, although without understanding what it meant [ICC]. It was an emphatic affirmation of what Pilate said [My, NTC].

QUESTION—Does οὐδὲ ἓν ῥῆμα 'not…even one charge' mean that he did not answer any accusation or that he did not speak a word?

1. It means he did not answer even one charge or accusation [BECNT, Lns, NIBC, NICNT, NTC, TH, WBC; ESV, NASB, NET, NIV, NLT, NRSV].
2. It means he did not answer by saying even one word [BNTC, NAC, NIGTC, PNTC, TRT; CEV, GW, KJV, NCV, REB, TEV].

DISCOURSE UNIT—27:15–31 [NCV]. The topic is Pilate tries to free Jesus.

DISCOURSE UNIT—27:15–26 [CEV, GW]. The topic is the crowd rejects Jesus [GW], Jesus is sentenced to death [TEV], the death sentence [CEV].

DISCOURSE UNIT—27:15–23 [ESV, NRSV]. The topic is the crowd chooses Barabbas [ESV], Barabbas or Jesus? [NRSV].

`27:15` Now at (the) festival the governor was-accustomed[a] to-release a-prisoner to[b]-the crowd, (anyone) whom they-wanted. `27:16` And at-that-time they-had a-notorious[c] prisoner, called Jesus Barabbas. `27:17` They having-come-together, Pilate said to-them, "Whom do-you-want (that) I-should-release for-you, Jesus Barabbas or Jesus the-one called Messiah?" `27:18` For he-knew that they had handed him over because-of envy.[d]

TEXT—Manuscripts reading Ἰησοῦν Βαραββᾶν 'Jesus Barabbas' are given a C rating by GNT, to indicate that choosing it over variant texts reading only Βαραββᾶν 'Barabbas' was difficult. The name 'Jesus' is included by NICNT, NIGTC; CEV, NET, NRSV, REB, TEV. It is included in brackets by GNT as well as by BECNT, WBC.

LEXICON—a. pluperfect act. indic. of ἐθίζω (LN **41.26**) (BAGD p. 234): 'to be accustomed to' [BAGD, BECNT, BNTC, NIGTC, PNTC, WBC; ESV, NASB, NET, NRSV], 'to be in the habit of' [**LN**; TEV], 'to be wont' [KJV], 'to carry out a custom, to maintain a tradition' [LN], not explicit

[CEV, GW, NCV]. This verb is translated by a phrase: 'it was (the governor's) custom' [NICNT; NIV, NLT], 'it was customary' [NTC; REB]. This verb means to carry out a custom or tradition [LN].

b. There is no lexical entry in the Greek text representing the word 'to', but it is supplied in translation to show the relationship indicated by the dative case of τῷ ὄχλῳ 'the crowd'. It is translated 'to' [BECNT, BNTC, NICNT, NIGTC, NTC, PNTC, WBC; KJV, NET, NLT], 'for' [ESV, NASB, NRSV], not explicit [CEV, GW, NCV, NIV, REB, TEV].

c. ἐπίσημος (LN 28.31) (BAGD 2. p. 298): 'notorious' [BAGD, BECNT, LN, NTC, WBC; ESV, NASB, NET, NIV, NLT, NRSV], 'notable' [BNTC, NIGTC, PNTC; KJV], 'well-known' [NICNT; CEV, GW, TEV], 'infamous' [BAGD], 'known to be very bad' [NCV], 'of some notoriety' [REB], 'outstanding, famous' [LN]. This adjective denotes the quality of being well known or outstanding, either because of positive or negative characteristics [LN].

d. φθόνος (LN 88.160) (BAGD p. 857): 'envy' [BAGD, BECNT, BNTC, LN, NIGTC, NTC, PNTC, WBC; ESV, KJV, NASB, NET, NIV, NLT], 'jealousy' [BAGD, LN; NRSV], 'rivalry' [NICNT], 'malice' [REB]. The phrase διὰ φθόνον 'because of envy' is translated 'because they were jealous' [CEV, GW, NCV, TEV]. This noun denotes a state of ill will toward someone because of some real or presumed advantage experienced by such a person [LN].

QUESTION—What does the adjective ἐπίσημος 'notorious' mean here?

It means that he was notorious [BECNT, ICC, LN, Lns, My, NAC, NIBC, NTC, TH, WBC; ESV, NASB, NCV, NET, NIV, NLT, NRSV, REB], although it is possible that it means that he was well-known or famous [BNTC, NAC, NICNT, NIGTC, PNTC, WBC; CEV, GW, KJV, TEV]. It means that he was well-known, and may actually have been held in high esteem as a revolutionary [EBC, NICNT]. He had become well known as a leader in an insurrection [PNTC].

QUESTION—Who was it that came together in v.17?

It was the crowds who had assembled to petition the governor for the release of a prisoner [EBC, ICC, My, NIGTC, PNTC, TH, TRT, WBC]. Pilate called the Sanhedrin together, in order to meet with him with and representatives of the people who had already approached him to petition for the release of a prisoner [Lns].

QUESTION—What does Pilate mean by describing Jesus as 'the one called Messiah'?

It indicates that he himself does not believe the claim [WBC], and it may even express contempt [EBC] or sarcasm [TH]. He probably thinks that Jesus does not deserve the title [NAC]. He hoped that the crowd would be positively affected by the consideration that Jesus might be the Messiah [BNTC, Lns, NICNT, NTC, PNTC], though he does not necessarily endorse the claim [NICNT].

27:19 While- he (was)-sitting on-the judgment-seat,[a] his wife sent (a-message) to him, "(Let-there-be) nothing[b] (between) you and that innocent[c] man, for today I have suffered much because-of a-dream about him."

LEXICON—a. βῆμα (LN 7.63) (BAGD 2. p. 140): 'judgment seat' [BECNT, LN, PNTC; ESV, KJV, NASB, NET, NLT, NRSV], 'judge's seat' [NCV, NIV], 'judgment throne' [WBC], 'judge's bench' [BNTC], 'judicial bench' [BAGD, NIGTC, NTC], 'judgment hall' [TEV], 'judgment place' [LN], 'tribunal' [BAGD]. The phrase ἐπὶ τοῦ βήματος 'on the judgment seat' is translated 'in court' [REB], 'hearing the case' [NICNT], 'judging the case' [CEV, GW]. This noun denotes a raised platform mounted by steps and usually furnished with a seat, used by officials in addressing an assembly, often on judicial matters [LN].

   b. μηδέν (LN 92.23): 'nothing' [LN]. The phrase μηδὲν σοί 'let there be nothing between you' is translated 'have nothing to do with' [BECNT, BNTC, NIGTC, PNTC; ESV, KJV, NASB, NET, NRSV, REB, TEV], 'don't have anything to do with' [NTC, WBC; CEV, NIV], 'don't do anything to' [NCV], 'don't get involved with' [NICNT], 'leave (that innocent man) alone' [GW, NLT]. This adjective is a negative reference to an entity, event, or state [LN].

   c. δίκαιος (LN 88.12) (BAGD 3. p. 196): 'innocent' [BAGD, BECNT; all versions except ESV, KJV, NASB], 'righteous' [BNTC, LN, NICNT, NIGTC, NTC, PNTC, WBC; ESV, NASB], 'just' [BAGD, LN; KJV]. This adjective describes being in accordance with what God requires [LN].

27:20 Now the chief-priests and the elders[a] persuaded the crowds that they-ask-for Barabbas but that-they-destroy[b] Jesus. **27:21** But answering, the governor said to-them, "Which of the two do-you-want (that) I-release for you?" And they-said, "Barabbas." **27:22** Pilate says to-them, "What then shall-I-do (with) Jesus the-one called Messiah?" All (of them) say, "Let-him-be-crucified!" **27:23** And he-said, "Why, (what) evil[c] has-he-done?" But they-shouted all-the-more saying, "Let-him-be-crucified!"

LEXICON—a. πρεσβύτερος (LN 53.77) (BAGD 2.a.β. p. 700): 'elder' [BAGD, LN; all translations except CEV, GW, NCV], 'leader' [CEV, GW], 'older leader' [NCV]. This noun denotes a person of responsibility and authority in matters of socio-religious concerns, both in Jewish and Christian societies [LN].

   b. aorist act. subj. of ἀπόλλυμι (LN 20.31) (BAGD 1.a.α. p. 95): 'to destroy' [BAGD, LN, NIGTC, PNTC, WBC; ESV, KJV], 'to have (someone) executed' [BECNT, NICNT, NTC; NIV], 'to have (someone) killed' [NET, NRSV], 'to have (someone) put to death' [REB, TEV], 'to put to death' [BNTC; NASB]. This active verb is translated as passive: 'to be killed' [CEV, NCV], 'to be put to death' [NLT]. It is translated as a

noun phrase: 'the execution of (Jesus)' [GW]. This verb means to destroy
or to cause the destruction of persons, objects, or institutions [LN].

c. κακός (LN 88.106) (BAGD 1.c. p. 397): 'evil' [BAGD, BECNT, BNTC,
LN, NIGTC, PNTC; ESV, KJV, NASB, NRSV], 'wrong' [NICNT, NTC;
GW, NCV, NET], 'crime' [CEV, NIV, NLT, TEV], 'bad thing' [WBC],
'harm' [REB], 'bad, harmful' [LN]. This adjective describes what is bad,
with the implication of being harmful and damaging [LN].

QUESTION—What is the subject of the clause 'but that they destroy Jesus'?
The subject of the sentence is the Jewish crowds, just as in the previous
clause 'that they ask for Barabbas' [PNTC, WBC]. They were to seek Jesus'
death [NTC, PNTC] or to cause it to come about [TH].

DISCOURSE UNIT—27:24–31 [NET]. The topic is Jesus is condemned and
mocked.

DISCOURSE UNIT—27:24–26 [ESV, NRSV]. The topic is Pilate delivers
Jesus to be crucified [ESV], Pilate hands Jesus over to be crucified [NRSV].

27:24 And Pilate having-seen that he-is-accomplishing[a] nothing, but rather
(that) a-riot[b] is-beginning, having-taken (some) water he-washed (his)
hands before the crowd, saying, "I-am innocent[c] of the blood[d] of-this
(man); see-to-(it)[e] yourselves." **27:25** And answering all the people said,
"His blood (be) on[f] us and on our children!" **27:26** Then he-released
Barabbas for-them; but having-flogged[g] Jesus, he-handed- (him) -over so-
that he-be-crucified.

TEXT—Manuscripts reading τούτου 'this (man)' are given a B rating by GNT
to indicate it was regarded to be almost certain. Manuscripts reading τούτου
δικαίου 'this just person' are followed by KJV.

LEXICON—a. pres. act. indic. of ὠφελέω (LN **68.33**) (BAGD 2.a. p. 900): 'to
accomplish' [BAGD, BECNT, BNTC, **LN**; NASB], 'to achieve'
[NIGTC], 'to gain' [ESV], 'to prevail' [KJV], 'to do' [LN; NCV, NET,
NRSV]. The phrase 'accomplishing nothing' is translated 'getting
nowhere' [**LN**, NICNT, PNTC, WBC; NIV, REB], 'not getting anywhere'
[NTC; GW, NLT], 'there was nothing he could do' [CEV], 'it was no use
to go on' [TEV]. This verb means to be successful in accomplishing some
goal [LN].

b. θόρυβος (LN 39.42) (BAGD 3.b. p. 363): 'riot' [LN, NICNT, NIGTC,
NTC; all versions except CEV, KJV, NIV], 'uproar' [BAGD, BECNT;
NIV], 'disturbance' [BAGD, BNTC], 'tumult' [PNTC; KJV], 'clamor'
[WBC], 'turmoil' [BAGD]. The phrase θόρυβος γίνεται 'a riot was
beginning' is translated 'the people were starting to riot' [CEV]. This
noun denotes disorderly behavior of people in violent opposition to
authority [LN].

c. ἀθῷος (LN 88.316) (BAGD p. 21): 'innocent' [BAGD, BECNT, BNTC,
LN, NICNT, NIGTC, NTC, PNTC, WBC; ESV, KJV, NASB, NET, NIV,
NLT, NRSV], 'guiltless' [BAGD, LN], 'not...guilty' [GW, NCV], 'not

responsible' [TEV], 'clean' [REB], not explicit [CEV]. This adjective
describes not being guilty of wrongdoing [LN].

d. αἷμα (LN 20.83) (BAGD 2.a. p. 22): 'blood' [BAGD, BECNT, BNTC,
NICNT, NIGTC, NTC, PNTC, WBC; ESV, KJV, NASB, NET, NIV,
NLT, NRSV, REB], 'killing' [LN; GW], 'death' [NCV, TEV], 'murder'
[LN]. The phrase Ἀθῷός εἰμι ἀπὸ τοῦ αἵματος τούτου 'I am innocent
of the blood of this man' is translated 'I won't have anything to do with
killing this man' [CEV]. This figurative use of αἷμα 'blood' means to
deprive a person of life by violent means [LN], that is, to kill [BAGD].

e. aorist act. impera. of ὁράω (LN **13.134**) (BAGD 2.b. p. 578): 'to see to
(something)' [BAGD, **LN**, NIGTC, PNTC; ESV, KJV, NASB, NRSV,
REB], 'to deal with' [BECNT], 'to answer for' [BNTC], 'to take care'
[BAGD; NET], 'to see to it that something happens, to arrange for
something to happen' [LN]. The phrase 'see to it yourselves' is translated
'it's your responsibility' [NICNT, WBC; NIV, similarly NLT], 'you are
the ones doing/causing it' [CEV, NCV], 'this is your doing' [TEV], 'do
what you want' [GW], 'that's your problem' [NTC]. This verb means to
take responsibility for causing something to happen [LN].

f. ἐπί with accusative (LN **90.17**) (BAGD III.1.b.γ. p. 289): 'on' [BAGD,
BECNT, BNTC, LN, NICNT, NIGTC, PNTC; ESV, KJV, NASB, NET,
NIV, NRSV, REB], 'upon' [BAGD, **LN**, NTC, WBC]. The phrase τὸ
αἷμα αὐτοῦ ἐφ' ἡμᾶς 'his blood be on us' is translated 'we take the
blame/responsibility for his death' [CEV, NLT], 'let the responsibility for
his death fall on us' [TEV], 'we will be responsible for his death' [NCV],
'the responsibility for killing him will rest on us' [GW]. This preposition
indicates the one upon whom responsibility falls [LN].

g. aorist act. participle of φραγελλόω (LN 19.9) (BAGD p. 865): 'to flog'
[BAGD, BNTC; NRSV], 'to have flogged' [BECNT, NICNT, NIGTC,
NTC; NET, NIV, REB], 'to scourge' [BAGD, PNTC; ESV, KJV], 'to
have scourged' [WBC; NASB], 'to have whipped' [GW, TEV], 'to whip,
to beat with a whip' [LN]. The phrase Ἰησοῦν φραγελλώσας 'having
flogged Jesus' is translated 'he ordered Jesus flogged' [NLT], 'he ordered
his soldiers to beat Jesus with a whip' [CEV], 'Jesus was beaten with a
whip' [NCV]. This verb means to beat severely with a whip [LN].

QUESTION—To whom does 'all the people' refer?
It refers to the entire crowd that was present there [BECNT, EBC, NAC,
PNTC, TH, TRT], including their leaders [TH]. When those people added
that Jesus' blood would also be on their children they were not passing
responsibility for his death down through the generations. By involving their
children they were showing their deep commitment and seriousness about
demanding the death of Jesus [NIGTC].

DISCOURSE UNIT—27:27–66 [NICNT, PNTC]. The topic is the death and
burial of Jesus [NICNT], the death of Jesus [PNTC].

DISCOURSE UNIT—27:27-56 [BECNT]. The topic is the crucifixion.

DISCOURSE UNIT—27:27-32 [NASB]. The topic is Jesus is mocked.

DISCOURSE UNIT—27:27-31 [ESV, NIV, NLT, NRSV, TEV]. The topic is the soldiers make fun of Jesus [TEV], Jesus is mocked [ESV], the soldiers mock Jesus [NIV, NLT, NRSV].

DISCOURSE UNIT—27:27-30 [CEV, GW]. The topic is the soldiers make fun of Jesus.

`27:27` **Then having-taken Jesus into the praetorium,[a] the soldiers of-the governor gathered the whole cohort[b] around him.** `27:28` **And having-stripped him, they-put-around him a-scarlet[c] robe,** `27:29` **and after having-woven a-crown from thorns, they-put (it) on his head and a-reed[d] in his right hand, and having-knelt before him they-mocked[e] him, saying, "Hail, King of the Jews!"** `27:30` **And having spat on him, they took the reed and -were-striking him on the head.**

LEXICON—a. πραιτώριον (LN 7.7) (BAGD p. 697): 'praetorium' [BAGD, BNTC, NIGTC, PNTC, WBC; NASB, NIV], 'governor's residence' [BECNT; NET, REB], 'governor's headquarters' [NTC; ESV, NRSV], 'governor's palace' [NCV, TEV], 'guard room' [NICNT], 'headquarters' [NLT], 'fortress' [**LN**; CEV], 'palace' [**LN**; GW], 'common hall' [KJV]. This noun denotes a governor's official residence [LN].

  b. σπεῖρα (LN 55.9) (BAGD p. 761): 'cohort' [BAGD, BECNT, BNTC, LN, NICNT, NIGTC, WBC; NASB, NET, NRSV], 'company' [PNTC; REB, TEV], 'company of soldiers' [NIV], 'rest of the troops' [CEV], 'troop' [GW], 'battalion' [ESV], 'regiment' [NLT], 'band' [NTC; KJV], 'band of soldiers' [LN], not explicit [NCV]. This noun denotes a Roman military unit of about six hundred soldiers, though only a part of such a cohort was often referred to as a cohort [LN].

  c. κόκκινος (LN **79.29**) (BAGD p. 440): 'scarlet' [BAGD, BECNT, BNTC, **LN**, NIGTC, NTC, PNTC, WBC; all versions except GW, NCV], 'red' [BAGD, LN, NICNT; NCV], 'bright red' [GW]. This adjective refers to the colors scarlet and red. The scarlet robe may have implied a high military rank [BAGD].

  d. κάλαμος (LN 3.55) (BAGD 2. p. 398): 'reed' [BECNT, LN, NIGTC, PNTC; ESV, KJV, NASB, NRSV], 'stick' [NICNT, NTC; CEV, GW, NCV, REB, TEV], 'reed stick' [NLT], 'staff' [BAGD, BNTC, WBC; NET, NIV], 'stalk' [BAGD]. This noun denotes the stalk of a reed plant [LN].

  e. aorist act. indic. of ἐμπαίζω (LN 33.406) (BAGD 1. p. 255): 'to mock' [BAGD, BECNT, BNTC, LN, NIGTC, NTC, PNTC, WBC; ESV, KJV, NASB, NET, NIV, NRSV], 'to make fun of' [BAGD, NICNT; CEV, GW, NCV, TEV], 'to ridicule' [BAGD, LN], 'to jeer' [REB]. This verb is translated by a phrase: 'in mockery' [NLT]. This verb means to make fun of someone by pretending that he is not what he is or by imitating him in a distorted manner [LN].

QUESTION—What and where was the praetorium?

This noun denotes the official residence of a governor [BAGD, LN, NAC]. The praetorium could have been either the palace of Herod in the western part of the city or the fortress Antonia northwest of the Temple area [BAGD, BECNT, BNTC, LN, NAC, PNTC, WBC]. It was probably the old palace of Herod on the west side of the city [EBC, NICNT, NIGTC, WBC]. It was the fortress Antonia [Lns, My].

QUESTION—How many men would have been in 'the whole cohort'?

Although a cohort at full strength would number up to six hundred soldiers, here the expression probably only refers to all the soldiers who were then present [BNTC, EBC, Lns, PNTC, TH, WBC]. It was probably not all 600 members of the cohort [ICC, Lns, NICNT, NTC, WBC], but it was certainly a large number of hostile men [ICC, WBC]. This word could also refer to a smaller detachment of 200 soldiers [PNTC]. Matthew may not be using the term in its technical military sense [NICNT], or he is just using the term more loosely [NIGTC].

QUESTION—What is the significance of the color of the robe?

In this passage the scarlet robe may have implied high military rank [LN]. It was a reddish purple robe such as soldiers or travelers would wear [NAC]. The ancients did not distinguish between colors as we do, so the robe could be described as either 'scarlet' or 'purple' [EBC]. The color was probably somewhere between scarlet and purple [TRT]. Here it was probably the red cloak of a Roman soldier [BNTC, EBC, ICC, Lns, NIBC, NICNT, NIGTC, NTC, TH, WBC], used in mockery of Jesus being dressed like a king [EBC, Lns, PNTC, TRT, WBC]. The scarlet color was close to the purple that kings would wear [NIBC, PNTC]. It was a reddish-purple robe such as soldiers or travelers would wear [NAC]. The red dye was much cheaper than the purple dye used for royalty [NICNT].

DISCOURSE UNIT—27:31–44 [CEV, GW, NET]. The topic is the crucifixion [GW, NET], Jesus is nailed to a cross [CEV].

27:31 **And when they-had-mocked him, they-stripped him (of) the robe and put-on him his-own clothes and they-led- him -away to crucify (him).**

DISCOURSE UNIT—27:32–44 [ESV, NCV, NIV, NLT, NRSV, TEV]. The topic is Jesus is crucified [NCV, TEV], the crucifixion [ESV, NIV], the crucifixion of Jesus [NRSV].

27:32 **And going-out, they-came-upon a-man (from) Cyrene Simon by-name. They-pressed-into-service[a] this man that he-carry his cross.**

LEXICON—a. aorist act. indic. of ἀγγαρεύω (LN 37.34) (BAGD p. 6): 'to press someone into service' [BAGD, BECNT, BNTC, LN, NIGTC; NASB, REB], 'to dragoon' [NICNT], 'to compel' [LN, PNTC; ESV,

KJV, NRSV], 'to force' [NTC, WBC; CEV, GW, NCV, NET, NIV, NLT, TEV], 'to compel someone to carry a load' [LN]. This verb means to force civilians to carry a load for some distance (in NT times Roman soldiers had the authority to enforce such service) [LN].

QUESTION—From where were they going out?

They were leaving the city [EBC, Lns, My, NICNT, NTC, TH, TRT]. They were leaving the praetorium [NIGTC].

QUESTION—What did Simon actually carry?

He would have carried only the cross-beam of the cross [BECNT, BNTC, EBC, ICC, NAC, NIBC, NICNT, NIGTC, PNTC, TH, WBC]. A few think he would have carried the entire cross [Lns, NTC, TRT].

DISCOURSE UNIT—27:33–56 [NASB]. The topic is the crucifixion.

27:33 **And having-come to a-place called Golgotha, which means Place of-a Skull,** **27:34** **they-gave him wine to-drink, with gall[a] having-been-mixed-in; but having-tasted (it), he-did- not -want to-drink (it).** **27:35** **And having-crucified him, they-distributed his clothes by-casting lots,[b]** **27:36** **and sitting-down they-kept-watch over-him there.**

TEXT—Manuscripts reading βάλλοντες κλῆρον 'casting lots' are given an A rating by GNT to indicate it was regarded to be certain. Manuscripts that add another clause about fulfilling the words of the prophet, etc., are followed by KJV.

LEXICON—a. χολή (LN **8.75**) (BAGD 1. p. 883): 'gall' [BAGD, BECNT, BNTC, **LN**, NIGTC, NTC, PNTC, WBC; ESV, KJV, NASB, NCV, NET, NIV, NRSV, REB], 'bitter gall' [NLT], 'a bitter substance' [TEV], 'a drug to ease the pain' [CEV], 'a drug called gall' [GW], 'bile' [BAGD]. The phrase οἶνον μετὰ χολῆς 'wine...with gall' is translated 'drugged wine' [NICNT]. This noun denotes the bitter yellowish liquid secreted by the liver and stored in the gall bladder. It is possible, however, that in Matthew 27:34 the reference is not specifically to gall but to a substance with an especially unpleasant taste [LN].

    b. κλῆρος (LN 6.219) (BAGD 1. p. 435): 'lot' [BAGD, BECNT, BNTC, LN, NICNT, NIGTC, NTC, PNTC, WBC; ESV, KJV, NASB, NCV, NIV, NRSV, REB]. The phrase βάλλοντες κλῆρον 'casting lots' is translated 'throwing dice' [GW, NET, NLT, TEV], 'gambling' [CEV]. This noun denotes a specially marked pebble, piece of pottery, or stick employed in making decisions based upon chance [LN]. The lots were possibly marked pebbles [NAC], and it would be similar to throwing dice [NAC, NTC].

QUESTION—What is gall, and why was it mixed with wine?

Gall could have been a pain-killing drug [BNTC, Lns, NAC, NICNT, PNTC; CEV]. Myrrh was mixed in to drug the victim and thus make the soldiers' job easier [Lns]. What Mark describes as wine mixed with myrrh was a different drink, offered to help dull the pain [WBC]. The offer of wine mixed with gall was not an act of mercy but of further torment by the Roman soldiers [EBC, ICC, NIGTC, WBC]. Mark indicates that it was myrrh that was mixed in, which describes what it actually was, whereas Matthew calls it 'gall' to describe the bitter taste and to link it to Psalm 69:21 [EBC, Lns, NTC], indicating that, like David, Jesus looked for sympathy but did not find any [EBC]. It was something bitter mixed into the wine, but not necessarily something intended to ease the pain [TH]. The women of Jerusalem would provide myrrh to mix with the wine to dull the pain, but the soldiers, as one last act of cruelty, mixed gall with it to make it bitter [NIBC]. It may have been a poison, and the offer would have been an invitation to hasten his own death by drinking the poison [ICC].

QUESTION—Why did Jesus not want to drink of the wine?

It probably contained a pain-killing ingredient, and he did not want to diminish his suffering [BECNT, BNTC, NAC, NICNT, NTC]. He wanted his mind to be clear through the entire ordeal [Lns, TRT]. It was too bitter to drink [My].

QUESTION—What was the cross like?

Crosses could be like an X, or like a T, but this one was probably like the traditional cross. [BECNT, EBC, ICC, Lns, My, NIBC, NICNT, NIGTC, NTC, WBC], and Jesus would have been suspended several feet above the ground [EBC, Lns].

QUESTION—Why did the soldiers keep watch?

They wanted to prevent anyone from coming to rescue the crucified man before he died [EBC, BNTC, Lns, NAC, NIBC, NICNT, NIGTC, NTC, PNTC, TH, WBC].

27:37 **And above his head they-put the written charge[a] against-him: "This is Jesus, the King of the Jews."** **27:38** **Then two criminals/insurrectionists[b] were crucified with him, one on his right and one on his left.** **27:39** **The-ones passing-by were-reviling[c] him, shaking[d] their heads** **27:40** **and saying, "You who (are-going-to) destroy the temple and in three days rebuild-it, save yourself! If you are the Son of God, come-down from the cross."**

TEXT—Manuscripts reading καὶ κατάβηθι 'and come down' are given a C rating by GNT to indicate that choosing that reading over variant texts that omit the καί 'and' was difficult. The καί 'and' is included by BECNT, NICNT, PNTC; GW, ESV, KJV, NASB, NCV, NET, NIV, NRSV, TEV. It is omitted by BNTC, NIGTC, NTC, WBC; CEV, NLT, REB.

LEXICON—a. αἰτία (LN **56.5**) (BAGD 2.a. p. 26): 'charge' [BAGD, BECNT, BNTC, LN, NICNT, PNTC; ESV, NASB, NCV, NET, NIV, NLT, NRSV, REB], 'accusation' [**LN**; GW, KJV, TEV, 'crime' [WBC], 'cause' [NIGTC], 'indictment' [NTC], 'complaint, ground for complaint, reason for capital punishment' [BAGD]. The phrase 'the written charge against him' is translated 'a sign that told why he was nailed there' [CEV]. This noun denotes the content of legal charges brought against someone [LN].

b. λῃστής (LN 57.240, 39.37) (BAGD 1. p. 473): 'criminal' [CEV, GW], 'robber' [BAGD, LN (57.240), NTC; ESV, NASB, NCV, NIV], 'bandit' [BAGD, BNTC, NICNT, NIGTC, PNTC; NRSV, REB, TEV], 'outlaw' [NET], 'highwayman' [BAGD, LN (57.240)], 'thief' [WBC; KJV], 'revolutionary' [BECNT; NLT], 'insurrectionist, rebel' [LN (39.37)]. This noun denotes one who robs by force and violence [LN (57.240)] or it denotes a person who engages in insurrection [LN (39.37)].

c. imperf. act. indic. of βλασφημέω (LN **33.400**) (BAGD 2.b.δ. p. 142): 'to revile' [BNTC, **LN**; KJV], 'to blaspheme' [LN, NIGTC, NTC, WBC], 'to taunt' [BECNT], 'to insult' [GW, NCV], 'to hurl insults' [NIV, TEV], 'to abuse' [NICNT], 'to hurl abuse' [NASB], 'to shout abuse' [NLT], 'to deride' [ESV, NRSV], 'to defame' [NET], 'to jeer' [PNTC; REB], 'to say terrible things' [CEV]. This verb means to speak against someone in such a way as to harm or injure his or her reputation (occurring in relation to persons as well as to divine beings) [LN].

d. pres. act. participle of κινέω (LN 16.2) (BAGD 2.a. p. 432): 'to shake (the head)' [BAGD, BECNT, BNTC, LN, NICNT, NIGTC, NTC, PNTC, WBC; CEV, GW, NCV, NET, NIV, NRSV, TEV], 'to wag (the head)' [ESV, KJV, NASB, REB], 'to shake (the head) in mockery' [NLT]. This verb means to set something in motion, with the nature of the movement dependent upon the object in question [LN].

QUESTION—What does λῃστής 'criminals/insurrectionists' mean here?

These were revolutionaries, insurrectionists [BECNT, EBC, NAC, NICNT], or rebel guerillas [EBC]. They may have been insurrectionists [ICC, WBC]. They would have been involved in terrorism and assassination [NAC], and may have been involved in hostility toward Rome along with robbery and plunder [BNTC]. They were robbers [Lns, NIGTC, NTC, TH], brigands, and may have been involved in a resistance movement [PNTC].

QUESTION—What does shaking the head express here?

It indicates disapproval [Lns, WBC], scorn [NICNT, TH, WBC], arrogant contempt [NTC], mockery [ICC, My, NIGTC].

27:41 Likewise[a] also the chief-priests, along with the scribes and elders, mocking said, **27:42** "He-saved[b] others, (but) himself he-cannot save; he is the King of Israel, let-him-come-down now from the cross and we-will-believe in him. **27:43** He-has-put-his-trust[c] in God, let-him-deliver[d] him now, if he-wants[e] him; for he said, 'I-am Son of-God.'" **27:44** And likewise also the criminals/insurrectionists being-crucified with him were-insulting[f] him.

TEXT—Manuscripts reading βασιλεὺς Ἰσραήλ ἐστιν 'he is King of Israel' are given a B rating by GNT to indicate it was regarded to be almost certain. Manuscripts reading εἰ βασιλεὺς Ἰσραήλ ἐστιν 'if he is the king of Israel' are followed by CEV, KJV, NCV.

LEXICON—a. ὁμοίως (LN 64.1) (BAGD p. 568): 'likewise' [BAGD, BNTC, LN, PNTC; KJV], 'in the same way' [BAGD, BECNT, NICNT; GW,

NASB, NET, NIV, NRSV, TEV], 'in a similar way' [WBC], 'similarly' [BAGD, NIGTC, NTC], 'so' [BAGD; ESV], not explicit [CEV, NCV, NLT, REB]. This adverb describes being similar to something else in some respect [LN].

b. aorist act. Indic. of σῴζω (LN 21.18) (BAGD 1.a. p. 798): 'to save' [BAGD; all translations], 'to preserve' [BAGD], 'to rescue' [BAGD, LN], 'to deliver, to make safe' [LN]. This verb means to rescue from danger and to restore to a former state of safety and well being [LN].

c. perf. act. indic. of πείθω (LN 31.82) (BAGD 2.a. p. 639): 'to put trust in' [BNTC, NICNT, PNTC; NASB], 'to trust in' [BAGD, BECNT, LN, NIGTC, WBC; ESV, KJV, NCV, NET, NIV, NRSV, REB, TEV], 'to trust' [CEV, GW, NLT], 'to place trust in' [NTC], 'to depend on' [BAGD, LN], 'to put confidence in' [BAGD], 'to rely on, to, to have (complete) confidence in' [LN]. This verb means to believe in something or someone to the extent of placing reliance or trust in or on [LN].

d. aorist mid. (deponent = act.) impera. of ῥύομαι (LN 21.23) (BAGD p. 737): 'to deliver' [BAGD, BECNT, BNTC, LN, NTC, PNTC, WBC; ESV, KJV, NET, NRSV], 'to rescue' [BAGD, **LN**, NICNT, NIGTC; GW, NASB, NIV, NLT, REB], 'to save' [BAGD; CEV, NCV, TEV], 'to preserve' [BAGD]. This verb means to rescue from danger, with the implication that the danger in question is severe and acute [LN].

e. pres. act. indic. of θέλω (LN 25.102, 25.1) (BAGD 4.b. p. 355): 'to want' [BECNT, BNTC, LN (25.1), NICNT, NIGTC, PNTC; all versions except ESV, KJV, NASB], 'to like' [BAGD, LN (25.102)], 'to have' [KJV], 'to take pleasure in' [BAGD], 'to delight in' [WBC; NASB], 'to enjoy' [LN (25.102)], 'to desire' [LN (25.1), NTC; ESV]. This verb means to take pleasure in something in view of its being desirable [LN (25.102)]. It can also mean to desire to have or experience something [LN (25.1)].

f. imperf. act. indic. of ὀνειδίζω (LN 33.389) (BAGD 1. p. 570): 'to insult' [BECNT, LN; GW, NASB, TEV], 'to revile' [BAGD, BNTC, NTC; ESV], 'to rail at' [NIGTC], 'to speak abusively' [NET], 'to ridicule' [NLT], 'to upbraid' [PNTC], 'to chide' [WBC], 'to taunt' [NRSV, REB], 'to cast in the teeth' [KJV], 'to heap insults upon' [BAGD; NIV], 'to reproach' [BAGD]. This verb means to speak disparagingly of a person in a manner which is not justified [LN].

QUESTION—What meaning is intended by εἰ θέλει αὐτόν 'if he wants him'?

1. It refers to whether or not God wants him [BNTC, Lns, NICNT, NIGTC, NTC, PNTC; ESV, NCV, NIV, NLT, REB] or delights in him [BECNT, WBC; NASB], or likes him [My], or has any interest in him [NTC]. The opposite would be that God disowns him; he will not have him [Lns]. It reflects the meaning of the original Hebrew of Psalm 22:8, which has to do with whether or not God delights in him [WBC].

2. It refers to whether or not God wants to save him [BECNT, TH; CEV, GW, NET, NRSV, TEV].

DISCOURSE UNIT—27:45–56 [CEV, ESV, GW, NCV, NET, NIV, NLT, NRSV, TEV]. The topic is Jesus dies on the cross [GW], Jesus dies [NCV], the death of Jesus [CEV, ESV, NIV, NLT, NRSV, TEV], Jesus' death [NET].

27:45 Now from (the) sixth[a] hour darkness was over the whole land[b] until (the) ninth hour. **27:46** And about (the) ninth hour Jesus cried-out[c] with a-loud voice saying, "Eli, Eli, lema sabachthani?" that is, "My God, my God, why have-you-forsaken[d] me?"

LEXICON—a. The phrase δὲ ἕκτης ὥρας…ἕως ὥρας ἐνάτης 'from the sixth hour…until the ninth hour' [BECNT, BNTC, NICNT, NIGTC, NTC, PNTC, WBC; ESV, KJV, NASB, NIV] is also translated 'at noon…until three o'clock' [CEV, NLT], 'at noon…until three in the afternoon' [GW], 'from noon on…until three in the afternoon' [NRSV], 'at noon…and/which lasted for three hours' [NCV, TEV], 'from noon until three' [NET], 'from midday…which lasted until three in the afternoon' [REB].

b. γῆ (LN 1.79) (BAGD 4. p. 157): 'land' [BAGD, BNTC, LN, NICNT, NIGTC, NTC, PNTC, WBC; all versions except CEV, NCV, TEV], 'earth' [BECNT], 'region' [BAGD, LN], 'country' [BAGD; NCV, TEV], 'territory' [LN], not explicit [CEV]. This noun denotes a region or regions of the earth, normally in relation to some ethnic group or geographical center, but not necessarily constituting a unit of governmental administration [LN].

c. aorist act. indic. of ἀναβοάω (LN **33.81**) (BAGD p. 51): 'to cry out' [BAGD, BECNT, BNTC, **LN**, NTC, PNTC, WBC; ESV, GW, KJV, NASB, NCV, NIV, TEV], 'to cry aloud' [REB], 'to cry' [NRSV], 'to call out' [NIGTC; NLT], 'to shout out' [NICNT], 'to shout' [LN; CEV, NET], 'to scream' [LN]. This verb means to cry or shout with unusually loud volume [LN].

d. aorist act. indic. of ἐγκαταλείπω (LN 35.54) (BAGD 2. p. 215): 'to forsake' [BAGD, BECNT, LN, NIGTC, NTC, PNTC; ESV, KJV, NASB, NET, NIV, NRSV, REB], 'to abandon' [BAGD, NICNT, PNTC; GW, NLT, TEV], 'to desert' [BAGD, BNTC, LN; CEV], 'to reject' [NCV]. This verb means to desert or forsake a person, thus leaving that individual uncared for [LN].

QUESTION—What area of land does 'the whole land' cover?
It refers to the land of Judea [BNTC, EBC, NIBC, NICNT, NIGTC, PNTC, TH, WBC; NCV, TEV]. It refers to the whole earth [BECNT, Lns, My]. Whatever area it covered, it was very extensive [NTC]. The darkness symbolized judgment [EBC, ICC, Lns, NICNT, NIGTC, NTC, PNTC, WBC], or a great evil [NAC]. It symbolized judgment against sin, which at that time Jesus was bearing in himself [NTC].

QUESTION—What language was Jesus using in his cry from the cross?
It was Aramaic [EBC, ICC, NAC, NIGTC, WBC]. The word for God, *Eli*, is Hebrew, and *lema sabachthani*, is Aramaic [Lns, My, PNTC, TRT]. The

Hebrew word for God, *Eli*, may have come into use in Aramaic, in which case the whole saying would be in Aramaic [NICNT].

QUESTION—Why did Jesus have this sense of abandonment?

In bearing the sin of the world he was thereby separated from the Father, which prompted this cry of agony and abandonment [BECNT, EBC, Lns, NAC, NICNT, NTC, PNTC, TRT, WBC]. He had a sense of alienation from having the sins of the world upon him [NIBC]. Although this cry expresses the sense of a loss of contact with his Father, his use of 'my' with 'God' shows that it is not the expression of a loss of faith [NICNT].

27:47 **And some of-those standing there having-heard it, said, "This-man is-calling-for Elijah." 27:48 And at-once one of them ran, and taking a-sponge, and having-filled-it (with) sour-wine,[a] and having-put-it-on a-stick,[b] he-gave-it to-him -to-drink. 27:49 But the others said, "Wait,[c] let-us-see if Elijah will-come to-save[d] him."**

LEXICON—a. ὄξος (LN **6.201**) (BAGD p. 574): 'sour wine' [BAGD, BECNT, BNTC, **LN**, NTC, PNTC, WBC; ESV, NASB, NET, NLT, NRSV, REB], 'sharp wine' [NIGTC], 'cheap wine' [TEV], 'wine' [CEV], 'vinegar' [NICNT; GW, KJV, NCV], 'wine vinegar' [BAGD; NIV]. This noun denotes a cheap, sour wine that evidently was a favorite beverage of poorer people and relatively effective in quenching thirst. It is sometimes rendered as 'bitter wine' or 'sour juice' [LN].

b. κάλαμος (LN 3.55) (BAGD 2. p. 398): 'stick' [NICNT, NTC, WBC; CEV, GW, NCV, NET, NIV, NRSV, REB, TEV], 'reed' [BECNT, LN, NIGTC, PNTC; ESV, KJV, NASB], 'reed stick' [NLT], 'stalk' [BAGD], 'staff' [BAGD, BNTC]. This noun denotes the stalk of a reed plant [LN].

c. aorist act. impera. of ἀφίημι (LN 68.43) (BAGD 4. p. 126): 'wait' [BECNT, NIGTC, WBC; CEV, ESV, NLT, NRSV, TEV], 'to stop' [LN, NICNT], 'to hold off' [NTC], 'to let be' [PNTC; KJV], 'to leave alone' [GW, NET, NIV], 'to not bother' [NCV], 'to allow, permit, tolerate' [BAGD], 'to give up, to quit' [LN], not explicit [BNTC; NASB, REB]. This verb means to stop doing something, with the implication of complete cessation [LN].

d. future act. participle of σῴζω (LN 21.18) (BAGD 1.a. p. 798): 'to save' [BAGD, BECNT, BNTC, NICNT, NIGTC, PNTC, WBC; all versions], 'to rescue' [BAGD, LN, NTC], 'to deliver' [LN], 'to preserve' [BAGD], 'to make safe' [LN]. This verb means to rescue from danger and to restore to a former state of safety and well being [LN].

QUESTION—Why was sour wine used?

It was a common beverage among poorer people and was also fairly effective in quenching thirst [BAGD, LN, NICNT, NTC, TRT, WBC], even more effective than water [BAGD]. It was the sour wine that soldiers drank [EBC, ICC, NIBC, NICNT, NIGTC, PNTC, TH, TRT]. This was a cheap wine [TH].

QUESTION—Was this offer of sour wine a gesture of mercy or of mockery?

1. It was given in mockery [EBC, ICC, NTC], possibly in order to prolong Jesus' life, and with it, his agony [EBC, ICC, Lns].
2. It was probably given as an act of kindness [BECNT, BNTC, My, NAC, NICNT, PNTC]. It was given as a pain-killer [NAC]. Whoever gave the drink may have wanted to appear to be on the right side of things in case Elijah did come [PNTC]. It may have simply been done out of idle curiosity [NIGTC].

27:50 And[a] having-cried-out[b] again with-a- loud -voice Jesus gave-up[c] his-spirit. **27:51** And behold, the curtain[d] of-the temple was-torn-in-two,[e] from top to bottom, and the earth[f] was-shaken and the rocks were-split.[g]

LEXICON—a. δέ (LN 89.87): 'and' [LN (89.87), NTC; ESV, NASB, NIV], 'and then' [LN (89.87)], 'then' [GW, NET, NLT, NRSV], 'but' [BECNT, LN (89.124), NICNT, PNTC, WBC; NCV], not explicit [BNTC, NIGTC; CEV, KJV]. This conjunction indicates a sequence of closely related events [LN (89.87)], or it may mark contrast [LN (89.124)].

b. aorist act. participle of κράζω (LN 33.83) (BAGD 1. p. 447): 'to cry out' [BAGD, BECNT, BNTC, NICNT, NIGTC, NTC, PNTC, WBC; ESV, GW, NASB, NCV, NET, NIV], 'to cry' [KJV, NRSV], 'to cry aloud' [REB], 'to shout' [LN; CEV], 'to shout out' [NLT]. The phrase κράξας φωνῇ μεγάλῃ 'having cried out with a loud voice' is translated 'he gave a loud cry' [TEV]. This verb means to shout or cry out, with the possible implication of the unpleasant nature of the sound [LN].

c. aorist act. indic. of ἀφίημι (LN **23.109**) (BAGD 1.a.β. p. 125): 'to give up' [BAGD, BECNT, BNTC; NET, NIV], 'to yield up' [NTC, PNTC; ESV, KJV, NASB], 'to let go' [NIGTC], 'to release' [NLT]. The idiom ἀφίημι τὸ πνεῦμα 'to give up' means 'to give up one's life' [GW], 'to breathe one's last' [NICNT; NRSV, REB, TEV], 'to die' [**LN**; CEV, NCV], 'to stop breathing' [WBC]. The idiom ἀφίημι τὸ πνεῦμα 'to send away the spirit' is interpreted by some to mean a voluntarily laying down of one's life, but such an inference is not justified by normal Greek usage. It simply means 'to die' [LN].

d. καταπέτασμα (LN **6.160**) (BAGD p. 416): 'curtain' [BAGD, BNTC, LN, NICNT, NIGTC, NTC, PNTC, WBC; all versions except KJV, NASB], 'veil' [BECNT, LN; KJV, NASB], 'drape' [**LN**]. This noun denotes a hanging of cloth over an opening [LN].

e. aorist pass. indic. of σχίζω (LN 63.26) (BAGD 1.b. p. 797): 'to be torn in two' [BECNT, BNTC, LN, NICNT, NTC, PNTC, WBC; all versions except GW, KJV, NCV], 'to be torn' [BAGD], 'to be torn into two pieces' [NCV], 'to be split in two' [NIGTC; GW], 'to be rent in twain' [KJV], 'to be divided, to be split' [BAGD, LN]. This verb means to split or divide into two parts [LN].

f. γῆ (LN 1.39): 'earth' [BECNT, BNTC, LN, NICNT, NIGTC, NTC, PNTC; all versions], 'ground' [WBC], 'world' [LN]. This noun denotes the surface of the earth as the dwelling place of mankind, in contrast with the heavens above and the world below [LN].

g. aorist pass. indic. of σχίζω (LN **63.26**) (BAGD 1.b. p. 797): 'to be split' [BAGD, BECNT, BNTC, **LN**, NICNT, NIGTC, NTC, PNTC; ESV, NASB, NIV, NRSV], 'to be split open' [WBC; GW], 'to be split apart' [CEV, NET, NLT], 'to be broken apart' [NCV], 'to split' [REB], 'to split apart' [TEV], 'to be rent' [LN], 'to be divided, to be torn in two' [LN]. This verb means to split or divide into two parts [LN].

QUESTION—Does the idiom ἀφῆκεν τὸ πνεῦμα 'gave up his spirit' mean that he consciously and voluntarily released his spirit in death, or simply that he breathed his last, and died?

1. Jesus consciously chose to yield his life at that moment, indicating that he sovereignly governed even the moment of his death [EBC, ICC,NAC, NIBC]. It means that he breathed his last [NAC, NICNT], but the text also suggests that he voluntarily relinquished his life [Lns, NAC, NICNT, NIGTC, NTC, PNTC, TRT]. It is translated as indicating that he yielded up his spirit [PNTC; ESV, KJV, NASB, NLT].

2. It means that he died [BECNT, My, TH, WBC; CEV, NCV]. It is translated that he breathed his last [NICNT; NRSV, REB, TEV].

QUESTION—Which curtain was it that was torn?

It was the curtain that separated the Holy of Holies from the rest of the sanctuary [Lns, NIBC, NTC, PNTC, TH, TRT, WBC]. It could have been the curtain that separated the Holy of Holies from the sanctuary [BNTC, EBC, NICNT], or the curtain that separated the sanctuary from the court, but either one could symbolize the same things [BNTC, EBC]. Others think it was the curtain that separated the sanctuary from the outer court [ICC, NIGTC], which probably would have been visible from Golgotha [NIGTC]. It was probably the curtain that separated the court of the Jews from the court of the Gentiles [NAC].

QUESTION—What might the tearing of the veil in the temple symbolize?

It symbolized an unrestricted access to the presence of God that had become possible through Jesus' sacrifice of himself [NIBC, NTC, PNTC, TRT, WBC]. It probably symbolized God's judgment against the Jewish authorities [NIBC, WBC], and the eventual bringing to an end of the temple and its sacrifices [TRT, WBC]. It symbolized that God himself was removing the division between the two segments of humanity, Jew and Gentile [NAC]. It foreshadows the destruction of the temple in 70 AD [ICC]. Regardless of which curtain was being torn, the tearing would represent both the obsolescence of the old order, which the temple represented, as well as the opening of a new avenue of access to God in which Jesus himself is the new temple, the meeting place of God and man [EBC]. It symbolized the fact that the old order, represented by the temple, which up to that point had been the avenue for access to God, was giving way to the new order, in which Jesus' death as a ransom for many becomes the avenue for access to

God [NICNT]. It symbolized that the ministry of the Jewish high priest was at an end, and now Jesus was the new high priest [Lns, TRT]. It symbolized God breaking out of the temple in power, and foreshadowed the coming destruction of the temple [NIGTC].

27:52 The tombs[a] also were-opened, and many bodies of-the saints[b] who-had-fallen-asleep[c] were-raised,[d] **27:53** and having-come-out of the tombs after his resurrection they-entered into the holy city and appeared[e] to-many.

LEXICON—a. μνημεῖον (LN 7.75) (BAGD 2. p. 524): 'tomb' [BAGD, BECNT, BNTC, LN, NICNT, NIGTC, NTC, PNTC, WBC; ESV, GW, NASB, NET, NIV, NLT, NRSV], 'grave' [BAGD, LN; CEV, KJV, NCV, REB, TEV]. This noun denotes a construction for the burial of the dead [LN].

b. οἱ ἅγιοι (LN 11.27) (BAGD 2.d.γ. p. 10): 'saints' [BECNT, BNTC, NTC, PNTC, WBC; ESV, KJV, NASB, NET, NRSV], 'God's saints' [REB], 'God's people' [LN, NICNT; CEV, NCV, TEV], 'holy ones' [BAGD, NIGTC], 'holy people' [GW, NIV], 'godly men and women' [NLT]. The adjective ἅγιος 'holy' occurring in the plural as a substantive denotes the people who belong to God, and as such they constitute a religious entity [LN]. In using this term it is important to avoid an expression that means 'sanctified' since the focus is not upon a particular state of holiness, but upon a special relationship with God. Those who are spoken of as 'the saints' may also have to be admonished to become sanctified [LN].

c. perf. mid. or pass. (deponent = act.) participle of κοιμάομαι (LN 23.104) (BAGD 2.b. p. 437): 'to fall asleep' [BAGD, BECNT, BNTC, NIGTC, NTC; ESV, NASB, NRSV], 'to be asleep' [PNTC], 'to sleep' [KJV], 'to die' [LN, NICNT, WBC; GW, NCV, NET, NIV, TEV], 'to be dead' [LN], not explicit [CEV]. The phrase τῶν κεκοιμημένων...ἠγέρθησαν 'having fallen asleep were raised' is translated 'were raised from sleep' [REB]. This verb means to sleep, as a euphemistic expression for the state of being dead [LN].

d. aorist pass. indic. of ἐγείρω (LN 23.94) (BAGD 2.c. p. 215): 'to be raised' [BAGD, BECNT, BNTC, NICNT, NIGTC, NTC, PNTC, WBC; ESV, NASB, NET, NRSV, REB], 'to be raised from the dead' [NCV, NLT], 'to rise' [BAGD], 'to arise' [KJV], 'to be raised to life' [LN; CEV, NIV, TEV], 'to come back to life' [GW], 'to be made to live again' [LN]. This verb means to cause someone to live again after having once died [LN].

e. aorist pass. indic. of ἐμφανίζω (LN **24.19**) (BAGD 1.a. p. 257 'to appear (to)' [BECNT, BNTC, NIGTC, NTC, PNTC; all versions except CEV, REB, TEV], 'to be seen (by)' [**LN**, NICNT, WBC; CEV], 'to be made visible, to be made to appear' [BAGD, LN], 'to be caused to be seen' [LN]. The phrase ἐνεφανίσθησαν πολλοῖς 'appeared to many' is translated 'many/many-people saw them' [REB, TEV]. This verb means to cause to become visible [LN].

QUESTION—What were these tombs?

They were structures built for the burial of the dead [LN]. They had been carved out of the rock, and were above the surface of the ground [Lns, PNTC].

QUESTION—Were the 'saints' who were raised unusually holy people (such as prophets) or were they ordinary people who served God?

They were probably exceptional people such as patriarchs, prophets, or martyrs [WBC]. They were martyrs and spiritual heroes from the Old Testament era or the intertestamental era [EBC]. They were certain Old Testament believers [NAC], the holy ones of old [ICC, NIBC], certain holy people honored by Jewish tradition [BNTC].

QUESTION—To which event does μετὰ τὴν ἔγερσιν αὐτοῦ 'after his resurrection refer?

1. After Jesus' resurrection, these saints came out of the tombs and went into Jerusalem [BECNT, EBC, NAC, NICNT, NIGTC, PNTC; ESV, GW, KJV, NASB, NCV, NET, NLT, NRSV, REB].

2. At the time of Jesus' death and the splitting of the rocks by the earthquake these saints came out of the tombs, but it was only after Jesus' resurrection that they went into the city [Lns, My, NIBC, NTC, TH, WBC; CEV, NIV, TEV].

27:54 Now the centurion[a] and those with him keeping-watch-over[b] Jesus, having-seen the earthquake and the-things having-happened, they-were-greatly -afraid,[c] saying "Truly[d] this (man) was (the) Son of God[e]!"

LEXICON—a. ἑκατόνταρχος (LN 55.16) (BAGD p. 237): 'centurion' [BECNT, BNTC, LN, NICNT, NIGTC, NTC, PNTC, WBC; ESV, KJV, NASB, NET, NIV, NRSV, REB], 'officer' [CEV], 'army officer' [GW, NCV, TEV], 'Roman officer' [NLT], 'captain' [LN]. This noun denotes a Roman officer in command of about one hundred men [LN].

b. pres. act. participle of τηρέω (LN 37.122) (BAGD 1. p. 814): 'to keep watch over' [BAGD, BNTC, NICNT, NIGTC; ESV, NRSV, REB], 'to watch' [LN, PNTC, WBC; GW, KJV, TEV], 'to guard' [BAGD, BECNT, LN, NTC; CEV, NCV, NET, NIV], 'to keep guard' [NASB], not explicit [NLT]. This verb means to continue to hold in custody [LN].

c. aorist pass. indic. of φοβέομαι (LN 25.252) (BAGD 1.a. p. 862): 'to be afraid' [BAGD, LN, PNTC, WBC], 'to be/become frightened' [BAGD, BECNT, BNTC, NIGTC, NTC; CEV, NASB, NCV], 'to be terrified' [NET], 'to fear' [LN; KJV]. The phrase ἐφοβήθησαν σφόδρα 'they were greatly afraid' is translated 'they were terrified' [NICNT; GW, NET, NIV, NLT, NRSV, TEV], 'they were filled with awe' [ESV, REB]. This verb means to be in a state of fearing something [LN].

   d. ἀληθῶς (LN 70.3) (BAGD 1. p. 37): 'truly' [BAGD, BECNT, BNTC,
   LN, NIGTC, WBC; ESV, KJV, NASB, NET, NLT, NRSV], 'really'
   [BAGD, LN, NICNT; CEV, NCV, TEV], 'surely' [NTC; NIV],
   'certainly' [GW], 'in truth, actually' [BAGD]. The phrase 'truly this man
   was God's Son' is translated 'this must have been a son of God' [REB].
   This adverb describes being real and not imaginary [LN].
   e. υἱὸς τοῦ θεοῦ (LN 12.15) (BAGD 2.b. p. 834): 'the Son of God'
   [BECNT, NIGTC, PNTC, WBC; ESV, GW, KJV, NASB, NCV, NIV,
   NLT, TEV], 'God's Son' [BNTC, NICNT, NTC; CEV, NET, NRSV], 'a
   son of God' [REB]. This noun denotes one who has the essential
   characteristics and nature of God [LN].
QUESTION—Aside from the earthquake, what might 'the things having
   happened' be?
   In addition to the earthquake, they were frightened by the darkness [NTC,
   WBC], the splitting of the tombs [NTC, WBC], Jesus' loud cry [EBC,
   NICNT], and the manner in which he died [NICNT].
QUESTION—What did the Roman soldiers mean by the affirmation that Jesus
   really was the Son of God?
   Although they had little understanding of what it might mean that he was the
   Son of God, their fear made them receptive to Jesus' claim to that effect,
   which the soldiers had also heard about from the Jewish leaders who had
   rejected it [WBC]. Being aware that the Jewish leaders had mocked Jesus for
   claiming to be God's son, they concluded that the Jewish leaders were
   wrong, and Jesus was in fact God's son [Lns, NICNT, NIGTC]. After being
   terrified by the darkness and earthquake they may have concluded that God
   himself was angry and that this was no ordinary person. They may have even
   understood 'Son of God' in a messianic sense [EBC]. Because of the
   darkness and the earthquake they concluded that Jesus was a supernatural
   being [BECNT]. They might have been affirming that Jesus was a good and
   innocent man, and he was right to call God his Father [NAC]. They
   concluded that he was no mere man [NIBC, PNTC], but had a special
   relationship to God [PNTC]. They may have concluded that he was the son
   of a god in a pagan sense [My].

27:55 And many women were there, watching[a] from a-distance, who had-
followed Jesus from Galilee. (while) serving[b] him. **27:56** Among them were
Mary Magdalene, and Mary the mother of James and Joseph, and the
mother of-the sons of-Zebedee.
LEXICON—a. pres. act. participle of θεωρέω (LN 24.14) (BAGD 1. p. 360):
   'to watch' [NICNT, NTC, PNTC, WBC; GW, NCV, NET, NIV, NLT,
   REB], 'to observe' [BAGD, BECNT, BNTC, LN], 'to look on' [NIGTC;
   CEV, ESV, NASB, NRSV, TEV], 'to behold' [KJV], 'to look at' [BAGD,
   LN], 'to be a spectator of' [BAGD, LN]. This verb means to observe
   something with continuity and attention, often with the implication that
   what is observed is something unusual [LN].

b. pres. act. participle of διακονέω (LN 35.37) (BAGD 2. p. 184): 'to serve'
[BAGD, LN (46.13), NIGTC, WBC], 'to minister to' [BNTC; ESV, KJV,
NASB], 'to minister to someone's need' [NTC], 'to wait upon' [BAGD,
LN (46.13)], 'to care for' [BECNT, NLT], 'to care for someone's needs'
[NIV], 'to take care of' [LN (35.37)], 'to provide for' [PNTC; NRSV], 'to
look after' [NICNT; REB], 'to help' [NCV, TEV], 'to be of help' [CEV],
'to support' [GW], 'to give support' [NET]. This verb means to take care
of, by rendering humble service to [LN (35.37)], or to serve food and
drink to those who are eating [LN (46.13)].

QUESTION—Who was the mother of Zebedee's sons, and who were James and
Joseph?

The mother of Zebedee's sons may have been Salome [EBC, Lns, NIBC,
NICNT, NIGTC, NTC], who might possibly have been Mary's sister, which
would then make the disciples James and John Jesus' cousins [EBC, NTC].
James and Joseph may have been cousins of Jesus [Lns, NAC, WBC] or they
may have been Jesus' half brothers [BECNT, EBC, TRT]. Approximately
half of the women whose names were recorded in Palestine at this time were
either named Mary or Salome [NICNT].

DISCOURSE UNIT— 27:57-66 [BECNT; CEV, NASB]. The topic is burial of
Jesus [BECNT], Jesus is buried [CEV, NASB].

DISCOURSE UNIT—27:57–61 [ESV, GW, NCV, NET, NIV, NLT, NRSV,
TEV]. The topic is Jesus is buried [ESV, GW, NCV], the burial of Jesus [NIV,
NLT, NRSV, TEV], Jesus' burial [NET].

27:57 Evening having-come, there-came a- rich -man from Arimathea,
Joseph by-name, who was himself a-disciple of Jesus also. **27:58** Having-
gone to-Pilate, this (man) asked-for the body of Jesus. Then Pilate ordered
(it) to-be-given[a] (to him). **27:59** And having-taken the body Joseph
wrapped[b] it in a clean linen-cloth[c] **27:60** and placed it in his-own new
tomb, which he-had-hewn[d] in the rock; and having-rolled a- great -stone to-
the entrance of-the tomb he-went-away. **27:61** And Mary Magdalene and
the other Mary were there, sitting opposite[e] the tomb.

LEXICON—a. aorist pass. infin. of ἀποδίδωμι (BAGD 1. p. 90): 'to be given'
[BAGD, BNTC, NICNT, NIGTC, NTC, PNTC; CEV, ESV, GW, NASB,
NET, NIV, NRSV, TEV], 'to be given over' [WBC], 'to be granted'
[BAGD], 'to be turned over' [BECNT], 'to be delivered' [KJV]. This
passive verb is also translated as active: 'to give' [NCV], 'to release (it)'
[NLT], 'to have (it)' [REB].

b. aorist act. indic. of ἐντυλίσσω (LN 79.118) (BAGD 1. p. 270): 'to wrap'
[BAGD, LN; all translations], 'to wrap up' [BAGD]. This verb means to
enclose an object by winding something about or around it [LN].

c. σινδών (LN 6.155) (BAGD 1. p. 751): 'linen cloth' [BAGD, BECNT,
BNTC, LN, NIGTC, NTC, WBC; all versions except ESV, REB, TEV],

'linen shroud' [ESV], 'linen sheet' [REB, TEV], 'linen' [PNTC], 'cloth' [NICNT]. This noun denotes linen cloth of good quality [LN].

d. aorist act. indic. of λατομέω (LN **19.25**) (BAGD 1. p. 467): 'to hew' [BNTC, PNTC; NASB, NRSV], 'to hew out (rock)' [BAGD, LN, NTC; KJV], 'to cut' [BECNT, NICNT, WBC; ESV, NET, NIV, REB], 'to cut out' [NCV], 'to carve' [NIGTC], 'to dig out' [TEV], 'to cut rock' [**LN**]. This active verb is also translated as passive: 'to be cut' [CEV, GW], 'to be carved' [NLT]. This verb means to shape rock by cutting, either internally or externally [LN].

e. ἀπέναντι (LN 83.42) (BAGD 1.a. p. 84): 'opposite' [BAGD, BECNT, LN, BNTC, NICNT, PNTC, WBC; ESV, NASB, NET, NIV, NRSV, REB], 'in front of' [LN, NIGTC], 'across from' [LN, NTC; CEV, NLT], 'facing' [GW, TEV], 'over against' [KJV], 'near' [NCV]. This preposition describes a position over against an object or other position [LN].

QUESTION—Where was Arimathea?

It was twenty-two miles northwest of Jerusalem [BNTC, EBC, NAC, NIBC, NICNT, NTC], and in the Old Testament it was known as Ramathaim, the home of Samuel [EBC, Lns, My, NAC], also known as Rama [Lns, My]. It may have been Ramathaim [NTC, WBC].

QUESTION—Who is 'the other Mary'?

She is the one identified in v.56 as the mother of James and Joseph [BECNT, BNTC, ICC, Lns, My, NAC, NTC, PNTC, TH, TRT, WBC]. She was also Jesus' mother [TRT].

DISCOURSE UNIT—27:62–66 [ESV, GW, NCV, NET, NIV, NLT, NRSV, TEV]. The topic is the chief priests and Pharisees secure Jesus' tomb [GW], the tomb of Jesus is guarded [NCV], the guard at the tomb [ESV, NET, NIV, NLT, NRSV, TEV].

`27:62` **And on-the next-day, which is after the (day of) Preparation,[a] the chief priests and the Pharisees were-gathered-together before Pilate** `27:63` **saying, "Sir, we-remember what that deceiver[b] said while still-living, 'After three days I-will-be-raised.[c]'**

LEXICON—a. παρασκευή (LN **67.201**) (BAGD p. 622): '(day of) preparation' [BAGD, BECNT, BNTC, **LN**, NICNT, NIGTC, NTC, PNTC, WBC; ESV, KJV, NASB, NCV, NET, NIV, NRSV, REB], 'Friday' [LN]. The phrase ἥτις ἐστὶν μετὰ τὴν παρασκευήν 'which is after the day of Preparation' is translated 'which was a Sabbath' [**LN**; CEV, TEV], 'on the Sabbath' [NLT], 'which was the day of worship' [GW].

b. πλάνος (LN 31.9) (BAGD 2. p. 666): 'deceiver' [BAGD, BNTC, NICNT, PNTC, WBC; GW, KJV, NASB, NET, NIV, NLT], 'imposter' [BAGD, BECNT, NICNT, NTC; ESV, NRSV, REB], 'liar' [CEV, NCV, TEV], that which deceives' [LN]. This substantive refers to someone who deceives [LN].

c. pres. pass. indic. of ἐγείρω (LN 23.94) (BAGD 2.c. p. 215): 'to be raised'
[BAGD, NICNT, NIGTC, PNTC], 'to be raised again' [BECNT; REB],
'to be raised to life' [TEV], 'to rise' [BAGD, BNTC, WBC; ESV], 'to rise
again' [KJV, NASB, NET, NIV, NRSV], 'to rise from the dead' [NCV,
NLT], 'to arise' [NTC], 'to come back from death' [CEV], 'to be brought
back to life' [GW], 'to be raised to life, to be made to live again' [LN].
This verb means to cause someone to live again after having once died
[LN].

27:64 **Therefore command (that) the tomb be-made-secure[a] until the third
day; lest his disciples come and steal him and tell the people, 'He-has-been
raised from the dead,' and the last deception[b] will-be worse than the first.'"**
27:65 **Pilate said to-them, "You-have[c] a-guard (of soldiers); go make-(it)-as
secure as you-know-how." 27:66 And they, having-gone, made- the tomb -
secure, having-sealed the stone with the guard.[d]**

LEXICON—a. aorist pass. infin. of ἀσφαλίζω (LN **21.11**) (BAGD 1. p. 119):
'to be made secure' [LN, NICNT, NTC, PNTC, WBC; ESV, KJV, NASB,
NIV, NRSV, REB], 'to be secured' [BECNT, NIGTC], 'to be guarded'
[BAGD, **LN**], 'to be guarded closely' [NCV], 'to be securely guarded'
[BNTC], 'to be carefully guarded' [CEV, TEV]. This passive verb is
translated as active: 'to make secure' [GW], 'to secure' [NET], 'to seal'
[NLT]. This verb means to cause something to be secure in the sense of
something which could not be tampered with or opened [LN].

b. πλάνη (LN 31.10) (BAGD p. 665): 'deception' [BAGD, BECNT, BNTC,
NIGTC, NTC, WBC; GW, NASB, NET, NIV, NRSV, REB], 'fraud'
[NICNT; ESV], 'error' [KJV], 'lie' [CEV, NCV, TEV], 'deceit' [BAGD],
'misleading belief, deceptive belief, error, mistaken view' [LN], not
explicit [NLT]. This noun denotes the content of that which misleads or
deceives [LN].

c. pres. act. indic. of ἔχω (LN 57.1) (BAGD I.7.b. p. 333): 'to have'
[BAGD, LN, NICNT; ESV, GW, KJV, NASB, NRSV, REB], 'to take'
[BNTC, NTC, PNTC, WBC; NET, NIV, NLT, TEV]. The phrase 'you
have a guard' is translated 'you can have a guard' [BECNT, NIGTC],
'take some of your soldiers and guard the tomb' [CEV, NCV]. This verb
means to have or possess objects or property [LN].

d. κουστωδία (LN 55.13) (BAGD p. 447). 'a guard' [BAGD, LN]. The
clause σφραγίσαντες τὸν λίθον μετὰ τῆς κουστωδίας 'having sealed
the stone with the guard' is translated 'by sealing the stone and setting a
guard' [ESV, REB], 'by putting a seal on the stone and posting/leaving
the guard' [NIV, TEV], 'by sealing the stone in the entrance and putting
solders there to guard it' [NCV], 'they placed a seal on the stone and
posted the soldiers on guard duty' [GW], 'and along with the guard they
set a seal on the stone' [NASB], 'sealing the stone, and setting a watch'
[KJV],. The whole verse is translated 'So they sealed the tomb and posted

guards to protect it' [NLT], 'So they sealed it tight and placed soldiers there to guard it' [CEV], 'So they went with the soldiers-of-the-guard/guard and made the tomb secure by sealing the stone' [NET, NRSV]. This noun denotes a group of soldiers serving as a guard [LN]. It denotes a guard composed of soldiers [BAGD].

QUESTION—What was the first deception?

They would have been referring to his claim to be Messiah [BNTC, EBC, My, NIBC, NICNT, NTC, PNTC, TH, TRT], and God's son [BNTC, NIBC], as well as his teaching that deviated from that of the Jewish establishment [NICNT]. It would have been his teaching about himself [ICC], the claims of his earlier ministry [NIGTC]. The first deception in their minds was Jesus' previous works and teaching [NAC].

QUESTION—Does Pilate mean that they have their own guards, or that they can have a guard of Roman soldiers?

1. He is telling them that he will provide a guard of Roman soldiers [BECNT, BNTC, ICC, Lns, My, NAC, NIBC, NIGTC, NTC, PNTC, TH, TRT, WBC]. The temple guard would have no authority outside the temple area, so the guard would have to be provided by the Roman governor [NTC].

2. He is reminding them that they have their own guards and should use them [EBC, NICNT].

QUESTION—How was the stone sealed?

The seal would have been an official wax seal and cord [EBC, NAC, NIBC, NTC]. The seal would have been clay [BECNT, My] or wax [BECNT, NICNT]. It was marked with official seals that would indicate if the stone had been moved [My, TRT, WBC].

DISCOURSE UNIT—28:1–20 [NAC, NIGTC, PNTC; NET, REB]. The topic is the resurrection [NAC, PNTC; NET, REB], resurrection and commissioning [NIGTC].

DISCOURSE UNIT—28:1–15 [BECNT, EBC; NASB]. The topic is the resurrection of Jesus [BECNT], the resurrection [EBC], Jesus is risen! [NASB].

DISCOURSE UNIT—28:1–10 [NICNT, PNTC; CEV, ESV, GW, NCV, NIV, NLT, NRSV, TEV]. The topic is the empty tomb and the risen Jesus [NICNT], the women at the tomb [PNTC], Jesus comes back to life [GW], Jesus rises from the dead [NCV], the resurrection [ESV, NIV, NLT, TEV], the resurrection of Jesus [NRSV], Jesus is alive [CEV].

28:1 And after (the) Sabbath, at-the dawning towards the-first (day of the) week, Mary Magdalene and the other Mary went to-look-at the tomb. **28:2** And behold[a] there-was a-great earthquake, for an-angel of the Lord had-come-down from heaven, and after-approaching he-rolled-back the stone and sat upon it. **28:3** And his appearance[b] was like lightning, and his clothing white as snow. **28:4** And the-ones on guard were-shaken[c] for fear of-him and they became like dead-men.[d]

LEXICON—a. ἰδού (LN 91.13): 'behold' [BNTC; ESV, KJV, NASB], 'look' [LN, PNTC, WBC], 'suddenly' [BECNT, NICNT, NTC; CEV, GW, NET, NLT, NRSV, REB, TEV], 'listen, pay attention, come now, then' [LN], not explicit [NIGTC; NCV, NIV]. This particle is a prompter of attention, which serves also to emphasize the following statement [LN].

b. εἰδέα (LN **58.14**) (BAGD p. 220): 'appearance' [BAGD, BECNT, BNTC, **LN**, NICNT, NIGTC, NTC, PNTC, WBC; ESV, NASB, NET, NIV, NRSV, TEV], 'face' [BAGD; NLT, REB], 'countenance' [KJV], 'form' [LN]. This noun is translated as a verb or verb phrase: '(he) looked/was (bright as lightning)' [CEV, GW], 'he was shining (as bright as lightning' [NCV]. This noun denotes appearance as the form of that which is seen [LN].

c. aorist pass. indic. of σείω (LN 25.233) (BAGD 2. p. 746): 'to be shaken' [NICNT, NIGTC, WBC; NET], 'to be stirred up, to be caused great anxiety' [LN]. This passive verb is translated as active: 'to shake' [BECNT, BNTC, NTC; CEV, GW, KJV, NASB, NCV, NIV, NLT, NRSV, REB], 'to tremble' [PNTC; ESV, TEV]. This verb is a figurative extension of meaning of 'to shake' (16.7) and it means to cause extreme anxiety and apprehension [LN].

d. νεκρός (LN 23.121) (BAGD 1.a.α. p. 534): 'dead (men)' [BECNT, BNTC, NTC, PNTC, WBC; ESV, KJV, NASB, NCV, NET, NIV, NRSV, TEV], 'dead (people)' [NIGTC], 'dead' [BAGD, LN; CEV, REB], 'corpse' [NICNT], 'lifeless' [LN]. The phrase ἀπὸ δὲ τοῦ φόβου …ἐγενήθησαν ὡς νεκροί 'for fear…became like dead men' is translated 'were…deathly afraid' [GW], 'they fell into a dead faint' [NLT]. This adjective describes being dead [LN].

QUESTION—What is the force of ἰδού 'behold' in this verse?

It indicates something happening suddenly [BECNT, NICNT, NTC, TH; CEV, GW, NET, NLT, NRSV, REB, TEV]. It calls attention to something unusual [Lns, WBC]. It introduces vividness to the account and draws attention to what is happening at the tomb [PNTC]. It gives dramatic force [NICNT].

QUESTION—Does v.2 describe what the women saw, or only what they found had happened?

They did not witness the earthquake or the angel's descent, both of which occurred before their arrival [EBC, Lns, NAC, NTC, NIBC, PNTC]. They also did not see the opening of the tomb [Lns, NAC, NIBC, NTC, PNTC].

QUESTION—What is the relation between the angel's descent, the earthquake, and the moving of the stone?

The earthquake is associated with the descent of the angel [NAC, NICNT, NTC, TH, TRT, WBC]. The descent of the angel caused the earthquake, after which the angel rolled the stone away [NTC, TH, TRT]. The angel himself moved the stone away [BNTC, Lns, NICNT, PNTC]. The earthquake occurred before the angel descended or rolled the stone away [NIBC]. The angel's action of moving the stone may have caused the earthquake [BECNT]. It was the earthquake that moved the stone [ICC, NAC, NIGTC]. The angel shook the earth to move the stone [NIGTC]. The earthquake shows the significance of what was happening [BNTC], that it was cosmic [NAC], and apocalyptic [WBC], a direct intervention of God [NICNT].

QUESTION—Was the earthquake a means of releasing Jesus from the grave?

It had nothing to do with freeing Jesus from the grave [BECNT, BNTC, EBC, Lns, NAC, NTC, WBC]. The rolling away of the stone was intended to allow witnesses to see that Jesus had risen, not to allow Jesus to escape [BECNT, BNTC, EBC, ICC, Lns, NICNT, NIGTC, NTC, PNTC, WBC].

QUESTION—In what sense were the guards like dead men?

They were paralyzed by terror [BNTC, NAC, PNTC, TH]. They may have fainted from the shock [BECNT, Lns, NTC, WBC]. There is irony in the fact that those who were assigned to guard a dead man became like dead men, while the one they were guarding was now alive [BECNT, ICC, NICNT, NIGTC, TH, TRT, WBC].

28:5 But the angel having-spoken[a] said to-the women, "You, do- not -be-afraid; I-know that you-are-looking-for Jesus the-one having-been-crucified. **28:6** He-is- not -here; for he-was-raised, just-as he-said. Come, see the place where he-was-lying.

TEXT—Manuscripts reading ὅπου ἔκειτο 'where he was lying' are given an A rating by GNT to indicate it was regarded to be certain. A variant reading is ὅπου ἔκειτο ὁ κύριος 'where the Lord lay' and it is followed by KJV only.

LEXICON—a. aorist passive (deponent = act.) participle of ἀποκρίνομαι (LN 33.28, 33.184): 'to speak, to declare, to say' [LN 33.28], 'to answer' [BECNT, BNTC, LN (33.184), PNTC, WBC; KJV], 'to reply'[LN (33.184)], not translated [all versions except [KJV]. This verb means to introduce or continue a somewhat formal discourse [LN (33:28)] or 'to respond to a question asking for information' [LN (33.184)].

QUESTION—In what sense did the angel 'answer' the women?

They had not said anything that the angel might answer, but he did respond to their situation [NICNT, NIGTC, PNTC]. He was responding to their astonishment and fear [Lns, My]. He was responding to the fact that the guards were terrified, as the women had seen, to tell them not to be afraid like the guards [NIGTC]. It simply means that he spoke [EBC].

QUESTION—What is the function of the emphatic ὑμεῖς 'you' in the angel's command to the women not to be afraid?

It distinguishes them from the guards, and emphasizes that contrast between them [BNTC, ICC, Lns, My, NICNT, NIGTC, NTC, PNTC, WBC]. He was telling them not to be afraid as the guards were [BNTC, My, NIGTC, WBC]. While it was fitting that the guards should be afraid, the angel had come to help these women, not to terrify them [PNTC]. It adds emphasis [Lns, TH].

QUESTION—Is there any significance in the use of the present tense of the imperative 'do not be afraid'?

The present tense indicates that the action is presently occurring, and should stop [Lns, NTC, TH].

QUESTION—Who is the agent of the passive verb ἠγέρθη 'he was raised'?

He was raised by God the Father [BECNT, ICC, NTC, PNTC, TH, WBC]. It is not passive in meaning, but is active intransitive in meaning: he arose [Lns].

QUESTION—What is the point of the angel's comment 'just as he said'?

It reminds them of Jesus' promises and predictions of his resurrection [EBC, ICC, Lns, NICNT, NIGTC, NTC, PNTC, TRT, WBC], and emphasizes that what has happened was not unexpected, but was something Jesus knew about all along [PNTC]. It implies a gentle reproach as well [BNTC].

28:7 **And-then go-quickly (and) tell his disciples, 'He-was-raised from the dead, and behold, he-is-going-ahead-of[a] you to Galilee; there you-will-see him.' Behold[b] I-(have)-told[c] you."**

LEXICON—a. pres. act. indic. of προάγω (LN 15.142) (BAGD 2. b. p. 702): 'to go ahead' [NICNT, NIGTC, NTC, PNTC, GW, NASB, NCV, NET, NIV, NLT, NRSV, REB, TEV], 'to go before (someone)' [BAGD, BECNT, WBC; ESV, KJV], 'to precede' [BNTC], 'to go prior to, to go away beforehand' [LN]. The phrase προάγει...εἰς τὴν Γαλιλαίαν, 'he is going ahead...to Galilee' is translated 'he is on his way to Galilee' [CEV]. This verb means to go prior to someone else's going [LN].

b. ἰδού (LN 91.13): 'behold' [BNTC; NASB], 'look' [LN, PNTC, WBC], 'see' [BECNT; ESV], 'take note' [GW], 'now' [NTC; NCV, NIV], 'lo' [KJV], 'listen' [LN; NET], 'remember' [NLT, TEV], 'pay attention' [LN], not explicit [NICNT, NIGTC; CEV, NRSV, REB]. This particle is a prompter of attention, which serves also to emphasize the following statement [LN].

c. aorist act. indic. of λέγω (εἶπον) (LN 33.69) (BAGD 2.c. p. 226): 'to tell' [BAGD, BECNT, BNTC, NTC, PNTC, WBC; all versions except NRSV], 'to say' [BAGD, LN, NIGTC], 'to speak, to say' [BAGD, LN]. The phrase ἰδοὺ εἶπον ὑμῖν 'Behold, I have told you' is translated 'That/this is my message to/for you' [NICNT; NRSV]. This verb means to speak or talk, with apparent focus upon the content of what is said [LN].

QUESTION—To which disciples were they to take this news?

Although there were other disciples, here he is referring to the eleven [BNTC, Lns, NAC, NICNT, NIGTC, NTC, PNTC].

QUESTION—What is significant about the fact that the first people to know of Jesus' resurrection were women?

It adds credibility to the gospel accounts because if the story had been fabricated the witnesses would almost certainly have been men since in that time the testimony of women was not valued or even considered valid [BECNT, ICC, NAC, NICNT, PNTC, WBC]. This forms a contrast with the male disciples, who were far too fearful to have planned to steal the body [NIGTC].

QUESTION—What is the significance of the statement, 'Behold, I have told you'?

It adds solemnity to what the angel has told them [ICC, My]. It adds weight to what Jesus had said earlier, and which the angel repeated to the women; that is, 'Jesus said it, and now I am saying it' [NIGTC]. It indicates an end to what the angel will say and do, and now the responsibility for action is given to the women [NICNT, NTC, PNTC]. It emphasizes the authority of the angelic revelation [Lns, NICNT, PNTC], so as to remove any trace of doubt [Lns]. It indicates that he has fulfilled his mission [BNTC]. It confirms the angel's message [TH].

QUESTION—Where does the angel's message to the disciples end?

1. It ends with 'there you will see him', and the following statement 'Behold I have told you' is addressed to the women [BECNT, BNTC, Lns, NICNT, NIGTC, NTC, PNTC, TH, TRT, WBC; GW, NCV, NET, NIV, NRSV, REB, TEV]. The first two occurrences of the plural pronoun 'you' v.7 are directed toward the disciples, and the last one is directed toward the women [TH]. The statement that he is going ahead of them to Galilee is probably applied to the women as well as to the disciples [WBC].

2. It ends with 'He was raised from the dead'; the following statement 'He is going ahead of you to Galilee' resumes his speech to the women, though the plural pronoun 'you' includes the disciples as well the women [NIGTC].

28:8 And having-departed quickly from the tomb with fear[a] and great joy,[b] they-ran to-tell his disciples. **28:9** And behold, Jesus met them and said, "Greetings[c]!" And they came (to him), took-hold[d] of his feet, and worshiped[e] him. **28:10** Then Jesus said to-them, "Do- not -be-afraid; go (and) tell my brothers that they-(should)-go to Galilee; and-there they-will-see me."

TEXT—Manuscripts reading καὶ ἰδού 'and behold' are given a B rating by GNT to indicate it was regarded to be almost certain. A variant reading is 'and as they went to tell the disciples, behold' and it is followed by KJV.

LEXICON—a. φόβος (LN **25.251**) (BAGD 2.a.α. p. 863): 'fear' [BAGD, BECNT, BNTC, **LN**, NICNT, NIGTC, NTC, PNTC, WBC; ESV, GW,

KJV, NASB, NET, NRSV], 'awe' [REB], 'alarm, fright' [BAGD]. The phrase μετὰ φόβου 'with fear' is translated 'frightened' [CEV, NLT], 'afraid' [NCV, NIV, TEV]. This noun denotes a state of severe distress, aroused by intense concern for impending pain, danger, evil, etc., or possibly by the illusion of such circumstances [LN].

b. χαρά (LN **25.123**) (BAGD 1. p. 875): 'joy' [BAGD, BECNT, BNTC, LN, NICNT, NIGTC, NTC, PNTC, WBC; ESV, GW, KJV, NASB, NET, NRSV, REB, TEV], 'gladness, great happiness' [LN]. The phrase μετὰ χαρᾶς μεγάλης 'with great joy' is translated 'very joyful' [LN (25.123)], 'very happy' [CEV, NCV], 'filled with joy' [NIV], 'filled with great joy' [NLT]. This noun denotes a state of joy and gladness [LN].

c. χαίρετε (LN 33.22) (BAGD 2.a. p. 874): 'greetings' [LN, NIGTC, PNTC, WBC; ESV, NCV, NET, NIV, NRSV], 'hello' [BAGD, BECNT, NICNT], 'hail' [BNTC, LN], 'all hail' [KJV], 'good morning' [NTC], 'peace be with you' [TEV]. This greeting is translated as a verb phrase: 'Jesus...greeted them' [CEV, GW, NASB, NLT], 'Jesus was...greeting them' [REB]. This word, which is actually the imperative form of the verb χαίρω, functions as a formalized expression of greeting, implying a wish for happiness on the part of the person greeted [LN].

d. aorist act. indic. of κρατέω (LN 18.6) (BAGD 1.b. p. 448): 'to take hold of' [BAGD, BECNT, BNTC, NICNT, NIGTC, NTC, PNTC; ESV, GW, NASB, NCV, NRSV, TEV], 'to hold on to' [LN; CEV, NET], 'to grasp' [BAGD, WBC; NLT], 'to clasp' [NIV, REB], 'to hold by' [KJV], 'to seize' [BAGD, LN]. This verb means to hold on to an object [LN].

e. aorist act. indic. of προσκυνέω (LN 53.56) (BAGD 5. p. 717): 'to worship' [BAGD, BECNT, LN, NIGTC, NTC, PNTC, WBC; all versions except GW, REB], 'to bow before' [NICNT], 'to kneel before' [REB], 'to bow down and/to worship' [LN; GW], 'to prostrate oneself in worship' [LN], 'to prostrate oneself before, to do reverence to' [BAGD]. This verb means to express by attitude and possibly by position one's allegiance to and regard for deity [LN].

QUESTION—Does the adjective μέγας 'great' modify only 'joy' or both 'fear' and 'joy'?

1. It modifies only 'joy' [BECNT, BNTC, ICC, Lns, NIBC, NICNT, NIGTC, NTC, PNTC, TH; all versions]. 'Fear' is masculine in gender whereas 'joy' and 'great' are feminine [Lns].

2. It modifies both nouns [My].

QUESTION—What is the meaning of ἰδού 'behold' in v.9?

It indicates that Jesus 'suddenly' appeared [BECNT, EBC, NICNT, NTC; CEV, GW, NET, NLT, NRSV, REB, TEV]. It indicates that something remarkable suddenly occurs [NICNT, NTC]. It shows the surprise the women felt [Lns]. It gets the reader's attention [WBC], expressing vividness [PNTC] or emphasis [NIGTC].

QUESTION—Does προσεκύνησαν 'worshipped' mean only that they knelt before him or that they actually worshipped him?

They worshiped him [BECNT, EBC, ICC, Lns, NAC, NICNT, NIGTC, NTC, PNTC, TH, WBC; CEV, ESV, GW, KJV, NASB, NCV, NET, NIV, NLT, NRSV, TEV]. They regarded him to be divine [Lns, PNTC]. It means that the women knelt before him, but the element of worship is clear also [NICNT]. It means that they knelt before him [REB]. This was a sign of submission [My, NIBC] and reverence [My].

QUESTION—What does Jesus' use of 'my brothers' imply?

It expresses his love for them [BECNT, Lns, NICNT, NIGTC, TH]. It shows his patience with them, and that he welcomes them back into a restored relationship despite their having deserted him [BECNT, Lns, NICNT, NIGTC]. It shows that he has forgiven them [ICC]. He has referred to his disciples as 'brothers' before, and the fact that he continues to do this indicates that he forgives them for having abandoned him [NICNT, NTC, WBC]. He expresses love toward those who had abandoned him and treats them as equals [NAC]. He has already referred to all his disciples, not just the apostles, as his brothers in previous passages (12:49–50, 25:40) [EBC, NICNT, PNTC], and those who have allegiance to him are considered 'family' [PNTC]. Even in his risen state he still holds to the family relationship [NIBC], and is bound to them in brotherly ties [BNTC].

DISCOURSE UNIT—28:11–15 [PNTC; CEV, ESV, GW, NCV, NET, NIV, NLT, NRSV, TEV]. The topic is the report of the guard [CEV, ESV, NLT, NRSV, TEV], the guards' report [NET, NIV], the guards report to the chief priests [GW], the soldiers report to the leaders [NCV], the soldiers silenced [PNTC],.

28:11 (As the women) were-going, behold, some of-the guard having-come into the city told[a] the chief-priests all that-had-happened. **28:12** And when-they-had-come-together with the elders, and taken-counsel, (they) gave a-large-sum[b] (of) money to the soldiers, **28:13** telling (them), "Say, 'Having-come by-night his disciples stole- him -away[c] (while) we were-sleeping.' "

LEXICON—a. aorist act. indic. of ἀπαγγέλλω (LN 33.198) (BAGD 1. p. 79): 'to tell' [BAGD, LN, PNTC; CEV, ESV, GW, NCV, NET, NLT, NRSV, TEV], 'to report' [BAGD, BECNT, BNTC, NICNT, NTC; NASB, NIV, REB], 'to announce' [BAGD, NIGTC], 'to recount' [WBC], 'to show' [KJV], 'to inform' [LN]. This verb means to announce or inform, with a possible focus upon the source of information [LN].

    b. ἱκανός (LN **59.12**) (BAGD 1.a. p. 374): 'large sum' [BAGD, BECNT, BNTC; NASB, NET, NIV, NRSV, TEV], 'quite a large sum' [WBC], 'good sum' [NICNT], 'considerable sum' [**LN**, NTC, PNTC], 'sufficient sum' [ESV], 'large amount' [GW, NCV], 'enough' [NIGTC], 'a lot' [CEV], 'large' [BAGD, LN; KJV], 'sufficient' [BAGD], 'much' [BAGD]. The phrase ἀργύρια ἱκανά 'a large sum of money' is translated 'a large bribe' [NLT], 'a substantial bribe' [REB]. This adjective describes a

relatively large quantity, probably implying what could be expected under
the circumstances [LN].

c. aorist act. indic. of κλέπτω (LN 57.232) (BAGD p. 434): 'to steal
(someone) away' [BECNT, NTC; ESV, KJV, NASB, NIV, NRSV], 'to
steal' [BAGD, BNTC, LN, NICNT, NIGTC, PNTC, WBC; CEV, GW,
NCV, NET, NLT, REB, TEV]. This verb means to take secretly and
without permission the property of someone else [LN].

QUESTION—What would be included in 'all that had happened'?

They would have seen the angel and the empty tomb [EBC, NICNT, PNTC,
TH, WBC], and the stone being rolled away [TH], and probably witnessed
the earthquake [EBC, TH, WBC], but they would not have seen the
resurrection [EBC].

QUESTION—What would be the problem with a story such as the one the
guards were told to spread?

There could be severe consequences for Roman soldiers who slept while on
guard duty [BECNT, BNTC, EBC, NAC, NIBC, NIGTC, PNTC, TH, TRT,
WBC], which would also be true if they were in fact Jewish temple police
[NICNT]. There is also the problem that if they had truly been sleeping they
would not have known of someone stealing the body [BECNT, EBC, My,
NICNT, NIGTC, NTC, PNTC, TH, WBC]. It is hard to believe that all the
guards would sleep so soundly that they would not be aware of Jesus'
disciples turning the heavy stone on its side and taking the body away [Lns,
NTC].

28:14 If this is-heard[a] by the governor, we-will-persuade[b] him and cause-
you -to-be free-of-worry.[c] **28:15** And having-taken the money, they did as
they-had-been-instructed. And this story has-been-spread[d] among (the)
Jews to this-day.

LEXICON—a. aorist pass. subj. of ἀκούω (LN 33.212) (BAGD 3.b. p. 32): 'to
be heard' [LN; NET], 'to be reported' [BECNT, NIGTC], 'to come to the
ears' [BAGD, NICNT, PNTC; ESV, KJV, NASB, NRSV], 'to reach the
ears' [BNTC, NTC; REB], 'to come to the attention' [WBC], 'to be
informed' [BAGD], 'to be received as news' [LN]. This passive verb
phrase is translated as active: 'if the governor hears' [CEV, similarly GW,
NCV, TEV], 'if this report gets to the governor' [NIV]. This verb means
to receive information about something, normally by word of mouth [LN].

b. fut. act. indic. of πείθω (LN 33.301) (BAGD 1.d. p. 639): 'to persuade'
[LN, NTC, PNTC; KJV], 'to undertake the necessary persuasion'
[NIGTC], 'to satisfy' [BAGD; ESV, NCV, NET, NIV, NRSV], 'to
pacify' [BAGD, BECNT, BNTC], 'to make it alright' [NICNT], 'to win
over' [NASB], 'to conciliate' [BAGD, WBC], 'to take care (of it)' [GW],
'to talk with' [CEV], 'to put matters right with' [REB], 'to convince (a
person that someone) is innocent' [TEV], 'to convince' [LN]. This verb

means to convince someone to believe something and to act on the basis of what is recommended [LN].

   c. ἀμέριμνος (LN **25.226**) (BAGD 1. p. 45): 'free from/of concern' [LN, NIGTC], 'free from anxiety' [PNTC], 'not worried' [**LN**], 'out of trouble' [BAGD, BECNT, BNTC, NTC; ESV, NASB, NET, NIV, NRSV], 'blameless' [WBC], 'without worry, unworried' [LN]. The phrase ὑμᾶς ἀμερίμνους ποιήσομεν 'cause you to be free from worry' is translated 'so that you will not need to worry' [NICNT], 'You won't have anything to worry about' [CEV, similarly GW, TEV], 'we will...secure you' [KJV], 'save you from trouble' [NCV], 'see you do not suffer' [REB], 'you will have nothing to be concerned about' or 'you will not have to be worried' [LN]. This adjective pertains to not being concerned or anxious [LN].

   d. aorist pass. indic. of διαφημίζω (LN 33.214) (BAGD p. 190): 'to be spread' [NIGTC; ESV, GW, NCV], 'to be spread about' [BAGD, LN], 'to be spread around' [NICNT; TEV], 'to be spread abroad' [PNTC], 'to be widely spread' [BECNT, NTC; NASB], 'to be spread widely' [WBC], 'to be circulated' [BNTC], 'to be widely circulated' [NIV], 'to become widely known' [REB], 'to be commonly reported' [KJV], 'to be told' [NET, NRSV], 'to be made known' [BAGD]. This passive verb phrase is translated as active: 'still tell each other this story' [CEV]. This verb means to spread information extensively and effectively concerning someone or something [LN].

DISCOURSE UNIT—28:16–20 [BECNT, EBC, NICNT, PNTC; CEV, ESV, GW, NASB, NCV, NET, NIV, NLT, NRSV, TEV]. The topic is commission by the risen Lord [BECNT], the risen messiah and his disciples [EBC], Galilee: the messianic mission is launched [NICNT], the great commission [PNTC; ESV, NET, NIV, NLT], Jesus gives instructions to the disciples [GW], Jesus talks to his followers [NCV], Jesus appears to his disciples [TEV], the commissioning of the disciples [NRSV], what Jesus' followers must do [CEV].

28:16 And[a] (the) eleven disciples went to Galilee, to the mountain[b] where Jesus had-directed them. **28:17** And-having-seen him, they-worshiped[c] (him); but some doubted.[d]

LEXICON—a. 'now' [BNTC, WBC; ESV, NRSV], 'so' [NTC; NET], 'then' [KJV, NIV, NLT], 'but' [BECNT, LN (89.124), PNTC; NASB], not explicit [NICNT, NIGTC; CEV, GW, NCV, REB, TEV]. This is the most commonly used particle when a simple connective is desired [LN].

   b. ὄρος (LN 1.46) (BAGD p. 582): 'mountain' [BAGD, BECNT, BNTC, LN, NIGTC, NTC, PNTC, WBC; all versions except TEV], 'hill' [BAGD; TEV], 'hills' [NICNT]. This noun denotes a relatively high elevation of land, in contrast with βουνός 'hill' (1.48), which is by comparison somewhat lower [LN].

   c. aorist act. indic. of προσκυνέω (LN 53.56) (BAGD 5. p. 717): 'to worship' [BAGD, BECNT, LN, NICNT, NIGTC, NTC, PNTC, WBC; all versions except GW, REB], 'to fall before someone in worship' [BNTC], 'to bow down and worship' [LN; GW], 'to kneel in worship' [REB], 'to prostrate oneself in worship' [LN], 'to prostrate oneself before, to do reverence to' [BAGD]. This verb means to express by attitude and possibly by position one's allegiance to and regard for deity [LN].

d. aorist act. indic. of διστάζω (LN 31.37) (BAGD 1. p. 200): 'to doubt' [BAGD, BECNT, BNTC, LN, NIGTC, NTC, WBC; CEV, ESV, KJV, NET, NIV, NLT, NRSV, TEV], 'to have doubts' [BAGD; GW], 'to be doubtful' [NASB, REB], 'to be hesitant' [NICNT], 'to hesitate' [PNTC], 'to be uncertain about' [LN]. The phrase οἱ δὲ ἐδίστασαν 'some doubted' is translated 'some of them did not believe it was really Jesus' [NCV]. This verb means to think that something may not be true or certain [LN].

QUESTION—What relationship is indicated by δέ 'and'?

It is transitional [BNTC, NICNT, NIGTC, NTC, TH, WBC; CEV, ESV, GW, KJV, NCV, NET, NIV, NLT, NRSV, REB, TEV]. It indicates contrast [BECNT, EBC, Lns, PNTC; NASB]. The contrast is between the disciples as opposed to the Jews and their plotting with the guards at the grave [PNTC]. It shows contrast between the falsehood of the previous verses and what is about to be narrated [ICC]. The fraudulent story about the stolen body contrasts with the disciples' obedience to Jesus as shown by their going to Galilee [EBC].

QUESTION—Who were the some who doubted?

1. It refers to some, but not all, of the eleven disciples [BECNT, BNTC, ICC, Lns, My, NAC, NICNT]. Though some were doubtful or hesitant, all of them worshipped [My].

2. It refers to all the eleven disciples, who in some way or other were unsure or hesitant [TH, WBC].

3. It is possible that the people referred to by 'some' could be other disciples besides the eleven [EBC, PNTC], and who, not having had the experience of seeing Jesus alive after his resurrection as the eleven had, were more hesitant to move from fear and unbelief to full faith and rejoicing [EBC].

QUESTION—What were they doubtful about?

They were not sure that it was Jesus [BNTC, Lns, My, NIBC, NIGTC, NTC, TH, TRT; NCV]; and it may refer to what happened initially when they saw him from a distance [NIBC, NTC]. Recognition of Jesus and faith in him may have come in stages for some [ICC]. This is more a matter of hesitation than sheer unbelief [NAC, PNTC, WBC]. All of the disciples were in a state of hesitation, indecision, and uncertainty about what recent events might mean, but this is not the same as the doubt of unbelief [WBC]. This verb expresses uncertainty and hesitation, and it may be that they doubted Jesus to some extent or were hesitant to worship him [BECNT]. They are unsure how to act in the presence of a supernaturally manifested person who is so holy and exalted [NAC]. This kind of hesitation is a disorientation that comes from a situation that is overwhelming and strange, but is not necessarily

unbelief, since in the one other passage in Matthew where this word occurs
(14:31–33) it is also linked with worship; in this instance they were unsure
how to respond to Jesus, who was at the same time familiar but also different
[NICNT]. It is possible in the same setting, just as in 14:31–33, to have
doubts as well as to worship [NIGTC].

28:18 **And having-approached Jesus spoke to-them saying, "All authority**[a]
in heaven and on earth has-been-given to-me. **28:19** **Therefore go**[b] **make-**
disciples[c] **(of) all nations,**[d]

LEXICON—a. ἐξουσία (LN 37.35) (BAGD 3. p. 278): 'authority' [BAGD; all
    translations except KJV, NCV], 'power' [KJV, NCV], 'authority to rule,
    right to control' [LN], 'absolute power, warrant' [BAGD]. This noun
    denotes the right to control or govern over [LN].

  b. aorist pass. (deponent = act.) participle of πορεύομαι (LN 15.10): 'to go'
    [LN; all translations]. The participle πορευθέντες 'having gone' is
    translated as an imperative: 'go' [all translations except GW], 'wherever
    you go' [GW]. This verb means to move from one place to another, with
    the possible implication of continuity and distance [LN].

  c. aorist act. impera. of μαθητεύω (LN **36.37**) (BAGD 3. p. 485): 'to make
    disciples' [**LN**; all translations except NIGTC; KJV, NCV], 'to make a
    disciple of' [BAGD], 'to disciple' [NIGTC], 'to teach' [BAGD; KJV], 'to
    make followers' [NCV], 'to cause people to become followers' [LN]. This
    verb means to cause someone to become a disciple or follower of
    someone else [LN].

  d. ἔθνος (LN 11.55, 11.37) (BAGD 1. p. 218): 'nation' [BAGD, LN (11.55);
    all translations except CEV, NCV, TEV], 'people' [BAGD, LN (11.55)],
    'people of all nations' [CEV], 'all people in the world' [NCV], 'all
    peoples everywhere' [TEV], 'heathen, pagans' (in the plural) [LN
    (11.37)]. This noun denotes the largest unit into which the people of the
    world are divided on the basis of their constituting a socio-political
    community [LN (11.55)]. In the plural this noun often denotes those who
    do not belong to the Jewish or Christian faith [LN (11.37)].

QUESTION—Who is the agent of the passive verb ἐδόθη 'was given'?
    God the Father gave the authority [BECNT, EBC, NAC, NICNT, TH,
    WBC]. This granting of authority echoes Dan 7:14 [BECNT, EBC, ICC,
    NAC, NIBC, NICNT, NIGTC, NTC, WBC]. Though Jesus was not lacking
    in authority during his earthly ministry, the difference here in this passage is
    that his authority is now exercised over the whole universe, in a conscious
    allusion to the 'Son of Man' passage in Daniel 7:13–14 [EBC]. Jesus no
    longer had the limitations that were his during his earthly ministry [PNTC].

QUESTION—What relationship is indicated by οὖν 'therefore'?
    It indicates that Jesus' universal authority is the basis of his giving his
    followers a universal mission [BECNT, BNTC, EBC, Lns, ICC, NIBC,
    NICNT, NIGTC, PNTC, WBC]. It indicates that Jesus' authority and

continuing presence with them are what enable them to make disciples [NTC, WBC].

QUESTION—Does the participle πορευθέντες 'having gone' indicate a circumstantial relationship or function as an imperative?

It functions as an imperative [EBC, NAC, NTC, PNTC, TH, WBC; all translations except GW]. This participle and the two following take on imperatival force because of the imperative 'make disciples' [PNTC, WBC].

QUESTION—What is involved in making disciples?

It means to teach others to hear, understand, and obey what Jesus taught [BECNT, EBC], which is primarily about ethics [BECNT, NIBC], especially the ethics expressed in the Sermon on the Mount [NIGTC]. They are to teach others to obey Jesus' interpretation of the Old Testament law as the basis for their living as the people of God [NICNT]. It is to call people to learn from and follow Jesus such that their lives are different because of their relationship to him [PNTC]. It includes evangelism, but more importantly involves the task of nurturing and teaching, particularly teaching those who are discipled to follow after righteousness as described in the teaching of Jesus [WBC]. Making disciples involves a balance between evangelism and Christian nurture, and the real heart of disciple making is teaching obedience to all that Jesus commanded [NAC]. In the gospel of Matthew the idea of discipleship is important, with the noun 'disciple' occurring 72 times [TH].

QUESTION—Does the plural noun ἔθνη 'nations' mean 'heathen, pagan' or is it simply a reference to the nations of the world?

It refers to the nations of the world [BECNT, EBC, ICC, Lns, My, NAC, NICNT, NIGTC, PNTC, TH, TRT, WBC; all versions]. It is a reference to all the nations of the world, which would include Israel [BECNT, EBC, ICC, NICNT, NIGTC, WBC]. It means everyone everywhere, with no distinction [EBC]. They have a world-wide mission [BNTC].

baptizing them in the name of the Father and of the Son and of the Holy Spirit,

QUESTION—What is the relation of the two participles 'baptizing' and 'teaching' to the primary imperative verb 'make disciples'?

These participles take on imperatival force because of the imperative 'make disciples' [BECNT, Lns, TH, WBC]. Baptizing and teaching describe the process of how disciples are made [BECNT, Lns, NIBC, NICNT, NTC, TRT]. Baptizing and teaching people to obey all Jesus' commands are what discipling involves [ICC, NAC]. They are ways of fulfilling the command to make disciples [TH]. The activities of 'baptizing' and 'teaching' are not the means of making disciples, but they do characterize that discipling [EBC, PNTC]. Teaching is subordinate to baptizing, meaning that ethical teaching must always accompany the administration of baptism [My].

QUESTION—Is there any significance in the fact that αὐτούς 'them' is masculine plural, as opposed to being neuter as would be necessary to agree grammatically with 'nations'?

It indicates a shift in perspective away from a focus on nations to a focus on individuals [NAC, WBC]. If the focus was still on national groups the pronoun would be the neuter αὐτά [WBC].

QUESTION—What is meant by baptizing εἰς 'in' the name of someone?

It means to come into a relationship with that person [ICC, NICNT, NTC, PNTC] and into a new allegiance to him [NICNT]. They are to come into a relationship with him in accordance with what he has communicated about himself [NTC]. Matthew's use of εἰς, which more often has the connotation of 'into', suggests coming into a relationship with and under the lordship of the person or persons named [EBC]. From that point on the existence of the person baptized is ruled by the one or ones into whose name he or she is baptized [WBC]. Here it means to be associated with Jesus' power and authority [NAC]. It means to be baptized in connection with the revelation of the Father, the Son, and the Holy Spirit [Lns]. It means to come into a comprehensive commitment to and solidarity with someone [NIGTC]. It means to give full worship and loyalty to them, to acknowledge the blessings of the Father, Son, and Holy Spirit, and to pledge allegiance to them [BNTC]. 'Name' represents the essential nature of the person, and by being baptized in the name of the Father, Son, and Holy Spirit, the baptized believer is introduced into special fellowship and dependence upon them, and expresses the idea that the name into which they are baptized is the sum total of their belief and confession [My]. To baptize in someone's name is to baptize by the authority of that person [TH].

QUESTION—What significance is there in the fact that the word 'name' is singular?

It shows the essential unity of the three [Lns, NICNT, PNTC, NTC, WBC]. It speaks of unity as well as diversity within the Trinity [NAC]. It also indicates that, since the Son is named along with the Father and the Holy Spirit, the Son is worthy of worship [NICNT]. There is no significance in the fact that 'name' is singular [NIGTC, TH, TRT].

28:20 teaching[a] them to-obey[b] all (things) that I-have-commanded[c] you. And behold,[d] I am with you all the days until the end of-the age.[e]"

TEXT—Manuscripts reading τοῦ αἰῶνος 'of the age' are given an A rating by GNT to indicate it was regarded to be certain. A variant reading includes ἀμήν 'Amen' and it is followed by KJV only.

LEXICON—a. pres. act. participle of διδάσκω (LN 33.224) (BAGD 2.e. p. 192): 'to teach' [BAGD, LN; all translations]. This verb means to provide instruction in a formal or informal setting [LN].

    b. pres. act. infin. of τηρέω (LN 36.19) (BAGD 5. p. 815): 'to obey' [BECNT, LN; NCV, NET, NIV, NLT, NRSV, TEV], 'to observe' [BAGD, BNTC, NTC, PNTC; ESV, KJV, NASB, REB], 'to keep'

[BAGD, NICNT, NIGTC, WBC], 'to do' [CEV, GW], 'to keep commandments' [LN]. This verb means to continue to obey orders or commandments [LN].

c. aorist mid. (deponent = act.) indic. of ἐντέλλομαι (LN 33.329) (BAGD p. 268): 'to command' [BAGD, LN; all translations except CEV, NCV, NLT], 'to teach' [NCV], 'to tell' [CEV]. This verb is translated as a noun: '(my) commands' [NLT]. This verb means to give definite orders, implying authority or official sanction [LN].

d. ἰδού (LN 91.13): 'behold' [ESV], 'lo' [KJV, NASB], 'remember' [GW, NET, NRSV], 'surely' [NIV], 'be sure of this' [NLT], 'look, listen, pay attention' [LN], not explicit [CEV, NCV, REB, TEV]. This particle is used to emphasize the importance of something [LN].

e. αἰών (LN 67.143) (BAGD 2.a. p. 27): 'age' [BAGD, BECNT, BNTC, LN, NICNT, NIGTC, NTC, PNTC, WBC; ESV, NASB, NCV, NET, NIV, NLT, NRSV, TEV], 'world' [CEV, KJV], 'time' [GW, REB], 'era' [LN]. This noun denotes a unit of time as a particular stage or period of history [LN].

QUESTION—What is the force of ἰδού 'behold' in this verse?

It emphasizes the truth of the following statement [EBC, NIGTC, PNTC; NIV, NLT]. It emphasizes the special character of the promise that follows [Lns, WBC]. It emphasizes that what follows is something that they should be careful to remember [BECNT, NTC, TRT; GW, NET, NRSV] and carry out [My].

QUESTION—How does the ending of Matthew's gospel relate to the beginning of it?

Jesus' promise to be with them always forms an inclusio with Matthew 1:23 at the very beginning of the gospel account, where Jesus was to be known as Immanuel, 'God with us' [BECNT, EBC, ICC, NAC, NIBC, NICNT, NIGTC, NTC, PNTC, WBC]. Matthew's gospel begins and ends with announcements from angels [BECNT].

QUESTION—What is meant by 'the end of the age'?

It is the consummation of history [BECNT, EBC, Lns, TH, WBC], marked by the return of Jesus [NIBC, WBC], the time of final judgment of the wicked [BECNT, NIBC, WBC], and of reward for the righteous [WBC]. It refers to Christ's return [NAC].

CPSIA information can be obtained
at www.ICGtesting.com
Printed in the USA
BVHW041529160322
631532BV00019B/568